FOREVER HONG KONG

FOREVER HONG KONG

A Global City's Decolonization Struggle

CHING KWAN LEE

Harvard University Press

Cambridge, Massachusetts
London, England
2025

Copyright © 2025 by the President and Fellows of Harvard College
All rights reserved
Printed in the United States of America
First printing

EU GPSR Authorised Representative
LOGOS EUROPE, 9 rue Nicolas Poussin, 17000, LA ROCHELLE, France
Contact@logoseurope.eu

Library of Congress Cataloging-in-Publication Data

Names: Lee, Ching Kwan, author.
Title: Forever Hong Kong : a global city's decolonization struggle / Ching Kwan Lee.
Description: Cambridge, Massachusetts ; London, England : Harvard University Press, 2025. | Includes bibliographical references and index.
Identifiers: LCCN 2024051843 | ISBN 9780674290198 (cloth) | ISBN 9780674300712 (pdf) | ISBN 9780674300729 (epub)
Subjects: LCSH: Hong Kong Protests, Hong Kong, China, 2019- | Decolonization—China—Hong Kong—History. | Protest movements—China—Hong Kong—History—21st century. | Hong Kong (China)—Politics and government—1997- | Hong Kong (China)—Colonial influence—History. | Hong Kong (China)—History—20th century. | Hong Kong (China)—History—21st century.
Classification: LCC HN740.H65 L44 2025 | DDC 951.2506/12—dc23/eng/20250218
LC record available at https://lccn.loc.gov/2024051843

In loving memory of my mentor Michael Burawoy, forever inspiring

You must go on. I can't go on. I will go on.
Samuel Beckett, *The Unnamable*

念念不忘　必有迴響
《一代宗師》

CONTENTS

INTRODUCTION 1

1 COLONIAL MYTHOLOGIES 17

2 PRACTICING POSTCOLONIALITY 58

3 "HONG KONGERS": (RE)BORN IN ACTION 119

4 BENDING THE ARC OF VIOLENCE 170

5 "BE WATER" GOES GLOBAL 231

6 TO BE CONTINUED 271

Notes 291
Acknowledgments 323
Index 325

FOREVER HONG KONG

INTRODUCTION

A POPULAR UPRISING IN 2019 FOREVER changed Hong Kong, a tiny dot on the world map but a giant heartbeat in the global economy. Deep in the soul of the city and its people, something fundamental had shifted, and there would be no going back, for better or for worse. That year, in the crucible of massive mobilizations demanding freedom, democracy, and autonomy, the city finally jettisoned its 180-year-long standing as a "borrowed place, borrowed time," first under British and then Chinese rule.[1] Rallying around the stirring slogan "Liberate Hong Kong, Revolution of Our Times," people braved the armed forces' endless rounds of tear gas, water cannons, and rubber and live bullets with peaceful marches, barricades, Molotov cocktails, urban guerrilla tactics, and trench warfare. The protests also gave birth to the trappings of a new culture: an anthem, a sign language, idioms, a font style, a dress code, mascots, color symbols, declarations, and an explosion of graffiti and public art. Most improbably, an embryonic vision for a political economy independent of China emerged.

The revolutionary mood in 2019 Hong Kong was reminiscent of another earth-shattering event that captivated the world three decades ago. As one veteran Reuters journalist put it, "It feels like another Tiananmen moment. Anything is possible!"[2] That parallel alone was too much for the largest Communist regime on earth to stomach. After a year of rebellion, Beijing unleashed its proverbial nuclear option, issuing a hard-lined National

Security Law that annihilated the movement and the city's liberal institutions. Hong Kong now stands on the edge of a precipice, and China risks a fatal blowback to its own global ambition. Paradoxically, the collective trauma Hong Kongers sustained had also resurrected the city, reclaimed for the first time by the people as theirs forever—an identity, a homeland, a cause. This book is the story of the circumstances and people behind this stunning turn of events. More than just another social movement, 2019 was both the peak of the city's ongoing decolonization struggle decades in the making and the opening salvo of a new era of confrontation between Western neoliberal capitalism and Chinese state capitalism. Among global cities of the world, Hong Kong is uniquely located at the interface of these two juggernauts, benefiting from their windfall riches when they cooperate while suffering from the ravages when they clash. The Hong Kong story is thus a window into the sociopolitical impacts of this epoch-defining geostrategic contest.

Not in my wildest dreams could I foresee my birthplace plunged into this upheaval. Nor could I anticipate the stroke of providential luck that brought me back to the city, after more than twenty years in the United States, on June 16, 2019, the day two million fellow citizens took to the street in the largest demonstration to take place in Hong Kong. The year before, when I accepted an offer to join the faculty of a local university, I had no idea that I would be literally walking into history. During the following two years, I was an observer and a participant, caught in an unforgettable swirl of mobilizations and countermobilizations, wild swings of emotions, and sights and sounds the city had never witnessed, all under the watchful eyes of the world media. Even as I write this book, I still feel the visceral energy and surrealness of those times.

Hong Kong as Puzzle: Another Kind of Decolonization

The events of 2019 have spawned a cottage industry of monographs and nonfiction books, some offering robust political economic analyses, others biographical portraits of prominent protesters. Among these are Ho-fung Hung's *City on the Edge,* Louisa Lim's *Indelible City,* Shibani Mahtani and Timothy McLaughlin's *Among the Braves,* Edmund Cheng and Samson Yuen's *The Making of Leaderful Mobilization,* Antony Dapiran's *City on Fire,* and Stephen Vine's *Defying the Dragon.* All these writings interpret the 2019 protest as mass resistance against the Chinese Communist regime, a quixotic popular bid for freedom and democracy. This approach is not incorrect but incomplete, for it captures the moment but not the movement, the appearance but not the essence of the uprising.

I argue in this book that 2019 was no ordinary movement: it was the zenith of a two-decade-long agitation whose purpose went way beyond universal suffrage and electoral reforms. What was at stake was Hong Kong itself as a political project. More than a narrow demand for democracy and freedom, Hong Kongers strived for the fundamental right for self-determination. They rethought taken-for-granted truths about their own city, challenged inherited norms that had long defined the realm of the political, and gradually dared to see themselves as historical agents who could envision previously unimaginable destinies. Therefore, their resistance amounts to a decolonization struggle. Unraveling the historical process through which Hong Kong citizens embarked on decolonization, this book also demonstrates that the target of their activism was not just mainland China's political economic domination but also core legacies of British colonization and the more recent crisis of neoliberal capitalism. Hong Kongers have fought a broader fight against what I call the "double coloniality" coproduced and reproduced by British and Chinese rule, embedded in institutional arrangement in and beyond the state, and implanted in people's habits of thought and collective predispositions even after a formal change of sovereignty.

That a decolonization struggle happened in Hong Kong is a puzzle at many levels. First, decolonization had long been an impossible option not just for the colonizers but also for the colonized. For the former, both Britain and the People's Republic of China (PRC) had strong geopolitical and economic interests in keeping Hong Kong a colony. But even the colonized people found themselves in a catch-22 situation: the alternative to colonial rule was Communist rule. One of the most iconic anticolonial, anticapitalist radical thinkers described this plainly in 1970: "If you truly believe in a liberal democracy like many others all over the world, the colonial government is your enemy. But unless you like to enjoy the mainland style of life in Hong Kong, you have to live under the feet of your enemy."[3] Oppression was relative. The majority of the local population in the post–World War II era were refugees and immigrants fleeing the Communist regime, and the colonial enclave and free port of Hong Kong was a refuge. When the Sino-British treaty that ceded part of Hong Kong to Britain ended in 1997, Britain and

China simply exchanged sovereignty over the city. The majority of locals actually preferred the status quo of colonialism. Given that, at this critical juncture of British betrayal and imminent Communist rule, there was neither an anticolonial nor an anti-Communist mass movement, it is stunning that over the next two decades, Hong Kong became a "city of protest," all while maintaining its status as Asia's premier financial center and the gateway to mainland China, itself the new powerhouse of the global economy.[4] What made "impossible decolonization" possible and desirable for the people once they were under national Chinese rule, rather than alien British rule? This is the central puzzle this book addresses.

Beating hearts of capitalism, global cities are not supposed to be places of protest. So what explains a Janus-faced Hong Kong where profits and protests have thrived together since the 1990s? As capitalist accumulation becomes ever-more financialized and spatially dispersed, global cities are coordinating sites providing producer services to transnational corporations headquartered there. Social polarization often follows: concentration of high-income transnational professional elites enjoying affluent lifestyles, leading to gentrification of residential and commercial spaces, coexisting with low-wage, often informalized or migrant labor providing personal and corporate services.[5] These capitalist logics drove Hong Kong's wealth and socioeconomic inequality, well documented in statistics. Aggregate wealth and income figures have long placed the city at the top among major economies in the world (for example, ranked thirteenth highest in per capita income in 2023), as did the level of income inequality (for example, ranked the eighth most unequal in 2016).[6] But global city theories cannot explain Hong Kong's politicization. What is the link between global city and political activism?

As protests have become more prevalent, scholars naturally apply theories of social movement and contentious politics to make sense of the wave of popular mobilizations since the 1997 handover. Adopting the literature's theoretical agenda and its influential arsenal of descriptive concepts—political opportunity structure, collective action frames, cycles of protests, emotional mobilization—a vibrant literature on social movements has emerged in Hong Kong studies. Many scholars zero in on the process of "mobilization"—people's ability to organize, recruit, lead, communicate, network, frame, and strategize to achieve their goal.[7] Yet, these studies inherit the blind spot of the parent literature: they do not explain the *subjects* of collective action and their political orientations.⁸ Important questions are given short shrift. Why do people want to mobilize in the first place? Why and how did Hong Kongers jettison their collective submission to colonial rule and turn themselves into decolonizing subjects?

Rather than fitting Hong Kong realities into theoretical agendas responding to other times and places, and thereby reinforcing its epistemic subalternity as a colony, this book takes a different approach.⁹ It looks at the Hong Kong story through the lens of "decolonization" for two reasons. First, the term accurately denotes the goals of the people—to disentangle their politics from the institutional, ideological, identification, and affective confines of the colonial order, past and present, and to make claims for an alternative, self-determining future. Second, poignantly, Chinese officials themselves defined their governance problem as one of decolonization. They have long argued that the "deep structural problem of Hong Kong" was the failed "return of the people's heart and mind in the process of decolonization." At stake for China is not just securing political, economic, and military domination but the eradication of people's colonial "beliefs, values, meanings, belonging and affects and the legitimacy these establish."¹⁰ After cracking down on the 2019 movement, "decolonization" has become the unifying leitmotif deployed by mainland officials, scholars, and policymakers to justify their purge of the city's "colonial" institutions, culture, and ideology. To strengthen patriotism to the nation and to Hong Kong requires "complete and thorough removal of the influence of colonial governance so that the Chinese national constitution can plant deep roots in people's hearts."¹¹

Decolonization, as both the political and discursive fields of struggle, has been and will continue to be the cornerstone of politics in Hong Kong and the PRC for the foreseeable future. But in the context of Hong Kong, it has a different character than in most of the academic literature, which has primarily focused on European colonialism and African anticolonial struggles. In particular, the case of French colonialism in Algeria was immortalized in classic works by Franz Fanon and Pierre Bourdieu, among others.¹² The African experience of colonization, marked by unmitigated physical violence, slavery, dehumanizing racism, land dispossession, economic exploitation, massacres, and concentration camps, elicited equally bloody anticolonial movements. Hong Kong's decolonization story, even at its most explosive in 2019, did not remotely compare to the level of physical violence or economic deprivation found in its African counterparts. As a matter of fact, the city's outsize affluence had made unrecognizable the colonial violence inflicted by both Britain and China on institutions, ideologies, and identities rather than bodies of color. The corresponding decolonization struggle that had intensified in the shadow of a booming financial economy was also therefore a messier, more ambivalent, and more civilized process, a far cry from scenes of African carnage.

Decolonization Is Back

More than half a century after the global wave of independence, the long shadows of colonialism still fuel many popular struggles. Across the postcolonial world, the language of decolonization is widely used by politicians and activists to protest ecological destruction, linguistic and cultural decline, exploitative foreign investment, and corporate land grabs, as well as to demand reparations and the repatriation of cultural objects.[13] Persistent racial hierarchies and violence against people of color and immigrants in the West have sparked social movements condemning the legacies of slavery and racial capitalism. Students and scholars in the United States and Europe are calling for decolonizing the curriculum and academic disciplines, becoming deeply reflexive of the role knowledge production plays both in the perpetuation of and the liberation from colonial domination.

Theorists such as Anibal Quiyano, Walter D. Mignolo, and Catherine Walsh make the distinction between colonization—that is, taking political and economic control over a dependent territory and people through military conquest—and coloniality—a matrix of power dispersed throughout society—in relations of inequality, culture, and knowledge production, bolstering and reproducing domination beyond the strict limits of colonial administration. It follows that decolonization and decoloniality are analytically distinguishable: "while 'taking hold' of the state was the fundamental task of decolonization," the fundamental task of decoloniality is "to liberate knowing and becoming what coloniality of knowledge and being prevents to know and become."[14] As this book shows, this conceptual distinction is important to the Hong Kong experience: the popular struggle there targeted both the colonial political order and colonial cognition, and while the people had not been successful in capturing the state—that is, installing democratic reform and overturning the government-corporate ruling bloc—they had already begun the task of dismantling the colonial hegemonic worldview they inherited. They embarked upon a "liberation of knowing and becoming."

For all its analytical insight, however, I do not deploy the term "decoloniality," which, as it has been formulated by the aforementioned theorists, privileges the epistemic over material practices and political economic analyses of decolonization. Decoloniality as they define it also entails a sweeping normative political project at odds with the empirical case at hand.[15] Instead of giving causal primacy or interpretive priority to epistemology and ontology, treating them as first movers in political thought and life, Hong Kong's decolonization had a more "worldly" genesis.[16] Popular resistance was triggered by political economic ruptures, which then led to cognitive and ideological ruptures, and not the other way around. Besides, Mignolo and colleagues' decolonial vision—delinking from the West, rejecting westernization, privileging the pluriverse of distinct civilizations and epistemologies—departs substantially from Hong Kong citizens' vision of decolonization. In the face of Chinese Communist colonization, a total rejection of "colonial modernity"—that is, liberal democracy, capitalism, and citizenship—would be dire. This book shows how the Chinese regime, adopting the positionality of historical victimhood at the hands of Western imperialism, has couched its current colonization of Hong Kong in decolonial terms, in order to de-westernize the people's values, mentalities, and knowledge imposed by British colonialism. Beijing's appropriation of the rhetoric of decoloniality parallels the global Far Right movement's "dangerous reanimation of ethnic-cultural, religious, Eurocentric, nationalist, and other mythologies normalizing rootedness and othering non-belonging."[17] Inasmuch as decolonial scholarship trains its critique singularly on historical European and American colonialisms, the case of Hong Kong is a reminder that imperialistic aspirations do not hail exclusively from the West. Other contemporary instances of non-European colonial aggressions include Russia's invasion of Ukraine, as well as Georgia and Chechnya; India's encroachment in Kashmir; and Israel's colonization of Palestine.[18] There is no romance in non-Western civilizations or "native" epistemology. In sum, to avoid the unnecessary entanglement with the controversial baggage of "decoloniality," I use the terms "decolonization," "anticolonial," and "decolonizing" to denote the liberation struggle against colonial domination in both political economic relations and collective cognition and subjectivity.

In sociology, too, decolonization as a subject of inquiry has made a comeback. Inspired by racial justice movements, there have been lively debates on "decolonizing" sociological knowledge and its canons.[19] A new wave of historical sociology has foregrounded empire, colonialism, and racial capitalism in the constitution of modernity and sociological knowledge of the metropoles, as well as sociology's complicity in perpetuating the colonial project.[20] This book was not initially motivated by these debates, although its findings are relevant to them. For instance, Hong Kong's experience of double colonization by both European and Eastern powers illustrates different ways of deploying "race" as a method of domination. What the literature has emphasized is racism as a "politics of difference" in European and American colonialisms, but Chinese colonization in Hong Kong shows that racism also works through a logic of "coercive sameness," alongside other nonracial forms of colonial othering (for example, flexible objectification and ethnicization) that are no less pernicious.

This book centers the colonized subjects, in keeping with decolonial sociology. Its premise is that "Those who live the colonial difference not only act but also produce knowledge and construct theory . . . through embodied practice and from the ground up, turning the dominant precept of reason and its geography and geopolitics on its head."[21] The sociologist Jose Itzigsohn calls this a margin epistemology.[22] But which subjects? In recent scholarship, the subjects are mostly the anticolonial political elite, intellectuals and theorists. Examining other cases of improbable decolonization, such as the Haitian Revolution and the Liberian independence movement or postcolonial Ghana and Tanzania, these historical studies focus on how the intellectual and political leaders in a racialized world order fostered radically different justifications for freedom and independence and instituted themselves as novel subjects in the world system as free, self-governing black people.[23] In this book, my subjects are not the elite and their texts but ordinary insurgent citizens with their historical subjectivity and embodied action. Without an overarching theory, they grew into a decolonization political force via praxis and reflexivity, one protest at a time, over more than twenty years. Just like the Luddite croppers, handloom weavers, and utopian artisans resisting industrialization in England, so empathetically captured by E. P. Thompson, Hong Kong protesters' insurrection may be foolhardy and quixotic, but their aspirations were valid on their own terms.[24]

This does not mean I can simply impose an irreducible capacity for self-determination or a simple-minded voluntarism on the people. As scholars in subaltern studies and postcolonial studies have shown, recovering the subject of decolonization from below has to attend to the complex terrain of the colonial context, one in which "the subject arrives at a sense of 'identity' not by the property of his own social being but always mediated through symbols and signs . . . discourse and forms of knowledge which colonialism produces."[25] The stories in this book show how double coloniality had insidious and stubborn impacts, and how breakthroughs were always punctured by ambivalences in the evolution of Hong Kongers' decolonizing subjectivities. Most people, including many young activists, relished the legacy liberal institutions of British colonialism and found themselves rooting for China's rightful claim to development and recognition in the world community. They only *became* subjects of decolonization, and not without trepidation, first as they reacted to neoliberal capitalism's crisis and then as they were betrayed by the bankruptcy of China's promissory note of "One Country, Two Systems."

Decolonial writings in cultural studies and philosophy have a tendency to cast the decolonizing subjects and their resistance in glorifying and heroic lights. The acclaimed political philosopher Achille Mbembe writes about their "will to community": "to stand up on one's own and to create a heritage . . . making possible the manifestation of one's own power of genesis, one's own capacity for articulating difference and for expressing a positive force."[26] The following account indeed reveals many moments of such irrepressible human spirit playing out in a global city against two colonialisms. But these laudable decolonial subjects did not emerge from thin air. How did they manage to shake off the colonial power that have not just dominated but constituted them? How did they achieve epistemic or cognitive autonomy from the colonizers and amass political capacity for change? As a sociologist, my goal is to analyze and theorize the conditions under which the decolonization subjects arise and evolve, with all their flaws, hesitations, and limitations. Hong Kong is arguably a paradigmatic case for this purpose as a kernel of its historical experience with colonialization and decolonization presents itself as a comparative puzzle. The structure of colonial domination before and after the 1997 handover was strikingly similar, consisting primarily of a ruling bloc of oligopolistic business and colonial elite, an executive-led autocratic polity, and a hierarchy of social power based on racial or ethnic othering. Yet, the former period was marked by popular acquiescence, even consent, whereas the latter persistent and daring defiance. Why?

The Argument

To foreshadow what the following historical and ethnographic analysis would make clear, five observations can be highlighted at the outset. First, colonialism as an objectively repressive and morally reprehensible system of power was not always subjectively experienced as such. It did not necessarily or automatically produce anticolonial or decolonizing subjects. In Hong Kong, the near absence of anticolonial agitation during the quarter century before the transfer of sovereignty was due to a colonial hegemony forged by Britain and China to realize their respective interests. This rule by consent based on four tenets—prosperity and stability; rule of law; free-market utopia; and China as destiny—produced among the colonized subjects entrenched complacency and pragmatic acquiescence to the status quo determined by the two colonial masters. Second, it took severe economic and political ruptures to shake off the lull of material comfort and spur cognitive ruptures that led people to question the political and moral foundations of colonial hegemony. Hong Kong, as a global city brokering global capitalism and global China, was hard hit by crisis and contradictions originating from both systems in the post-1997 period. Third, at the forefront of this budding decolonizing movement was not a class actor but a generational one: the world-facing, postcolonial youth coming of age after 1997. Arguably and paradoxically, their political interest and agency were constituted by a new temporality imposed by the new sovereign. As China promised limited autonomy for the city until only 2047, out of an expediency to exploit Hong Kong's western institutions for its own global agenda, the young generation became the largest stakeholders in this time-sensitive struggle for the future. Fourth, once started, the decolonizing movement developed its own momentum and grew in capacity and reflexivity. Citizens turned colonial truth claims into rights claims, battling various forms of violence, and over time expanded their political aspirations beyond the boundaries set by the colonial rulers. First person accounts demonstrated overwhelmingly that their decolonial subjecthood arose out of participation in mass action, and not primarily through ideological persuasion, cultural identification or communal imagination. Finally, intensifying geopolitical rivalry between China and the West generated exogenous political and moral leverage for the passionate minority of activists to enroll the pragmatic majority in an ever-expanding struggle, as evinced in the 2019 protests. In a nutshell, both the old and new colonial masters, their collusion and their competition, dialectically contributed to the making of the decolonial subjects for whom colonial mythologies were both a source of aspiration and an object of transcendence.

This book begins the story of decolonization by establishing the benchmark features of colonization in Hong Kong. Chapter 1 argues that beneath the facade of formal British colonial rule, Hong Kong's situation should be understood as "double colonization," with China as a secondary but perennial phantom colonizer. After a century of colonial repression and neglect, and despite their ideological animosity, the two big powers found common interest in cementing a colonial hegemony since the 1970s. This hegemonic order was founded on four tenets: stability and prosperity, rule of law, free-market utopia, and China as destiny. This chapter offers a historical and thematic sketch of Hong Kong politics, economy, and society by way of juxtaposing the claims of these four foundational myths and the more complex and inconvenient colonial realities they glossed over. The importance of these colonial mythologies, which were embraced by the people at large and unevenly embedded in institutions, was that they purportedly described what Hong Kong was and prescribed what the people wanted. When I talk about the decolonization struggle in subsequent chapters, I am talking about the historical process whereby the colonized challenged these pillars of subjugation that had for decades defined the permissible boundaries of the political.

Chapter 2 zeroes in on the "interregnum," the period (circa 1997–2017) when the old colonial master had exited and the new had not yet consolidated itself. It traces the genesis of Hong Kong's decolonization struggle to the political economic ruptures triggered by the crisis and contradictions of neoliberal capitalism in the late 1990s and not, as most analyses presumed, the aggression of the Chinese Communist regime. The first decade after the handover saw the ravages of the Asian financial crisis, the bursting housing bubble, and corporate downsizing, inflicting doubts about "stability and prosperity" among the middle-class masses. At the same time, the diffusion of the global justice movement to Hong Kong inspired social activism seeking an alternative vision of a good society beyond "free-market utopia" and profit-driven developmentalism. Then, in the second post-handover decade, the China factor became the decisive trigger of popular rebellion. The contradictory imperatives and impulses (wavering between development and securitization, globalism and nationalism) of Beijing's global China project led to policy interventions targeting Hong Kong's institutions, ideology, and identities. Popular grievances and mass resistance grew and radicalized, building on mobilizations in the previous decade. Along the way, the cardinal principles of "China as destiny" and "rule of law" were eroded by actions on both sides. Against the background of political economic ruptures, this chapter focuses on the biographies and voices of the activists in order to explain how a decolonizing subjecthood arose in Hong Kong. From the annual 1989 vigils and July 1, 2003, rally to the preservation of Star Ferry and Queen's Pier (2007–2008), the anti-Express Rail Link protests (2009–2010), antiprivatization and Occupy Central (2011), the anti–national education campaign (2012), Occupy Central with Love and Peace (2013), the Umbrella Movement (2014), and the Fish Ball Revolution (2016), among others, a postcolonial generation had ignited a process of engaging and contesting entrenched colonial myths, turning them into rights claims and demands beyond the confines of double coloniality. By setting an end date for "One Country, Two Systems," the Communist regime created a generation who would bear the brunt of the city's unsettled future and therefore were the most determined to fight for it.

The souring of China's relation with the US-led West since around 2017 created a perfect storm for Hong Kong's decolonization struggle to expand and climax in 2019. Chapters 3, 4, and 5 go inside the 2019 movement to examine what made the pragmatic majority join the struggle previously spearheaded by the passionate minority of the younger generations and how their joint action pushed the decolonization struggle to new heights and in new directions. Chapter 3 documents the wide range of interests, identities, and emotions propelling citizens from different social strata, generations, and political orientations to the streets. They all had stakes in resisting the extradition bill and faced mainland China as the structural source of their discontent. Through sustained participation in different forms over six months, Hong Kongers were (re)born as members of a political community in action. This chapter also analyses the four mechanisms of solidarity that allowed the movement to sustain its political momentum: mechanical solidarity based on like-mindedness and compassion; reflexive solidarity based on conscious overcoming of past fragmentation; organic solidarity based on a division of labor and mutual dependence; and "quotidienization" of resistance. But the 2019 movement also had a dark side, which can be called "coercive solidarity," whereby minority voices were suppressed.

Chapter 4 tracks the evolution of this political community's engagement with an essential element in anticolonial struggles the world over: violence. If, before 2019, the majority of the populace still believed in the rule of law as the opposite of violence, then after the events in 2019, that binary distinction broke down irreparably. Three forms of violence were at the heart of Hong Kong's decolonization struggle: police, market, and institutional. First came the police use of disproportionate force with impunity, which united the citizenry as victims and challenged their entrenched beliefs in a stark opposition between "law and order" and "violence and chaos." Through mass participation in different kinds of public action involving varying degrees of legality, the experiential and moral boundaries of violence and nonviolence were blurred. In particular, I explore the experience and meanings of violence among the "brave warriors," the frontline youth who risked their lives and futures by battling the police. Instead of the cathartic effects of violence, which, according to Franz Fanon, free the colonized from their feeling of inferiority and humiliation, the Hong Kong youths spoke of sacrifice, discipline, and moral obligations. Several months into the uprising, pained by the heavy toll exacted by violent street clashes, citizens called for three other campaigns to bend the arc of violence and steer the struggle off the streets. These attempts included a political consumer movement called the "yellow economy" made up of pro-democracy businesses, a new union movement aimed at democracy in the workplace, and an election campaign called "35+" seeking to use constitutional rules to paralyze the government. Activists' and citizens' promotion for and regime repression against these activities revealed the previously hidden colonial violence inherent in the oligopolistic market economy and the proestablishment election system.

In Chapter 5, I turn to the "international front" of the decolonization struggle through an inside look at five types of activism: crowdfunding for global advertisements, advocacy for international sanctions, lobbying the United State Congress for passing the Hong Kong Human Rights and Democracy Act, cross-movement solidarity building, and diasporic activism. Once again, the postcolonial generation provided the impetus behind these mobilizations, often with essential but unexpected support from the previous generations of émigré activists whose quiet groundwork became a legacy to build on. Their activisms punctured the colonial mythology of "China as destiny" and unleashed a search for alternative political visions that are still amorphous and tentative. Finally, the conclusion chapter summarizes the major historical characteristics and sociological mechanisms constitutive of Hong Kong's decolonization experience. (expand) It also contrasts two opposing visions of decolonization that will shape the future of Hong Kong and China. On the one hand, for Chinese Communist intellectuals and officials, decolonizing Hong Kong is both a method of nationalizing a formerly colonized borderland and a part of statecraft for building an imagined China-centered world empire. On the other hand, Hong Kong activist intellectuals talk of decolonization as a project of achieving relational equality through building institutions and alliances at the local, national, and transnational levels. How these imaginaries will be realized, or not, is beyond the scope of this book. But they all intimate the significance of Hong Kong's ongoing decolonization.

Method

The research for this book was carried out from 2019 to 2023, on the streets and in archives, in and outside of Hong Kong. For nine months (June 2019–May 2020), I observed and participated in many street rallies and befriended and interviewed a representative range of citizens who played different roles in the movement. After mass demonstrations subsided in mid-2020, due first to social distancing and pandemic-induced regulations and then to the National Security Law, I continued to interview people in and outside Hong Kong, including exiled dissidents and activists against whom the government had issued arrest warrants and bounties. The time lapse between 2019 and 2023 allowed me to piece together the movement's multiple and simultaneous moving parts, something an ethnographer could never fully cover as events were happening. Having access to both real-time developments and reflections in their aftermath combined two opportunities for knowledge. Whereas the ethnographic moment captures what people did and thought inside the struggle without knowing the future, their recollections and reflections add insights to historical knowledge. Archival research in London and the secondary scholarship on Hong Kong provided the material for reconstructing the nature of pre-1997 colonial hegemony.

The subjects in this book include prominent leaders and iconic activists, as well as citizens who were not public figures but whose experiences and points of view I found representative of the broader public. Both during and after 2019, many people teared up talking about what happened. Everyone seemed to have witnessed particularly selfless acts by fellow citizens that moved them to the core. After the crackdown by the regime, the destruction of Hong Kong pained them as much as the realization that their memories of 2019 were fast receding. Rather than being "faceless" and "leaderless," the movement could be described more accurately as a mosaic of the multitudes in which every tiny dot was a center of leadership and capacity. To protect the subjects of this study in the era of the National Security Law, all names in this book are fictitious except for those who expressly wanted to be identified. Their courage to speak truth to power is also part of Hong Kong's anticolonial struggle.

I hope this book will be of interest and value not just to scholars but to Hong Kongers and others who care about this international city. Emphatically, though, this work is *not* a celebratory chronicle by a Hong Konger nostalgic for her fallen homeland. Nor is this a China-bashing exercise: Hong Kong people's fight for decolonization also targeted basic tenets of British colonialism, not just China's more recent encroachment. In short, my twin objective is to render, from within the struggle, an empathetic and intimate account, and from the outside, a dispassionate sociological analysis on how the decolonization of this global city has unfolded and intensified, what made its political capacity possible and its agenda desirable, what it has achieved, and where it has fallen short. This, I believe, is what Hong Kongers need and want, not a starry-eyed eulogy to mirror Communist propaganda. I also hope this book contributes to what many people in it wanted to do: leave a legacy of resistance.

Finally, this is a book for the global public. Hong Kong has always belonged to the world, not in juridical terms of sovereignty enshrined in international treaties but in every other way. When I expressed this view in a public forum in 2020, the Chinese Communist propaganda machine launched a smear campaign against me and others. But the fact of the matter is, thanks to its centuries-old open economy, its geopolitical location between East and West, and its bilingual culture, countless people from all over the world have visited, sojourned, worked, studied, grown up, and gotten married in the city. Hong Kong's fate touches all who have connections to it. At a time when the Chinese Communist regime is keen on rewriting the city's history, asserting, for instance, that "Hong Kong has never been a British colony," the world needs to be mindful.[27] Franz Fanon has long noted, "Colonialism is not content to impose its laws on the colonized country's present and future.... With a kind of perverted logic, it turns its attention to the past of the colonized people and distorts it, disfigures it, and destroys it."[28] It is no accident that Milan Kundera also arrived at the same observation about Communism, famously reminding us that "the struggle of man against power is the struggle of memory against forgetting."[29] History and memory are at the heart of Hong Kong's struggle in the throes of renewed colonization.

CHAPTER ONE

COLONIAL MYTHOLOGIES

HONG KONG IS A MAGNIFICENT ENIGMA. For a taste of its most accessible and mundane beauty, just stand in the middle of the city to take in the splendor of the nighttime Victoria Harbour. True to its century-old reputation as the crown jewel of the British empire, the city always sparkles with a panache all its own. The competitive energy of lit-up corporate powerhouses standing shoulder to shoulder along the waterfront is modulated by the rugged mountain ranges that wrap around the city, itself the densest tapestry of humble residential lights. The symphony of their reflections in the water, and the buzz of ordinary life connecting everything, horizontally and vertically, complete this masterpiece of a landscape. "I don't think I will ever tire of this view," wrote Chris Patten in his diary with a longing befitting a last governor overseeing the empire's retreat.[1] He knew better than most that what lay incongruously behind the glamor was the city's enduring coloniality.

Throughout the centuries, politicians, historians, and social scientists have coined evocative terms to describe the city's enigma—"borrowed place, borrowed time," "edge of empires," "East meets West," "capitalist paradise," "cauldron of world cultures," "Cold War's contact zone," and more. In one way or another, they all pointed to the contradiction that one of the most affluent and cosmopolitan economic centers of the world has never left the political dark age of colonialism. After the British handed over the city's sovereignty to the People's Republic of China in 1997 and the city received a promissory "One Country, Two Systems" note with a 2047 expiration date, new entries to this rich lexicon have added another layer of colors and intrigue. Metamorphized over two decades, Hong Kong has become a "city of protest," a "city on the edge," a "rebel city," and the "restive frontier of global China." The most unforgettable rebellion erupted in 2019: six months of thunderous million-strong uprisings on the streets, followed by another six months of unrelenting if subdued defiance, only to be starkly arrested by Beijing's crackdown in mid-2020. How and why did the colonized become rebellious decolonizing subjects? More specifically, why did a decolonization struggle not happen under foreign British rule but under Chinese national sovereignty? Bucking a global trend, Hong Kong was made an exception to the wave of decolonization in the post–World War II era. When the British began to withdraw belatedly in the mid-1980s, the preparation was not for the colony's independence but for its absorption into another country. Delayed and denied from above, why did decolonization from below in this British colony of nineteenth-century pedigree return in recent decades with a vengeance against an aspiring Chinese empire coming of age in the twenty-first century? Second, unlike other anticolonial struggles, the main social force demanding change was not a national bourgeoisie championing independence, a racialized and exploited working class, or a dispossessed and wretched peasantry. It was a political generation coming of age in the transition from British to Chinese rule. What accounts for the formation of their decolonizing subjecthood?

Forever a Colony: The Durable Structure of Double Colonization

Historians have generally defined decolonization as the process whereby colonial powers transferred institutional and legal control over their territories and dependencies to formally sovereign nation-states. They speak of waves and patterns of decolonization so varied in methods, agents, goals, and consequences that the phenomenon defies generalizations.[2] In the late eighteenth century, the American and Haitian Revolutions were the first successful challenges to colonialism. Napoleonic upheavals in Europe so weakened Spain and Portugal that European settlers from Mexico to Chile expelled their imperial masters. By 1825 the Spanish and Portuguese empires were shadows of their former selves. Then came Cuban independence in 1902, and the white settler colonies (Canada, Australia, New Zealand, and South

Africa) were granted internal autonomy by the British Parliament's passage of the Statute of Westminster in 1931. Between 1945 and 1989, over one hundred new independent states were born. In Asia and Africa, national independence movements also made claims to alternative civilizations as a counterpoint to the modern capitalism from where imperialism developed. But such empowering rhetoric "also subordinated other claims for justice and equality to the nation as the representative of a civilization."[3] Nation building was therefore a process of the nationalist elites establishing hegemony over marginalized "fragments" of the nation. Hong Kong was one such "fragment" in China's nation-building project.

The age of decolonization was formally endorsed by the 1960 United Nations' Declaration on the Granting of Independence to Colonial Countries and Peoples. In those days in Hong Kong, progressive reformers, mostly liberal-minded expatriates and Chinese elites, formed various clubs and parties to demand constitutional changes, from increased electoral representation in the legislature to Hong Kong as a self-governing dominion within the Commonwealth. Yet, when the PRC gained a permanent seat at the United Nations in 1971, Beijing quickly maneuvered to remove Hong Kong and neighboring Macau, a Portuguese colony, from the United Nations' list of non-self-governing territories, thereby depriving these cities of the right to self-determination.[4]

British acquiescence to China's Hong Kong policy at the United Nations epitomized a broader pattern of what I call "double coloniality." In legal terms, British sovereignty over Hong Kong was formally recognized in international treaties.[5] But in practice, and especially at critical junctures, the China factor loomed so large in London's calculations that it was more accurate to speak of the China presence as a case of phantom colonialism, opaque but always haunting. Sino-British collusion, collaboration, competition, and conflict coproduced and reproduced colonial rule in Hong Kong.[6] This double coloniality makes Hong Kong's experience unique, for it meant that the local populace was subjected to two colonial masters with shared interests, despite their antagonism. It also made the 1997 formal transfer of sovereignty peaceful and amicable. China had insisted that Britain hand over a Hong Kong with its original political economic system intact because it wanted to inherit the same structure of colonial domination. Yet, to the dismay and bafflement of Beijing, even as the structural features of colonial domination remained largely the same under both British and Chinese rule, mass resistance erupted only under the latter. More than once, top Chinese Communist officials responsible for Hong Kong affairs asked the public: why did you not rebel under the British when you had even less democracy? Their diagnosis—that the people's "heart and mind" had not reverted to China—correctly pointed to the breakdown of popular consent as the crux of the problem. But why and how did subjectivity and subjecthood change under the same power structure of colonial domination?

This chapter first offers a thumbnail sketch of the similar structure of colonial rule in both pre- and post-1997 Hong Kong to establish the fact that the city has remained a colony, regardless of its formal change in jurisdictional status. A consequential crack in this repressive power structure developed during the last quarter century of formal British control when the colonial government quietly set off a decolonization process from above, one that fostered a colonial hegemony without fundamental change in the structure of colonial rule. This chapter then explains the four mythologies constituting this colonial hegemony. The rest of the book tracks how events since 1997 dismantled these pillars of popular consent through a process of decolonization from below.

Historians have established the contour of Hong Kong's colonial power structure: a ruling bloc consisting of British colonial officials and British merchant capital controlled the economy and the legislature and imposed a repressive rule-by-law regime over the local population made up mostly of waves of refugees from mainland China. Crucially, though, mediating between the colonial bureaucracy and Chinese society was a local Chinese business elite class that worked at the edge of both the British and the Chinese empires and the cracks within them. Rewarded with privileges—land grants and commercial monopolies—by the British, they became co-opted collaborators in the colonial establishment, gaining recognition by contributing to war funds and organizing festivities in honor of British royalties while also dominating the local community via philanthropic, religious, and cultural institutions. As a ruling alliance, "Chinese merchants, British merchants, and colonial officials were all interested in the expansion of capitalism in Hong Kong and China."[7] The structural domination of the business-bureaucratic bloc has endured since 1997, even though the cast of character has been replaced. The erstwhile comprador class, homegrown tycoons and politicians groomed or co-opted by the Chinese Communist Party, have joined hands with mainland state capitalists and their representatives to dominate a still-oligopolistic market economy. At the grassroots levels, "united front" organizations and foot soldiers have penetrated working-class neighborhoods with their extensive patron-clientelist networks offering petty material benefits and services in exchange for political allegiance.

The political system has remained decidedly autocratic across the two periods of colonial rule. From the beginning of colonial rule in 1842 to the present day, it has been executive led—headed by either a governor appointed by London or a chief executive appointed by Beijing, who then selected his own advisors, forming the Executive Council. This draconian system is marked by the conspicuous absence of universal suffrage and the people's right to self-determination, both of which have long been enshrined as universal human rights in international covenants. The legislature under both British and Chinese rule has been returned by a hodgepodge of electoral rules over the years, including appointments, indirect election, and functional constituencies elections available only to professional and business groups. Popular votes have never returned more than half of the legislators. Direct election for a limited number of seats (eighteen out of sixty) in the legislature did not happen until 1991, only six years before the end of formal British rule.[8]

Like other colonial regimes, race was an organizing principle of power and "colonial othering." From racial segregation in residential patterns to membership in social clubs in the early decades of colonial rule, the color bar assured expatriate domination in senior civil service (until the 1990s). English was the only official language (until 1974) in a majority-Chinese society in which Britons and Europeans formed a privileged elite.[9] A peculiar racialization of the Chinese was used to justify autocracy. The local population was deemed unsuited for political participation thanks to their purported traditional culture. As late as 1966, a British Parliamentary report still referenced Confucian classics to conclude that for the Hong Kong Chinese, the relationship between the government and its people was analogous to one between parents and children, a shepherd and his flock. It argued that "This traditional concept does not contemplate the direct participation of the population in the organization or processes of government."[10] This was how the colonial regime justified the absence of popular direct election to even the lowest rung of the political system until the 1982 district board election (for only one-third of seats). After 1997, race and colonial othering have operated with a new logic. Instead of racial difference, the Communist regime uses racial commonality, in the form of Han nationalism, as its justification to resume sovereignty. In the official discourse, Hong Kongers are the descendants of the Yellow Emperor, the common ancestor of all Han Chinese bounded by blood ties. The relation between the Chinese mainland and Hong Kong is therefore similarly naturalized as biological and primordial, expressed in the phrase "blood is thicker than water." Under this racialized nationalism, only "patriots" (i.e., supporters of the Chinese regime) can rule Hong Kong, and opposition political leaders are assailed as "traitors" of the Han race.[11] In the eyes of Beijing officials, British colonialism has made Hong Kong people lesser Chinese, with lifestyle, mentality, and culture too alienated from the Chinese nation. As with other ethnic minorities under Chinese sovereignty, the policy solution is coercive assimilation, including systematic nationalistic education and ideological indoctrination targeting the younger generations.

Colonial othering goes beyond racialization. What Aime Cesaire termed "thing-ification" can be found under both British and Chinese rule, as Hong Kong people and society have been objectified as an instrument, a "one-dimensional" (a la Herbert Marcuse's one-dimensional man) society whose raison d'être was to serve the economic needs of its two masters—trade and profits for the British and foreign exchange, intelligence, and external connections for the Communist mainland.[12] At multiple junctures of political agitation before 1997, Beijing, no less than London, was adamant in repressing and punishing pro-China activists who dared to destabilize the colony, lest the city's economic functions be disrupted. The British colonialists celebrated the Hong Kong Chinese as the model *Homo economicus*, whose defining qualities were industriousness and entrepreneurship. Similarly, the Communist regime's policy toward Hong Kong was famously and publicly summed up as "full utilization, long term planning." Hong Kong and its people were dehumanized and instrumentalized as "the goose that lay the golden egg." After 1997, as China's interest pivoted toward global integration and the inflow of capital, technology, and trade, Hong Kong has been made the "other" system under the "One Country, Two Systems" framework. Its promised autonomy has always been conditional on its service to the need of the country, and hence its abrupt termination in 2020 in the aftermath of the 2019 uprising, when national interest called for confrontation with the West.

These structural features of repressive domination underpinning double colonial rule were fertile soil for resistance. Throughout much of formal

British sovereignty, as we see in the next section, popular unrest spurred by political events in the mainland and in Taiwan, as well as social discontent against the colonial government, regularly rocked Hong Kong society. Especially in what historians call the "fiery 1970s," stirrings of a self-conscious albeit marginalized "anticolonial" movement were evident in the campaigns for the use of Chinese as an official language and to protect Diaoyutai. Yet, two factors had prevented full-blown rebellion against the British. First, repression was relative. Bearing witness to decades of political atrocity committed by Communist China next door had kept Hong Kongers' anticolonial sentiment at bay. Between colonialism and Communism, people found the former a lesser evil. Second, as London strategized for a glorious exit in 1997, it made deliberate efforts since the 1970s to create a rule by consent. Social and government reforms, infrastructural investments, and initial steps toward democratization took place just as the Hong Kong economy successfully transformed itself from an industrial colony to a global financial center, allowing the elites to share prosperity, no matter how unequally, with the people. Under these colonial situations, people's pursuit of material wealth, comfort, and social mobility became their most salient orientation, with political aspiration and anxiety playing subdued second fiddle. It was during this period that Britain and China orchestrated a colonial hegemony in which consent outweighed coercion. If a decolonization movement did not happen before 1997, it was largely due to the success of this hegemony in producing the popular experience of colonialism as a benign force and the colony as a miracle city. After 1997, the busting of these myths also motivated resistance to the colonial regime now under Chinese sovereignty. The next section unpacks the core elements of this hegemony with two objectives: to show that these myths sanitized and simplified Hong Kong's colonial experience but created consent and to establish the benchmarks for tracking changes in experience and subjectivity after 1997.

Debunking Colonial Mythologies

At the heart of the colonial hegemony in Hong Kong were four presumably nonnegotiable, taken-for-granted principles that formed the basis of popular consent and set limits to legitimate political behavior. They were stability and prosperity, rule of law, free-market utopia, and China as destiny. Both London and Beijing had shared interests in orchestrating and perpetuating what citizens had also come to hold proudly as their "core values." In actuality, these principles were mythologies manufactured and articulated by the political, economic, and cultural elites through intellectual leadership and material concessions. Their discursive constructions of reality rang true because they were not based on lies, but selective appropriation of historical facts and marginalization of alternative voices.

The four foundational myths were the cornerstones of the Hong Kong legend that it has always enjoyed "prosperity and stability," the quintessential definition of a good society wanted and cherished by the local Chinese. British colonialism provided the essential institutions for achieving this good society because it brought to Hong Kong the "rule of law," civil liberty, a clean bureaucracy, and a "free and competitive capitalist economy." Freedom, not democracy, was the people's top priority. Due to the population's Chinese descent and China's insistence on its historical sovereignty, China is the ineluctable destiny of Hong Kong.

As a regime of truth consolidated since the early 1970s, these four claims had exerted powerful holds on people's self-image and collective imagination of their city. Paradoxically, under varying historical circumstances, these myths motivated both colonial submission and decolonizing rebellion. On the one hand, they secured people's submission by setting limits to the terrain of feasible and desirable political action, as if they issued a menacing warning: "don't rock the boat!" On the other hand, emotional investment in these ideologies also spurred citizens' protests against their erosion and violation by Beijing after Britain's exit. And through popular mobilizations, new visions beyond the four tenets emerged. For each of these components of colonial hegemony, I explain its contents, makers, and effects, based on both old and new scholarship in Hong Kong studies. It should be clear from the following that Britain and China coproduced these mythologies through cooperation, conflict, and complicity. The popular struggles that would emerge after 1997 were "decolonizing" in that they aimed at or resulted in the dismantling, however uneven and incomplete, of these mythologies.

Prosperity and Stability

As Hong Kong's signature catchphrase, "prosperity and stability" (繁榮安定) had been used as a description of the city's achievement, the people's definition of a good society, and their common aspiration. It was the leitmotif played up to the world and local audiences by both Britain and China with pomp and pageantry. At the handover ceremony on June 30, 1997, Prince Charles, representing Queen Elizabeth II, declared that "Hong Kong has shown the world how *dynamism and stability* can be defining characteristics of a successful society. These have together created a great economy which is the envy of the world." The Chinese president, Jiang Zemin, representing the new sovereign, also pledged that "China and all the countries and regions that have investment and trade interests here will continue to work for the *prosperity and stability* of Hong Kong."[13] But it was the colonial reckoning by the last governor on the last day of empire in the territory that best articulated "prosperity and stability" as a narrative of achievement embraced by Hong Kong Chinese with the help of British institutions:

> The restless energy, the hard work, the audacity of the men and women who have written Hong Kong's success story—mostly Chinese men and Chinese women. They were only ordinary in the sense that most of them came here with nothing. They are extraordinary in what they have achieved against the odds. As British administration ends, we are, I believe, entitled to say that our own nation's contribution here was to provide the scaffolding that enabled the people of Hong Kong to ascend: the rule of law; clean and light-handed government; the values of a free society; the beginnings of representative government; and democratic accountability. This is a Chinese city, a very Chinese city with British characteristics. No dependent territory has been left more *prosperous* . . . and most *stable* too.[14]

The myth of prosperity and stability was coproduced by the Sino-British political elite and local academics and found resonance in the media and the public. Tracing its emergence in local newspapers, John Wong showed that the phrase first appeared in Hong Kong's major English newspaper, the *South China Morning Post,* in the aftermath of World War II, citing a British legislator's comment on Hong Kong's role in postwar "Far Eastern prosperity and stability." In the late 1960s, the paired notion appeared in the Chinese press not just as the unilateral effort of the colonial government to court public support but as "the joint product of the colonial regime and Hong Kongers who concomitantly crafted the notions and promoted acquiescence to continued British colonial rule after the disconcerting experience of 1966 and 1967."[15] The real explosion of the term in public discourse happened in the early 1980s, during the Sino-British negotiations on the future of Hong Kong. The rhetoric of prosperity and stability became the terms of the two countries' bargaining chips and their competition for legitimacy and popularity among the angry and anxious Hong Kong population excluded from the negotiation table. From 1983 to 1984, references to prosperity and stability more than doubled in the English and Chinese pro-business presses and tripled in the local pro-Beijing press, signaling that "the Chinese regime was an equal, if not the dominant, partner in enshrining the cherished values as a slogan in Hong Kong's collective mindset."[16]

Scholarly work also lent scientific gravitas to the narrative of prosperity and stability as Hong Kong's reality and ideology. The most influential and definitive treatise was *Politics and Society in Hong Kong* (1982), written by the sociologist Siu-kai Lau, one among the first generation of local-born but US-trained social scientists. He set out to explain Hong Kong as a "twentieth-century miracle" singular in its achievement of political stability under highly destabilizing conditions: rapid economic growth, urbanization, a colonial regime professing laissez-faire and social noninterventionism, all of which had led to political breakdowns and exclusionary regimes in the Third World. A key to resolving the Hong Kong puzzle of stability was his canonical notion of "utilitarian familism," denoting the normative and behavioral tendency of Hong Kong Chinese to put familial prosperity above all else. Based on his and others' survey data collected in the 1970s, Lau's portrait of Hong Kong society spotlights people's fetishism of material wealth, short-term time horizons, social avoidance, political aloofness and apathy, and obsession with social stability, which they saw as the primary responsibility of the government.[17] Thanks to this Chinese cultural trait, even an alien, inflexible, undemocratic colonial bureaucratic polity was spared the challenge of popular mobilization for social service and political participation that was characteristic of many developing countries.[18] Poignantly, Lau concluded that "perhaps the *most* important factor underwriting political stability in Hong Kong is ... the stabilizing effects of political passivity and apathy. As a society composed of a huge number of mutually 'isolated' familial groups ... mobilization of the Chinese people into sustained, large-scale political action is almost an impossible mission."[19]

Lau's analysis was the most parsimonious and systematic, but his diagnosis echoed other scholars, both expatriate and Chinese, writing at the time. They all underscored the successful marriage of British colonial managerialism and purportedly innate Chinese familialism, producing a depoliticized but highly materialistic, industrious, and stable society.[20] But was the "prosperity and stability" so celebrated by the elite an accurate description of Hong Kong society's experience and aspiration? This section argues that prosperity and stability was a mythology resulting from a tunnel vision that falsely generalizes the short 1970s–1990s to the entirety of Hong Kong's colonial trajectories, thereby drastically flattening and obfuscating its variegated historical experiences and popular aspirations over more than a century.[21] Contradicting the myth of stability and prosperity, Hong Kong historiographies had chronicled the eruption of major incidents of social and political unrest every few years in almost every decade prior to the 1970s. Social surveys had also painted a complex range of citizen demands beyond wealth and order.

From the founding moment of the colony in the mid-nineteenth century, the combination of antiforeign sentiment and resentment of the colonial government's exorbitant demands provoked a general strike by the Chinese in 1844 in response to a poll tax and individual registration ordinance.[22] Poverty and misery against the background of foreign wars with China spawned social unrest led by the coolies, boatmen, dockyard workers, sedan chair pullers, hawkers, domestic servants, and Triad secret societies. As political turmoil flared in the mainland at the end of Qing rule—the Sino-French War, the Sino-Japanese War, the Hundred Days' Reform, and the Boxer Uprising—antiforeignism turned into popular nationalism in Hong Kong. The colony, thanks to its economic and intellectual ties to the West, famously became the revolutionary base for Westernized intelligentsia, barristers, physicians, and merchants aiming at overthrowing the Manchus and the gentry-scholar-official political order. Propelled by a nationalistic concern for China and their own class interests, these elitist nationalists, including Sun Yat-sen and other Cantonese revolutionaries, recruited the more literate segment of Hong Kong's laboring masses, the mechanics, traders, artisans, and coolies, into revolutionary organizations such as the Siyi Association and Tongmenhui.

The successful 1911 revolution inspired a new republican patriotic fever and political consciousness at the grassroots level. Widespread disorder gripped Hong Kong, compelling Governor Lugard to invoke emergency powers under the Peace Preservation Ordinance in 1911. These outbursts against colonialism included a three-month-long tram boycott in 1912–1913 and the anti-Japanese May 4 boycott by merchants and students in 1919. During the "roaring 1920s," when postwar inflation and a boom in production strengthened labor's bargaining power and grievances against racialized class exploitation became politicized, Hong Kong workers pulled off an impressive total of forty-two strikes between 1920 and 1922. By any historical standards, these were large-scale political actions: a nineteen-day strike by mechanics in dockyards, factories, and utilities companies; a 10,000-strong seamen's strike lasting two months; and a general strike by a quarter of the entire labor force in 1922 that reduced Hong Kong to a ghost town and a dead harbor. But it was the general strike-boycott from June 1925 to October 1926 that "came close to ruining Hong Kong and liquidating British interest in South China. . . . It was a gigantic political protest sponsored by the [Chinese Communist Party-Kuomintang] United Front in Canton using economic warfare against British imperialism. At its peak, the movement, drawing some 250,000 Hong Kong strikers and the families back to the Canton Delta, paralyzed the colony."[23] Demanding the end of unequal treaties, universal suffrage, and freedom of speech and association, the Hong Kong strike was a direct response to the May 30 incident in Shanghai involving the killing of Chinese workers by Japanese management and citizens by British police in the international settlement.

In the 1930s, as China battled against Japan's invasion, boycotts, street protests, and labor strife erupted in Hong Kong, involving thousands of seamen, dockworkers, and students and even turning deadly on a few occasions. After the Japanese occupation of Hong Kong, which lasted from December 1941 to August 1945, thousands of workers in the largest dockyards launched the first wave of strikes in 1946 over rehabilitation allowances and an eight-hour workday. Then electricity and ferry workers struck over race-based disparity in pay and disrupted power supply and transportation in the city. In 1947, which local newspapers described as the "year of the great labor movements," Hong Kong saw "wave after wave of labor actions" by peak tramway workers, cotton weavers, dairy farmhands, tobacco workers, and taxi and bus drivers.[24] After a particularly bloody strike by the tramway workers in January 1950, where 800 police confronted thousands of workers and supporters with tear gas and batons, the colonial regime resorted to repressive measures, especially deportation of labor unionists, to restore industrial peace.[25]

Beyond labor discontents, livelihood issues from squatter evictions and shantytown fires to ferry fare hikes fueled social disturbances in post–World War II Hong Kong. The antieviction riot of squatters in the Kowloon Walled City (1948), the Tung Tau fire and the subsequent riot sparked by a comfort mission from China (1952), and the Shek Kip Mei shantytown fire (1953) mounted enormous pressure on colonial governance. More explicitly politicized unrest happened in 1952 and 1956 on the occasions of the two National Days respectively celebrated by the PRC and Taiwan. The 1956 Kowloon and Tsuen Wan riots were particularly bloody, resulting in eight deaths and a hundred serious injuries. Confrontations flared up between sympathizers and unionists of the two parties, as well as between the rioters and the colonial police. These were violent events entailing arson, physical assaults, looting, and mobs attacking union headquarters, factories, and public transportation. Police had to use tear gas, curfews, and military troops to restore order.[26] As the first postwar locally born generation came of age, social discontent triggered by the Star Ferry and Hong Kong telephone fare increase in 1966 evolved into multiday demonstrations, marches, hunger strikes, and riots.[27] Finally there were the watershed 1967 riots. Beginning as an industrial dispute in an artificial flower factory in Kowloon in April, violent clashes ensued between the workers and the police in May after intervention and mobilization by the pro-Communist trade unions. A protest statement issued by the Chinese Ministry of Foreign Affairs, followed by a sympathetic editorial in the *People's Daily*, emboldened local leftists to action. Seizing the frenzy of the Cultural Revolution in the mainland, local leftists launched a self-professed anticolonial violent struggle. A four-day general strike was called, and the use of some 1,200 genuine bombs and more than 8,000 suspected bombs paralyzed the entire city. The police responded with massive arrests of rioters and raids on Communist premises, reinforced by emergency legislation and the deployment of British troops. By the end of the riots, 51 were dead, 4,500 were arrested, and 465 were imprisoned for unlawful assembly.[28]

One thing is clear in this broad-stroke sketch of popular resistance from the late 1880s to the late 1960s. Hong Kong was *not* a land of prosperity and stability where an apolitical Chinese society coexisted with a law-bound colonial bureaucracy. Quite the contrary, what prevailed was poverty and instability and persistent, even violent, conflicts between a politically conscious populace and an aloof and autocratic alien regime. The 1966 and 1967 riots were the last straw in a century-old chronicle of political and social unrest that compelled a fundamental reorientation of colonial rule from one

1.1 Demonstrators at the Star Ferry concourse before the march to Kowloon on April 5, 1966. The placards read, "second day of hunger strike," "oppose fare increase," and "release detainees." Historians reckoned this incident as the first homegrown anticolonial social protest.
CREDIT: South China Morning Post

of neglect, distrust, and repression toward service, communication, and consultation. In the wake of the two violent and deadly riots, the colonial regime admitted its failure to secure active public support and legitimacy, especially among the younger generations. No longer prone to partisan politics rooted in the CCP and KMT rivalry as their parents were, the locally born youth (between the ages of fifteen and twenty-five) nevertheless lacked a sense of security, belonging, and civic responsibility to Hong Kong.[29] Murray MacLehose, who arrived as governor in 1971, explained his assessment and strategy to London:

> One feature that strikes me as salient is that though Hong Kong is the home of over 4 million who have to a greater or lesser extent rejected China, a large proportion have not fully accepted Hong Kong. A new

generation is growing up—55% of our population is under 25—and is demanding more from Government, often rightly. Like any other government this one must govern by consent and must do so without the aid of the electoral system. If that consent is to be retained, not only must legitimate demands be satisfied, but the population must be convinced that such satisfaction is genuinely the objective of Government. The need is not only for administrative action producing physical results; there is also a need to secure the active confidence of the population. We cannot aim at national loyalty, but civic pride might be a useful substitute.[30]

But it must be emphasized that pressure from below did not fully account for the reformist turn under the MacLehose governorship (1971–1982). The impetus for reform stemmed as much, if not more, from British strategic calculation toward China. Governors before MacLehose (for example, Alexander Grantham and David Trench) had been reluctant to pursue political and social reform in Hong Kong out of their own conservatism, their sense of vulnerability to Chinese military aggression, and fear of creating a mobilized and self-governing populace, which would upset the PRC.[31] But when MacLehose assumed his post in 1971, he understood that his was a "government in a hurry"; he stated, "A maximum degree of economic progress and tranquility in the Colony, and international respect for it, must be achieved during the run-up to the proposed attempt to negotiate about its future with the Chinese in the mid-1980s."[32] If not, the lack of assurance about the future would cause "investment and employment to drop . . . the Colony could rapidly go downhill to a point at which it became valueless to either the United Kingdom or China, and probably ungovernable, and thus invite Chinese intervention."[33]

Even though MacLehose resisted pressure from the governing Labour Party in London to democratize the legislature and impose radical reforms in labor rights and social security, his reign still witnessed transformative social programs.[34] These included the ten-year housing program driving the development of new towns, the introduction of nine-year free and universal education, the setting up of the Independent Commission Against Corruption, improving social services, freeing the media from government control, installing overt and covert mechanisms of public opinion collection, launching grassroots community campaigns to foster a Hong Kong identity, and more. These policies coincided with Hong Kong's successful metamorphosis from an industrial colony during the Cold War to a global city of high finance brokering post-Mao China's opening and integration with the world capitalist order. To top it all, MacLehose's keenly sensitive publicity campaigns created "a public image of Hong Kong as a much more liberal society than the communist mainland, thereby maximizing Britain's leverage in its future negotiations with China."[35]

The credence of prosperity and stability was largely rooted in people's collective memory of the MacLehose era as the city's golden years. But once again, memory and myth have a tendency to eclipse messy and inconvenient reality. Yes, overall GDP growth often exceeded 10 percent from 1968 to 1997. After adjusting for inflation, median income skyrocketed 36 percent during 1976–1981, 11 percent during 1981–1986, and a whopping 144 percent from 1986 to 1996.[36] These impressive growth statistics attested to the regime's capacity to fund social spending, make possible material concessions to the general masses, inspire boundless optimism, and craft a diagnosis of prosperity and stability focusing on colonial enlightenment and benevolence. Yet, the Hong Kong economic miracle was punctuated by erratic recessions caused by the oil crisis in the 1970s, stock market crashes in 1973 and 1987, and an exchange rate collapse in 1983 during the Sino-British negotiation.[37] The undeniable general prosperity prevailing from the 1970s to the 1990s was also accompanied by a steep rise in inequality, with the GINI coefficient climbing from 0.42 in 1971 to 0.52 by 1997.[38]

Finally, the *desirability* of prosperity and stability as the ultimate and singular definition of a good society among Hong Kong residents has been exaggerated. The MacLehose era was actually also Hong Kong's "fiery era," a term cultural historians used in reference to the bloom of social activism articulating alternative visions and values.[39] In tandem with the dominant ideology of prosperity and stability, progressive and socially concerned university students, teachers, Trotskyists, anarchists, community organizers, independent unionists, radical Catholic clergy, and critical artists forged a vibrant culture of dissent. After the Communist-controlled Left lost popular support in the aftermath of 1967, social movements and periodicals emerged under a variety of banners—anticolonialism, anti-imperialism, anticorruption, class struggle, social awareness, and learning about China. Their causes were wide ranging, from the use of Chinese as an official language, the extradition of the corrupt chief superintendent Godber, and the recognition of

1.2 Students demonstrated outside the city hall, with the Star Ferry Pier in the background, demanding the adoption of Chinese as an official language on March 14, 1971.
CREDIT: South China Morning Post

Chinese sovereignty over the Diaoyutai territory against Japanese claims to autonomy for school administrators, labor rights, housing rights for boat people, police reforms, and so on.[40] The colonial government was concerned enough to establish the Standing Committee on Pressure Groups in order to monitor the activities of these activist groups and either place their leaders under surveillance or co-opt them into the large number of advisory committees.[41] Most importantly for our purpose, their activisms challenged the monolithic myth about Hong Kongers' political apathy and crass materialism to the exclusion of other values.

It was not only the educated elite or rebellious youth who aspired to a good society defined by fairness, equity, and democracy, in addition to stability and prosperity. Surveys based on representative samples found that in 1985, 55 percent of the respondents agreed or strongly agreed that a good society was one where there was not much difference in incomes, and 64 percent found the gap between rich and poor in Hong Kong to be too large. A total of 50–56 percent of the respondents agreed that political leaders elected by the people would perform a better job and knew better what was good for Hong Kong than the current undemocratic system. While the majority (53 percent) of those polled disapproved of confrontational protests against the government, a plurality (47 percent) approved of radical actions to force changes in government policies.[42]

These historical and survey data alluded to a complex Hong Kong mentality that far exceeded the one-dimensional vision encapsulated by the "prosperity and stability" myth. But in an undemocratic political system, these yearnings remained an inchoate structure of feelings without systematic articulation to rival the dominant narrative. Hence, there was a widespread sense of collective disempowerment. Longitudinal survey data collected throughout the 1980s bear this out: 73–85 percent of respondents consistently expressed a "paralyzing sense of political powerlessness."[43] People of my generation who came of age in the 1970s and 1980s would remember living in a schizophrenic atmosphere of pride and anxiety, in which "prosperity and stability" was always uttered in the same breath with "a crisis of confidence."[44] Looking back, the popular obsession with prosperity and stability should be understood as the sublimation of Hong Kongers' persistent sense of powerlessness and resignation in determining their destiny. Making a virtue out of necessity, and trying to reconcile the contradiction between economic affluence and poverty in political agency, Hong Kongers invested morally and emotionally in the prosperity and stability myth as part of their self-limiting survivalist ideology.

Rule of Law

Hailed as the bedrock of the Hong Kong way of life, the rule of law was widely perceived as the most valuable asset Britain has bequeathed to the colony. The rule of law was deemed the institutional foundation of its other core values: freedom, human rights, justice, integrity and transparency, plurality, respect for individuals, and professionalism.[45] An important corollary of the rule-of-law narrative was that law-based governance was more important than democracy as a guarantor of freedom. That was why popular demands for democratization (defined as one person, one vote) before 1997 had remained weak.[46] Except for an episodic surge in support for electoral reform in the immediate aftermath of the 1989 Tiananmen Square massacre, Hong Kongers had acquiesced to what a prominent public intellectual called "virtual liberalism"—that is, mistaking limited negative freedoms for the real freedom to self-determination and full-fledged democracy.[47] The powerful hold of this myth engendered a behavioral consequence: Hong Kongers' engrained law-abiding dispositions. Until recent years, political activism had to be polite politics that observed the boundary of the law, otherwise it risked alienating the masses.

The centrality of the rule of law as a ruling ideology in a British colony is hardly remarkable. What is puzzling about the Hong Kong case is its indigenization as a local mythology embraced by the people. Tracing the myth's genealogy is a revelatory journey for the locally born like myself because the history of the law, like the history of the city itself, never made it to our curriculums, including that of the oldest law school in the territory.[48] The following discussion shows the stark discrepancy between the rhetoric of the "rule of law" and the reality of "rule by law" throughout most of the colony's existence.

Historians of the British empire have long documented that imposing the rule of law was "Pax Britannica's most potent elixir," liberal imperialism's "compulsory gospel," "a moral conquest, more striking, more durable, and far more solid than the physical conquest renders it possible. It exercises an influence over the minds of the people in many ways comparable to a new religion."[49] And as in other colonies, laws in Hong Kong bestowed legitimation on state violence to codify difference, curtail freedoms, expropriate land and property, and crack down on dissent and disobedience. Racial segregation and race-based prejudice were enshrined in legislation related to residency, public health, and mobility in the early decades of colonial rule.[50] Since then, the law has never ceased to be the principal means of suppressing political demonstrations and subduing organized labor.[51]

In the post–World War II era, largely due to the presence of Communist China as an external and internal threat, Hong Kong was exempted from human rights reform throughout the British empire. Even when Britain extended the European Convention on Human Rights to its colonies in the 1950s, restraining the use of emergency powers, Hong Kong was excluded. Officials there argued that "(o)ngoing violence and threats there from presumed Communist agitators" called for "a complete negation of human rights."[52] The detention and deportation regulations passed in 1956 and 1962, repealed only in 1995, which allowed the governor to detain and deport undesirable aliens without trial, were so draconian that they prompted reviews by the British Colonial Office. Among the seventeen Emergency Regulations issued in 1966–1967, one in particular stands out for its blatant denials of the rule of law and sobering reminders of how seamlessly colonial legality was transferred from British to Chinese hands today. Regulation 31 allowed the colonial secretary in Hong Kong to detain a person for up to a year without trial or reason; on expiry, detention could be renewed (repeatedly) for a further year. Indeed, in 1967, fifty-two leftist leaders were detained at the Victoria Road Detention Centre (the "White House"), many for over a year, in solitary confinement, and without trial.[53] Fast tracking to 2021 and under Chinese rule, forty-six democratic activists were arrested in a mass raid and detained for over two years before their trial began in 2023.

Even in periods without major civil unrest, draconian regulations allowed for mass detention without trial in the name of controlling criminal activities. For instance, between 1956 and 1960, some 32,000 were detained.[54] In 1973, because of the oil crisis, emergency regulations were passed to strengthen executive control over all walks of life.[55] Due to the deep and pervasive embeddedness of CCP and KMT affiliates and operations in Hong Kong civil society, the law cast a wide net for maintaining order. In addition to a wide variety of Emergency Regulations, the Education Ordinance, the Education Regulations, the Telecommunication Ordinance, and the Film Censorship Regulations were used to close schools and newspapers; deregister teachers; deport editors and school administrators; prohibit the display of symbols and flags of a political nature; censor textbooks, curriculums, news content, and scripts of dramatic performances; ban films for political reasons (well into the late 1980s); and jail citizens for inflammatory speeches, posters, and other nonverbal dissemination of undesirable ideas.[56] Other British colonial-era laws that would come back to haunt the 2019 protesters included the Sedition Ordinance (1938), which was later incorporated into the Criminal Ordinance, and the Public Order Ordinance (1967) amended in 1997. Many of these offences are now proscribed in the 2020 National Security Law.

The China factor in Hong Kong's double coloniality functioned more than just as a threat justifying draconian laws. The colonial government also had to strike a delicate balance between deterrence and appeasement, cajoling and bargaining, competition and confrontation. Appeasement with China was invoked by governors and local elites alike as a major reason for dismissing democratization as "inopportune" for four decades after the end of World War II.[57] A siege mentality of the colonial government and Britain's realization of Hong Kong's vulnerability loomed larger than any explicit objection

1.3 Police clashed with citizens at the Protect Diaoyutai protest in Victoria Park, July 7, 1971.
CREDIT: South China Morning Post

from the Communist leadership as an explanation for the lack of progress in representative government. As a matter of fact, Mao Tse-tung did not object to the idea of allowing democracy in Hong Kong, saying in an interview with a British reporter in 1946 that "so long as your officials do not maltreat Chinese subjects in Hong Kong, and so long as Chinese are not treated as inferior to others in the matter of taxation and a voice in the Government, I am not interested in Hong Kong, and will certainly not allow it to be a bone of contention between your country and mine."[58] In reality, it was not so much objection from China but the colonial government's worries about the potential dangers arising from Chinese politics infiltrating an elected legislature in Hong Kong that led Governor Grantham to abandon the constitutional reform proposal started by his predecessor, Governor Young, and endorsed by community groups from the left and right. Subsequent colonial administrations stuck to a risk-averse strategy of "masterly inactivity" in order to keep peace with China.[59] Sir David Trench (governor from 1964 to 1971) did not mince words when he said, "Every single policy—social, political or economic—is colored by China's nearness, China's attitudes, and the consequent difficulty of being certain of an assured future. . . . The situation demands great realism in all our thinking. . . . Hong Kong cannot afford the luxury of making mistakes, and particularly of well-meant mistakes, in any of its policies."[60] Paradoxically, therefore, the watchful presence of the PRC with irredentist ambitions acted as a disciplinary force to impede colonial rule from degenerating into a police state because any domestic crisis of its own making would risk its own survival.[61]

Beginning in the 1970s, bargaining with China became the strategic consideration of the colonial government. Foreseeing the need to engage Beijing in discussing Hong Kong's future, and to maximize London's leverage, MacLehose realized he had to win a popularity contest against China over its subjects. Part of his hegemonic project was to mark a moral boundary between a stable, law-based government in Hong Kong and a corrupt, unruly, rule-by-man regime on the mainland. The establishment of the Independent Commission Against Corruption became a landmark event in the genesis of the rule-of-law myth. Aimed at rooting out rampant corruption in the police force and other government departments, the commission's aggressive anticorruption campaigns were hugely popular. It became an icon of the principle of equal treatment before the law—a narrow definition of the rule of law—even though some of its high-handed measures against the defendants were criticized for violating the common-law principle of presumption of innocence.[62] Still reeling from the horror of indiscriminate violence during the 1967 riot, MacLehose's agenda of law-based and welfare-oriented government, emphatically without enhancement of political freedom and civil liberty, won the competition with China for the hearts and minds of Hong Kongers. The colonial government was so successful in establishing colonial hegemony that when the PRC and the UK began their torturous negotiations over Hong Kong's future between October 1982 and September 1984, the vast majority of the population preferred remaining a British colony to returning to China. Polls showed that 95 percent opted for the status quo, 64 percent for Chinese sovereignty under British administration, 37 percent for Hong Kong independence, and only 26 percent for full return to China.[63]

In order to not upset China, when Britain ratified the International Covenant on Civil and Political Rights and extended it to Hong Kong in 1976, little effort was made by the local government or London to announce its extension and to amend local laws in accordance with its provisions. Quite the contrary, the UK added the reservations that deprived Hong Kong citizens of the right to self-determination and the right to the development of representative government.⁶⁴ Only after Margaret Thatcher capitulated to Deng Xiaoping's insistence of recovering Chinese sovereignty over the entirety of Hong Kong did the British launch an eleventh-hour electoral reform to democratize what was then a legislature by appointment only into one "constituted by elections" as stipulated in the Joint Declaration signed in 1984.

But China's most earth-shattering impact on Hong Kong's rule of law came in the wake of the deadly crackdown on the 1989 Tiananmen protests. To assuage widespread panic and boost business confidence in the colony facing an imminent return to a brutal regime, the Hong Kong government proposed a Bill of Rights to establish a human rights jurisprudence. Besides the Bill of Rights Ordinance (BOR) itself, the Legislative Council passed a number of pieces of legislation to protect the provisions of the Bill of Rights covering equal opportunities and employees' rights to representation and collective bargaining, as well as extending international human rights treaties to Hong Kong, including rights of the child, women, and prisoners.⁶⁵

It should now be clear that the British colonial practice of the rule of law in Hong Kong always took into account the China factor. "China was probably the greatest friend and foe for all Hong Kong governors," remarked legal historian Michael Ng. "Whilst keen to keep a foot in the door of a huge potential market for British traders, the colony's governors had for a century been wrestling with what they perceived as potential state security risks flowing across the border.... Most of the political censorship laws and measures curtailing freedom of expression were designed to nip 'the China problem' in the bud, although what that problem was shifted over time."⁶⁶

Thanks to the BOR in 1991, the final years of British rule were marked by an unprecedented explosion of rights legislation, accompanied by a rigorous but ironic discourse about the rule of law as an entrenched feature of life in Hong Kong. If the function of a myth is "to transform history into nature," the oratorical cunning of the last governor, Chris Patten, who arrived in 1992, made him the master mythmaker of the "rule of law" as a self-evident essence of Hong Kong society. Taking a refreshingly confrontational approach to China, Chris Patten, a professional politician of the Conservative Party, tried to maximize the pace and space for electoral democracy and legal reforms under the framework of the Joint Declaration. Whether motivated by the desire for a glorious imperial retreat or a genuine commitment to democracy and human rights, Patten was singularly instrumental in cultivating Hong Kong's self-proclaimed "rule of law" identity as a society.

The legal scholar Carol Jones observes that this tide of belief in the rule of law rose as confrontation with the PRC intensified after Patten's appointment. The conflict with mainland China over Patten's reforms sent people scrambling for protective barriers around Hong Kong's "way of life."[67] Reiterated many times in almost all his public addresses, policy speeches, and media interviews over a five-year period, Patten hammered into the popular mind a message made up of interconnected terms. The rule of law was the "bedrock of your way of life." It guaranteed fair and equitable treatment for everyone and produced "a safe and secure environment for the individual, for families and for businesses to flourish." Hong Kong was a "decent, open, plural society living in freedom under the rule of law." No one was above the law, "no politician, no business leader, no Governor"; the law served everyone. The rule of law was the community's "most prized possession." As a master of mythic discourse, Patten managed to create a tunnel vision of 150 years of colonial rule based only on the last few years and convinced the populace not to question the British legacy to Hong Kong—a free-market economy, the freedom of the individual, the rule of law, and democracy.[68]

One of the major political and behavioral consequences of the rule-of-law myth is a law-abiding, conservative political culture. People show a moral obligation to follow the procedures and letters of the law regardless of their opinion about the law. Comparing two random surveys between the 1980s and 2010s, Hong Kong's legal culture seems to have become more compliant, perhaps because the 1990s had boosted people's confidence in the legal system. In 1985, 47 percent opined that they should obey the law even if the law is wrong because law-abiding citizens are necessary for an orderly society, while 21 percent opted for disobedience even if they had to face prosecution and jail time.[69] By 2017, 80–90 percent of respondents emphasized compliance with the law regardless of their opinion about the law and a preference for peaceful means to resolve conflicts.[70] Such law-abiding culture is also in evidence when citizens take political action. Polite politics and social discipline have remained the norm through the decades until the very recent past. Remarkably, between 1975 and 1995, even though "there were on average 182 public protests, processions and demonstrations every year, less than 1.5% led to even minor violence. From 2002 to 2012 the total number of public protests processions and demonstrations each year has increased from 2303 to 7529. The number of participants prosecuted was trivial: 29 in 2002 and 31 in 2012."[71]

The point is this: despite more than a century of rule *by* law, where colonial Hong Kong was subjected to a variety of draconian laws aimed at repressing civil liberty and political dissent, Hong Kongers subscribed, in ideology and action, to the myth that the rule *of* law has always been in the DNA of the city. The historical reality, as the legal historian Michael Ng concluded in his detailed study of political censorship and information control under British rule, is that "the freedom of expression enshrined in English case law never fully applied, if it applied at all, to Hong Kong simply because the law was superseded by numerous pieces of legislation imposing political censorship. . . . Independence of the judiciary was also a textbook doctrine rather than a reality in colonial Hong Kong. . . . The deep structural connection between the executive and the courts continued until less than a decade before Hong Kong's retrocession to China."[72]

Free-Market Utopia

The myth of Hong Kong as a free-market paradise was made world famous by the Nobel laureate Milton Friedman. In his landmark 1980 television series, *Free to Choose*, against the backdrop of Victoria Harbour, he declared in one of the opening scenes of the first episode, "If you want to see how the free market really works, *this* is the place to come."[73] He also wrote glowingly about his favorite economy: "Hong Kong, a Crown colony of Great Britain, should be the modern exemplar of free markets and limited government . . . Hong Kong has no tariffs or other restraints on international trade. . . . It has no government direction of economic activity, no minimum wage laws, no fixing of prices. . . . Hong Kong—a speck of land next to mainland China containing less than 400 square miles with a population roughly 4.5 million people. . . . Yet they enjoy one of the highest standards of living in all of Asia."[74]

For the local population, it was financial secretary (1961–1971) John Cowperthwaite's strident adherence to the doctrine of laissez-faire economics, and the coinage of the term "positive noninterventionism" by his successor, Philip Haddon-Cave, that had the most lasting impact. Recycled in numerous government papers, policy speeches, academic writings, and the media, laissez-faire economics—i.e., low taxes, small government, free trade, and avoidance of a Western-style welfare state—did more than explain Hong Kong's success and sanctify the government's approach to the economy.

The colonial elite used it as a political strategy and an ethical principle. As an economic doctrine, colonial officials argued that it provided a pro-business environment that granted maximum freedom for the pursuit of profit, the accumulation of personal wealth, competition-driven efficiency, and meritocracy. But it also meant no state resources for corporate bailouts and no protection or support for industries. In the absence of democracy, this fervent free-market ideology took on an ethical role of creating a clear distinction between "public" and "private" interests and thus was the basis of a social compact guaranteeing political and economic fairness.[75] The principle of a laissez-faire economy often equipped the government with a convenient excuse for doing nothing when faced with public demands for government action. The free-market ideology was of course at the center of the last governor's many influential rhetorical flourishes. Patten's agenda-setting policy speech in 1992 reflected Thatcher's neoliberalism:

> The success of the economy is central to all our hopes. We must do nothing to jeopardize it. Our prescription for prosperity is straightforward. We believe that businessmen not politicians or officials make the best commercial decisions. We believe that low and predictable taxes are the best form of investment incentive. We believe that government spending must follow, not outpace, economic growth. We believe in competition within a sound, fair framework of regulation and law.[76]

Unencumbered by the transfer of sovereignty, Hong Kong's economy was ranked the freest in the world for twenty-five consecutive years by the Heritage Foundation since 1995.[77] The index evaluates 177 countries in four broad policy areas that affect economic freedom: rule of law, government size, regulatory efficiency, and open markets.

But Hong Kong was not always a free-market utopia. First, the colonial government did intervene in the economy, albeit in covert ways, from the 1950s to the 1970s. Hidden state subsidies such as public housing, provision of education and medical care, rent control, and price negotiations for foodstuffs imported from China amounted to social wages that contributed significantly to capitalist accumulation and Hong Kong's takeoff as a low-cost manufacturing center.[78] Also, industry-specific policy interventions abound. Banking ordinances were enacted to regulate the unruly expansion and reckless practices of the banking sector, which saw periodic crisis from the 1960s to the 1980s. In the mid-1960s, when some local Chinese-owned banks failed, "the colonial government rescued and repaid the depositors to curb the potential for serious political unrest."[79] In the 1970s, regulations were issued on deposit-taking companies down to their interest rates agreements. A new Banking Ordinance was enacted in 1986 after a wave of banking crises erupted in the 1980s. In agriculture, too, the colonial government proactively organized marketing organizations and agricultural cooperatives and provided low-interest credit and cheap fertilizers in order to incentivize local food production and reduce dependence on Chinese food imports in the 1950s and 1960s. Sometimes, politically motivated economic policy took the form of a calculated refusal to intervene. The prime example was the government's rejection of manufacturers' strong lobbying for dedicated industrial land and the establishment of an industrial bank. The persistent bias against industries and industrial upgrading was due to the historical dominance of pro-British trading and banking interests in politics. State manipulation to "domesticate" industrial interests included marginalizing the oppositionist Chinese Manufacturers' Association and creating an obedient Federation of Hong Kong Industries.[80]

Aside from the discrepancy between the rhetoric of nonintervention and the reality of intervention, the free market was a myth because of its presumed but erroneous corollary that the free market means a fair and competitive market. The truth is that monopolies and oligopolies had long been pronounced and persistent, with the largest British companies in firm control of the commanding heights of the Hong Kong economy. In the 1970s "about half the total value of Hong Kong's public listed companies was accounted for by the Jardine and Swire Groups, together with Hutchinson Whampoa and Wheelock Marden.... Their chiefs or delegates sit on all the key bodies in the Colony . . . a tiny group that manipulates the money supply, the stock exchange and the government."[81] After the handover, even when these traditional British firms were totally eclipsed by Hong Kong Chinese and mainland state enterprises and a fair amount of deregulation was introduced after the 1980s, the business-government alliance remained intact. To this day, cartels and oligopolies dominate the banking, telecommunications, television, and even supermarket industries.[82] Most egregious is the property sector, where four companies are kings. The government's monopoly on land in the city has maintained a tight supply of land to keep prices high, and land sales have generated 40 percent of its revenue. The Sino-British agreement has entrenched this high land price regime for another fifty years. Behind Hong Kong's famously low income tax rate of 15 percent, a key source of much of its reputation as a free-market economy, lies a colonial relic of land monopoly by the special administrative region (SAR) government. By 2014, Hong Kong ranked at the top in *The Economist*'s "crony-capitalism" index.[83]

If the existence of a free-market utopia is questionable, so is the claim that it is the reason for Hong Kong's prosperity. The latter had much to do with external political economic conditions: the Cold War world economy and its embargo on China; the influx of waves after waves of refugees desperate for jobs; the arrival of skilled industrialists from Shanghai bringing with them capital, technology, and later multinational trading networks in an emergent international subcontracting system; and the US opening of its markets for East Asian imports as a containment strategy against Communism.[84] Since the 1980s, Hong Kong's rise as a global city was again not due to laissez-faire but was the fruit of a long historical accumulation of connectivity and expertise on international trading, banking, finance, legal, and informational services first to inter-Asia and then China trade.[85]

As an ideology, the official "free market" narrative glossed over people's ambivalence about laissez-faire. A territory-wide poll in 1988 found that the public accepted the principle of noninterventionism in general but "they were obviously not prepared to accept wholesale the distributive outcome of the market, as they want the government to regulate business activities to prevent fraud and tax the rich more heavily."[86] Moreover, the public was not sure how laissez-faire led to economic success. Siu-kai Lau and Hsin-chi Kuan, based on their longitudinal survey data, observed in 1990 that the free market "is regarded as the indispensable means by which Hong Kong achieved its economic success, even though the exact manner in which laissez-faire contributes to economic growth is not clear in the public mind. Accordingly, laissez-faire in Hong Kong is only weakly grounded in ideological argumentation."[87]

For decades, the rationality of free-market competition had been so hegemonic that it had set a salient limit to politics. "So successful was the colonial administration in making laissez faire and minimal economic and social intervention an integral part of the Hong Kong outlook," writes Leo Goodstadt, "that not a single serious political party in Hong Kong sought to challenge the legitimacy of this old-fashioned set of doctrines or their primacy in economic management before 1997."[88] The possible reasons for the lack of political demands for government intervention prior to 1997 included the robust growth of the economy keeping afloat even the most marginalized, the public's sense of powerlessness in influencing public policy, and the general support for capitalism among a population of refugees fleeing Communism. By the last years of the British colonial era, empirical data already showed a gross disparity between government and popular conceptions of laissez-faire, with the public demanding a highly interventionist government. As we see in the next chapter, the free-market spell on Hong Kong politics would only be broken after 1997, evinced by the formation of political parties running on socioeconomic equity platforms—the League of Social Democrats in 2006, the Labour Party and People Power in 2011.

China as Destiny

The idea that Hong Kong was on a preordained path of "decolonization without independence," due to be returned to Chinese sovereignty, had long been propagated by both China and Britain as the city's self-evident destiny. But in reality, this seemingly inevitable outcome had been jointly engineered by the two colonial masters, often by preempting, absorbing, and repressing its alternatives. Through it all, China and Britain colluded, not always amicably, and even competed in maintaining Hong Kong's status as an undemocratic colony from which they both derived immense interests. Neither wanted self-determination for Hong Kong, originally a political possibility endorsed by the United Nations' decolonization agenda in the 1960s. China's maneuvering and Britain's acquiescence aborted that possibility. Even before Hong Kong's future surfaced as an explicit diplomatic agenda, the colonial government always took pain to reassure China that its policy would steer clear of any possibility of full democracy and its presumed consequence, self-determination. Then, in the 1970s and 1980s, Britain pursued a two-pronged approach to ensure its maximum leverage in negotiating with China over Hong Kong's future. On the one hand, continuing its autocratic colonial rule, London endorsed China's insistence on excluding Hong Kong citizens from the negotiation table and precluded them from gaining the right of abode to Britain via the new Nationality Act. On the other hand, to augment its bargaining chips and prepare for a glorious exit, the colonial regime began to instill civic pride, local belonging, political participation, and communication as substitutes to the unattainable ideals of national loyalty and democracy. The consequence was the incongruous—and, for the people, rather painful—juxtaposition of a strong local identity of Hong Kongers as a distinct and proud community and a choiceless submission to the self-fulfilling prophecy of "China as destiny." A retrospective gaze at this history reveals the multiple junctures at which the destiny of Hong Kong could have changed course.

The first time the British recognized the future of Hong Kong as a problem was during the Pacific War. As the supreme commander of the Allied powers' "China theater," Chiang Kai-shek began negotiation with the British over the status of Hong Kong in 1942. After a century of humiliations, the KMT's public position had always been to end unequal treaties and recover lost territories. With the support of the United States, agreements were signed in 1943 among China, Britain, and the United States that China reserved the right to raise the question of the New Territories after Japan's defeat.[89] That scenario never came to be, as the British, rather than the KMT, liberated Hong Kong in August 1945, and China descended into civil war. With the imminent victory of the CCP, Communist emissaries in Hong Kong made it clear that unequal treaties were invalid, but Hong Kong was "a matter left by history" to be resolved when the time was ripe. The Communists had long valued the colony as a regional center from which to coordinate their revolutionary struggles and transmit directives to neighboring countries. After the founding of the PRC in 1949, Mao's policy "to defer the seizure of the colonial bastions of Hong Kong and Macao because of their economic value to China" had remained intact, even reaffirmed, through the turmoil of the Korean War and the Cultural Revolution. Seeing as irrelevant the technical legal distinction between the New Territories as a ninety-nine-year lease due to expire in 1997 and the rest of Hong Kong as a permanent concession, the Communist regime took a bifurcated approach to Hong Kong. Rhetorically waving the lofty banner of anti-imperialism as the Third World leader of the international Non-Aligned Movement, Beijing in practice took a calculated and expedient stance of "fully utilizing Hong Kong for the long term."[90]

On this the CCP found tacit mutual understanding with the United Kingdom. A British cabinet paper in 1949 made clear that Hong Kong's primary value was, echoing the instrumentalism of the CCP, as "a free port and place of exchange between China and the rest of the world." The paper prescribed a pragmatic rather than a principled approach to Hong Kong until the day

China would raise the issue of retrocession. It reckoned that "Before 1997 the United Kingdom Government of the day will have to consider the status of Hong Kong. But we are surely not justified some two generations in advance of the event in attempting to lay down the principles which should govern any arrangement which it may be possible to reach with China at that time."[91] As the United States refused to commit to defending Hong Kong against a possible Chinese invasion during the Cold War, Britain was cornered into a position of risk-averse governance, always anxious to appease China and avert its infiltrations in the colony. In short, throughout the post–World War II period, British colonial rule had all along assumed China to be Hong Kong's destiny, an inevitable and invincible force.

Yet, from 1949 through the 1960s, there was no lack of local stirring and international pressure supporting Hong Kong's cause of democratization and self-determination. Vocal "reformers" formed political associations and parties: the Reform Club (1949), Chinese Reform Club (1949), Hong Kong Civic Association (1955), Hong Kong United Nations Association (1955), Democratic Self-Governing Party (1963), Socialist Democratic Party (1964), and Hong Kong Labour Party (1964). Led by scions of the comprador class, expatriates, missionaries, and British-trained Chinese lawyers, these civic groups publicly criticized the colonial regime's abuse of emergency regulations to deport dissidents and dissolve legitimate organizations. Demanding the same kind of popular representation reforms granted to other British colonies, they lobbied MPs in London and engaged them in public debates during their visits to Hong Kong. The most colorful and radical of them was Ma Man Fai, the scion of the Sincere Department Store chain known for his flawless English and traditional Chinese attire. His United Nations Association (UNA) of Hong Kong advocated the ultimate goal of internal self-rule through universal suffrage. Criticizing the colony as a "paradise of plutocracy," the UNA's farsighted proposals in 1960–1961 included the creation of Hong Kong citizenship for all long-term residents, irrespective of race and nationality, as a guarantee for voting and other civic rights, as well as free universal elementary and secondary education so that all citizens could assume the responsibility of democratic government.[92] Not gaining much traction among the local populace, their efforts targeting Britain also proved futile. In London, the minister of Commonwealth affairs argued in 1966 that "because of Hong Kong's peculiar relationship with China, it would not be possible to think of normal self-government and not possible, therefore, to consider an elected Legislative Council."[93] An accompanying working party report on local administration released by the ministry in 1967 even cited Confucian classical references to justify the lack of direct political participation in the process of government, as Chinese traditional culture considered the relationship between government and people analogous to that between parents and children or between a shepherd and his flock.[94] Finally, the riots in 1966 and 1967 provided the last nail in the coffin, giving the colonial regime the perfect excuse to prioritize stability and order over democratization and liberalization.

This local striving, however marginalized, for constitutional change and eventual self-rule happened at a time when an international drive toward complete decolonization of all territories designated as "trust" or "non-self-governing" under the United Nations Charter was at its peak. Hong Kong was designated as a non-self-governing territory in 1946 and administered by Great Britain. In 1960, the UN General Assembly unanimously passed Resolution 1514, or the Declaration on the Granting of Independence to Colonial Countries and Peoples, stating, "All peoples have the right to self-determination; by virtue of that right they freely determine their political status and freely pursue their economic, social and cultural development. . . . Immediate steps shall be taken, in Trust and Non-Self-Governing Territories or all other territories which have not yet attained independence, to transfer all powers to the peoples of those territories, without any conditions or reservations, in accordance with their freely expressed will and desire without any distinction as to race, creed or color, in order to enable them to enjoy complete independence and freedom."[95]

Reaffirmed by the International Court of Justice and major international treaties, Resolution 1514 had come to be recognized as an authoritative expression of international customary law and the legal basis for the decolonization policy of the United Nations. The resolution also enabled the creation of a special committee to oversee the implementation of its principles and the use of elections to determine the will of the people. When the PRC joined the UN in 1972, it was appointed as a member of this special committee due to its long history of anticolonial struggle. In March 1972, China sent a letter to the Special Committee requesting the removal of Hong Kong and Macau from the category of colonial territories.[96] Despite disagreement among members of the Special Committee on China's request, the pro-China Tanzanian chairperson of the Special Committee glossed over the diversity

COLONIAL MYTHOLOGIES   49

of opinions to endorse China's request as the recommendation of the committee. As a result, the issue was not presented to the General Assembly for individual discussion, and the Special Committee report was summarily approved on November 2, 1972, by the General Assembly as Resolution 2908. Hong Kong and Macau were excluded from the list of territories to which the Declaration on the Granting of Independence was applicable.

Britain's position on this issue has remained a mystery to this day. It cast one of the five no votes, against ninety-nine yes votes, in the General Assembly, mostly as a political gesture. In substantive terms, Britain did not put up any fight against China. The only input it had was a letter sent to the secretary general after the passage of Resolution 2908 stating that the legal status of Hong Kong remained the same and Britain would discontinue the practice of transmitting information on Hong Kong as a non-self-governing territory in light of the resolution. While historians do not find any archival record about Britain's calculation specific to this decision about Hong Kong, a special report commissioned by the Thatcher administration on the eve of the Sino-British negotiations in the 1980s did underscore Britain's overall policy to appease China. The prospect of détente with the PRC in the early 1970s was tantalizing, compared to the rather unpalatable alternative of confronting Beijing over Hong Kong as a territory slated for self-government.[97]

Rather than a predetermined given, the destiny of Hong Kong was contested in the 1970s. Notwithstanding the UN resolution, a decade later, Britain under Thatcher would try to negotiate for a de facto continuation of its rule rather than returning the colony to Chinese administration. In the meantime, the colonial government continued to hedge its and Hong Kong's position with ambivalence. The most illustrative example was its governance of water supply. Touted as the unyielding material foundation of the "China as destiny" myth, Hong Kong's dependence on China for the supply of water was actually the result of political decisions rather than an act of nature. From 1959 to 1978, the colonial government created a localized self-sufficient water network by building and upgrading the Plove Cove reservoir, the High Island reservoir, and the world-class Lok On Pai seawater desalination plant. At the same time, as a medium-term solution to alleviate specific droughts such as those in 1959 and 1962–1964, the government also accepted China's politically motivated offer of supplying water to Hong Kong from the Dongjiang and Shenzhen reservoir. Maintaining water self-sufficiency was costly, compared to importing cheaper Chinese water, but the colonial government had one goal in mind: to minimize the risk of being reliant on China. A paradigm shift in water policy occurred in the early 1980s when financial concerns overshadowed political security considerations. The government abandoned desalination, ceased the construction of new reservoirs, and cut back on catchment areas. In 1985, Chinese supply of water reached 50 percent of total water consumption, and the rate increased to 76 percent in 1997.[98] Hong Kong had both become dependent on Dongjiang water and found itself needing to compete for it with other cities in Guangdong province.

Besides water, Chinese food supply was often cited as the basis of Hong Kong's inevitable reliance on the mainland for basic survival. Again, this was a myth because the historical fact is that China never gained total control over Hong Kong's food security. As a free port, the city has been able to import a variety of food products from virtually anywhere. The colonial government even devised a rice control scheme to increase supply and build up a stockpile through imports from Thailand and elsewhere, with the explicit aim of preventing a Chinese monopoly of rice supply. The local seafood industry consistently provided more than 50 percent of local consumption, and local supply of vegetables actually increased to more than 50 percent of total consumption throughout the colonial period. The only exception was livestock, for which imports from China had always accounted for more than 60 percent and in some years reached 80 percent.[99] Regardless, over the decades, official CCP propaganda tended to exaggerate the importance of Chinese food supplies, calling China's food export company Ng Fung Hong the food basket of Hong Kong and the Chinese food-delivery trains the lifelines of Hong Kong. During the colonial era, despite the public remaining indifferent, if not hostile, to the Communist state, there was a growing acceptance that China had a strong hold over the people of Hong Kong.[100]

Another episode illustrating the open-ended rather than pre-determined nature of Hong Kong's political destiny is the contestation over Hong Kongers' nationality and citizenship. In a short span of five years, Hong Kong people saw their citizenship changed from the standard category of British subjects holding British passports with limited partiality-based right of abode in Britain to British Dependent Territories citizens (BDTC) under the British Nationality Act (1981) without right of abode. Then, in 1986, in the wake of the Sino-British negotiations and with Chinese endorsement, Hong Kong residents were given a new nationality category, called British National (Overseas), or BNO. This status came packaged with a new passport to be

COLONIAL MYTHOLOGIES 51

used as a travel document, without British nationality or right of abode in the United Kingdom or the right of transmissibility to the next generation but with British consular protection in third countries other than Hong Kong or mainland China. While the 1981 Nationality Act was motivated by a general hostility toward non-white immigration from Hong Kong, as well as Malaysia, Singapore, and India, the BDTC and BNO statuses were Hong Kong–specific categories that had resulted from intense lobbying by Hong Kong legislators at that time and compromises by China and Britain in response to a crisis of identity and confidence among Hong Kongers.[101] These compromises and conflicts signaled, once again, the political genesis and legal inventiveness in the making of Hong Kongers' nationality and citizenship statuses. Nothing was historically inevitable.

A final example attesting to the historical contingency of Hong Kong's future was Margaret Thatcher's encounter with Deng Xiaoping on September 24, 1982. The UK Foreign and Commonwealth Office had always held the view that Hong Kong was indefensible militarily and the permanently ceded territories were economically unviable without the New Territories (or 92 percent of the Hong Kong land mass). Yet, buoyed by her victory in the Falklands War with Argentina just a few months earlier, Thatcher refused to surrender British sovereignty over Hong Kong Island and Kowloon. She was backed by international laws. Pointing out the two countries' mutual interest in maintaining prosperity and stability in Hong Kong, she boldly asserted Britain's superiority in achieving this goal because the majority of Hong Kongers preferred the colonial status quo. Deng not only staunchly enunciated his position that the time was ripe for resuming China's nonnegotiable sovereignty over all of Hong Kong, he even divulged to Thatcher that in the disastrous scenario where serious instability happened in Hong Kong in the next fifteen years of transition, the Chinese government would bravely tackle the disaster and be compelled to revise the time and mode of retrocession.[102] Famously, their meeting ended in such distressing discord that when Thatcher fell on the steps of the Great Hall of the People on her way out, the media harped on the shock she suffered from Deng.

In the following weeks, the Foreign and Commonwealth Office proposed giving economic incentives to China—concessional loans and assistance with building the Guangdong nuclear power plant and energy development projects in northwest Chinese—if China agreed to Britain's extended rule after 1997 under a new Sino-British cooperation agreement to substitute for the nineteenth-century treaties. This bold proposal for continued British administration of the Colony well into the future in exchange for fully reverting Hong Kong's sovereignty to China prompted Thatcher to urge London officials to consider moving the status of Hong Kong Island and Kowloon "closer to independence" so that citizens would be accustomed to governing local affairs in the face of possible Chinese pressure. In early 1983, she went on to urge the governor and foreign minister to promptly promote the goal of Hong Kong independence or self-rule through democratization in the next five years so that people would be willing to defend their existing way of life and stand up against Beijing. In another meeting, Thatcher even said, "A number of alternatives could be put to the Hong Kong people in a referendum ... they could be offered the choice between Chinese sovereignty plus Chinese administration, Chinese sovereignty plus British administration or other formulae. If they voted for Chinese sovereignty and British administration, this could be a useful card to play with the Chinese."[103]

During the twenty-two rounds of long and tumultuous Sino-British negotiations from July 1983 to September 1984, punctuated by diplomatic stalemates, stock market slumps, exchange rate slides, and citizens' panic buying of essentials on several occasions, different possibilities for Hong Kong's future were put forth and discussed by the colonial elite in Hong Kong and London. These included the Singaporean model of self-rule before its independence in 1965, an international consultative committee serving as a buffer institution between Beijing and Hong Kong, and other "credible elements of a British presence."[104] They were ultimately abandoned due to the intransigence of the Chinese government, which at one point announced it would impose a unilateral solution if agreement was not reached within one year. The fact that these options were even envisioned attests to the mythic nature of the claim that China is Hong Kong's inevitable and self-evident destiny. At various points in history, this outcome was far from certain.

In short, it was politics rather than destiny that made China Hong Kong's new sovereign. Without representation or participation in the high-stakes closed-door negotiations, Hong Kongers felt utterly powerless about the Joint Declaration. Signed by the premiers of both countries in December 1984 and registered with the UN as an international agreement, the document formally transferred sovereignty of the colony from Britain to the PRC. Its three annexes outline a fifty-year blueprint for Hong Kong's autonomy as a free port and economy, its executive-driven political system, and liberties based on the common law, all to be unchanged and enshrined in a Basic Law to be drafted by Beijing's appointees during the transition.[105] As "China as destiny" became a fait accompli, a gloomy view of the future prevailed in the mid-1980s. A territory-wide representative survey in 1986 described an "intense pessimism" taking hold. More than half of the respondents predicted a downward turn in living standards, 60 percent expected a reduction in freedom, 57 percent anticipated a reduction in civil rights, and 52 percent saw the degeneration of the judicial system. Only one-third thought that the status quo could remain unchanged for fifty years, and a mere 17 percent were optimistic that Hong Kong people could enjoy a happy and blissful life after 1997. What is noteworthy about this general pessimism was its incongruous coexistence with a strong sense of local capacity and identity. The same survey found that citizens believed that Hong Kongers were able to govern well (62 percent), even though only 22 percent expected the Chinese government to allow them to govern the city themselves.[106] While Hong Kong independence was deemed outside the realm of political possibility, longitudinal survey findings from 1985 to 1995 confirmed that the majority (varying between 50 percent and 64 percent) of the Hong Kong population identified themselves as "Hongkongese," consistently outnumbering those who identified themselves as "Chinese" (varying between 24 percent and 36 percent), with an average of 15 percent saying "both."[107]

The Tiananmen massacre in 1989 only darkened the horizon and heightened people's angst, driving an exodus of the middle class. From 1985 to 1997, 576,000 emigrated, mostly to Canada, Australia, New Zealand, and the United States.[108] After two mass demonstrations, each with over one million citizens, in support of Beijing students' demands for democracy in 1989, the majority of Hong Kongers stayed and acquiesced to the choiceless reality imposed on them. Distrustful of the new political class vying for positions in the suddenly democratized political system, they chose to pour their energy into seizing the seemingly unlimited economic opportunities opened up by the China boom. Occupying the front-row seats in the spectacle of China's rise in the world economy, and honing their traditional skills in bridging both, Hong Kongers, along with much of the West, embraced China's turn to capitalism and rooted for its collateral potential for political and social liberalization.

Without putting up any resistance, social and political activists saw the transition to Chinese rule as a moment of another kind of boom—the opening up of a political opportunity structure. Progressive and liberal intellectuals and politicians talked up the vision of "reunion in democracy," that is, the idea that Hong Kong's democratization would inspire a similar process on the mainland. From district board elections in 1982 to functional constituencies elections by corporate bodies in the Legislative Council in 1985 and direct election of eighteen and then twenty Legislative Council seats in 1991 and 1995, the electoral game absorbed a whole generation of political activists coming of age in the late colonial period into institutionalized politics. Former social workers, student leaders, and grassroots community activists championing housing rights and rights for hawkers, teachers, and workers jettisoned social movements for political parties and electoral seats as vehicles of progressive change. As these politicians became full-time salaried legislators with regular access to media, public-funded staff, and office resources, their parties became increasingly reliant on mainstream middle-class support to deliver the largest possible number of votes to keep them in their positions. Middle-class conservatism—minimal labor rights, lean welfare, and conciliatory relation with China—became the political mainstream.

The Poverty of Historical Agency

This chapter has revealed how many of the historical myths about Hong Kong run counter to reality. Instead of a people enjoying prosperity and stability, the city's politicized citizenry had witnessed and participated in decades of sociopolitical unrest and economic instability; instead of rule of law, people were subjected to an illiberal rule-by-law regime; instead of a free and competitive capitalism, Hong Kong's economy was long dominated by an entrenched oligopolistic expatriate elite; and rather than a predetermined outcome, its return to Chinese sovereignty was the result of political contestations between China and Britain. But the successful mythologization of prosperity and stability, rule of law, free-market utopia, and Chinese sovereignty as Hong Kong's essence and destiny defined the ethos of Hong Kongers on the eve of the 1997 transition. Despite rising local identification, expressed in popular culture, cinema, music, and literature, there was a lack of historical agency.[109] People felt that they did not control their own history. They were predisposed to lean heavily on adaptation for survival. The cultural critic Law Wing Sang had attributed this "localism without subjectivity" to what he calls "passive reunification" with China, or the absence of a genuine decolonization movement.[110] Despite incipient anticolonial agitations in the 1960s and 1970s, mentioned in previous sections, popular attempts to rethink and reject the colonial order did not happen until the rise of the postcolonial generations who would unleash a new subjectivity in the midst of political and economic structural transformation. Many young activists would come to blame their predecessors for surrendering Hong Kong to the Communist regime without even putting up a fight. But as this chapter has shown, the historical consolidation of these colonial myths put severe social constraints on what the older generation of activists could accomplish. During the years leading up to 1997, the general population was enthralled by the imminent China boom and Britain's eleventh-hour democratization of the Hong Kong political system.

To get an insider's glimpse of political activism in the 1980s and 1990s, and to empathize with what people at that time saw as within the realm of possibility in those days, consider the case of Lee Wing-tat, a key political figure at the center of Hong Kong democratic politics during and after the transition. Beginning as a student activist at the University of Hong Kong in the late 1970s, Lee was among the first generation of elected politicians, first in the Regional Council in 1986 and then on the district board in 1988. A cofounder of what would become the largest pro-democracy political party in Hong Kong in 1990 and one of the first directly elected legislators in the Legislative Council in 1991, his two-decade-long career as a legislator (until 2012) included a stint as the chairman of the Democratic Party in 2004–2006. When we met in London in 2022, he recalled the historical and social constraints for political activism and a very different public perception of China in those days:

> Today [2022] young people accused my generation of not fighting for Hong Kong's independence, and simply surrendered Hong Kong to China. But they have no idea what kind of society we were facing then. In the 1980s, I was already part of the democracy movement, but not in the very frontline. There were Uncle Wah [Szeto Wah], Martin Lee, Yeung Sum.... We faced many constraints people today do not see. The world is not a blank sheet of paper, and you get what you draw. In those days, the most powerful forces were Britain and China. Even Thatcher had to yield to China. Yes, China was poor but

they were willing to fight the Korean War at all cost. Most of the Hong Kong people had not touched a gun and there was no mass movement to speak of. In the mid-1980s, very few citizens showed up in public rallies or forums about Hong Kong's future or democracy. One or two hundred was considered a big number. The so-called milestone event, the Ko Shan convention in 1986, drew only seven hundred, even though we claimed there were a thousand. By the standard at that time, it was already unprecedented. Uncle Wah had a motto: "don't wear a big hat if you don't have a big head." We had little popular support and no bargaining chip. In 1987–1988, me and my party colleagues went to Xinhua News Agency to protest, and you know how pathetic, we only had one hundred or so people. It's so embarrassing in front of the cameras of BBC and other international media that we decided to bring more banners to create the illusion that there were more people.

So the imagination for an independent Hong Kong was not meaningful in a depoliticized society. Even the idea of democracy was very remote to most people at that time. Only the elite among the middle class were passionate about it. The business sector only cared about the China market. It was not until 1989 Tiananmen that a million people went on the street.

China then was also very different from today. In the 1980s, the CCP was relatively tolerant. Because it wanted international support, it presented a liberal face to the outside world. I still remember when Martin [Lee] was appointed to the drafting committee of the Basic Law, his proposal of including international judges on the Court of Final Appeals was accepted by Beijing! You look around the world, no country would accept foreign judges in its courts, not even the US. This tells you how much CCP wanted to convince the world it was a liberal force. I myself really aspired to the slogan of "Hong Kong people ruling Hong Kong." I was then a thirty-something district board councilor, and step-by-step through elections, I could envision myself becoming an official. You could say today I was naive, but the atmosphere in those years was indeed hopeful for us democrats. Uncle Wah and Martin also thought the CCP was negotiable. After 1989, we realized for the first time that CCP could not be trusted because it was willing to kill its own people to protect its power. Since then, I always add a question mark at the end of whatever the CCP announced.

Election to us was a means to fight the CCP because election was not just about getting seats; it's a process and a tool to mobilize a democracy movement. Hong Kongers were awakened by 1989; they talk politics now. Since then, we have had a mass base, which made a big difference. Once a system of mass election was put in place, we all had to build up mass support. And if this base was robust, even when the CCP wanted to crack down, we hoped they'd be hesitant. Of course, today, we know we miscalculated.[111]

Under Chinese rule beginning in 1997, while Lee and his generation of politicians became part of the establishment, the hegemonic colonial order began to buckle. To Beijing's dismay, Hong Kong would no longer be the proverbial goose that only lays golden eggs. People's emotional investments in the foundational myths that Beijing had helped produce and sustain would come back to haunt them when a different reality presented itself. The dialectic of double coloniality, from a force of consent to one of resistance, would be triggered by the crisis and contradictions of both neoliberal capitalism and Chinese state capitalism hitting Hong Kong as the bridge between them.

CHAPTER TWO

PRACTICING POSTCOLONIALITY

WITH THE FORMAL ENDING OF BRITISH COLONIZATION in 1997, Hong Kong entered an uncharted territory of decolonization without independence. It became a postcolony, officially a special administrative region in the People's Republic of China under a "One Country, Two Systems" (OCTS) framework until 2047. With self-determination out of the question, the postcolony was given a consolation prize—fifty years of "Hong Kong people ruling Hong Kong" (港人治港). Despite its ring of naivete, this tantalizing mantra was uttered as much by the British as the Chinese political elite. It made them look honorable, claiming that a premier global city finally emerged from the dark age of colonialism. What they might not have expected was the seriousness with which the Hong Kong people, especially the younger generations, took and practiced postcoloniality. The two decades since 1997 would see the rise of a decolonizing subjecthood, spearheaded by the postcolonial youthful generations and then proliferated through waves of social mobilization to the rest of the population. Hong Kong's younger generations could have chosen the path of least resistance—to become the most well-positioned *Homo economicus* to exploit the immense markets opened up by "Chimerica," the growing symbiosis between China and America. Why did resistance become attractive, even obligatory?

To pry open the links between political economic changes and transformation in political subjectivities, this chapter paints a generational portrait in collective action. Through a collage of personal stories, it documents how people made sense of the political economic conditions they were thrown into and made history out of them. The chronology of protest events in post-1997 Hong Kong has often been written with little illumination on the ideas, values, feelings, and (mis)calculations of the key activists. As a result, the logic of practicing postcoloniality remains a black box. This chapter brings them into the spotlight. My focus is on the organizers and leaders of major protests, for their mobilization capacity still mattered in those years before mass protests went "leaderless" in 2019. They formed a passionate minority who, despite their numerical marginality, forcefully put on the public agenda ideas and actions that would slowly but surely transform the pragmatic majority. The following narrative is organized chronologically, weaving together an analytical thread structured around the chipping away of the four colonial myths and a subjective thread about people's agencies. It shows how double coloniality evolved in the post-handover period and how the transformation from colonized to decolonizing subjects was the uneven and unintended consequence of years of activism. The concluding section reviews, in conceptual terms, the specific conditions making this decolonization struggle possible.

Interregnum between Two Colonialisms

The volatile period between the exit of one colonial master and the consolidation of another can be conceptualized as an "interregnum." This was originally a monarchical term denoting the periods between the death of one regent and the ascension of the next. In the writings of Antonio Gramsci and other Marxist analysts, it refers to a period of uncertainty and disagreement among the dominant elite in which former ideologies, while maintaining institutional power, lose traction and become disoriented. "The old is dying and the new cannot be born, in this interregnum a great variety of morbid symptoms appear," famously observed Gramsci about the crisis-ridden liberal capitalist order in the interwar period.[1] As in other instances of interregnum (for example, post-2008 neoliberalism), the power elite faced a crisis of authority: loss of public support and internal ideological division, leading to deep political dysfunction.[2]

In Hong Kong, the interregnum from British to Chinese colonialization was likewise plagued with crises and contradictions, which paradoxically unleashed unintended consequences and opportunities in society. The governing elites, both locally and in Beijing, oscillated between two contradictory objectives: developing Hong Kong into a global city and transforming it into a patriotic Chinese territory. The CCP regime juggled rendering Hong Kong a tool for its globalization and economic liberalization agenda and subjugating the city to its sovereignty and nationalistic agenda. The former imperative called for "othering" Hong Kong and the latter "assimilating" it. Complicating Beijing's dilemma of autonomy or control was the United States. To protect American commercial interests in Hong Kong after Britain's exit, the Hong Kong Policy Act was passed in 1992 stipulating US certification of the continual existence of autonomy in Hong Kong as a condition for renewing Hong Kong's status as a separate customs and trade entity from China.[3] As a rising China at that time still depended on Hong Kong as an indispensable channel for accessing the global market, foreign direct investment, financial services, and sensitive technology, Beijing had no choice but to retain the institutional trappings of late British colonialism: common law, civil liberty protection, a politically neutral civil service, a free press, and professional law enforcement. Yet, from time to time, it could not contain its coercive assimilation impulse. "Othering" Hong Kong meant keeping intact the political and civil liberty for younger generations to put the reigning ideology "Hong Kong people ruling Hong Kong" into practice. "Assimilating" Hong Kong meant intervening into its rule-of-law and free-market economy, nationalizing its education and curriculum, and eroding civil liberty.

Beyond the confusion arising from competing elite agendas, during the same period, crises and contradictions emanating from two global economic forces—capitalist neoliberalism and global China—also upset Hong Kong's status quo and propelled the younger generations onto a path of decolonization from below. During the first decade (circa 1997—2007) of the interregnum, it was global neoliberalism and its countermovements that politicized Hong Kong and broke the hold of colonial hegemony on which China had planned to build. The Asian financial crisis, the precursor of the 2008 Wall Street meltdown, hit Hong Kong just months after the handover in 1997 and punctured the myth of prosperity and stability. Its devasting economic effects were aggravated by the mismanagement of the SARS epidemic in 2003, which led the alienated middle class to demand more accountable governments and democratic rights. Soon, the flipside of global neoliberalism in the form of the antiglobalization movement arrived in Hong Kong as well, inspiring a vision of "the good society" critical of the primacy of the free-market economy, developmentalism, prosperity, and stability. At the forefront were members of the so-called post-1980s generation. Advocating progressive ideas of democratic planning and rights to the city, they explicitly branded their agenda in decolonial terms, targeting the entrenched alliance of capitalists and bureaucratic elite since colonial times. Empowered by social media and communication technology spreading around the world at the turn of the millennium, they introduced a new paradigm of nonviolent direct action that pushed the limits of Hong Kong's polite and legalistic protest culture.

During the second decade (circa 2008–2018) of the interregnum, it was global China that instigated waves of mass mobilization. The CCP became more assertive with its global agenda—using economic statecraft to export overcapacity through outbound investment and loans for infrastructure construction, coopting foreign elites through patron clientelism, shaping public opinion by media ownership and social media campaigns, and sponsoring educational institutions abroad. Hong Kong became one of Beijing's many targets of penetration.[4] Thanks to its sovereignty over the territory, China's encroachments in all these arenas were more pernicious and effective than in places such as Africa, Latin America, or Southeast Asia, resulting in backlashes that were stronger than those found elsewhere. Pushing back at China's colonial agenda of institutional transplant and identity transformation targeting education, law, and electoral reform, one social movement after another erupted. Often on the frontier of resistance were activists with self-identification labels—the post-1990s generation, the autonomous generation, or the cursed generation. Notwithstanding these internal differentiations, they were all digital and social media natives, claiming a birthright to a free, liberal, democratizing, and postcolonial Hong Kong. A popular feeling of being recolonized by mainland China was palpable, not just because of the influx of Red capital in major sectors of the economy. Beijing's stalling, even reversal, of electoral reform proved particularly devastating. Popular discontent grew in tandem with political capacity and localist tendencies among the younger cohorts for whom China was no longer the inevitable destiny. Toward the end of the interregnum, when the regime weaponized the law and bureaucratic rules to suppress young localist politicians' electoral prospects, the last bastion of colonial hegemony—the rule of law—began to crumble. If these resistance struggles were originally reacting to the violation of values enshrined in the colonial mythologies, over time they developed new aspirations transcending the confines of that colonial hegemony.

1989–2003: Cracks in "Stability and Prosperity"

The first core element of the colonial hegemony to be shaken was stability and prosperity. Two crises happening respectively a few years before and after 1997—the Tiananmen Massacre on June 4, 1989, and the mass demonstration on July 1, 2003—undermined the routine expectations of prosperity and stability and opened the way for new political subjectivities. These events triggered a mass awakening to the fragility of Hong Kong's stability and prosperity and the need for democracy, which had for so long been considered a secondary and dispensable luxury.

The Tiananmen incident in 1989 was the most serious political crisis in the history of the People's Republic of China and had a deeply distressing impact on Hong Kong. In the spring of 1989, Chinese students and urbanites took to the streets in major cities to protest corruption, inflation, and the lack

2.1 On May 21, 1989, the day after martial law was declared in Beijing, a million Hong Kong citizens marched on the streets to support the students demonstrating in Tiananmen Square.
CREDIT: South China Morning Post

of political liberalization, which ended in the imposition of martial law and a military crackdown on June 4. Hong Kong citizens bore witness to the events through around-the-clock news coverage. They launched waves of ad campaigns and donation drives for funds and resources, assisted with smuggling protest leaders on the run out of the mainland after the crackdown, and, most impressively, joined three million-strong solidarity marches in May and June in support of the movement. The bloody crackdown left such a strong emotional imprint on Hong Kongers that the June 4 vigil organized by the Alliance in Support of Patriotic Democratic Movements in China became a fixture in the city's political calendar for the first time in 1990 and endured for the next thirty years. The iconic image of a "sea of candlelight" in Victoria Park, where an average of a hundred thousand people gathered annually (until it was banned in 2020), was reported worldwide and became a constitutive element of Hong Kongers' collective memory and identity.[5] Political scientists agreed that Tiananmen was the historic event that enlightened the Hong Kong citizenry about the importance of democracy as a defense against deadly state atrocity under one-party rule. In its aftermath, four out of five citizens favored a speedier democratization, even at the risk of confronting Beijing. The political party United Democrats was formed in 1990, winning Hong Kong's first direct election for the legislature in 1991 in a landslide.[6]

Another shock to the collective psyche came just a few months after the official departure of British colonists. Hong Kong's open economy was caught off guard in the Asian financial crisis originating from Southeast Asia. For all its reputation as the textbook illustration of successful free-market capitalism, Hong Kong was not prepared to deal with the tumble of neoliberalism right after the handover. Deregulation of the financial markets fed speculative bubbles in housing, land, currency, and stocks around the world. In Hong Kong, the absence of political unrest against the Sino-British agreement and the dissipation of a feared crisis of confidence over the city's future fueled even bigger bubbles in the markets. The red-hot frenzy to buy property was so outlandish that family members had to take turns in long queues day and night to have a chance to buy overpriced condos still on the drawing boards. Then, out of the blue, the regional financial tsunami originating in Thailand and South Korea hit just a few months after the handover. It marked the first time during the extended and almost uninterrupted economic boom and development in the postwar decades that Hong Kong saw a recession and its middle-class families experienced a reversal of fortune. A rapid 40 percent downturn in stock prices was followed by a 40 percent drop in property prices by the end of 1997 and the Hong Kong currency under attack by overseas speculators.[7]

Those years also saw major corporations and government civil service restructured and downsized. As their peers elsewhere, Hong Kong's middle class (administrators, managers, and professionals) confronted rapidly diminishing career prospects and job security. When the SARS epidemic, which originated in China, hit in 2003, taking the lives of 299 residents, property prices plunged once again. Dwindling numbers of Asian tourists meant a surge in the unemployment rate and the liquidation of small businesses. The much-trumpeted touchstone of Hong Kong's way of life, "prosperity and stability," began to unravel. And citizens blamed the SAR government and the chief executive's ruling alliance for a number of policy blunders, from housing to education to cultural infrastructure, in the face of this crisis.[8]

While citizens were still reeling from the neoliberal maelstrom, the Hong Kong political elite, handpicked by China for their loyalty and subservience, proved incapable of weathering the storms. Adding insult to injury, some of the high officials, in an attempt to placate Beijing's imperial impulse to control the city, made the ill-timed proposal to enact a National Security Law. At that time, Beijing was rattled by the rise of a pro-independence party in Taiwan since the late 1990s and the color revolutions in former Communist states in the early 2000s were. Passing a local legislation stipulated by Article 23 of Hong Kong's Basic Law would assuage Beijing's worries. But the secretary for security's proposal backfired badly. Protected by the Bill of Rights and a police force respectful of people's right of assembly, civil society organizations galvanized the simmering popular anger against the government into a historic show of force on July 1, 2003. Half a million citizens poured, orderly and feisty, onto the streets, demanding "power to the people." The two-and-a-half-mile march from Victoria Park to the government headquarters took a full day to complete. When the Liberal Party representing the local business sectors defected to side with civil society, the government backed down, shelved the bill, and dismissed chief officials, forcing the resignation of the chief executive. Having scored this unprecedented victory, the annual antigovernment July 1 rally, together with the June 4 vigil, would become a tradition in the city's civic life for the following three decades.

A New Normal of Protests for Democracy

For all the euphoria they generated, we should not overestimate the subversiveness of these peaceful rallies or their transformative impact on Hong Kongers' political culture. On-site polls found that the majority of participants in the July 1 rallies in the early 2000s hailed from the college-educated middle class and were below fifty years old, with the largest cohort from the thirty-to-forty-nine age range.[9] Compared to the colonial period, they had evolved from attentive spectators of politics to attentive analysts and occasional activists. Yet surveys and focus group interviews revealed that some of the deep-seated negative ideas about politics continued to pervade even the most politically active citizens.[10] More generally, sociologists agreed that after 1997, the middle class had new grievances, becoming aware of the need to articulate and defend their interests and casting doubt on the legitimacy and credibility of their long uncritically accepted Hong Kong–style market-driven capitalism.[11] Yet anger did not translate into sustained political activism. In the words of a long-time observer of the middle class, they remained "rearguard"—"hesitant, confused, and vacillating in their opinions, unfocused and discontinuous in their actions ... politically irritable, but ... have no political passion."[12] Finally, critical intellectuals also questioned the performative tendencies of the July 1 marches, arguing that the ritualistic spectacle merely expressed a "pseudo public sphere." A wide range of groups showed up in the rally but did not engage in any substantive debates or collaboration across their diverse agendas.[13]

Unbeknownst to these critics, the July 1 marches and June 4 vigils, ritualistic as they were, actually had an enduring political impact on the impressionable young children tagging along with their parents. As they grew up to become activists in the student and localist movements, many would remember these events as formative. The effects of annual rituals on the postcolonial generation did not predominantly stem from the concrete political ideas and policy controversy spotlighted each year by the sea of placards and protest songs. Instead, these marches inspired a spirit of collective resistance and a sensitivity to social issues. Eddie Chu Hoi-dick, one of the most prominent activists during the interregnum, traced his interest in social movements to the June 4 vigils, July 1 rallies, and numerous other small rallies around the handover. He recalled with a trademark grin, "For me and my generation, we experienced June 4 as children in Primary 6 or junior high. We personally witnessed society's total mobilization and that experience of street protests made us see politics not as dangerous but as obligatory. When I was in college, even though I did not participate in the student union or other campus organizations, I still joined the July 1 demonstrations."[14]

Leo Tang, a future leader in the student and union movements, had his first memory of political participation in 2003: "My mom took me and my sister to the July 1 rally. I only have vague memory about the rally, but since then I developed a cognitive sensitivity about our political situation. Growing up, we just took for granted that mass demonstrations was a 'minimum charge' [against the government]. The real enlightenment was when schools were closed during SARS that year. Without classes, our teachers could not give us other kinds of homework except newspaper clippings. Every day I devoured the news in the *Apple Daily* and read a ton of criticisms against Chief Executive Tung. It's funny how awakening happened when formal schooling stopped!"[15]

Mass rallies' effects of enlightenment and empowerment even reached youngsters from underprivileged backgrounds. Residing in far-flung public housing projects, working-class youths did not routinely venture into the glittering heart of Hong Kong Island where Victoria Park, the default assembly place for rallies, was located. Such a trip was a prohibitively expensive and psychologically alien expedition. But when Nathan Law turned seventeen, he went with a group of friends from his home in Tung Chung, a new town on Lantau Island near the airport. Nathan, who emerged as a student leader during the Umbrella Movement and would go on to become the youngest elected legislator in Hong Kong's history, only to be disqualified a few months later by Beijing's retroactive intervention in 2016, spotlighted his first June 4 vigil as a coming-of-age experience:

> Where I was raised, there wasn't much hope or feeling of agency. My parents both had to work very hard to earn a living. . . . We lived in government-subsidized public housing, and I had limited opportunities to see beyond our closed world. . . . I was seventeen when I first went [to the rally]. Like many Hongkongers, attending the vigil represented a coming of age experience for me. . . . Most of all it represented the beginning of my maturity. . . . That day I read every word on every leaflet, and my heart wept with every story. That day I learnt what it truly meant to feel solidarity, and to be a Hongkonger with a

free spirit. It was my first education in politics and the power of political activism.[16]

It was during those years that "lawful protests" became the gold standard of collective action. The political experimentation of the postcolonial generation would not have been possible without the institutional resilience of Hong Kong's civil liberty in the first decade after the handover. The police routinely issued the "no-objection notification," required by the Public Order Ordinance, to the organizer of the annual July 1 rally, the Civil Human Rights Front. According to the Civil Human Rights Front's records, it was not until 2011 that the police began to restrain unruly protest behavior (that is, unauthorized assembly, unlawful assembly, and violation of public order). Forty-five people were charged that year, more than the total from 1997 to 2010.[17] Even though, from 2011 onward, police imposed more conditions and restraints in the no-objection notification—increasing the scope of forbidden areas and reducing the duration of the rally and the number of road lanes protesters could occupy—the right to the annual July 1 rally was never denied or questioned until the 2020 National Security Law.

Not that the activists were all legalistic and conservative, but they were concerned with staying within the limits deemed acceptable by the vast majority of Hong Kong citizens. The president of the Federation of Students in 1989–1990, To Kwan Hang, admitted that the Beijing student movement taught him what civil disobedience was. However, he also realized Hong Kong was not ready for civil disobedience. On the one hand, the citizenry would not support anything against the law, and on the other, the regime was still so respectful of civil liberty that there was no need for civil disobedience.[18]

2005–2010: Challenging the "Free-Market Utopia"

After 2003, even as the economy gradually rebounded, stimulated by a number of preferential economic initiatives "gifted" by Beijing, prosperity and stability became increasingly out of reach for the vast majority of the citizenry.[19] The question "whose prosperity and stability?" entered public debates as Hong Kong's ascendance to global city status brought aggravated social polarization specific to this type of political economy.[20] As commanding nodes of global capital providing specialized producer services such as finance, law, insurance, advertising, and accountancy, global cities are notorious sites of heightened inequality. These postindustrial cities, where middle-class manufacturing jobs have disappeared, attract a high concentration of workers at the top and bottom of the occupational hierarchy. In Hong Kong, widening income gaps between the top and bottom occupations bred social discontents. Social surveys during this period found that more than 80 percent of the respondents deemed inequality "serious" while more than 70 percent deemed it "unjust."[21] In other words, it was not just middle-class homeowners saddled with negative equities but the general working population and the young who found the narrative of prosperity increasingly illusive.

The scale and concentration of economic distress in the post-1997 decade began to break down another foundation of colonial hegemony: Hong Kong is a free-market utopia. Critical voices emerged to question the legitimacy and fairness of Hong Kong's market economy, especially its foundations of favoring tycoons and major corporations. While foreign-born businesspeople, Chinese tycoons, and colonial rulers had always formed an entrenched governing alliance under British rule, the post-handover government's hands became ever visible. The economic elite were *seen* leveraging Beijing's support to override or derail public policies, such as increasing housing supply. Blatant partiality and favoritism to the landed elite's profiteering in commercial and residential real estate had cast a long shadow on ordinary people's lives. Extravagant infrastructure projects, such as the West Kowloon Cultural Area, the harbor reclamation, and the project called Cyberport, were found to entail questionable tenders and ended up delivering lucrative profits to the leading developers. The term "real estate hegemony," coined by a real estate insider-turned-author, entered everyday parlance with a vengeance, lending the public a powerful discursive shorthand to articulate widespread grievances against the ruling elite.[22] Media spotlights on the downtrodden in cage houses and partitioned apartments vividly captured the visceral pains of the human suffering inflicted by grotesque inequality.

Several high-impact social movements in the second half of the 2000s directly questioned market-driven developmentalism, especially in relation to land use and urban planning. Ironically, it was government policies to bolster Hong Kong as Asia's premier global city that gave birth to these agitations. First, Hong Kong followed in the footstep of other cities around the world at that time to develop a "cultural economy."²³ It aimed to create a new growth sector by turning culture, art, and heritage into an industry that could also boost tourism. Historical buildings were identified and refurbished for retail, entertainment, and community uses, with the private sector bearing the cost and capturing the profits of redevelopment. This inadvertently invigorated community interests in local history and collective memory.

The second consequential policy flowing from the government's global city agenda was hosting the sixth World Trade Organization ministerial meeting in 2005. The government budgeted about HK$300 million for the event, hoping it would help raise the city's international profile.²⁴ But as the WTO ministers arrived, the transnational antiglobalization movement also descended. For about a week in December 2005, more than two thousand South Korean farmers, together with an alliance of global civil society groups, demonstrated the power of a highly organized, disciplined, adaptive, and confrontational movement. This global event became the catalyst for local civil society to break the taboo of confrontational activism. Steeped in the tradition of polite and law-abiding marches, Hong Kong activists and citizens alike were mesmerized by this totally different model of protest—occupying roads and public spaces, breaking police cordons, making weapons with onsite objects, building triangular barricades with roadside fences, bracing tear gas canisters with umbrellas and cling wrap, using humble gestures of bowing and kneeling in the marches through town, and engaging the public with joyful music and dance performances. It was a revelation. In the protests to come, Hong Kongers would lift many pages from the South Korean farmers' playbook, mimicking their shrewd combination of militant and affective tactics.

Soon the unintended consequences of these two policies converged. Young activists put into practice what they learned from the anticapitalist global justice movement to protect heritage spaces and architecture. They campaigned against the reclamation in Victoria Harbour (which significantly narrowed the harbor to create space for prime real estate) and the demolition of the Central Police Compound (the first colonial structure built in 1841 symbolizing the early colonial criminal justice system), Wedding Card Street (a neighborhood housing a cottage industry specialized in the printing of wedding cards), the Star Ferry Pier (an iconic and busy pier with a Westminster-style clock tower), the Queen's Pier (a colonial ceremonial structure for the landing of British governors and royalties), and Tsoi Yuen Village (a small community of elderly farmers slated for clearance to make way for a high-speed rail connecting Kowloon to the mainland). Self-styled "progressive localists" posited an opposition between "people's" space in the dual sense of common folks and autonomous citizens demanding participatory planning and urban developmentalism imposed by a business-government growth coalition. Activists reminded fellow citizens of their right to urban space as a repository of people's history and livelihood, recalling, for instance, that the 1966 hunger strike took place at the Star Ferry Pier and that Wedding Card Street and Tsoi Yuen Village respectively represented a local folk industry and an alternative lifestyle eliminated by undemocratic planning. According to two academics heavily involved in these mobilizations, the goal was "preserving now" by promoting people's reidentification with the locality and regaining control over everyday life in situ, to be liberated from neoliberal commercialization and the statist colonial past.[25]

Eddie Chu, an iconic leader of the first wave of the localist movement, wrote in a newspaper that those behind the Star Ferry and Queen's Pier campaigns (December 2006–July 2007) considered the protests a "reckoning with the culture of colonial governance." He explained to his readers how all the colonists from Britain, an oceanic power, chose to arrive by water, landing at the pier, to project Britain's intimidating military prowess and demand submission of its colonial subjects. More ominous, he alerted the readers, was that the government's new plan also included a Chinese army pier as part of a new architectural cluster consisting of the government and police headquarters. He deplored that all along it was the same colonial governance expressed in land use, something he realized after, not before, he took part in the preservation campaign. He wrote, "After occupying the Queen's Pier for five months, it [the pier] became a map for finding our historical agency. Following its routes, I found the way to our colonial past. In the process of contesting the current government, I also discovered the new colonial era we are in. If I had not been involved in all the details of both the new and old ways of colonial power, I would not have realized my own keen desire to find a path to autonomy."[26] In a public forum with then secretary of land development and future chief executive Carrie Lam, Eddie Chu famously proclaimed the people's right to preserve their history: "Queen's Pier is a landmark of Hong Kong's social movement. Hong Kongers must stand on this spot in order to tell our own story."[27] In another meeting with the culture secretary, he and other activists framed their opposition in anticolonial terms: "The colonialists did not let us have a sense of history, and now this government still denies us our sense of history. What kind of government are you?"[28]

Global Origins of Localism

The collective biographies of this cohort of the postcolonial generation point to the preponderant influence of neoliberal globalization, the global justice movement, and the accidental nature of their decolonial activism. They were oblivious to Hong Kong's own history of anticolonial struggle, describing their radicalism as without lineage, "like a birth out of rocks."[29] This ahistoricism among even the most rebellious youth spoke volumes about the effectiveness of colonial hegemony. They had no theory of change other than the action model of the antiglobalization movement. Only in the process of action did they educate themselves and others about colonialism and undemocratic planning and come to see their reincarnation in the present. The global origins of their decolonial subjectivity would be eclipsed and forgotten in the following decade as the China factor loomed larger than ever. But to obliterate this lesson is to forego a major political resource of Hong Kong as a global city.

Graduating from college in the late 1990s, core members of these movements sought careers in global nongovernmental organizations (NGOs), international journalism, and transnational alternative media activism. This generation was exposed to transnational political values and applied them to local issues. The establishment of *Hong Kong In-media* in 2004 was a local response to a global movement. The Hong Kong activists consciously appropriated the model of media activism from global and regional examples: Independent Media Center (Indymedia), a transnational media activism network formed after the anti-WTO protests in Seattle in 1999; MediAct from South Korea; Malaysiakini from Malaysia; and Cool Cloud Collective in Taiwan.[30]

A key figure in the preservation movement, Chow Sze-chung, joined Greenpeace in Hong Kong as a full-time staff member after earning his master's degree at Lingnan University in 2004 while volunteering at *Inmedia*. Letting on a tinge of nostalgia, he recalled, "Those were the years of July 1, 2003, and Lee Tong Street redevelopment. I was surrounded by teachers and alumni who tried to turn media into mobilization, journalism into activism. . . . It was very popular then to talk about the antiglobalization protests in Seattle as a reference, the power of digital video cameras and citizen journalists. Then in 2005, when the WTO meeting in Hong Kong gave us a real-life situation to apply these ideas, Eddie, me, and others formed a small group to organize our reporting. As witnesses and reporters, we had to be on site, which means we were also participants. That's how we produced many 'action reports.' . . . What I learned from Greenpeace was the power of spectacle after spectacle, very media driven. Through Inmedia, our propaganda became very effective and quick. We put something out today, tomorrow there would be legislators and crowds descending on our protest site."[31]

For him and others, localist ideas and decolonizing subjecthood emerged not from theory or academic studies but from the process of, in Chow's words, "daring to make a decision about my destiny. Once I charged into the demolition site and stopped the government, I found myself in a historical space. My favorite act was renting a boat which we called 'The Localist' and invited different kinds of marginalized Hong Kong residents—Filipino domestic workers, new immigrants, ordinary workers—to reenact the landing at Queen's Pier. We turned it to a plebeian space through action. Action is historical reflection. . . . Having witnessed the South Korean farmers, I had a strong feeling to want to create our own history, and I felt I personally could resist, block, and achieve something. It's a new feeling for me . . . I did not have a term for it at that time. We did not know anything about the history of local social movements; there was no local reference for what we were doing. Only later in cultural studies did I learn about 'historical subject' or 'theories of resistance.'"[32]

Similarly for Eddie Chu, collective action led to cognitive liberation, decolonial subjectivity, and most important of all, historical agency: "Growing up under colonial rule, and knowing the Sino-British Declaration already set down the roadmap for our future, we always thought there was nothing we could do to change Hong Kong. This was the background for me to go to Iran, Palestine, and Afghanistan, to be a global citizen, pursuing justice, so I don't have to deal with Hong Kong. But the moment I charged into the Star Ferry construction site and climbed up the excavator, I suddenly realized that was the first time I made a decision to resist, the first time I made a decision for Hong Kong. I could resist and stop something from happening. . . . I wanted to be a global citizen, doing justice anywhere is fine. But now I realize only a

PRACTICING POSTCOLONIALITY 73

Hong Kong person, not any American, would charge into the Star Ferry site that day. There is something only locals can contribute to local politics."[33]

The Star Ferry protest only lasted several days. They did not have any formal organization or clear plan of action. During the Queen's Pier campaign a few months later, the core group of thirty to forty activists named themselves Local Action. Like a commune, they decided to camp out at the pier day and night for three months. It was only then that Eddie began to educate himself about local history:

> I went daily to the Public Records Office and university libraries, to compile historical data to put into the brochures we used for our guided tours. Several foreign residents joined us to explain colonial architecture and how the use of public space was part of colonial strategies. The Queen's Pier, the city hall, and the Edinburgh Place form a cluster of colonial architecture representing the reopening of colonial rule after World War II. I then collected pictures of the pier over time and showed how they affected Hong Kong's civil society. Different protests—blind workers' strike, the protect Diaoyutai campaign, and the hunger strike in 1966—had happened there. I was really genuinely excited by the new historical information I collected. The excitement was contagious. I was able to charm and excite many secondary school liberal studies teachers who brought countless groups of their students to our guided tours. From there we influenced many young students. I always said to them, "We are all Hong Kongers, but you and I did not know all this history. Don't you find this fascinating?" Actually, such ignorance was both fascinating and unreasonable. How could I be in my twenties, doing something seemingly radical, but know nothing about this place?[34]

These post-1980s-generation activists also took a page, quite literally, out of the global justice movement's manual—direct action. Chow Sze-chung pointed out that "When we started the Star Ferry preservation campaign, our brand of direct action was the composite of Greenpeace and Korean farmers. Greenpeace was part of the battle in Seattle, and our friends working there had manuals about how to chain yourself to the ground, how to create dramatic social impact with a small number of people.... We could not adopt all the militant strategies of the Korean farmers, such as charging at the police with sharp objects. We only adopted their foreplay—ascetic walks, jumping into the sea, festive chanting and drums. At that time, activists and the police in Hong Kong saw each other as opponents but not enemies to harm."[35]

The tolerance of the police and the government was a crucial enabling condition for the rise of a protest culture and the politicization of the postcolonial generation. In the mid-2000s, rule of law and freedom of association still prevailed. The cost of rebellion was negligible, a conscious calculation on the part of the activists. Chow witnessed that, "The police were very polite: they removed us from the construction site and left us outside the fences. We continued to gather there. When more people came, they hustled us to move further away. Every time they did that, they ended up helping us expand the size of the crowd surrounding us! . . . Carrie Lam personally came to our occupation site and debated with Eddie on a public forum. This made the government's eventual clearance look much more reasonable."[36]

During those years, arrests by police seldom resulted in prosecution. Most of the time, activists were carried away from the scene of a protest by police who behaved cordially. Eddie was arrested several times, including during the anti–West Rail campaign with massive crowds encircling the Legislative Council (the Old Supreme Court Building) and the Government House. Looking back at that time fifteen years later, he deplored, "It's quite unimaginable today that the police at that time never pressed charges of unlawful assembly even in those situations. The atmosphere then was not acrimonious or deadly oppositional. I even felt that the government thought of social movements as social reforms. It was still finding a way to deal with social movements. I had this theory: the CCP already controlled things like elections and universal suffrage, so the government could act as an umbrella to shield a space for social protests, so that people could shift attention away from those nonnegotiable matters such as election."

It bears emphasizing that for almost two decades after 1997, civil liberty and freedom of association were largely intact, and a crackdown on protests was preempted thanks to China's need to preserve a liberal and West-facing Hong Kong to facilitate its global rise. In the minds of the activists, the legal risks of protest was often weighed against their own threshold of tolerance. Y. C. Chen, another core activist of Local Action, alluded to the prevailing common law protection for civil rights at that time in Hong Kong as a big emboldening factor for them: "In Hong Kong, we know arrests do not necessarily mean prosecution. After consulting our lawyers, we know we can pay the price. Under the Public Ordinance Order, the penalty for blocking the streets is normally twenty-four months of public service order or fine of several thousand dollars. It's nothing."[37] The personal risk for rebellion would escalate drastically as rule-of-law protection receded equally quickly in the years leading up to 2019.

Passionate Minority and Pragmatic Majority

Among the general public, the preservation campaigns by progressive localists did not inspire the kind of critical decolonial reflections they championed. Instead, their highly visible actions triggered an outpouring of collective memories about a leisurely walk along the waterfront for a first date, a less crowded and less competitive but prosperous Hong Kong, the pomp and pageantry of the queen's visits in the good old days of colonial rule. The Chinese Communist press reacted by admonishing such sentiment as "ideologically backward colonial nostalgia," promoted by a minority of colonial servants. Despite such discordance, the issues of coloniality and decoloniality entered the public imagination and would return in later protests as the terms of discursive contestations between Hong Kong and China.

Perturbed by socioeconomic inequity and emotionally supportive of the passionate minority's localist campaigns, the pragmatic majority still subscribed to the liberal creed of free-market rationality and acquiesced to market outcomes, no matter how unequal. Throughout the 2000s, collective mobilizations against neoliberal policies, such as the privatization of public assets, from airports, subways, and tunnels to malls in public housing estates and hospitals, were fringe affairs, attended by small crowds of a few hundred to a maximum of two thousand. The public often denigrated anti-neoliberalism protests as quixotic and futile attempts to "block Planet Earth from rotating" (阻住地球轉, a Cantonese slang), recalled Y. C. Chen, the organizer of many of these rallies. A Taiwan- and US-trained urban studies scholar of Malaysian Chinese descent, Y. C. had just arrived in Hong Kong in 2004 to assume a faculty position at a local university. Inspired by Manuel Castells's seminal *City and the Grassroots* and Taiwan's democratization struggles, he threw himself into these protests only to find very little popular resonance. With a few radical social workers and academics, Y. C.

organized marches, signature campaigns, and public forums criticizing the price hikes that would follow the privatization of government assets. He deplored that, "Our biggest march saw two thousand mostly elderly supporters who were already organized by the community activists. But we were met by one thousand real estate brokers who wanted to sell retail storefronts. They always scolded us, 'Don't block the earth's rotation!'"[38]

Similarly, in 2011, when Jaco Chow, a twenty-something leftist organizer, together with a dozen anarchists and Tankies, launched the Occupy Central movement in solidarity with Occupy Wall Street and antiausterity occupations in Europe, they did not get as much as a whisper from the public. Pitching tents for three hundred consecutive days on public grounds under the landmark building housing the headquarters of the Hong Kong Shanghai Bank, the group did not entice more than a couple hundred participants. Jaco was not surprised that "When we had public forums and band shows, only friends and students of the organizers would come. At most, we got between one hundred and three hundred participants. We were just some rebellious young people trying to plant a flag, to put forth something strange, maybe for future movements. Several years later we saw some ripple effects: a Facebook page called 'Youth supporting universal social insurance scheme,' a march targeting the financial secretary's budget speech, etc. But most of the time, the masses just found us weird."[39]

So entrenched was capitalist hegemony in Hong Kong society that a substantial challenge to the cardinal principle of "free market" rationality would not emerge until 2019. Only then did leveraging the market for political struggle and fighting "Red capital" (that is, capital from mainland China) become a conscious and collective strategy to sustain popular protests.

The stirrings of the post-1980s generation in the mid-2000s had the most consequential impact on the cohorts to follow. For example, Joshua Wong, who would in a few years attain international fame during the anti–national education campaign in 2012 and the Umbrella Movement in 2014, told me when we met in 2015 that Eddie Chu's anti–West Rail campaign in 2009–2010 was what opened up his vision for political action, even though he was only fourteen years old at the time and only read about the movement in the news.[40] Like many other student activists, he was spurred to "do something" by the city's extreme socioeconomic inequality and personal encounters with the underclass. His father was a devout Christian, and Joshua often accompanied him on his visits to the elderly, underprivileged families, and children

PRACTICING POSTCOLONIALITY   77

with special needs. Joshua had an epiphany on a Saturday visit to a senior citizens' home he had visited a year before:

> A few dozen octogenarians had already taken their seats in a big circle in the day room, expecting us. I recognized the same peeling pastel walls and tattered furniture from a year ago; I saw the same faces staring back at me; the home was every bit as short-staffed, the amenities as dated and the residents as lonely and destitute as they were when my father and I left them last time we came. My eyes welled up despite myself, but deep down I was more angry than sad. . . . It wasn't fair that my family could live in a middle-class neighborhood, attend a fancy megachurch and go on overseas holidays while nearly a fifth of the local population struggled below the poverty line, with barely enough to eat and no decent home to live in.[41]

Inspired by a political-junkie classmate, Joshua spent his summer in 2009 reading news feeds on his phone about local politics and the electoral system structurally designed to guarantee control by big business and the professional sectors. He wrote in his memoire that, "I felt angry and frustrated that such a blatantly unjust system had been allowed to fly under the radar for so long. I also came to realize that everything that's wrong with Hong Kong—from old-age poverty to skyrocketing property prices and the wanton destruction of historic buildings to make way for pork-barrel redevelopment projects—was attributable to a single culprit: our unaccountable government and the lopsided electoral system that created and facilitated it. It did not take me long to turn my political awakening into action."[42]

Soon, Joshua and his fellow high school students would find the occasion to mark their own place in Hong Kong's history of resistance. It is important to note that even though they were younger than the post-1980s generation and reacting to a new set of conditions, socioeconomic inequality was central to both cohorts' critique of Hong Kong's postcolonial reality.

2012 Anti–National Education: Questioning Chinese Identity

As we have seen, during the first decade of post-1997 Hong Kong, the crisis of global neoliberalism and its countermovement were the main drivers for collective mobilizations that led to the initial unraveling of the colonial myths of "prosperity and stability" and "free-market utopia," the emergence of the postcolonial generation as active agents of history, and their critique of persistent coloniality. During the second post-1997 decade, it was the imperatives and dilemmas of China's global project in controlling Hong Kong's economy, education, and electoral reforms that spurred popular resistance. Along the way, regardless of the actual outcomes of these struggles, the tenets of "China as destiny" and "rule of law" began to lose their credence.

The interventionist turn in China's Hong Kong policy originated from the political economic challenges Beijing faced by the mid-2000s, but especially in the post-2008 world. From the beginning, Deng Xiaoping's blueprint of "One Country, Two Systems"—whereby a liberal world-facing society is allowed a high degree of autonomy under a one-party Communist state—was only an expedient strategy to achieve China's economic opening by leveraging global capitalism for its own development. Beijing's impulse to fully control Hong Kong's affairs and ensure people's loyalty to the central government was held in check by its need to maintain Hong Kong's autonomy, a condition demanded by the United States via the Hong Kong Policy Act of 1992. This legislation prescribed that the city would need to keep its autonomy in order to be treated as a separate economic entity from the rest of China. But things began to change in the years following the 2008 financial crisis. On the one hand, the crisis exhausted China's export-led model of economic growth, exacerbated its overcapacity problem, threatened its performance-based legitimacy, and produced enormous pressure on China to intensify its global expansion, including Hong Kong, as mitigation. On the other hand, Beijing's concern with national security also grew in the wake of the color revolutions in former Eastern European Communist regimes, rebellions in Tibet and Xinjiang, and the Arab Spring.[43]

Locally, the July 1, 2003, rally was a wake-up call for Chinese officials responsible for Hong Kong. Legal scholars and researchers, including Jiang Shigong and Cao Erbao, were dispatched to the city to offer a diagnosis and a policy solution. The former would pen theoretical papers advocating strong sovereign control from the center as a step to revive a Confucianist empire while the later oversaw the organizational expansion of the Liaison Office, Beijing's outpost in Hong Kong, and the formation of a second governing team consisting of mainland cadres. At the heart of their diagnosis was young Hong Kongers' lack of identification with China and their nostalgia for colonial rule.[44] In 2011, the Hong Kong government announced the curriculum guidelines for "moral and national education" to be made mandatory in 2012, with the goal of cultivating students' patriotic feeling toward China.[45] For high school students and their middle-class parents, this proposal was a frontal assault to their long-cherished right to a high-quality liberal education, which was a ticket to upward mobility and competitive careers. "Against brain-washing education" instantly became the unifying call of Hong Kong society, while top Chinese officials denounced it as "separatist thought" resulting from 150 years of British "colonial brainwashing."[46]

For fifteen-year-old Joshua Wong, news of this curriculum felt like a declaration of war, not least because up to that point, he had been taught that he should be a concerned citizen. He explained, "National education hit very close to home for me. It was the first government policy that deliberately targeted and directly impacted my classmates and me. I was a key 'stakeholder'—a term we had just learned in liberal studies class. . . . And if the people who had the most to lose didn't speak up, who else would?"[47] This remark well illustrated how the government's contradictory policies—both civic and patriotic education—created a critical mind and decolonial subjectivity in Joshua.

In May 2011, together with a schoolmate named Ivan Lam, Joshua launched a Facebook group called Scholarism—"'scholar' because we were a student group and 'ism' to signal a new way of thinking (and to give the name more gravitas)." Within a year, they had ten thousand followers, and a legion of high school volunteers handed out flyers throughout Hong Kong, speaking through microphones in street booths accented by snappy graphics and banners. They found eager allies among parents, professional teachers' groups, and university students who were united in their objection to the "brainwashing" and "spoon-fed patriotism" of the textbooks for national education. In these texts, China's Communist government was described as a progressive and selfless regime upholding stability and prosperity. Multiparty democracy in the West was dismissed as a chaotic, conflict-ridden system that victimized ordinary citizens, and controversial episodes such as the 1989 student movement (and the associated Tiananmen Massacre) were ignored.

When these high school activists sought the advice of the post-1980s generation who a few years earlier had pulled off their stunning series of localist campaigns, it was not their decolonization rhetoric but their action repertoire that they found appealing. From renting loudspeakers to strategizing the use of public space, managing rumors, planning for overnight security,

2.2 People demonstrated in Hong Kong in July 2012 to protest the introduction of "moral and national education" curriculum in the territory's public schools. The banners read, "Withdraw brainwashing education."
CREDIT: *Kyodo News* / Getty Images

direct action tactics, and even hunger strikes, Scholarism inherited a reservoir of local practices and turbocharged them with digital velocity and youthful fearlessness. Police restraint toward their rallies also contributed to their risk-free attitude. "There were no conflicts or clashes during those large rallies. The same police officers always stationed in the same spots, and after a while, we recognized each other's familiar faces. I even greeted them and struck up some small talks with them," recalled Lilly, a core member of Scholarism, who found that kind of civility hard to believe from the perspective of 2020.[48]

Social opposition to patriotic education quickly mushroomed to encompass a broad coalition of over twenty civic groups, consisting of the main professional teachers' union, the Federation of Students, religious bodies, parents' groups, and a loose network of veteran student movement leaders. After weeks of massive protests—including the 90,000-strong July 29 parade, followed by a ten-day marathon protest with 32,000 angry citizens participating and culminating in the 120,000-strong September 1 Occupy Tamar outside the government headquarters and a hunger strike—the SAR government conceded. Moral and national education would be optional, not compulsory.[49] The immediate legacy of the anti–national education protest was euphoria and empowerment of the young. "It gave every freedom-loving citizen a shot in the arm and reminded them that they didn't need to roll over and play dead in the face of bad government policies. Real change could happen if we worked together," wrote Joshua Wong, now a household name, a political star, and a history maker.[50] He knew winning the battle was not the same as winning the war, and very soon he would start a new campaign for electoral reform.

The Local Genesis of Resistance

Unlike the post-1980s generation, who were "globalists" drawing inspiration from the antiglobalization movement, the cohort that Scholarism represented were born, quite literally, digital natives. Access to social media on mobile digital devices made them aware of the color revolutions, the Arab Spring, and Occupy Wall Street, but these events did not feel as relevant or urgent as the threats to their birthright—freedom in their native city. China was an intruder rather than their destiny, but Chinese students in 1989 were also an inspiration for some of the activists. Along with the Hong Kong citizenry, they were sympathetic to the Chinese students' quest for democracy—going to June 4 vigils in Victoria Park with their parents was part of their childhood memories—and were emotionally swayed by a rising China at the time of the Beijing Olympics (2008) and the World Expo in Shanghai (2010).

Born in 1996, Melanie, a soft-spoken Scholarism member, attributed the beginning of her political awareness to the many years of June 4 rallies she attended: "My parents are very liberal, and they took me to June 4 vigils almost every year. My dad is a schoolteacher, and my mom took me to shop at the Teacher's Union supermarket where a statue of the Goddess of Liberty was a fixture. June 4 kept popping up in my mind, and I searched online about it. I did not know all the history, but June 4 in a nutshell was about brave students standing up and dying for liberty and democracy in the face of a repressive government. . . . My parents were university students in 1989. They told me about writing letters to people in the mainland to explain to them what had happened. Even my apolitical grandfather joined the June 4 rally. So I knew this must be some event."[51]

Unlike the old generations of Hong Kongers, Tiananmen was a lesson less in dictatorship's deadly force than in students' youthful spirit of resistance. Instead of weighing the balance of power and chance of failure and concluding that Hong Kongers had no hope, the young had a moral commitment. Melanie encountered this generational contrast firsthand: "When we handed out flyers in the neighborhoods, older people would often say to us, 'You can't beat the Communist Party.' But I did not think too much about that. Win or lose, we need to do something. Even if in the end we lost everything, we could still say we had tried to fight."[52]

Fighting against Beijing's imposition of the propaganda-like curriculum of national education did not imply a wholesale rejection of China. Two Scholarism activists, Ivan and Lilly, were ambivalent about, even proud of, China in those years. Like many secondary school students joining school-sponsored tours to personally experience a globalizing and prosperous mainland, they rooted for Team China during the Beijing Olympics and visited the World Expo in Shanghai. It was only when the anti–national education campaign proved to be the beginning rather than the end of China's retreat from "One Country, Two Systems" that the postcolonial generations came to realize the incompatibility between being Chinese and being Hong Kongers.

For Brian Leung, a graduating high school student at the time and a future leader of the localist student movement, the anti–national education campaign crystallized the identity conundrum at the heart of this campaign: "I was among the two hundred thousand occupying Civic Square. This movement made me ask myself if I was a Chinese or a Hong Konger. Why were Hong Kong people so upset and unwilling to be educated as Chinese nationals? I began thinking if we could separate our identities as Hong Kongers from the Chinese. Behind people's objection to the brainwashing curriculum was something more fundamental: i.e., Hong Kongers at their core did not have the entrenched identity to be Chinese; our identity was distinct from 'Chinese.'"[53] In a few years' time, Brian would emerge as an intellectual leader among students at the University of Hong Kong, promoting the idea of a "Hong Kong nation," inspired by Benedict Anderson's constructivist argument of the nation-state as "imagined communities."

For the high school students of Scholarism, popular culture, not cultural theories, fortuitously shaped their political agency. Many were avid fans of anime and video games depicting moral contests between good and evil. In that universe, when an evil force or external enemy attacked, ordinary young people had no choice but to muster their courage and strength to strike back and protect their homes. "We suddenly became adults because we encountered a monster," explained one Scholarism member about their audacity to take on the largest Communist Party in the world. Joshua Wong himself was a marvel of digital existence and efficiency, constantly multitasking with different electronic gadgets, moving seamlessly from media interviews to WhatsApp messaging, telephone calls, and face-to-face chats while attending public forums, having dinners with his comrades, and, of course, playing his favorite video game, Goddard. "Facebook is my library," he told me back in 2015.

Unsurprisingly, Scholarism was obsessed with social media and public visibility. According to Lilly and Ivan, two hunger strikers at the height of the campaign, "For each action, our goal was always to catch eyeballs, create a strong media impact. Say, when we forced the curriculum issue on all the establishment political parties, we would visit them and each time we'd bring a 'gift,' a prop to ridicule them. For example, we visited Regina Ip's party, we gave her a broom [her nickname due to her hairstyle]. Or when we had a signature campaign, we did not just send in stacks of papers with the signatures. We cut out all the signatures and pasted them on a big black banner to wrap around the concrete flower bed outside the Liaison Office. We wanted it to be photogenic. In our meetings we mostly focused on images that drew the maximum numbers of likes on Facebook. We were social media natives and could leverage its evolution. We studied Facebook's algorithm as it moved from text to image to videos, and we adjusted accordingly to make sure we plan our action to generate nice pictures or videos. When Facebook promoted its 'live' feature, we posted more 'live' broadcasts because we knew Facebook would send notifications to all. So there was a time when many people watched our live events."[54] Despite their lack of an international strategy, international support poured in. Photos from major cities around the world showing young people posing with their hands crossed above their heads, the signature gesture of the movement, flooded the Facebook page of Scholarism as well as concerned parents' groups.

The local social media platform called Golden was their training ground to engage in uncensored, humorous, and no-holds-barred discussions of anything under the sun—food, entertainment, tabloid news, current affairs, and politics. Information about anything was just one click away. One member described the learning machine that was Scholarism:

> In our meetings, we were very goal oriented, everything we did, we thought about how to enhance our political capacity, to expand our halo, how to develop social movement. Actually, as students, we project very loud soundbites. . . . You may think these fifteen-year-olds wouldn't know a thing, let alone political capacity. But I can guarantee you, if you spent one week with Scholarism, you'd have enough vocabulary to PK [debate] the pan-dem "old seafood" [Cantonese homonym for obsolete elderlies]. Every day we process a large amount of information, and we watch many interviews to prepare for many interviews.[55]

For all their courage, moral clarity, and inventive capacity, these young student activists were not immune from the tensions that plagued many other social movements. It was no secret that Scholarism had an autocratic streak. Decision-making was controlled by a few at the apex of a three-tiered hierarchical structure: the executive committee, members, and volunteers. For instance, the decision to stage a hunger strike was made by a handful of people in the executive committee. When they put it to a vote among the members and the majority returned a no vote, they forced another round of discussion and managed to reverse the decision by a second round of voting. Sometimes, action decisions were so time sensitive that meetings were deemed not practical. At the end of the Civic Square occupation on September 1, 2012, Lee, who had camped out there for days, was shocked to learn of a sudden decision to retreat from the square, announced by the leadership on Facebook. There was no prior warning or discussion among the many small groups. He observed wryly that, "Power was concentrated in the hands of Ivan, Joshua, Yanki and Lilly. The four also controlled external liaison and communication with the alliance."[56]

Seeking media exposure sometimes had a negative effect on members. Among the few male students sent to staff street booths, Lee noted the predominance of girls speaking on behalf of Scholarism. Joshua explained to him that it was because the media found girls in uniforms from elite schools participating in social movement an appealing angle. While Lee did not see this as particularly objectionable at that time, it left a bad taste when he recalled it years later. There was even an "antiwomen" culture, according to Melanie, among the guys who talked a lot about girls having long legs and gossiped about members' relationships with women. She was distraught "when some of us brought this to the table for discussion, the guys just dismissed this issue as divisive, saying we spoil the atmosphere, interfering people's wanking."[57]

Finally, despite standing together as allies addressing the massive crowds, there was little discussion or consensus among high school students, university students, and parent groups about what education should entail. The Scholarism cohort opposed nationalistic education from the position of liberal studies and the civic education and did not frame their campaign in terms of anticolonial resistance. But their ally, the Federation of Students, hoisted a banner demanding "anticolonial, anti-national education" at their class boycotts. In an op-ed article, the student union president of the Chinese University of Hong Kong pointed to the similarity in the "brainwashing logic" between British colonial education and Chinese national education. "In the national education curriculum guideline, there is only descriptions of political system and bureaucratic ranks, with no mention of citizens' duty to participate in public affairs; national history only focuses on economic development of major cities . . . no different from colonists' mythology trumpeting of Hong Kong's economic miracle. . . . National education is just the amplification of the colonial logic of slavish education. So how can we resist national education without also resisting colonial education?"[58]

Zooming out from the classrooms and university campuses, Hong Kong society at large at that time (2011–2012) was engulfed in simmering anger about another kind of Chinese colonization, pejoratively termed "yellow locust invasion." The massive influx of mainland Chinese tourists—soaring from 15.5 million in 2003 to 54 million in 2013—had exceeded the capacity of a city of 7 million. Pregnant mainland Chinese women occupied public hospital beds, and altercations erupted between local Hong Kong residents and mainland visitors in congested subway trains, shops, and streets. The government's failure to regulate their entry and mitigate their negative impacts on local residents' everyday lives gave rise to anti-China and anti-mainland Chinese sentiments strong enough to birth a nativist political movement that would grow and evolve into a pro-independence localist movement in subsequent years. From around 2012, local residents at border towns had organized a number of vigilante "reclaim protests" to physically harass mainland parallel traders hauling suitcases of goods across the border.

The year 2012 also witnessed Beijing's blunt intervention in the chief executive election to install its own candidate, C. Y. Leung, as well as the detention of prominent human rights activists Zhao Lianhai and Ai Weiwei and the torture and mysterious death of Li Wangyang, a prisoner detained for his Tiananmen activism, after an interview with a Hong Kong television station. All these events fueled an unprecedented wave of anti-China sentiment, and the "Hong Konger" identity grew in inverse proportion to people's trust in the central government, according to surveys. Antimainlandization became the main campaign platform in the 2012 Legislative Council elections. In the eyes of many, autonomy under the "One Country, Two Systems" blueprint had turned elusive, whereas "the political gap between a more oppressive China and a more liberal, efficacious, and participative Hong Kong populace was ever-widening."[59] These political currents were amplified by popular writings of academics and university students that coined and popularized concepts such as "localism" and "Hong Kong nationalism." This discourse systematized what were previously inchoate structures of feelings and crystallized a vision of Hong Kong's destiny against and beyond China. However, mainstream society and pan-democratic forces deemed it too radical and unrealistic. Ethnographic research and surveys routinely confirmed the appeal of ethnonationalism, family ties, and transborder living experiences among the Hong Kong citizenry experiencing intensified socioeconomic integration with the mainland.[60] Relating to China with ambivalence and openness rather than total rejection, the citizenry wanted to make one last effort to demand autonomy under the constitutional framework of OCTS.

Fifteen years after the handover, citizens' discontent with the SAR government's failure to circumvent Chinese erosion of Hong Kong's autonomy and civil liberty convinced many about the importance of realizing a full democracy before it was too late. The Basic Law, Hong Kong's mini-constitution under Chinese sovereignty, stipulated universal suffrage for the election of the chief executive and the Legislative Council but without a timetable. In 2004 and 2007, Beijing hardened its position by reinterpreting the Basic Law in a way that in essence created more procedural hurdles for electoral reforms, giving the National People's Congress Standing Committee (NPCSC) the power over the initiation and approval of universal suffrage. In 2009–2010, the Democratic Party brokered a political reform bill with

2.3 During the annual July 1 demonstration in 2013, some citizens waved the official flag of colonial-era Hong Kong to protest against "Chinese colonists."
CREDIT: AP Photo / Vincent Yu

Beijing, essentially expanding the number of elected seats in the legislature without fundamental change in the structural power held by Beijing. This bill fractured the pan-democratic camp and utterly alienated the young generation from the mainstream democrats whose compromise was widely condemned as a betrayal.[61] Even moderate public intellectuals were frustrated by many years of Chinese abrogation to deliver the constitutional promise of universal suffrage. Several months after the success of the anti–national education campaign, on January 16, 2013, law professor Benny Tai penned a newspaper article announcing a civil disobedience campaign called Occupy Central with Love and Peace (OCLP) to force Beijing to the bargaining table, in anticipation of yet another iteration of a reform proposal to be issued by Beijing in August 2014.

2014 Umbrella Movement: Legalistic Resistance's Last Stand

Inspired by Martin Luther King Jr.'s 1963 action in Birmingham, Alabama, Benny Tai envisioned "10,000 people sitting down in Hong Kong's central business district, hand in hand, submitting to police arrest one by one. . . . We want to solidify a momentous civil force that amounts to a political crisis, to compel the CCP to make a rational decision after calculating the cost and benefits of full democracy, and be willing to negotiate with the Hong Kong democrats. . . . Another goal is to awaken people's moral compass. For too long, even though more than 50 percent of citizens pledged support for democracy in opinion polls, only a tiny minority are willing to make personal sacrifice in action. That's why there was never adequate political pressure on China to change its position on universal suffrage. We want a critical mass of people to take action in the spirit of self-sacrifice."[62]

To the rather conservative and law-abiding populace, Occupy Central was as radical as a nuclear bomb thrown in a calm sea. The core element of what Tai called the "ultimate weapon of maximum impact" was a series of "deliberation days" culminating in a public referendum on various models of nominating the chief executive. Joined by the sociology professor Chan Kin Man and the Reverend Chu Yiu Ming, forming the so-called Occupy Trio, Tai would lead the planned occupation and then surrender to the police. Their spirit of sacrifice was intended to awaken the population to the cause of democratization and add pressure on Beijing.[63] For the postcolonial generations, such preplanned, preannounced, conciliatory peaceful occupation was too little too late. But the Occupy Trio knew the public would not go along with anything more radical. A wide spectrum of pro-democracy organizations and activists, including the post-1980s progressive localists, Scholarism, and the Federation of Students, supported OCLP by holding deliberation circles in their own communities, running training camps on nonviolent confrontation with the police, and actively debating three proposals—civic nomination, nomination by an enlarged nomination committee, or multiple channels of nomination—for the final public referendum.

A public referendum on June 22, 2014, with more than 790,000 citizens participating, returned "civic nomination" as the preferred option. Initiated by Joshua Wong's Scholarism and supported by the Federation of Students, this outcome was deemed subversive and was vocally denounced by Beijing. It dared to go beyond the Basic Law's prescription of "nomination by a broadly representative committee according to democratic procedure." Faced with such popular pressure, the State Council in Beijing doubled down on centralizing power. In a white paper issued in June 2014, officials introduced the notion of "comprehensive jurisdiction" held by the central government in all matters about Hong Kong and stated that "one country" is the source of "two systems." Then, on August 31, the National People's Congress decided to impose additional screening rules on the candidates running for chief executive, bluntly rejecting the option of civic nomination preferred by the electorate. With this fateful decision, all bets were off, and one could almost hear a collective cri de coeur in Hong Kong. That evening, the two generations of activists shared a stage in a public rally of a few thousand people, condemning the death sentence Beijing had pronounced for Hong Kong democracy and hailing the end of an era of democratic movements and the beginning of an era of resistance.

Two weeks later, harnessing the palpable outrage among the young and pro-democratic populace, the Federation of Students, under the leadership of Alex Chow, Lester Shum, and Nathan Law, initiated a week-long class boycott on all eight university campuses, followed by Scholarism leaders, Joshua Wong and Ivan Lam, calling for similar boycotts among high school students. On September 26 they decided to escalate the movement by charging into Civic Square, the site of thunderous rallies during the anti–national education campaign in 2012. Protests against their arrests rapidly grew, sparking confrontations with the police and spurring the Occupy Trio to immediately launch their much-heralded OCLP campaign. To support the students, more people poured into the streets on Sunday, September 28, many wearing goggles and raincoats, with umbrellas in hand and cling wrap for eye protection against pepper spray. Around six in the evening, to everyone's surprise, riot police wearing helmets and gas masks began firing a total of eighty-seven canisters of tear gas at unarmed citizens. Shell-shocked, angry, and indignant, even more citizens came to Admiralty, where the government headquarters and the chief executive's office were located among corporate headquarters in upscale commercial towers. Refusing to leave, citizens began seventy-nine days of occupation in Admiralty and nearby Causeway Bay, as well as in Mongkok across the harbor in Kowloon. The centrality of Hong Kong in global finance drew intense media attention from around the world. Soon foreign journalists coined the term "Umbrella Revolution," spotlighting the ubiquitous umbrellas that people carried to defend themselves. Protesters revised the term to "Movement" to signal its reformist rather than revolutionary agenda. When *Time* featured a cover image of the boyish-looking seventeen-year-old Joshua Wong, taken by the renowned

2.4 The Umbrella Movement erupted on September 28, 2014, after the police shot eighty-seven cannisters of tear gas at citizens' peaceful protests against China's new electoral restrictions.
CREDIT: AP Photo / Wally Santana

war photographer James Nachtwey, the movement also acquired a face, youthful and rebellious, as captivating as Hong Kong's neon-lit cityscape.

By Hong Kong standards, the Umbrella Movement was stunning and singular in scale, duration, and visibility. At the peak of the movement, some 20 percent of the city's 7.2 million residents had participated in one form or another. Lasting seventy-nine days around the clock, protesters pitched 2,500 tents blocking off some of the busiest roads in downtown Hong Kong and Kowloon. A vast majority of participants were under forty years of age— 40 percent were twenty-five or younger and another 40 percent were between twenty-six and forty. A quarter of participants were current college students, and 73 percent of all participants reported some college education. Yet their subjective class status was lower than their objective educational attainment; 47 percent of all participants identified themselves as belonging to the lower classes. Despite a lack of revolutionary intent, Umbrella participants scored high (mid-seven on a ten-point scale) on their sense of belonging to Hong Kong and low (mid-two on a ten-point scale) on their sense of belonging to China.[64]

Despite nerve-wrecking rumors of military crackdown in the early days of the occupation, the SAR government responded by attrition. Specifically, Beijing first made it clear that there was unified support among the political and economic elite for the embattled chief executive. Then, pro-regime organizations were on hand to host their own rallies, disrupting the occupied areas and demanding the "restoration of business and order." Court injunctions filed by pro-establishment business groups reframed the protests from a political event to a judicial dispute, shifting the burden of clearance from the police to the judiciary. The legal profession and the media soon warned the protesters that mass defiance of court orders would be a direct affront to the rule of law, the ultimate safeguard of their rights.[65] In essence, the regime ingenuously and effectively mobilized popular support for two of the core pillars of colonial hegemony—stability and prosperity and rule of law—to subdue the movement.

After the occupied sites were cleared by bailiffs and the occupiers were carried away by the police, student leader Alex Chow lamented Hong Kong people's entrenched submission to "the common-sense reasoning that economic development is important, and development needs stability, and stability needs cooperation with the regime."[66] Throughout the occupation, public support was ambivalent, hovering below 30 percent at the beginning and plunging to a single digit by December 2014. He reckoned that "The middle class blamed the suffragists for rocking the economic boat and putting the lofty ideals of a few people above the livelihood of all people."[67] They were also scared by the Communist propaganda machine's dire warnings of an impending recession brought on by the protests.[68]

Despite their radical rhetoric of "autonomous destiny," the activists themselves were careful not to openly question the inevitability of "China as destiny." They took pains to stay within the parameter of "One Country, Two Systems," demanding only that China deliver its promises. To assuage Beijing's ire, a tactical decision was made to replace the original slogan of "Self-Determining Destiny" (insinuating independence) with "Autonomous Destiny" (autonomy was promised in the Basic Law). The substance of their demands was also about political reform rather than regime change.[69] At that time, the entanglements of economic interests and political identities among China, the West, and Hong Kongers conspired to stall any public questioning of Chinese sovereignty. For their part, officials in Beijing tried to balance the contradictory objectives of keeping Hong Kong both a Chinese and a global city. On the one hand, they issued strong condemnations of the occupation as a Western-instigated "color revolution" and made false claims about Joshua Wong receiving training by the US Marines and funding from the CIA. On the other, not long after the encampment started, Beijing's "middlemen" were sent to convey a message to the movement leadership that there would be "no concession, no bloodshed."[70] Meanwhile, foreign governments and corporations, revelling in China's multibillion-dollar plans to build intercontinental infrastructure, had little interest in supporting the protest movement.

Student leader Nathan Law was at the center of these crosscurrents and attested that "public announcements by the Federation of Students in 2014 . . . always began with 'under the framework of one country two systems.' We did not say anything about Hong Kong independence or foreign forces. At that time, international support was nil. Britain was talking about a 'golden era' with China. Obama did not offer a word of support; the US political establishment was all silent because they were all very friendly to China. And the European Union cared even less. We only had media and academic attention. For a long time, Hong Kong politicians consciously avoided reaching out to foreign countries for support because people would call them 'traitors of the Han people' colluding with foreign forces. Martin Lee was an example. Such stigmatization had a chilling effect on all of us, especially me as a political novice. Also among the general population, before the rise of localism, most people still identified themselves as somehow connected to China, as Chinese, so you don't want to be cast as a traitor of your people. Only after the rise of localism did we [young politicians] not worry about the label of traitor. It was only after 2014 that we could imagine Hong Kong as the world's Hong Kong, and not China's Hong Kong."[71]

Under the Umbrella: Class Difference and Strategic Frictions

While the Umbrella Movement failed to obtain any concession from Beijing on democratic reform, it unmistakably brought to public view the internal fissures among the protesters on the basis of class and strategy. If these fragmentations undermined the movement, they also challenged citizens with a solidarity learning curve. In the next chapter, we will see how people converted formerly paralyzing divisions into hard-won lessons in the 2019 protests. But first, we need to understand, from inside the Umbrella Movement, the contentions around class and strategy, and what they revealed about the enduring structural roots (i.e., persistent socioeconomic inequality and the pernicious effect of colonial legality) of the overall decolonization struggle.

First, expressions of discontents against inequality fell along class lines. Even though the Umbrella Movement was not explicitly anticapitalist, the Federation of Students representing university students always included in their public statements a critique of the colonial "party-state-capitalist bloc" as the structural cause of Hong Kong's predicament before and after 1997. In a public statement at the beginning of the class boycotts on September 22, 2014, students assailed China for grafting the old colonial mentality onto Hong Kong's current system: "It glorifies the colonial principles of 'small government big market,' 'executive-leadership,' 'no change for 50 years' as shields against popular demands for social justice and redistribution . . . CCP embraces the relics of colonial mentality." It went on to explain that under "Chinese imperialism," any demands for democracy would be rejected by the colonial rationale of protecting business and industrial interests and protecting Hong Kong as an economic city without need for belonging. The statement continued, "We still do not have political subjectivity; we still have not dismantled the colonial political economic structure that steeply favors the establishment elite; we have not completed our path of decolonization."[72]

During the week of class boycotts, impromptu and mobile "democracy classrooms" popped up on campuses and in open spaces near the government headquarters. Among the many lectures delivered by intellectuals during these teach-ins, quite a few explicated the anticolonial nature of the movement. For instance, one speaker said, "What does 'anti-colonial' mean in the slogan 'anti-colonial screening'? It does not mean anti-Chinese or colonization by Mainlanders. Real 'anti-colonial' is fighting against a political economic system that privileges the Chinese-Hong Kong capitalist class. This is not a struggle against a national or ethnic group, but a class struggle. Because the government denies us the right of civic nomination, and through a low tax regime and the absence of welfare and labor protection we pass our wealth to the rich."[73]

Progressive ideologies informed the prefigurative practices at the Admiralty protest site. Occupiers carried out political experiments that realized aspects of the ideal society in the here and now, illustrating a yearning for an alternative to the city's hallmark free-wheeling, individualistic, competitive capitalism. The tents at Admiralty formed self-identified "villages," innovatively named after political slogans or characteristics of the organizers. Occupiers built communal facilities, replete with electricity, chargers, and Wi-Fi; bathrooms furnished with a bathtub, curtain, and shower facilities; study areas; and a well-stocked library. Citizens and businesses donated massive amounts of food and water for free distribution in this urban commons where reciprocity and self-organization were the norms permeating every aspect of occupation life. Volunteers offered talks and classes on carpentry, sewing, metalwork, waste reduction, and democratic theories. There were defense and patrol teams, along with stations offering food, first aid, psychological counseling, plein air painting and calligraphy, street arts, poetry reading, impromptu dancing and singing performances, and more. Amazingly, urban farmers even planted vegetables, gesturing at a radical alternative to Hong Kong's dependency on food imports and corporate control of the urban landscape. The critique of capitalist rationality was downplayed in students' speeches and media talking points because they did not want to alienate the socially conservative Hong Kong public. However, economic inequality perpetuated by the elite as a hallmark of Hong Kong's past and present coloniality was consistently part of their political sensibilities.[74]

Alien to the abstract discourses of anticolonial, anticapitalist critique, working-class participants' grievances were expressed negatively and aggressively as hostility against mainlanders. In stark contrast to the Admiralty gestalt of civility and order, moralistic ideals, artistic creativity, and intellectual (some might say "elitist") dialogues, Occupy Mongkok was grassroots, rowdy, militant, almost anarchistic, and always transgressive. These characteristics stemmed from the site's urban ecology and the protesters' self-selection. Mongkok was a densely populated working-class hub known for its bustling night markets, street vendors, shady alleys, nightclubs, and affordable eateries. Triad societies, gangsters, undocumented immigrants, and sex workers rubbed elbows with the young, lower classes, and voyeuristic tourists seeking an exotic Hong Kong. When the subway at Admiralty was shut down on the first day of the occupation, netizens proposed Mongkok as an alternative site. By midnight, several thousand protesters besieged the intersection of Argyle Street and Nathan Road. Trucks were driven there to block a newly formed encampment area, which soon saw makeshift barricades marking its boundaries and a stage set up for people to make speeches. Participants in both sites were mostly young (58 percent in the eighteen-to-twenty-nine age group). Compared to Admiralty, Mongkok had a slightly higher proportion of male, self-identified lower-class protesters who lived in public housing.⁷⁵

Instead of eloquent statements issued by student organizations, Mongkok protesters expressed themselves in action and liberal use of foul language, which was explicitly disapproved of at Admiralty. Having spent seventy-four days occupying Mongkok while juggling a minimum-wage job in far-away Taipo, twenty-one-year-old Fire found himself right at home in this milieu. His parents were street hawkers selling fish balls (a local snack), and his family of five lived in a public housing unit of three hundred square feet. He felt that people like him could not "share the aura" at Admiralty. His lot was just the shadow of Hong Kong. Like many young people attracted to the Mongkok site, he was adamant that this resistance was not just about universal suffrage but their right to a basic livelihood. He had a simple conviction: Hong Kong people should come first. He could not accept the fact that noncitizen pregnant women, parallel traders, and mainland tourists were allowed to take away economic resources in Hong Kong while people like him were crushed and despondent. He was adamant that "Hong Kong's young people should not be the ones to shoulder this burden."⁷⁶ The burden he referred to was the same that the Federation of Students had in mind—sky-high property prices, stagnant wages, scarce social welfare, and grotesque inequality that disproportionately beset the working-class youth.

Fire also saw himself making a "sacrifice" for Hong Kong, although not in the same way as the Occupy Trio and the students at Admiralty. Whereas the intellectual elite's notion of "sacrifice" was to surrender themselves to the police at the end of their civil disobedience in order to awaken the public, Fire's sacrifice was physical—the bodily injuries and pains he sustained staving off police batons and thugs. Right from the beginning of Occupy Mongkok, on October 3, protesters encountered harassment and assaults by mask-wearing mobs, widely suspected to be gangsters and pro-China elements who had business and political interests in opposing the protests. The police also made several attempts to forcefully clear the site, wielding shields, batons, and pepper spray against occupiers who resisted with umbrellas, sticks, and metal fences. Injuries and physical and verbal skirmishes were common scenes in Occupy Mongkok. Making a virtue out of necessity, many embraced an ethic of militancy to counter the principle of nonviolence in Admiralty. Militancy entailed real, physical, and personal sacrifice, which to them was more authentic, morally superior, and more effective than passively sitting down, singing and talking, as the pan-democrats had done for twenty years without any result.

An amateur freestyle biker with two large earrings, Fire was in the front line, sustaining police beatings and numerous bruises on his arm, in the battle to reclaim Mongkok on October 17. Scornful of the idea that surrendering to police arrest was "responsible civic disobedience," he quipped, "The glory of Admiralty was exchanged with our blood.... The big stage only cares about the support of rich middle class who only talk but never take action.... There's no way I can accept being carried away by police. That's surrender. It generates no bargaining chip, no pressure on the government."[77]

Umbrella was Fire's first political act. But he was far from alone in taking pride in Mongkok's ethos of militancy and direct action in dealing with a repressive and unjust regime. Fighting along him in Mongkok was veteran protester Jaco Chow, one of the organizers of Occupy Central 2011. He was among a small circle of activists trying to radicalize Hong Kong's social movements. Their lot consisted of anarchists, left-leaning individuals, artists, and students. Concerned primarily with socioeconomic injustice and class inequality, but also frustrated by the sluggish pace of democratization, Jaco had turned to creating road blockages and storming government sites to escalate conflict and pressure. Occupy Mongkok therefore marked a turning point whereby this radical fringe of the postcolonial movement joined with the young localists to fight back at police and thug violence. As he said to me, "These freshmen had no prior political experience, no political affiliation, and no idea of us blocking the roads all these years. But in Mongkok, fights and altercations erupted constantly, every few days. At first we were only defending the site from the gangsters. But soon small teams of police came out of alleys to dismantle the tents and push us out without any reason. Of course we had to fight back numerous times. Many of these went unreported. Injured people just put their hands on the wound to stop the bleeding and walked away, and police did not make any arrest except on the last day."[78]

Jaco's assessment that Mongkok was the beginning of the militants' public visibility was independently corroborated by Ray Wong, a twenty-one-year-old interior design student who would soon become a vocal and visible militant founder of a pro-independence political party, the Hong Kong Indigenous. Ray was at the scene when the police were sent to demolish Occupy Mongkok and was certain that "it was the first time protesters proactively charged at the police, seeking confrontation, and not just passively subjecting themselves to police arrest. There were about one hundred to two hundred people on Shanghai Street. I asked those in the front row, one after another, whether or not they were ready to charge at the police. It's clear to me the mass sentiment then was 'we don't want to give in without a fight.' Wearing a mask, I climbed up to the fence railing and took the loudspeaker and talked for an hour to keep up their morale. It was the first time I saw protesters throw wooden boards and other objects at the police. At that moment, an important psychological barrier was overcome."[79]

The tactical difference between Admiralty and Mongkok, between bargaining and confrontation, might have arisen from different past experiences of resistance. Ivan, a Federation of Students leader tasked with communicating with the occupiers, saw the CCP as a "bargaining" partner: "We knew there was no sure win fighting the CCP, but we have a chance, so at least we could try. Every time a protest arises, CCP has to weigh different options. What we do is to increase its cost [of ignoring our demands]. Maybe it will work. They backed down in 2003 and 2012, didn't they? Our generation does not have the same fear of CCP as the older generation. They have memories of people made to kneel on broken glass. We have no such personal experience with the CCP, and 'newborn calves are not afraid of tigers.'"[80] But for Fire and Jaco, half a million people in the July 1, 2003, march, thirty years of pan-democrats, and the daily singing of protest songs in Admiralty all led to nothing. Only confrontation would bring political pressure.

Occupy Mongkok also represented a repudiation of Admiralty's hierarchical and centralized power structure. The so-called big stage at Admiralty was both a physical structure for people to make public speeches and a symbol of a centralized command controlled, rather ineffectively, by a coalition of civil society and the two student organizations called the Five-Party Platform. They took it upon themselves to set the rules for deliberation, accessing the microphone on the big stage and picketing the occupied site to ensure peaceful and rational behavior. For some, the centralized leadership was the antinomy of freedom and democracy because it excluded those with dissenting ideas and tactics. Ray Wong moved from Admiralty to Mongkok in the early days of Umbrella because of the former's "tyrannical" tendency. In Mongkok, he found real freedom.

> I was at first a rational and nonviolent protester. But I became very disappointed with Admiralty after they tried to stall protesters'

spontaneous action. A few days after Occupation began, I held up a sign asking people to gather near the Government Complex in order to stop the reinforcement of police supply. A marshal came to stop me, saying I should obtain permission of the big stage! Another time, about one hundred of us who were connected online wanted to block Lung Wo Road, to expand the occupy zone, and to encircle the Government Complex. We were again stopped by the big stage people. Also I started noticing that the big stage screened people who wanted to speak to the crowd. At first, they did not give them the microphone. When we protested, they had to let them talk, but they would then deliberately lower the volume of the speaker! Thereafter, for me the big stage meant repression. When I moved to Mongkok, I saw real freedom—three minutes on the stage for everyone; even the blue ribbons [the pro-establishment camp] got three minutes. We could act autonomously without anyone's approval. We had a very strong urge to do something; we were always thinking of action. One day, near the end of October, we thought of a foolish but playful way to block one more traffic lane—a group of us walked out to the middle of the road, dropped coins on the ground, and pretended to be slowly looking for them, holding up traffic. I felt very involved and hopeful that our action would bring change.[81]

Looking back at the tactical and organizational disagreement four years after the end of Umbrella, Brian Leung, the editor of a special issue on Hong Kong nationalism in the University of Hong Kong's student magazine, *Undergrad*, penned a thoughtful and critical analysis of the student leaders' elitism and their failure to understand the militants' rationale for confrontational tactics. As a participant at Admiralty's fringe areas, he witnessed how participants guarding the frontiers encountered more physical attacks by the police than those peacefully surrounding and protecting the big stage. These participants were living in the shadow of violence and sustaining an emotional toll not known to those at the core. Brian wrote, "Face to face stand off with the police, advancing and defending, sucking up pepper sprays and beatings by batons, milling around anxiously became our everyday life. Three o'clock in the morning, still half asleep half awake, people would be thrown into a war-like mode by adrenaline rush, every time they heard the slightest police movement. The rhythm of protest at the periphery and at the core was totally different. Whereas the masses at and near the core insisted on peaceful behavior and were pacified, those at the fringes had to endure physical and emotional violence."[82] This spatial logic, producing vastly diverse everyday realities, emotions, and strategies within the same movement, eluded the student leaders, whose elitism demanded a unified ethics for the entire movement. Without immersing themselves among the peripheral masses, they simply dismissed the militants as irrational and excluded them from speaking on the main stage.

Another student leader, Alex Chow, also admitted the failure of leadership. He attributed the students' rejection of violence to the situational pressure on them to build consensus among various factions and to secure public support by staying within the paradigm of lawful action. His own personal aversion to violent action was also a factor.

> Before the onset of Umbrella, many Federation of Students activists were self-professed radicals not that different from the militants in Mongkok. But once Umbrella began, and the masses were already taking action, we felt pinched in the middle by the many actors—the [Occupy] Trio, civil society, occupiers, militants, government—who projected onto the students a mediating, balancing, consensus-making strategic role.... When I heard that some occupiers wanted to escalate action by storming the chief executive office or committing a suicide attack at some government buildings with explosives, I just thought those were delusional ideas. I also could not overcome my own moral and psychological barrier to take these actions, especially because I thought most protesters and most citizens would not endorse them. You could say we did stay within the colonial boundaries of lawful action. Folks among the Five-Party Platform subscribed to these boundaries. Some even said Mongkok was another movement, 'Why should we care about them?'"[83]

Lastly, disagreement over tactics sometimes arose from differences in generational experience. Explaining their conviction about the effectiveness of nonviolent resistance, Chan Kin Man, one of the Occupy Trio, referenced the successful examples of Czechoslovakia's Velvet Revolution and Poland's self-limiting Solidarity movement, historical lessons in his youth.[84] But for the young militants in Mongkok, such as Ray Wong, Ukraine's Revolution of Dignity in Maidan in 2014 was more instructive. Ukraine was discussed among occupiers as a lesson about brave people willing to sacrifice and win through violent clashes with the police.[85]

Notwithstanding their differences, what protesters in Admiralty and Mongkok shared was their conscious attempt to leave a legacy for future generations. Student leader Chung Yiu Wah expressed a determination to nurture a local tradition of resistance: "Every generation should leave some legacy for the future generation. Just like we are today influenced by what our predecessors had experienced and done. Doesn't our fervent demand for democracy today stem from the half million strong rally in 2003, or the one million strong pro-students march in 1989, and twenty years of June 4th commemoration? I was born in 1992, the generation without first hand experience of 1989. But when I look back.... I feel our generation is doing the same thing: bequeathing resources of resistance. This time, it is for our own Hong Kong."[86] Echoing this sentiment but in very different way, Fire said he was proud of his participation because "in the future I could tell my grandchildren that grandpa shed blood defending Hong Kong. It was the first time I felt I was part of history, part of Hong Kong's destiny."[87]

Miraculously, the failure of Umbrella led to reflections on these differences that would resurface again in 2019, only this time they would be less a source of fragmentation than solidarity (see Chapters 3 and 4).

2016: Localism Against "China as Destiny"

After the bulldozers smashed the defiant banners "We will be back" and "It's just the beginning" in Admiralty in mid-December 2014, despondence set in among the participants. Not only did the protesters feel a deep sense of failure, as author Jason Ng observed, "when they went back to their parents and friends to face their judging eyes. They had nothing to show for their efforts. ... They failed to get any political concessions from either the SAR government or Beijing. The empty handedness turned into shame, and shame gave way to anger and contempt."[88] They also had to face the bitterness fanned by the militant localists who labeled everyone not agreeing with their combative tactics a "self-deluding leftard." The Occupy Trio, the student leaders, and other activists were formally charged under the Public Order Ordinance and were awaiting trial. In the wake of what many considered defeat, people asked what else could be done if seventy-nine days of occupation did not move the regime an inch toward universal suffrage.

Somehow, some citizens picked up the pieces and sustained the struggle in three "localist" directions: embedding the citizens' struggle in local communities, advocating "nativist" localism through militant street rallies, and forming new political parties calling for autonomy, even independence. In Beijing's eyes, the indomitable rise of these variegated currents of localism was an unacceptable challenge to Chinese sovereignty. To nip this energetic movement in the bud, Beijing and its agents in Hong Kong usurped the rule of law to punish the localists by criminalizing their street action and disqualifying them from running for election and from taking office even *after* they were duly elected. In imposing a rule *by* law in Hong Kong, Beijing shattered the binary between law and violence so foundational to its colonial hegemony. While localist consciousness in Hong Kong had emerged during bouts of social activism in the late 1960s and early 1970s, it was only in the 2010s, and especially in the post-Umbrella years, that localism became a political force of mass mobilization.[89] In what follows, I examine the genesis of these strands of "localism" taking root between the end of the Umbrella Movement and the eruption of the 2019 protests. Their enormous popular appeal signaled the bankruptcy of "China as destiny" myth as a ruling ideology.

Communal Localism

Social movements around the world have occurred in waves, with ebbs and flows. At times of low levels of mobilization, "abeyance structures" would form among activists to maintain social networks, identities, and visions that could revive the movement when conditions were ripe again.[90] Umbrella was no exception. Away from the limelight, a quiet flourish of post-Umbrella organizations developed in different occupational and geographical communities after 2014. Months-long encampments had provided fertile ground for people and groups to make connections, invent new vocabularies, and incubate collective visions. During Occupy, the post-1980s activists behind the Star Ferry and Queen's Pier preservation movements already promoted the "back to the community" idea. "Localism" meant long-term, labor-intensive activism at the grassroots level, at work and in everyday life. Among the forty-five or so post-Umbrella community organizations were Umbrella-2Neighborhood, Fixing Hong Kong, Wan Chai Commons, Tseung Kwan O Concerned Groups, and Post-Umbrella Moms and Dads. Some of these sought to win seats in district council elections, while others fostered a culture of civic participation or countered the vote-buying, petty handout campaigns by pro-establishment political parties.[91] An activist of the neighborhood repair service group Fixing Hong Kong vividly described their vision: "We are like soccer players who keep the spectators interested, so that one day they'd join the game. Or like a church keeping its door open and the lights on, so that people would come in one day."[92] Among professionals—lawyers, therapists, nurses, doctors, artists, insurance and financial service employees, accountants, architects, information technology workers, and urban planners—eighteen post-Umbrella organizations were formed. Bearing names such as Progressive Lawyers Group and Medicins Inspires, many of these encouraged their professions to participate in the elections of the functional constituencies and their respective election committees as a way to push for democratization from within the system.[93] As we will see, these organizations would provide ideological and organizational bridges between the 2014 and 2019 upsurges of activism.

Militant Localism

Taking a different tack and making more noise, quite literally, were the militant localists. The Umbrella Movement radicalized many young activists because its outcome convinced them OCTS was a scam. For Glacier, who was a freshman at the University of Hong Kong during Umbrella, the tipping point for her to lose faith in the current political system was the avalanche of tear gas and batons on September 26. Still reeling from the indignation years later, she recalled, "I was very, very angry. They shattered my trust in this society. We didn't do anything; we even held up our arms to show we were not using force. I felt it is right to resist, whether we have power or not."[94] Now that Beijing tore up the road map of OCTS, she and others felt liberated to find another path for Hong Kong—independence. She was one of the few female faces among the so-called militant localists who endorsed confrontational means to achieve their political goals. Localism was her answer to the "China as destiny" myth. Her fighting words were her proverbial weapons.

On a bustling Mongkok street, Glacier took the microphone and climbed the steps of a short ladder, surrounded by the yellow banners of Passion Times, a political organization representing militant localists. Without notes, poised and fearless, as her calm and youthful voice floated above the endless stream of pedestrians a few feet below, she tried to explain to Hong Kongers the need for a localist agenda. Occasional passersby shouted, "Well said, well said! Add oil, add oil!" Without losing a beat, she continued:

> Our job is to preserve Hong Kong's culture, not to let the evil claws of the CCP extend to our place. All around us, we can see the marks of mainland influences. All our neighborhood shopping centers all turn to sell luxury brands, LVs, cosmetics, baby formulas for parallel traders. We can lose no time to protect our Hong Kong. To protect our Hong Kong we don't need to go to the annual vigil at Victoria Park anymore. Why? Because for twenty-six years people had chanted "Rehabilitate June 4," "Release democratic activists," but there was no effect. Nil. . . . They [CCP] had not even responded once. Do we still want to waste our time to sit down, sing songs, light candles, and chant slogans? Is it realistic to expect CCP to suddenly kneel down and apologize to us that it was their mistakes to kill students with tanks in 1989? People forget that the essence of the CCP is to be totalitarian, to be undemocratic. . . . As Hong Kongers, what we can do is to protect and consolidate our own city, our streets, our culture, our identities, fight for our own democracy, build a democratic Hong Kong, build an independent Hong Kong. . . . What we need to do is to put up a real fight against the CCP as Hong Kongers. We already shed blood during the Umbrella Revolution. People were permanently injured, beaten up. How could we just let these sacrifices be?[95]

Glacier's turn to localism and independence as a political vision was commonplace among her generation. After Umbrella, militant localists in Occupy Mongkok regrouped online and on the streets to resume the series of community-specific "liberation" rallies that began around 2012. They arose from the anti-Chinese sentiments that had brewed for years since China opened the floodgate of individual tourists from the mainland to Hong Kong, ostensibly to revive the city's economy through tourism. The tourism industry registered double-digit growth, and the government promoted an economic dependency discourse in which Beijing was the benefactor.[96] Complaints against the influx of tens of millions of tourists overwhelming the capacity of local transportation and of pregnant women taking up hospital beds and other public facilities went unheeded by a government beholden to corporate and mainland interests. Then, since the mid-2000s, deadly food scandals involving baby formula and the prevalence of luxury counterfeits in mainland China created a huge market for smuggled consumer goods from Hong Kong. As these businesses thrived, commercial rent in border towns went up, and pharmacies and retail stores survived by catering to the army of suitcase-bearing traders exploiting the newly available tourist permits, ignoring the everyday needs of local residents.

The first call for vigilante action was posted on social media by a handful of mostly young local residents in September 2012. At the Sheung Shui train station, the penultimate stop before the border at Lo Wu, several hundred people gathered to pick on parallel traders, kicking their suitcases, blocking them from entering the train station gates, yelling expletives, and calling them "yellow locusts." These rallies spread to other border towns such as Fanling and Yuen Long. A concerned group focused on the North District was formed in 2013, raising fund for advertisements on buses, collecting statistics about parallel traders, and running local "theme tours" and photography contests exposing the negative impacts of parallel trade on local communities. "The mainstream media and the pan-democrats discriminated against us, accusing us of discriminating against mainlanders. But what's wrong with 'Hong Kong people first'?" fumed Leung Kam Shing, the convener of the first rally and a local organization that was still active as of 2022.[97]

The rank of militant localists grew during Occupy Mongkok, and they relaunched after the tents were removed. For them, Umbrella was proof that peaceful protests were totally useless, the Hong Kong government had no legitimacy, the law was unjust, China would never deliver the promise of democracy and autonomy, and an alternative paradigm of resistance was needed. One of the leaders of this nativist militant camp was Ray Wong, whose accidental yet also inevitable trajectory into localist politics was emblematic of the postcolonial logic of practice among many of his peers:

> My militancy and localism were reactions to pan-democrats' inaction. I was pushed to the front line because things happened and compelled me to react. We could win the battle against CCP. Chin Wan and Lian Yizen wrote about Hong Kong's significance for China. Beijing will stand to lose if OCTS fails. The problem was people did not listen, even mainstream pro-pan-democrats media such as Apple

Daily and Ming Pao boycotted us, marginalized us. They framed us as a bunch of crazy people.⁹⁸

As a teenager, Ray was more interested in girls, road biking, and saving up enough to be a globe-trotting backpacker than politics. But even as a bystander, he could not help being moved by Joshua Wong's hunger strike in 2012, annoyed by the drones of mainland tourists crowding the streets near his school, and impressed by the valiance of young people trying to storm the Legislative Council Complex (LegCo) to oppose the development plan for the northeast territory the summer before the outbreak of Umbrella. Then in Occupy Admiralty, he started managing an impromptu resource station when nobody else was available. Without planning or making an effort,

> Organically, I became part of a one-hundred-person action group that grew into a network of six hundred people. . . . We continued to discuss online. We anticipated a more radical movement in June, before LegCo discussion of electoral reform, to promote militant resistance to blow the whistle [to announce rallies]. But what kind of organization? At first, we were just a Facebook page called Localist Democratic Front. Then someone in the group who was an English major at CUHK proposed the English name "Hong Kong Indigenous." We just said OK, whatever. Ha ha! Then we collaborated with other local groups to liberate Tuen Mun, to break citizens' inertia.
>
> We wanted to make noise, to break the hegemony of the peaceful, rational, and lawful mode of resistance. The role of organization is to convene the gathering and let the masses unleash their will and energy. Responsibility for action resides with the individual, not with organizers. We cannot assume participants have no agency. We have to allow the masses to be spontaneous. Our organization at the beginning had no ambition to stand for election. That's why we did not have the burden to appeal to the moderate, the majority.⁹⁹

In late 2014, after the Umbrella encampments were cleared, fifty or so people responded to the call of Hong Kong Indigenous for a "Defend Ramen Shop" rally in Sheng Shui that involved walking around and cursing at parallel traders and police. In the ensuing months, there were more such protests in Tuen Mun, Yuen Long, and Shatin. Each time, Ray announced the end of the official march, leaving the masses to unleash their emotions and spontaneous rows and scuffles with mainlanders. Once police interfered, everyone's emotions would, without exception, flare up. He seemed to have mastered the delicate balance between organization and spontaneity in direct action and was elated when the government tightened the rules for mainland tourists. For him, militancy had delivered:

> Why liberation rallies? Parallel trade is the best policy arena to highlight to the public how an undemocratic government could ignore public interests and let social problems fester. We have exhausted all peaceful means, writing letters, speeches in legislature. It's time to use direct action to force the pharmacies to close their doors and harass the traders directly. Those liberation rallies in February and March [2015] were shots in our arms because China actually conceded to a certain extent. In May, the authorities canceled multientry individual tourist visas and allowed entry only once a week.[100]

Then came the fateful clashes with the police on the eve of the Lunar New Year in February 2016 in an incident known colloquially as the Fish Ball Revolution, after which the Hong Kong Indigenous and its two leaders shot to fame. Ray Wong and his comrade in arms, Edward Leung, mobilized their group's base to show up in Mongkok, together with other localist public figures, to patronize street vendors selling fish balls and other local snacks and protect them from harassment and citation by the sanitation officers. Suddenly, the peaceful and bustling festivity turned into an intense confrontation between the people and the police when the latter showed up in response to reports of a road blockage by a few individuals. Popular hostility toward the police in the wake of Umbrella easily boiled over. That night, verbal and physical altercations between hundreds of angry, mostly young people were initially contained when Edward, quick on his feet, justified the gathering of people by citing his right as an election candidate to host a campaign rally of under thirty people without advance police permission. Ray, as the spokesperson of Hong Kong Indigenous, also made a deal with the police and announced that both sides would withdraw. But soon, after both Ray and Edward left the scene, fighting resumed and intensified—bottles, sticks, and bricks dug up from pedestrian pathways were hurled at the police, who responded with batons, pepper spray, throwing bricks back at the protesters, and even two warning gunshots. By the time they returned, skirmishes had spread to other streets. Police footage showed them at the front line hurling shields and charging at the police. Chaos and carnage continued until the next morning. The police made ninety arrests, and eventually fifty were charged and thirty-one prosecuted.¹⁰¹ The chief executive denounced it as a "riot," a term that had not been used since the deadly 1967 disturbance by bomb-planting Communist sympathizers. The Department of Justice charged Ray and Edward for inciting and participating in riots, with maximum sentences of ten years. Both were granted bail, awaiting trial.¹⁰²

Localist Political Parties

Even before the Mongkok incident, Hong Kong Indigenous had become popular among the younger generation who found its militancy appealing and necessary. In internal meetings they discussed Mandela's Spear of the Nation and the difficulty of launching violent resistance in Hong Kong because it is very difficult to smuggle arms into the city. Guerrilla warfare also seemed out of the question. Still, Ray observed that citizens' threshold for violence kept rising in those years, because "each time protesters became more militant, triggering more militancy by the regime, more people accept more violence. . . . Taiwan has military drafts, and we think people should learn to build up their bodies and learn to combat. We took boxing classes together because we wanted to be able to push back at the police. It's really mild, but we were called 'militant' because Hong Kong has been so peaceful. Our goal was to find a maximum threshold to keep up political pressure without triggering military intervention by Beijing. Exactly what Lian Yizeng wrote about 'on the edges of violence.' In 2014, when Benny Tai kept referencing Martin Luther King Jr., we the militants on social media already criticized him for ignoring Malcom X. We talked about these on Facebook, My Radio, and our own digital radio called 'channel i.' When Edward spoke, typically a thousand or more people would be listening live!"¹⁰³

Edward Leung, a student at the University of Hong Kong who was battling depression and finding purpose in Umbrella, had joined the liberation rallies where the blue banners of the newly formed Hong Kong Indigenous were prominent. He and Ray hit it off very quickly because they had the exact same convictions.¹⁰⁴ But according to Ray, they were reluctant political leaders being thrusted to the limelight by the historical circumstances they did not anticipate. Edward's decision to run for election was made casually and serendipitously: "I (Ray) told him (Edward) my plan to backpack, but he convinced me not to waste the budding reputation of Hong Kong Indigenous. We were the most recognized among post-Umbrella organizations in terms of mobilization power; in just a few days we could pull off, say, an outdoor film screening in busy Mongkok. Then one day, in a core group meeting of a dozen people, Edward showed off his charm by giving a mesmerizing speech, basically saying we wanted to spread our beliefs among the people but the mass media discriminated against us. Facebook is not enough, and we must reclaim our discursive power. He said he's willing to run for election. I was only too happy to transfer my name recognition to someone so I can leave to backpack.... One day, he and I were lounging on a couch watching the vote count for that year's district council elections and we saw many votes went to the new party Youngspiration. We made a quick analysis: voters wanted new young faces because they were sick and tired of the pan-democrats. With one eye on the television, the other on our calendars, Edward said casually, 'Why don't we try the by-election in February? I don't have any papers to submit in February, so the timing should work.' Just like that! For us, it's a very easy decision. Election was a tool, a platform, a source of resources, to spread localist ideology, to strengthen our street action. Our imagination was that if the majority supported us the militants, there'd be enough political pressure forcing the government to give in."[105]

Charming and eloquent, Edward liked to sum up his election platform with a quartet of four-character Chinese phrases: resist tyranny with combat action (以武抗暴), differentiating Hong Kong from China (中港區隔), sovereignty belongs to the people (主權在民), and Hong Kong independence (香港獨立). In election debates, his oratory skills combined with his good looks always made him stand out. Echoing Glacier and Ray, whose turn to militant action and localist political visions resulted from reflections on the futility of past tactics and agendas that loyally stayed within the confine of OCTS, Edward's unvarnished and heartfelt speeches became the voice of his generation. On the campaign trail, he said,

> We believe in changing the future of Hong Kong with our own hands. Hong Kong is our home, it's what nurtures us. But we only see the rule of Basic Law crumbling. Promises on autonomy are nothing but empty words. We no longer have hopes for China. We can no longer

2.5 Ray Wong (first from the left) and Edward Leung (center) of Hong Kong Indigenous campaigned for Leung's candidacy in the 2016 by-election. Their slogan, "Liberate Hong Kong, revolution of our times," would become the rallying cry of the 2019 uprising.
CREDIT: Anthony Wallace / Getty Images

rely on old political parties and politicians. To fight an authoritarian regime is to put our lives on the line and allows no holdback. I feel that our past democratic movements had too many holdbacks, too many reservations. That's why we still do not have democracy. The peaceful, rational, and nonviolent movements can no longer shake up this regime. Indeed, no one wishes for violence to happen. But our only way out is using force against violence. What I represent is an ideal: it's the government who should be fearful of the people, for sovereignty rests with the people. We Hong Kongers are the rightful masters of this land. We shall reclaim Hong Kong; we shall lead a revolution of our times![106]

Rethinking Violence and Rule of Law

But how could a militant localist awaiting trial for his role in the Mongkok violence stand any chance of winning an election given Hong Kong's legalistic political culture? The general public was shell-shocked by the violence. A public opinion poll conducted two months after the incident showed that the majority of citizens, regardless of political identifications, did not support the Mongkok protesters. Even among the self-proclaimed localists, only 34.5 percent supported the protest. But significantly, across the board, more than two-thirds of all respondents saw the government as the root of the problem.[107]

Stunningly, Edward's popularity among the young and localist voters soared after the Fish Ball Revolution, indicating their distrust of the regime and their endorsement of a new level of combativeness in resistance, so long as it only targeted the police. Fish Ball made Edward famous, and his rallies grew in size. Only three weeks after the Fish Ball Revolution, he secured 66,524 votes (15 percent of the popular vote) in the by-election. Even though he did not win, this level of support almost guaranteed him a seat in the Legislative Council general election in September. In Edward, the post-Umbrella localist generation had found a hero, a visionary in word and action.

Besides Hong Kong Indigenous, several new political parties formed in 2015 also had their eye on the 2016 LegCo election, trying to tap into the reservoir of localist sentiment and mass-mobilization capacity revealed during Umbrella. Youngspiration was formed in January 2015 by Baggio Leung, a former president of the City University of Hong Kong student union. Its major campaign issue was the restriction of Chinese immigration to Hong Kong, as well as safeguarding Hong Kongers' interests, culture, and identity against mainland encroachment. The party scored an initial victory in the 2015 district council election when one of their nine candidates won a seat, inspiring Edward Leung to run. For the 2016 election, Youngspiration promoted a more radical goal: the right to self-determination for the Hong Kong nation, a platform no doubt influenced by other newly formed political parties.

In March 2016, Andy Chan Ho Tin and Jason Chow announced the formation of the Hong Kong National Party, the first political party ever to openly call for an independent republic of Hong Kong. Asserting that Hong Kong's colonial regime needed to be overthrown because it served the interests of China rather than Hong Kong, Chan and Chow urged Hong Kong people to construct their own nationality and nation by all effective and necessary forms of struggle. Modeled after other revolutionary parties, all members remained anonymous, except Chan and Chow, who traveled to

Japan and Taiwan to discuss the formation of an international alliance against PRC colonization. They also petitioned the US government to cancel the city's special status under the Hong Kong Policy Act in response to China's infringement of the city's autonomy.[108] All these boundary-shattering provocations put the National Party on the far end of a spectrum of localist parties.

A more moderate election platform was "self-determination," put forth by a political party called Demosisto in April 2016. Its leaders were Joshua Wong, who disbanded Scholarism in 2016, and Nathan Law, a Federation of Students leader. Quite bluntly, they declared the bankruptcy of "One Country, Two Systems": "Repeated atrocities (such as the NPCSC's didactic interpretations of the Basic Law and the mysterious disappearance of Hong Kongers within the city's borders) have led us to finally learn that we were all deceived by the PRC and that their fantasy of 'One Country Two Systems' was a mere illusory concept.... By employing popular referendum and seeking international support, we will push for the self-determination of Hong Kong to be included as an agenda in the international realm of politics. Hong Kongers must have a say in our own future, and must retain the right of self-determination."[109]

The political parties that emerged from the ashes of Umbrella popularized ideas such as self-determination, autonomy, independence, and nation building; all were visions for Hong Kong that openly defied Chinese sovereignty. The intellectual groundwork for their defiance was laid as early as 2011 with the publication of *On Hong Kong as City State* by Chin Wan, a previously unknown ethnologist at a second-tier local university. The author argued that Hong Kong had its own historical and cultural character distinct from China and that it was China that was economically dependent on Hong Kong, not the other way around. This paradigm-shifting inversion of the presumed hierarchy was subversive enough that the book became a sensation, and its arguments were eagerly embraced by many activists and ordinary young people. A few years later, in February 2014, the official journal of the undergraduate student union at the University of Hong Kong, *Undergrad*, published an issue titled "Hong Kong Nationality, Self Determination of Our Future." Its contributors explored ideas such as Hong Kong nationalism—based on civic values of democracy, freedom, and rule of law, as opposed to racialized Chinese nationalism based on blood, soil, and ancestry—and self-determination as enshrined in international conventions and as the basis for a legally binding referendum on the city's future.[110] Ten years later, the editor-in-chief of this issue, Brian Leung, explained to me how fractured, but also lively, the discursive terrain of localism was:

> In those days, we believed China was in the process of colonizing Hong Kong; but to the pan-dem mainstream and established leftist scholars, they would not accept this discourse of Chinese colonization. Perhaps because of their Chinese nationalism. We localist students also were alienated from the elitism of the Federation of Students. But we did not see ourselves the same as those populist suitcase-kicking protesters even though we were sympathetic. We were more interested in creating respectable and rational (you could even say "elitist") narratives. . . . We wanted to be provocative, to stimulate people's thinking. Our consensus was that we did not like to be called Chinese. Why can Chinese call themselves a nation but Hong Kongers cannot do the same? Nationhood was imagined, according to Benedict Anderson. Even the Chinese nationhood concept was imagined from piecing together the pseudoscience of race and the myth of Yellow Emperor. We knew it is awkward to even say the term "Hong Kong nation," but this was exactly the point—to provoke. In the West, ethnicity and nationality can be separated. Cultural descent and political allegiance are distinguishable. We were frustrated that in the Chinese-speaking world, these concepts are fused. The pro-establishment elite always challenged us by asking: do you use chopsticks, is your skin not yellow and your hair black?[111]

It was a time of intense ideological debates. Every week there would be talks at bookstores or public forums on the street, in different neighborhoods and campuses. There was a general expectation that democracy was around the corner. The Hong Kong National Party journal *Comitium* joined the theoretical discussions of Hong Kong nationalism and local identity by drawing on academic Sinophone studies and theories of nationalism. On the one hand, contributors to the journal challenged a China-centered nationalism imposed on populations sharing a Sinitic-language heritage and called out China's double colonization of post-1997 Hong Kong: "territorial colonization supplemented by ideological colonization in the conception of 'pan-Chineseness' and Chinese victimization, leaving the majority of residents fundamentally unable to recognize the colonizing process as such."[112] On the other, the journal also critically engaged the *Undergrad* argument for civic nationalism, arguing that through the process of anticolonial resistance, an ethnic communal identity constructing "China as the other" would emerge.

Among this cacophony of voices challenging China as Hong Kong's destiny, Edward Leung was perhaps the most forceful and influential. His message was that Hong Kongers must reclaim their "subjecthood" in a "decolonizing" struggle in the face of Chinese colonization. In a news media interview marking the twentieth anniversary of the handover, he deplored that

> Hong Kong is still a colony. Hong Kongers are a dominated people, whether by Britain or by China, who cannot determine their own destiny. Hong Kong has never experienced a decolonization process; the people were being decolonized.... Unlike Taiwanese who have subjecthood, Hong Kong people only think about emigrating when problems arise. But we need to stare straight into our reality: we are facing a regime that kills without blinking and the second-largest economy in the world that no country wants to oppose. On the other hand, our small city of seven million had to confront a country of 1.3 billion. We may not succeed, but in the process, we will make ourselves. That's our legacy.[113]

Elsewhere, in a 2016 double interview debating Chow Hang Tung, an organizer of the annual June 4 vigil who was critical of the localists' identity politics, Edward explained the need for prioritizing identity politics in Hong Kong's decolonizing struggle: "Because this is about decolonization, we cannot avoid identity politics. We wanted to begin a nation-building process. Before there is a nation-state, we need to have national identity, especially because Hong Kong is being subjected to Chinese colonialism. Decolonial struggle cannot identify with the colonialists' imposed identity—Chinese first and then Hong Kong. Second, ethnic nationalism is about where and who you were born, but we are for civic nationalism, meaning national membership is based on common values, lifestyle, language. This kind of civic nationalism is universal, including US and France. How can you say they are discriminatory? British colonial education policy made us learn about Chinese culture as a way to stabilize its rule and cultivated among us a cultural Chinese identity. But why do we only learn Chinese history and Chinese literature and not Hong Kong history and Hong Kong literature? Hong Kongers always thought Hong Kong independence is impossible because they never had adequate subjecthood; they are still bound by the sentiment of Great China and Chinese identity, especially the older generation. The British abandoned them, the Chinese dominated them, and they stayed mum, even though surveys showed more than 80 percent were against reunification, only 10 percent wanted reunification. We already missed 1997 as a historic opportunity to fight for our right to self-determination, including the option of independence. Why can't we seize the upcoming one in 2047? Hong Kong is our native home. Our priority, capacity, and responsibility are to fight for a democratic Hong Kong. Mainland Chinese should make their own choice."[114]

By 2016, Hong Kong independence was no longer a forbidden political fantasy but a publicly promoted electoral agenda. Not yet a majority proposition, this budding movement was gaining unmistakable traction among the young. A poll conducted by the Center for Communication and Public Opinion Survey at the Chinese University of Hong Kong in June 2016 showed 17 percent of all respondents and 40 percent of respondents between fifteen and twenty-four years of age supported Hong Kong independence.[115] Therefore, when the Electoral Affairs Commission rejected Edward Leung's candidacy application, together with that of Alan Chan of the Hong Kong National Party and several others, citing their pro-independence stance, the younger generation cried foul. Even after duly winning the election, two pro-independence legislators of Youngspiration were disqualified on account of their behavior during the swearing-in ceremony—unfurling a banner saying "Hong Kong is not China" and uttering words that signal Hong Kong independence. The grounds for their disqualification emerged after China's top legislative body, the NPCSC, interpreted a clause in the territory's constitution, which was soon applied to four more pro-democracy legislators. This move was widely condemned by the Hong Kong public. Two thousand lawyers dressed in black held a silent protest march against this blatant violation of the rule of law and autonomy. In 2018, when Edward Leung was sentenced to six years in jail for rioting and assaulting a police officer during the Fish Ball Revolution in Mongkok, and other young people received similarly harsh jail terms, the boundary between law and violence became even more ambiguous, if not totally blurred.[116] The 2019 uprising would exhume his campaign slogan, "Liberate Hong Kong, revolution of our times," to be the rallying cry for all protesters. In doing so, they immortalized him as their icon and declared that "payback day" would come.

The Making of Decolonial Subjectivities

In this chapter, we have seen how the four pillars of colonial hegemony—prosperity and stability, free-market utopia, rule of law, and China as destiny—were shaken to various degrees in the post-handover years. Popular mobilizations have erupted almost every year since, in response to a combination of political economic ruptures that are global, regional, national, and local in origin. Notably, during this twenty-year period, democracy and universal suffrage were not the only demands, and the Chinese Communist regime was not their only source of discontent. Remaking Hong Kong through decolonization became a political project. In chronicling how the people's decolonial praxis evolved, I have put front and center the experiences of the postcolonial generation, a passionate minority who spearheaded the rise of decolonial subjectivities in Hong Kong. The pragmatic majority, whether attentive spectators, occasional participants, wavering supporters, or ardent opponents, were inevitably affected by the accumulation of decolonizing actions and ideas. A few years later, as seen in the next chapter, many among this majority would become impassioned participants.

What lessons does this brief history of resistance suggest about the mechanisms and conditions allowing this decolonial process to take off? First, political economic ruptures were the material conditions that compelled popular reassessment of entrenched common sense, and Hong Kong had more than its fair share of ruptures. Global cities in general are susceptible to the volatility of the global economy, but Hong Kong, as a unique node bridging the West and China, has borne the brunt of the combined impacts of their crises and contradictions. On the one hand, there were shocks (the Asian financial crisis) and countermovements (anti-WTO, global social justice) originating from neoliberal capitalism. On the other, Chinese reform produced its own internal crisis (the Tiananmen Massacre), contradictory impulses of global integration ("One Country, Two Systems," liberal and civic education curriculum) and authoritarian nationalistic control (a national security bill, national and patriotic education, illiberal election rules, and criminalizing political dissent). These political forces were playing out in a deeply paradoxical institutional environment in which people still had wide latitude in exercising the civil right of assembly and protest, thanks to British liberal institutions and a mini-constitution stipulating democratization toward universal suffrage. The ruling ideology of "Hong Kong people rule Hong Kong" also interpellated, even extolled, the citizenry to become their own masters.[117]

Second, political economic ruptures induce ideological ruptures. The colonial hegemony that once produced and entrenched submission now inspired critique and resistance to its violation. Just as postwar French and British imperial ideologies of universal citizenship and development inspired West African laborers to make claims for equalization of salaries, benefits, and juridical treatment, thereby confronting the French and British governments with the burden of an empire of citizens, the so-called Hong Kong core values became the standards to judge, criticize, and rebel against their erosions under Chinese rule.[118] From the annual 1989 vigils and July 1, 2003, rally to the Star Ferry, Queen's Pier, and anti–West Rail protests, anti-privatization, and Occupy Central in 2011, the anti–national education campaign, the Umbrella Movement, and the Fish Ball Revolution, among others, Hong Kongers ignited a process of contesting colonial truth claims, turning them into right claims. But colonial legacies did not exhaust the world of political visions among citizens of a global city. Hong Kong activists in moments of ruptures were also inspired by contemporary struggles, from the Battle of Seattle and anti-WTO South Korean farmers to mainland China's Tiananmen students, Taiwan's Sunflower Movement, the Eastern European dissident movement, the Maidan protest in Ukraine, and black struggles in the United States and South Africa.

Third, and related to the idea of a dialectic of coloniality and anticoloniality, the colonial temporality (with expiration dates of 1997 and 2047) imposed on the city was an impetus for the decolonizing struggle in Hong Kong. Rather than class actors emphasized in the study of anticolonial struggles in Africa—a national bourgeoisie championing independence, a racialized and exploited working class, or a dispossessed wretched peasantry—in Hong Kong it was a demographic constituency I call the postcolonial political generation. Not only were they, like other political generations, bound up with the unfolding of a common destiny and shared "exposure to and participation in the social and intellectual symptoms of a process of dynamic destabilization," they also shared generational interests and identities defined by 1997 and 2047, respectively the end of British colonization and the end point of "One Country, Two Systems."[119] Bearing the brunt of the city's unsettled future, this generation had the largest collective stake in the city. As shown in this chapter (and the next), this generational interest cut across divides of class, gender, race, and religion, despite internal disagreement and tensions among a number of "generational units," forming what Mannheim called "a new generation entelechy."[120] As the face of this generation, Joshua Wong, made clear, "My generation . . . would have the most to lose if Hong Kong were to become like just another mainland Chinese city, where information is not freely shared and the rule of law is ignored. . . . Earlier generations, many of whom came here from mainland China, wanted one thing: a stable life. . . . The people of my generation want more. In a world where ideas and ideals flow freely, we want what everybody else in an advanced society seems to have: a say in our future."[121]

Fourth, decolonizing politics in Hong Kong was fraught with uneven consciousness, meanings, and visions of "decolonization." We have seen how the post-1980s generation consciously and publicly framed their action in "anticolonial" and "decolonizing" rhetoric. Their critique was against both neoliberalism and the authoritarianism inhered in Hong Kong's colonial order, before and after 1997. Then there were the later militant localists who talked pragmatically and expediently about decolonization against China (for example, Edward Leung) and civic nationalism as an antidote to China's ethnic nationalism (Brian Leung and other *Undergrad* authors). Less mentioned in their discourses was the complicity of British colonialism. Some ultraright localists used the term "yellow locusts" against Chinese visitors and immigrants to express their anger against China's colonization. Critics assailed their xenophobic behavior for reestablishing ethnic hierarchies as a self-defeating colonial project rather than a liberatory decolonizing one.[122] While some protesters waved the official flag of British Hong Kong to signal their preference for the previous colonial master over the current one and to demand "Chinese Colonialists Get Out," many citizens were not explicitly motivated by any grand vision of decolonization in joining protests. Their demands were mostly couched in concrete policy-specific terms: universal suffrage, anti–Article 23 legislation, anti–brainwashing education, anti–parallel trade, and more. Chinese officials reacted to this cacophony of decolonization discourses with equally contradictory rhetoric. On the one hand, they condemned popular demands to preserve historic architecture as "colonial nostalgia." On the other, they indicated their own inadmissible nostalgia for British colonialism in their constant laments about the disappearance of "rationality and harmony" (that is, no protests).[123] Citizens and Communist officials had understandings of colonization and coloniality that might be different from those of academics and intellectuals, but all were engaged in a struggle with Hong Kong's colonial order.

Finally, there was no guarantee that resistance would grow rather than atrophy thanks to tensions from within. This chapter has not shied away from the fact that various movements were plagued by internal dissension and acrimonious factionalism (for example, within the OCLP and among pan-democrats, organized students, progressive and militant localists, and the middle and working classes), failures of leadership (during the Umbrella Movement), and organizational cultures of sexism, authoritarianism, and elitism (Scholarism and the Federation of Students). With hindsight, however, such disagreements had the paradoxical effect of expanding the action repertoire and ideological spectrum of the city's political activism. Even failure in obtaining concessions from Beijing, when shared by all camps and factions, would turn out to be a unifying force. This was exactly what happened in 2019, when past discord became the raw material for collective reflection, solidarity, and reconciliation. How and why this positive turn of events happened is the subject of the next chapter.

CHAPTER THREE

"HONG KONGERS"
(Re)born in Action

THE PROTESTS IN 2019 WERE THE LARGEST and longest in Hong Kong's history and therefore had the most profound impact on Hong Kong people's collective identity as a political community. The scale of citizen participation meant that the decolonial struggle had proliferated beyond the most radical and active of the postcolonial generation to involve the pragmatic majority who had been on the sideline of the action up to that point. This chapter examines the variety of motivations and pathways leading different social groups to join the movement. The key question is: if 155 years of double coloniality had deprived Hong Kongers of their historical agency, why did so many break that shackle to reclaim their subjecthood in 2019? If a "will to community" is what decolonizing struggles the world over have in common, what did Hong Kong citizens envision it to be?[1] In a nutshell, I make three arguments. First, the Hong Kong experience shows that it was through *action*, not imagination, that a political community had arisen. Second, China, as the *structural* source of a wide variety of discontent, united a populace otherwise divided by heterogeneous interests, identities, and ideologies. Third, after two decades of capacity and legacy building, the decolonization movement did not just expand its social base in 2019: it developed a *reflexivity* among its various factions to produce an unprecedented level of solidarity and creativity. In a nutshell, the collective agent of decolonization had made a quantum leap as a political force.

Historical Contingency of a Political Rupture

In April 2019, the Hong Kong government under Carrie Lam introduced amendments to Hong Kong's extradition laws that would allow criminal suspects, including foreigners, to be sent to mainland China for trial. Opponents said the changes would put them at the mercy of the Chinese courts, which had a notorious record of arbitrary detentions, torture, and other human rights violations. The Hong Kong public, along with the United States, Canada, the US Chamber of Commerce, and the European Union, all voiced their opposition to the bill, which they argued would deal a serious blow to the city's rule of law and its status as a global financial hub. In May, legislators clashed over the bill, and in early June, more than 120,000 students, alumni, staff, and parents from 185 secondary schools signed a petition against it. On June 6, three thousand Hong Kong lawyers again took to the streets dressed in black. In light of the imminent reading of the bill in the Legislative Council, the Civil Human Rights Front, the organizer of the annual July 1 rally since 2003, called for a mass rally on June 9 to pressure the government to withdraw the bill.[2] One million citizens showed up and sparked a momentum of resistance that would grow in tandem with the regime's staunch refusal to compromise.

No one expected this level of popular rage, least of all the people themselves. After the summary disqualification of localist candidates and the imprisonment of those involved in the 2014 Umbrella occupation and the 2016 Fish Ball Revolution, civil society entered a period of depression, with no clear sign of revival. The structural imbalance of power between the sovereign and the people seemed insurmountable. The Hong Kong government seized this moment to push through several highly controversial policies that further subsumed Hong Kong to China's control. Citizens' disgruntlement was palpable, but action was feeble, for instance, against the "colocation" customs clearance at the high-speed train terminal located in downtown Kowloon. It practically allowed Chinese jurisdiction on Hong Kong's soil where local laws no longer apply, in clear violation of Article 18 of the Basic Law. Popular discontent simmered because colocation was tantamount to a zone of extraterritoriality. Still, in June 2018, when a march was called to protest this decision outside the LegCo Complex, only several hundred people showed up. Another policy that triggered mass criticism but little action was the mammoth land reclamation project called Lantau Tomorrow Vision. With a price tag equivalent to two-thirds of the city's fiscal reserve, many ridiculed the plan as "dumping money into the ocean," just another white elephant project to integrate Hong Kong with the Greater Bay Area while also boosting the bottom line of Chinese state contractors. To the dismay of the organizers, only a few thousand citizens joined the protest in October 2018.

These anemic responses must have emboldened the Carrie Lam administration to further Beijing's agenda of tightening its grip on Hong Kong, this time through the court. Even after the handover in 1997, there had been no provision for extradition between the Hong Kong and mainland judicial systems. A Reuters investigation, based on interviews with fifty Chinese officials and top Hong Kong officials, concluded that the push for an extradition bill came in 2017 from the Central Commission for Discipline Inspection spearheading Xi Jinping's antigraft campaign on the mainland.[3] One of the officials' targets, the Chinese billionaire Xiao Jianhua, had to be abducted from his luxury hotel in Hong Kong to the mainland due to the lack of a less politically damaging means of capturing fugitives. Since then, Chinese officials had been looking for an opportunity to close what was deemed a legal loophole. They found one in a murder case that happened in Taiwan in early 2018 involving a Hong Kong man who could not be charged by the Hong Kong police because of the lack of an extradition agreement with Taiwan. Carrie Lam used this case to argue for the need for new laws that could send fugitives back to both Taiwan and the mainland.

There was no single reason why this bill triggered a tsunami of protests. Some scholars explained the scale of mobilization by the universal threat the bill posed to everyone's freedom, the core of all core values for Hong Kongers.[4] But the 1997 handover and the denial of universal suffrage in 2014 arguably also posed a similarly universal threat without sparking any comparable level of resistance. Going inside the movement, I found a diversity of activism pathways among different social groups for whom the bill and China meant different things. Once they joined, action then generated its own dynamic prompting more action. The following first-person accounts by the protestors illustrate an alchemy of cognition, emotion, interest, belief, and reflection.[5] Social scientists with a penchant for theorization tend to

3.1 In the front line of protests were ninja-like black bloc youngsters, wearing helmets, gas masks, and googles, with umbrellas in hand, in anticipation of clashes with full-geared police.
CREDIT: Anthony Kwan / Getty Images

disaggregate these elements of collective action, using them as springboards for developing distinct schools of thought—from resource mobilization to postmaterialist identity politics to the cultural, emotional, and affective turns in theories. Yet, on the ground, people make history by combining, not isolating, these human faculties. The most potent episodes of collective action are only possible when people's body, mind, heart, and soul align and point them in the same direction. This was what happened in 2019.

As the Asian hub for international news organizations, the city's political turmoil instantly became a global spectacle with an around-the-clock live audience. All eyes were on the front lines of the urban battlefield. Many of these ninja-like black bloc youngsters formed a new cohort of "political freshmen"—high school students, even preteens, who were too young to join the Umbrella Movement in 2014. Donning their iconic goggles and gas masks fitted with filters in bright pink and yellow, their first political act was to take on full-geared riot police backed by the world's largest Communist regime. So captivating were their moral clarity, youthful fearlessness, and tactical ingenuity that it was easy to forget the invisible army behind them.

First-aid volunteers, rescue drivers, housewives, elders, office workers, bankers, lawyers, and small business owners played all sorts of supportive but critical roles in each protest. Their participation made this truly a people's uprising in size and representation. Some 36.4 to 45.6 percent of the population of seven million had participated in a movement that transcended divisions of class, generation, gender, religion, and race.[6] Their different trajectories into the protests can be read as a people's map of the city's surreptitious social structure. Springing from their respective social locations and collective biographies, but resisting China as a dominating structure for different reasons, a kaleidoscope of voices, emotions, interests, and beliefs coalesced on the streets every week from June 2019 to January 2020 and then more sporadically until May 2020 before being crushed by the enactment of the National Security Law on July 1, 2020. But the proliferation of the movement was not predetermined. As we shall see, it was the government's recalcitrance and the police's unrelenting violence beginning on June 12 that convinced the general public that they had to dig in and that this movement would be the endgame for Hong Kong's future. Had Carrie Lam withdrawn

3.2 Citizens encircled the Legislative Council Complex to block the second reading of the extradition bill on June 12, 2019.
CREDIT: AP Photo / Kin Cheung

Political Freshmen

"I used to dislike Hong Kong. People are rude and cold. Our teacher told us Hong Kongers had the lowest 'smiling' index in the world!" quipped fifteen-year-old Ben, a slight, short, boyish-looking secondary school student. A self-professed "Hong Kong pig" (港豬), he used to care only about food, video games, and sleep. Yet, in the summer of 2019, like tens of thousands of young people, Ben became an avid resister, vowing to fight for the city's freedom. These young activists talked and texted about "going to dreams" (去發夢), a code word for joining street protests. Their first taste of mass action was the million-strong June 9 march that made headlines around the world. With no agenda other than hanging out with his schoolmates, Ben stumbled into a miracle. Swept up by the sea of people united in their chants for freedom, Ben had an epiphany: "Hong Kong could be so lovely, and Hong Kongers could be so united!" When he saw small children marching with placards demanding "repeal the evil law" (a reference to the extradition bill), he was ashamed of his own earlier apathy.

Near midnight, as marchers were returning home, exhausted and exhilarated, they heard Chief Executive Carrie Lam's response: "I heard you, but the second reading of the bill will proceed as planned on Wednesday, June 12." Blasé and arrogant, Lam was woefully blind to the political volcano her signature callousness had detonated. On the day of the second reading, an estimated fifty thousand citizens arrived near the government headquarters, trying to block the roads and stop the legislators from accessing the LegCo Complex. As a novice, Ben went with several friends, without even a mask or umbrella. He was terrified when the police showered the crowd with endless rounds of tear gas and pepper spray. His friend with asthma fainted right next to him and was helped to the sidewalk by volunteer paramedics who cleaned his eyes. At one point, Ben came face-to-face with the riot police, who almost snatched him. Instead, he succumbed to the burning pain in his eyes caused by the tear gas. Wet from pepper spray, he vomited some red substance and lost consciousness for a few seconds until his friend pulled him back to his feet. Along with other protesters, Ben ran frantically away from the police, through the seemingly impenetrable thicket of tear gas, all the time yelling at the top of his lungs, "Run! Run!" Then came a magical encounter:

> As we retreated to the Admiralty MTR [Mass Transit Railway] station, a twenty-something bro took off his helmet, put it on my head, and said, "From now on, our future is in your hands. You will fight, and you cannot die." We looked at each other, tears swirling in our eyes. With a simple "add oil" [a Cantonese term for "keep going"], he disappeared into the white smoke around us. That day, I felt like I was dead but was resurrected.

From then on, Ben did not want to be the one who was saved but the one who would save others. No longer a Hong Kong pig, he vowed to put all his efforts into keeping Hong Kong free. In the months ahead, and along with many other youths, he would rapidly "evolve"—a witty and subversive invocation of Darwin's term by protesters to mark the *speed* of personal change—into a militant frontliner. What was truly amazing about Ben's almost religious initiation into this popular uprising was its banality. Many who had been to street protests remembered witnessing scenes of citizen solidarity and care that transformed, moved, and sustained them. For six months in 2019, the famously competitive ethos that animated the city's marble-lined malls, glittering towers of corporate headquarters, and neon-lit streets of bustling commerce dissipated. In its place, the grace of collective kindness enveloped the city, binding perfect strangers in chance encounters at a citywide march or neighborhood demonstration. Appellations of "bro and sis" (巴打、絲打) or "hand and feet" (手足), colloquial terms of endearment, became the new linguistic currency that facilitated numerous daily exchanges of care, assistance, and even sacrifice. The dreaminess of solidarity was as intoxicating as the people's political awakening was empowering. How did this metamorphosis come about?

High school students in Hong Kong, like their counterparts the world over, are a fun-loving bunch with budding talents and interests in things like music, sports, anime, video games, and, of course, romance. Disciplined by tremendous parental and social pressures to excel in examinations, there is little time for anything else. Those from lower-class families even have to squeeze in a part-time job to generate pocket money. Politics and social movements were the least likely objects on their radar. Even in the spring of 2019, when people began voicing concerns about threats to personal liberty, many heard of the bill as distant thunder. Then came a signature campaign by more than three hundred high school alumni groups that brought the call to action to the school gate. The organizers did not anticipate the overwhelming response they unleashed. Forty-year-old Francis, who called himself a "movement old hand," was one of the four initiators. A veteran activist of the anti-WTO protest in 2005 and the 2012 anti–national education campaign, he mobilized his old movement base among his five thousand Facebook friends. He drafted a statement, circulated it as a Google Doc, and collected HK$200,000 from alumni of 163 schools in one week. In the end, they collected more than one hundred thousand signatures endorsing an antiextradition statement that was published in *Ming Pao*, a Chinese newspaper that many high schools subscribed to for their students. He explained, "Many people are suffering from the posttraumatic syndrome after the Umbrella Movement. The signature campaign reignited their fire of engagement, reversed their depression, allowed them to break out of their isolation and powerlessness. It made them feel like 'I did something, with my real name.'"

But exactly *how* did a signature campaign spur young students to action? The campaign sparked curiosity because it came from their predecessors. But impersonal statements could equally easily be buried among their numerous school readings or tossed aside among the many mundane chores in their busy schedules. What were the personal or emotional connections between the bill and the signature campaign and these political freshmen?

For sixteen-year-old Little Shield (a nom de guerre), the extradition bill posed a direct threat to him and many people in Hong Kong. With a grin, he said mockingly, "You know how creative and irreverent young Hong Kongers are. We love to make fun of everything, like adding some curse words to the national anthem. Or teasing Xi Jinping as Winnie the Pooh. And I worried that these people would 'be disappeared' by this bill." Similarly, Sammy, who quit school after Form 3 (a junior high school level in the Hong Kong education system), was "forced by his friends" to join the march on June 9 after they saw his posts on Facebook criticizing the government and the education system. Unlike the experientially distant demands for universal suffrage during the Umbrella Movement, the extradition bill upset even teenagers because they saw it as directly impacting their everyday life. The personal and quotidian risks posed by the bill were widely shared among protesters from all walks of life.

The roots that connected young people to the movement had highly variegated, often serendipitous, beginnings. Quite a few were being dragged along by their friends to the first two protests in June, thinking it was just another hangout with buddies. Harry had just completed his school exams and was lounging in a study room near his home, enjoying the free air-conditioning and playing video games. Then someone gave him a flyer urging people to defend the LegCo Complex that night (June 11) to block the bill's second reading the following day. He reckoned that exams were over and he had time on his hands, so he decided to go for fun. Through Instagram, he rounded up the "naughty ones" from his class who happened to live in the same public housing estate. "Fourteen of us, all wearing black clothing, because that was the dress code recommended by people online. I still remember that was the first time I wore black pants in such hot summer weather," he joked. Harry would become a skilled and dedicated black bloc protester from that day on. A couple of months later, when we went to one protest together, he reprimanded me for not wearing two layers of pants: "The police like to tear off women's pants. You should have worn at least two layers. Some frontline sisses wear three!" Regardless, he complained often, "No one enjoys rallies. It's too hot and strenuous."

Similar serendipity sent Jenny, a precocious seventeen-year-old woman with a passion for poetry and literature, to the movement. She launched her own antiextradition signature campaign at her school after she saw on Instagram that her primary school friend had started one. Admitting her unabashedly childlike instinct, she told me, "I have always looked at her as my imaginary rival. If she could do it, I could too." But Jenny was quick to add another motive: "I recently attended a poetry workshop at the Chinese University. A friend from that workshop wrote a poem comparing the bill to a beast hiding in the cave and Hong Kong people still don't recognize this imminent danger. I began to pay attention." Despite her literary disposition and demure appearance, she attended almost every protest and march since June 9 and confessed to have accepted the use of principled violence by protesters after seeing, in person, the violence inflicted by the police on unarmed citizens on June 12.

During the month of June, the entire society was intensely focused on the extradition bill and elated by the massive turnout on June 9. Even the most apolitical and carefree students sensed the excitement, the peer pressure, and the obligation to care. Risk was then minimal, as large-scale peaceful marches

3.3 The common sight of teenage protesters in the front line, facing water cannons, tear gas, and bullet rounds and putting their future on the line, created a powerful moral force fueling social support for the movement.
CREDIT: Isaac Lawrence / Getty Images

had happened quite regularly in the past twenty years and were routinely given "no objection notice" by the police. On June 9, Doug, a seventeen-year-old Form 5 student, even chatted with some of the policemen standing next to him, pleading with them to open more lanes on Hennessy Road. He was stuck for hours in the massive crowd outside the Japanese department store Sogo, one of the default meeting places for protesters, because too many people had joined from all directions, blocking the march. A police officer responded politely, "We have to wait for instructions from our superiors. Please just wait to see what arrangements they make." This unremarkably pedestrian exchange left a deep impression on Doug because that was the last time he saw mutual respect and civility between citizens and law enforcement in the city.

After taking steps in protest for the first time, it was by no means inevitable that these young protesters would stay. As a matter of fact, for many uninitiated teenagers, fear was as palpable as excitement when marching peacefully among one or two million fellow citizens. "On June 9 I was afraid to see even traffic cops!" Fei recalled with embarrassment and disbelief after he "evolved" into a committed militant a month later. Jenny, the poet, was frightened even just handing out flyers opposing the extradition bill in Causeway Bay on the eve of the second reading. Donning a mask, she took pains to hide her school emblem badge with plastic stickers, afraid of being recognized. On June 12, even though she stayed at the back of the pack, mere rumors coming from the front about police unfurling their warning flags in orange and blue sent shivers down her spine. The mere sight of the police was nerve-racking enough for the young, raised as they were to respect the law. So why did trepidation not inhibit their participation? It turned out that fear was always felt, but it was neither the only nor the most powerful emotion.

First, according to some, the adrenaline rush during protests put their anxiety under control. Then, with characteristic playfulness and humor, many reported with relief that after being hit by tear gas for the first time, their body simply acclimatized amazingly well to the second and the third. To their delight, some found that "actually it wasn't that bad after the first hit. Once you realize water can wash it away, you just get prepared." Fifteen-year-old Lam observed that as he upgraded his gear from a flimsy N95 surgical mask to a professional 3M gas mask with 20926 filters, his fear remained but became manageable. After making up his mind to fight, he was proud that he was even able to "reverse my instinct. Instead of fleeing from tear gas canisters, I went toward them. My job as a 'firefighter' was to extinguish them with water, a traffic cone, or a small plate." Such rapid evolution of tactics was quite common until the police used up their tear gas inventory and, from around September, switched to their expired stockpile, which emitted extremely toxic chemicals.

By far the most common solution to manage fear was to willfully overcome it for a cause. In this process, the confrontation on June 12 became the ground zero of many a revolutionary life. "Shaken to the core" at multiple levels—kinetic, corporal, emotional, moral, and cognitive—by what they saw and experienced firsthand, there would be no going back for these impressionable young people. Ben was not the only one who was moved to tears by the spirit of solidarity and compassion among Hong Kongers. Amid the chaos of rubber bullets and pepper spray, different people encountered their personal moments of truth—a group of youngsters trying to convince a tender ten-year-old kid with a rubber shield in the front line to move to the back, first-aiders rushing toward the police to rescue the injured, male protesters bringing down an iron fence to let women and children flee the tear-gassed sites, and people giving up their PPE to those younger or more vulnerable. For those who had been there that day, "Hong Kong" became an embodied community over which they could claim ownership.

Witnessing the collective will to sacrifice and protect their own city overwhelmed young protesters, transforming them sometimes in very literal ways. Little Shield, a youth with the muscular build of a grown adult, confirmed his newfound militant identity by adopting a nom de guerre on June 12. He recalled, "That day, I only had a N95 mask. I did not even have a hard hat. Walking with the crowd, little by little, I found myself in the front line, helping to make roadblocks. Then I got hit with tear gas. Immediately a first-aider approached and cleaned my eyes with water. The schoolteacher who was hit in the eye by a rubber bullet fell right next to me. I was among those who helped him to the sidewalk. Then I just followed the flow of the crowd. Suddenly, an older guy shoved a half-sized synthetic shield to me. From then on, I took on the name Little Shield." When the crowd successfully blocked the legislature from functioning that day, Little Shield was convinced that "without the militants, the bill would have gone through the second reading. Who could say the militants are useless?"

More than just moved, startled, and infuriated, young protesters were also clear about the contrast between good and evil. It was an easy decision which side they wanted to be on: that of a peaceful unarmed citizenry insisting their million-strong voice be heard, not a recalcitrant government inflicting disproportionate violence. Wai, whom I would befriend in the months ahead, went to June 9 with two seniors in his school's running club. He was very proud of himself and the one million Hong Kongers, feeling for the first time that "I also can do something." The government's response convinced him that he had to go to the front line. And on June 12, the sudden eruption of massive tear gas and his scary encounters with the special tactical squad, nicknamed the Raptors, were baffling and clarifying at the same time. That was his first day in the front line, and what he saw steeled his determination to stay there. He was wandering around helping to distribute water, cling wrap, and other resources, stopping here and there to chat with strangers, even taking a nap. With instruction from fellow protesters, he learned to make steel barricades, especially the triangular variety. Then, around three in the afternoon, the police fired tear gas, and very soon he found a group of riot police charging toward him. Still shaken months later, he recounted, "It was the first time I was so close to the Raptors. I had only a face mask and an umbrella, and they attacked us without warning. They jumped over the median barrier and subdued several bros right next to me. I ran in full speed and turned toward Harcourt Road when I heard people shouting for help to build barricades and roadblocks. That day, I was actually very scared every minute. But I felt I have an obligation to come out, especially because I am an athlete. I can no longer afford to be a bystander. I missed my English exam that morning, so I had to repeat my Form 5.!"

Wai might have rubbed shoulders with Doug on June 12. When Doug completed the march on June 9, he was elated by the thought that "surely the government would back down." But when the chief executive thumbed her nose at a million people, his indignation and anger turned out to be transformative: "I changed from a pacifist to a frontliner on June 12. When I got to Tamar Park at 5:30 a.m., feeling lost, scared, and anxious, two-thirds of the park was already filled with people. They responded to the call to spend the previous night there to 'picnic.' I just wanted to encircle the LegCo Complex so that legislators cannot proceed with the bill's second reading. I had never thought that I'd be making and pushing iron barricades."

The fighter in him, emerging through some impromptu reactions to the immediate circumstances on the protest site, surprised even himself. At the beginning, he was just sitting on the lawn of Tamar Park. When he heard people yelling, "Tim Mei Avenue needs people!" he sprang into action. But there was a problem: hailing from a working-class neighborhood in Kowloon, he was unfamiliar with the geography of Hong Kong Island's posh central business district and did not know where Tim Mei Avenue was. So he just wandered around anxiously, trying to be helpful. When he saw protesters building barricades by bundling together fences removed from the sidewalks, he asked, "How can I help?" A man gave a terse command, "Make a triangle barricade. Push it to the front!" When Doug confessed that he did not know how, the man took out his smartphone and showed him a video clip about South Korean farmers pushing triangular barricades against the Hong Kong police during the 2005 anti-WTO protest. Doug watched, then taught himself to make the barricades with plastic zip ties. He spent the next hour making a whole row of barricades and pushed them to Lungwo Road, near the Convention Center. When he heard "LegCo needs people," he ran toward the Complex, and on the way, he picked up an abandoned gas mask on the ground. That moment became etched in his memory because "That was the first time I put on a gas mask. It was only later that I realized the mask would not work because one of the filters was missing. But I was too ignorant to know then."

For these novices, it was not an idea of Hong Kong or a political ideology that moved them to action. On the contrary, it was in and through action that they discovered a Hong Kong they loved and cared about. Doug, after making his first barricades, would go back to learn about the history of the WTO protests fourteen years earlier, when he was just a toddler. Harry, who taught me to wear multiple layers of pants, would likewise read up on Tiananmen and the Cultural Revolution, install the WeChat app popular in China, and begin his personal propaganda campaign to engage mainland netizens. He fed them many photos and reports to inform them of these forbidden histories. Others began reading online about the Umbrella Movement and other local political struggles that predated their birth. Becoming avid readers of current affairs and political news on LIHKG, an open online messaging and chat platform, some, like Harry, spent their spare time in bookstores, reading for free. As if hit by first love, many young people discovered a whole new dimension of their existence inside the movement and in action. This love is all the more powerful and seductive because many experienced a genuine sense of personal growth and societal purpose through collective struggle.

The Umbrella Generation

This internal logic of political participation, from emotional and kinetic mobilization to moral and cognitive awakening, was widely found among political freshmen. Among those more seasoned or experienced in protests and politics, especially the twenty- and thirty-somethings who were baptized by the Umbrella Movement in 2014, their pathways to 2019 were more colored by the hard lessons learned during and since that movement. As one of them put it eloquently, "If the Umbrella Movement was a thesis, the Fish Ball Revolution would be an antithesis, and the Anti–Extradition Bill Movement is a synthesis!"[7] Instead of teenagers' playful moniker of "Hong Kong pig," their autobiographical narratives always referenced "Umbrella." As a political cohort, the Umbrella generation was not limited to a biological age group. But, on the street, recognizable by their more mature outlook and physique, teenage protesters would address them by the deferential terms "elder bros" (師兄) or "elder sisses" (師姐).

One of the most unusual sights in the run-up to the clashes on June 12 was a hymn-singing marathon by several hundred Christians who regularly held prayer meetings near LegCo. For twelve hours, from dusk to dawn, they kept repeating "Sing Hallelujah to the Lord," the melancholy tune of which hung over the light rain enveloping Hong Kong. They knew even the Public Order Ordinance could not touch religious activities in public. Indeed, as police harassed and frisked young students in nearby subway stations, they did not dare to interfere with the Christians. Joseph, a forty-year-old devout Christian and full-time father, sang with a group under a bridge; the song was echoed by those on the bridge, and soon protesters nearby also joined. "It was so overwhelming, so moving. I had a strong feeling that Jesus Christ was there with us. . . . Actually," he laughed, "this hymn has many high notes, very difficult to sing repeatedly. I sang nonstop for two hours and had to quit. I returned early the next day and saw that many Christians spent the night there and continued 'Sing Hallelujah to the Lord' all morning."

Joseph traced his political enlightenment to the Umbrella occupation sites, even though he did not feel strongly about Umbrella's demands for universal suffrage. Instead, he was drawn to the young protesters' passion for building a utopian community, even in the face of an impossible fight to challenge the Communist regime. He wanted to join the progressive movement within the local Christian community. But he struggled with an inner sense of powerlessness as he observed the erosion of "One Country, Two Systems," as if 2047 had arrived ahead of its designated schedule. As a pastor, he was acutely aware of the wave of religious suppression and demolition of churches raging through the mainland, a harbinger of things to come in Hong Kong. Joseph witnessed that "Recently foreign ministers our church invited were denied entry. Other churches have the same experience. Xi wants to control everything, leaving us very little wiggle room. Compared to Umbrella, I feel my own survival is at stake in this movement."

Just like many political freshmen, what Joseph witnessed and experienced on June 12 turned his worldview upside down. He and a dozen other fellow Christians kept the singing marathon going, intentionally creating a "safety zone" for protesters in case violence flared up. Positioned with the group on the bridge connecting the LegCo building with the CITIC Tower and other surrounding office high-rises, he got a bird's-eye view of the changing police formation and protesters' reactions. His vivid depiction of that fateful day echoed many others who became ardent protesters:

> In the morning, when I saw the endless influx of citizens to the LegCo area, completely taking over all the lanes on Harcourt Road, all the familiar emotions came back—this was Umbrella 2.0! I was deeply touched. When we felt our dream for democracy and solidarity was crushed, I saw at that moment we could recover and try again. We kept singing, looking for hymns through our phone, and people would join the chorus when we sing the more familiar ones. Suddenly, around 2:00 p.m., things became very tense. People circulated the rumor that chaos would happen around 3:00 p.m. I was standing at the L-shaped corner at the end of the walk bridge, with a clear view of the bottom of LegCo. I saw the riot police guarding the front gate had changed their formation, put on their helmets, while those guarding the other side of the building had left, leaving only the steel barricades. A group of students saw the unguarded zone, rushed toward it, and cut the zip ties to move the barricade. Their coordination was adroit, fast, and organized. At the same moment, people on Harcourt Road began making triangular barricades, and a long human chain of supply was transporting umbrellas and helmets. The atmosphere was so intense that we all knew something was about to happen. We could sing no more. The next thing I saw was some protesters trying to break through police cordon outside LegCo; I was so excited to see their surge. I am a pacifist, and I could not tell if they were right or wrong at that moment. I just hoped they'd succeed, and I applauded and cheered them on together with the massive crowd. But how can citizens with just yellow helmets and umbrellas overcome full-geared riot police? Every forward step they took, the police pushed back. . . . Things became really chaotic. When I saw the police shot tear gas into the crowd outside CITIC Tower, I had to flee. That day, I only had a face cloth, no mask or anything. If the police charged toward the bridge, we would die. My friend warned me, if a Raptor comes after me, just run because Raptors will beat up anyone they see. My face cloth was useless. Soon my wife and I were on our knees, tears came rushing out our painful eyes. After a while, when we regained our balance, we ran toward Admiralty, and I saw the frantic

crowd rushing under our bridge, yelling, "Help," "Run," "People will die!" Some of them rushed up the stairs to the bridge. I was so scared that people would kill each other in a stampede. I felt death was upon us. Every entrance to those office buildings connected to the bridge was bolted. The police kept firing at the crowd that escaped to the locked entrance of CITIC Tower. We were about one hundred meters from them, but the tear gas was unbearably suffocating. I cannot image how painful it must have been for those in that crowd. I could tell the police were not trying to disperse the protesters. They were trying to kill them. From that day on, I totally changed my view of the Hong Kong police.

Joseph realized that June 12 had subverted his values and beliefs. For an avowed pacifist, it was a big revolutionary step for him to come to the realization that "violence is a relative concept." He sighed, "How can we talk about justice when fully armored police are allowed to attack unarmed citizens?"

An emotional hallmark of the Umbrella generation during the 2019 movement was their dialectical transformation from hopelessness to hope, powerlessness to power. The failure of the Umbrella Movement to bring about electoral reform (universal suffrage) sent many citizens and university students into a psychological abyss. The advance of ever more authoritarian control and institutional violence in its aftermath generated an atmosphere of utter powerlessness in civil society. But the massive turnout for the two June marches gave them a glimmer of hope and more.

Similar to the emotional dialectic energizing the Tahrir Square protests in 2011 in Egypt, the Umbrella generation's sense of defeat five years earlier evolved into empowerment in 2019. Their social media posts declared, "I have nothing to lose any more," "This is the endgame," and "There is no more retreat for Hong Kongers," prompting many to throw themselves wholeheartedly into the antiextradition movement. As seen in the last chapter, between the two movements, Beijing had shown its true colors, unilaterally abrogating its constitutional promise of universal suffrage. The futility of peaceful and patient occupation clarified for this generation born during the transition years that Hong Kongers had to defend their homeland and values by all means. The rise of localist ideologies, political parties, and charismatic leaders in the post-Umbrella years crystallized a new political vision pivoting toward Hong Kong independence.

Not far from Joseph among the crowd frontally attacked by tear gas on June 12 was another Umbrella survivor, Peggy, a tall and charming twenty-four-year-old. With a newly minted master's degree in education, she had just landed a well-paying teaching post in the summer of 2019. But she gave up her dream job to participate in the movement full-time. To pay the bills, she took on two part-time jobs with flexible hours, and she became one of a minority of frontline militant sisters, throwing Molotov cocktails. She spent so much time in the front line that her body was reacting to the tear gas residue. Four months into the protests, her mensural cycle became erratic. "For Hong Kong, I am willing to give up my future," she said, "I am willing to die."

The root of this commitment was Umbrella. A university freshman in 2014, Peggy was a fixture in the Admiralty protest site during the entire seventy-nine days of the occupation. She would go to Admiralty after class, then home for a quick shower and a change of clothes and then back to Admiralty, and still go to school the next day. This movement was an immense revelation and awakening to her: "People used to think that insisting on peaceful and rational means, securing popular support could bring about social change. But this is exactly what caused our generation so much suffering. You see it was only when students charged into the Civic Square that the movement saw its breakthrough. . . . After witnessing the demise of Umbrella, I plunged into a deep, long depression. Many people had the same experience. For a whole year, I did not want to read the news, until Edward Leung came along." If the charismatic localist and his slogan, "Liberate Hong Kong, revolution of our times," gave her hope, it was the suicide protest of Leung Ling Kit on June 15, which triggered the two-million-strong march the following day, that taught her about hopelessness and love for Hong Kong. She concluded, "How much despair and love for a place will drive a man to jump to his death? He sacrificed his life to counsel our government. How can we give up this movement now?"

For Alan, a twenty-seven-year-old customs officer and a student in an online degree program, Umbrella gave him his first taste of "doing something for Hong Kong." His government job limited his participation then, but he still visited the site thirty out of the seventy-nine days, according to his count. He reminisced how, "At the beginning, every time I went to the site, I teared up because I saw the beauty of Hong Kong people. Anyone in need of help would find help. Once I saw a group of protesters pushing a water-filled barricade up the slope of Cotton Road. That Sisyphus spirit overturned my

3.4 Women were equally active participants in the 2019 movement. Many endorsed a radical and militant style of resistance.
CREDIT: Kim Kyung Hoon / Reuters Pictures

stereotype of Hong Kongers as only money obsessed.... Mr. Leung's death hit me very hard; I simply could not accept it as a reality in a place that calls itself democratic and civilized. How desperate must he have become about the government, the system, and his own future before he would choose to end his own life?" With the imminent passage of the extradition bill, Alan believed that "this is Hong Kong's Endgame [referencing the fourth Avengers movie]. Hong Kong cannot lose anymore, and protesters can retreat no more. To resist is to save Hong Kong, to save our rule of law."

Bren, like Peggy, was a college freshman when Umbrella erupted. He was a natural militant who did not believe in peaceful sing-a-song protest. Therefore, toward the end of the occupation, on November 30, 2014, when the student leaders announced an escalation of action, he answered their call to block roads on Lungwo Road. Without any protective gear, only a clinical mask, he was chased by some thirty Raptors, who came "just a few meters from me. I was terrified, mortified, even after I successfully fled to safety. This episode made me a determined resister." He joined a post-Umbrella neighborhood organization seeking to remake local politics by electing democrats into the district boards, a statutory local governance body without legislative power. In his reflexive moment, he confessed, "Yes, I recognize my inner conflict; I am taking both roads: outside and inside the system."

More important than his action strategy was his ideological turn to localism: "I worshipped Edward Leung and the Hong Kong Indigenous [Leung's party]. When Leung called for mass support in Mongkok on the eve of the Chinese New Year in 2016, I went to help. I was among those who launched the first wave of attack against the police barricade. It was quite a funny scene. Edward and a few others announced they wanted to start an election rally, and after three shouts, everyone charged toward the police. Of course, our side collapsed quickly, beaten back by the police, and everyone just fled in fear. After that night, the police began searching and arresting many people. I was not arrested, but I lived in fear and despair for the next few months." Ever more a believer in Hong Kong independence, he formed a small team in 2019. They skipped the foreplay, the peaceful rallies, "to conserve energy" and showed up only toward the end for the real deal, equipped with protective or assault gear.

Bren, Peggy, and Alan were among several hundred protesters who stormed into the LegCo Complex on July 1, the annual holiday commemorating Hong Kong's return to China. So were political freshmen Wai and Fei. Condemned by the regime and the pro-China political elite as an unmitigated act of violence in violation of Hong Kong's rule of law, this episode had the ironic effect of awakening the public to the elusive boundary and questionable binary opposition between rule of law and violence.

Around eleven in the morning on July 1, Wai and his two schoolmates were among the two hundred protesters gathered under the covered entrance of the LegCo Complex shaped like a "pot bottom," as it would be nicknamed, discussing their action plans for the day. Early that morning, they had failed to interrupt the official flag hoisting ceremony in the nearby Golden Bauhinia Square. After a heated debate, three action proposals were presented: taking down the national flag from the square, barging into the cocktail party hosted by Carrie Lam in Kowloon, or storming LegCo. The third option won the most votes. Yet people were not sure how to break into the fortified structure. At around two in the afternoon, Wai and others made an assault cart by fitting a steel rod to a cardboard-collection cart. He took the lead to run it against the glass panels lining the exterior of the building. It was a defining moment for him as "More than twenty cameras were pointing at me! I was actually very scared because that's the first time in my life so many cameras were focusing on me. Also, I knew I was not prepared for the consequences of what I was doing. Soon, I retreated, and other protesters stepped forward." Several pan-democratic legislators arrived, trying to convince them to quit. One threw his body in front of the makeshift attack trolley, only to be shoved to the sidewalk, while another, in tears, reminded them that rioting would cost them ten years in prison. To no avail, some of these legislators broke down in tears watching protesters experiment with different methods to smash the glass and metal barriers.

Finally, around seven or eight in the evening, the militants began to make some headway with heavy-duty hammers, folded ladders, and shovels. Elated, Wai and others went in, scared to death because the police had been eerily absent the whole day and the unguarded LegCo looked like a trap: "We knew it might be an ambush, but we were exhilarated. People were shouting and cheering. I was overwhelmed, because I felt, 'Finally we Hong Kongers have taken back our LegCo!' It was very dark inside. Me and my friends held onto each other's backpacks to find our way around the first two floors. Soon, we were frightened and short of water, so we left the building."

Alan, the customs officer, was inside LegCo to support the frontline brothers, thinking that the more people there were, the safer it was for all. With excitement and anxiety, he recalled, "There was no big stage, so we were improvising every step along the way. We did not know the geography of LegCo. People were debating whether to stay in the main chamber or occupy the security room or to go deeper inside to allow more people in. It was euphoric. Immediately some protesters began trashing the furniture to vent their anger at the government. But very quickly, some people yelled at them, 'We are here not to vandalize! We are here to make a stand. We must insist we are not rioters.' I was so proud to see Hong Kongers keeping calm and rational even at that moment. People left cash after breaking the soda machine to get drinks. They trashed the portraits of the political elites but left the library and archive intact. Our values shine through." After about twenty minutes, Alan and his friends decided to leave, not ready to spend their youth in prison.

Peggy was also among those taking back the legislature that night. As a tall woman, she was in the front line among a mostly male crowd breaking in. She hesitated for a few seconds, considering the serious legal consequences, but decided that she must enter because "this is a once-in-a-lifetime opportunity. I texted my boyfriend once I got inside. This may be our last chance. The government has disqualified legislators we elected. Even my young students called the LegCo TrashCo.... People were ransacking the place, spray-painting graffiti everywhere, and I brushed past Brian Leung before he took his mask off and made that speech. I was too scared and I left."

Peggy was referring to Brian Leung, the only protester who revealed his identity while imploring the people not to leave LegCo. As we saw in Chapter 2, Brian was a participant in the Umbrella Movement and later became a vocal localist intellectual. But instead of politics, he decided to pursue an academic career in the United States. When protests broke out in 2019, he was a PhD student who returned to join the masses. That day, he reckoned that another failure like the last one would set back the popular momentum for democratization for years to come. Against the background of a defaced emblem of the Hong Kong SAR and a huge protest banner planted on the chairman's podium declaring "No Rioters, Only Tyranny," in front of a dense panoply of reporters and cameras, he called upon his fellow protesters to stay:

> If we retreat, we will become what the TVB calls "the rioters." They will be filming the destruction and the mess in the LegCo building and condemning us as rioters. Therefore, now we cannot split in this movement. If we win, we win it together.... If after careful consideration you could occupy with us, stay. The more people we are here, the safer we will be.... Let's urge people outside to come in and join us. Because there is no return for us after we get to this point. We cannot play flash mob anymore because it is a once-in-a-lifetime chance to occupy the LegCo. If you cannot stay, then use peaceful means to encircle the LegCo, use your bodies to protect us. If we go back to sleep in our air-conditioned rooms, then tomorrow morning nothing would happen in Hong Kong. Sacrifices in the past month will be in vain.... In the Sunflower Movement, after students occupied the legislature, adults, political leaders, and legislators came to protect them from the outside. So, students, don't be distracted. Get enough bros and sisses with the courage to join us in this chamber. The reason why I remove my mask is to let everyone know that we Hongkongers cannot lose any more. If we lost, our civil society would sink to the bottom for the next ten years.[8]

3.5 On July 1, 2019, Brian Leung, the only protester during the storming of the Legislative Council Complex to take off his mask, read out a declaration underscoring the five demands of Hong Kong citizens. After fleeing the city, he became a leader of the Hong Kong diaspora in exile.
CREDIT: *South China Morning Post*

What would go down in history that evening was not only Brian's impassioned plea or the declaration composed by a digital crowd on LIHKG and that he read out on behalf of the "Hong Kong protesters." It was a scene, livestreamed by Gwyneth Ho, a reporter for the online newspaper *Stand News*, that would become an indelible memory for millions of citizens, militants and pacifists alike. Minutes before armed police were to regain control of the LegCo building right after midnight, a dozen protesters who had already fled to safety risked their own lives to burst into the chamber again and extract four martyrs who had declared their determination to stay and face death. As the protesters shouted "Leave together," a young woman explained in a trembling voice to the *Stand News* reporter who was running with the group, "We are all very, very scared, but we are even more scared by the thought of not seeing these four tomorrow." Never mind that they didn't know each other.

That simple logic that, no matter what, you don't abandon others in harm's way moved many people to tears that night, including Alan, the customs officer, who watched the live report on the bus he took to go home after fleeing LegCo. He cried, "because I understood totally the fear she was talking about. The whole time I was afraid of being arrested, being injured, but my greatest fear was losing this place I call home. To me, July 1 was the turning point in this movement. It lifted the deep gloom I was in since Umbrella, because I discovered Hong Kong people's solidarity: no one split from the movement that night. When I exited the LegCo, I saw thousands of pacifist protesters sticking around, trying their best to defend us, the militants inside, from the advancing police. I saw hope for Hong Kong."

Even for the majority of Hong Kong citizens who were not physically present at the sites of action, the events on June 12 and July 1 were still powerful experiences. The avalanche of live videos on media platforms brought the heartbeats of the activists close to most citizens, albeit virtually. Foreshadowing the dynamic between the regime and the people in the months to come, the June 12 incident displayed in plain view the face-off of the people versus the despot, peace versus violence, the effectiveness of confrontational direct action versus the futility of peaceful institutional politics. During the storming of LegCo on July 1, what shone through amid the broken glass and vandalized symbols of power was the young protesters' principled violence, compassion, and solidarity. Perhaps more stunning than the event itself was public reaction to it. Opinion polls taken among the peaceful protesters registered a turning tide in support of the action that night.

The Middle Class and Professionals

If the political freshmen's political subjectivity as Hong Kongers was awakened through collective action in 2019 and the Umbrella generation were resuming the fight for a vision for Hong Kong nurtured during and since the 2014 Umbrella occupation, the political agencies of many of the middle-class and professional members of the movement were informed by their experiences in the workplace. Economic integration between Hong Kong and China in the post-1997 era had created many job opportunities for Hong Kong professionals to work for Chinese state and private companies and to travel to or station in China. Even as their careers and incomes became dependent on the mainland, these professionals were alienated from it. More powerful than any ideology, it was their personal experiences of discrimination and distrust by mainland Chinese employers, their knowledge of the "unprofessional" mainland way of business, and their insight into the mainland economy that consolidated their interest and identity as Hong Kongers through the "othering" of China.

A telling example was Tommy, who became a confirmed Hong Konger after hitting a glass ceiling in two Chinese-owned companies. The father of a three-year-old, Tommy summed up his dramatic political transformation over the past decade: "When I was young, I voted for DAB [Hong Kong's largest pro-China political party]. By 2016, I voted for Edward Leung [Hong Kong's most famous localist]." A marketing professional with a politically conservative family background—his father owned a factory in China during the early reform years—Tommy has worked for a Chinese-invested company and then a Chinese state-owned enterprise. He was not paying much attention to the Umbrella Movement, as his company had issued memos prohibiting employees from participating. Not attuned to political ideology, he was adamant about the ubiquitous glass ceiling faced by Hong Kongers like him. He grumbled, "At first there were still two Hong Kongers among senior management in the Chinese company. The Chinese boss thinks he only needs Hong Kongers for public relations and finance. Marketing? No need for Hong Kongers. I used to have a Hong Konger as my superior, but after he left, a mainlander replaced him. At the state owned company, it's even worse: none of the department heads was a Hong Konger. I did not even get a chance to see senior management. I realized no matter how hard we work, Hong Kongers can only be sidekicks in Chinese companies. This is how I began to establish my own identity as a Hong Konger." The fact that Tommy was a long-time resident in Sheung Shui reinforced this tendency. He and his family had front-row seats to the invasion of his neighborhood by parallel traders from across the borders. When he complained to the district councilor, the official only "retorted that parallel trade was good for the economy! The government turned a blind eye to all the chaos and inconvenience to local residents. So when Edward Leung mobilized the 'Reclaim Sheung Shui' protests, I voted for him in the 2016 by-election."

Like many middle-aged, middle-class citizens, Tommy's participation in the movement was hidden—he went to protests approved by the police whenever he could find childcare for his three-year-old. But he was also a keyboard warrior who leveraged his knowledge of the neighborhood to assist protesters. He would walk around, gathering and posting intelligence about riot police locations and little-known escape routes on a Telegram channel called "Sheung Shui schoolbus pick up."

To him, "Liberate Hong Kong, revolution of our times" meant returning Hong Kong's condition to the one under British rule, that is, using British institutions that can connect the city with the rest of the world. Universal suffrage was a must, whether Hong Kong was independent or part of China. If nothing else, China had itself made that promise in the Basic Law, Hong Kong's mini-constitution.

Thirty-something Freedom worked in the garment industry and had been traveling to the mainland for nine years. From day one, he hated it. But when he graduated from college, everyone was telling him that working in China was his generation's destiny. Since then, he had more knowledge about China and more time to reflect: "People went to China to invest and emptied all industrial resources from Hong Kong to China. As a consequence, our economy had to rely on finance and tourism. A small place does not have to be dependent on another bigger economy or country. Look at Israel. It survives despite being surrounded by Arab countries. Or Singapore. It can even sell water to Malaysia. It's possible if people try." His work experience led him to see a different China: the exodus of factories to Vietnam, Thailand, and Myanmar; the precipitous fall in exports; and the overall slowing of the Chinese economy. To him, the Chinese economy was in a downward trend, a bubble buoyed by speculations in the housing and stock markets. Despite the official rhetoric touting Hong Kong's reliance on China, Freedom thought it was the other way around. Hong Kong lays China's golden egg so that wealthy officials can launder their money and China can trade with the world. That's why, to him, "If we maintain our critical importance to China, we can continue to fight for autonomy, even independence."

Considering the risks he could personally take and his heavy travel schedule, Freedom played the role of rescue driver, picking up protesters fleeing from the police whenever he was in Hong Kong. He and his partner would wait near protest sites or subway stations shut down by the police. During an unauthorized mass rally on July 28 in Yuen Long to protest the indiscriminate terrorist assault by triads on passengers on July 21 in this border town, Freedom's car was one among many lining the main street. He did two rounds of pickups that day and was impressed by how polite his passengers were, even though "they were very exhausted, carrying lots of gear, but they still thought about letting others more in need to get into our car. Some even forced us to accept money."

His first rally had been July 1, 2003, when he was just a secondary school student. Like many of this generation, teachers and schools in those years were free to take a political stand on issues such as Tiananmen and even encouraged students to participate in public affairs. By the time of Umbrella, his work-related travel only allowed him to stay in the occupation zones on Saturday and Sunday. But he witnessed one critical moment of the movement that clarified his disdain for the peaceful, rational, and nonviolent camp. Two months into the occupation, radicals proposed an escalation to occupy Lungwo Road. He deplored, "The student leaders were not enthusiastic but went along anyway, I think, just to show escalation was useless. In the end, many protesters were injured when they clashed with the police. When we returned to the Harcourt Road occupy site, I saw people singing as if to announce to the world they split with the radicals, that they would continue their 'joyous resistance' and could care less about the injured." After Umbrella, Freedom became a passionate supporter of localist politicians such as Ray Wong, Baggio Leung, and Edward Leung, volunteering for their election campaigns, collecting donation, distributing flyers, and monitoring vote counts. After these leaders were disqualified by the government to run for LegCo office, forced into exile, and imprisoned, respectively, Freedom toyed with the idea of emigration but decided that the only place he felt at home was Hong Kong.

On July 21, he was among the crowd marching toward Sheung Wan, on the way to China's Hong Kong Liaison Office. Suddenly, some people began chanting Edward Leung's slogan, "Liberate Hong Kong, revolution of our times." It was the first time since June that this had happened. Freedom was moved to tears when he realized so many people still remembered Leung. Articulating a typical view I found among his cohort, livelihood under British rule was the yardstick to assess the one under Chinese rule:

> Recover Hong Kong means recovering the one before the handover. I had fond memory of those years. Even though I came from a grassroots family, we did not have to worry about livelihood. Government gave us enough support [housing and medical care] to raise a family. With a regular income, my dad could buy a flat. Not a luxurious one, but something decent. But now, even though I am so-called middle class, I do not see a good life ahead. In this housing market, I will have to work until my sixties and seventies for a tiny three-hundred-square-foot flat. Too many mainlanders have used up our resources. Local shops serve them rather than locals, and all these monopolies. . . . Before 1997,

people were able to live, did not have to sacrifice their family life to work in China; now people just survive, even with their greatest effort. We will need the rule of law and freedom we had then in order to restore Hong Kong.

Among Hong Kong's professional class, the most glamorous were the corporate executives, bankers, financial experts, and lawyers working in the Central District's Class A office towers and earning premium salaries, even share options. Ordinarily too busy and risk averse to demonstrate, these professionals nevertheless launched a series of lunchtime flash rallies called "lunch with you" via their Telegram groups in mid-November after the police sieged Polytechnic University, where thousands of students and protesters hunkered down. They were undaunted by the white terror permeating the corporate world at that time. Many companies had prohibited their employees from participating in protests, and high-profile dismissals of senior executives with liberal views had served as a warning to the rest. But that week, police violence against the students led many to take a stance. Starting at noon each day, designer suit–wearing bankers and accountants, female executives, lawyers, and office ladies in high heels began gathering in the heart of the central business district, the section flanked by Pedder Street, Queens' Road, and Des Voeux Road, where the imposing flagship stores of Louis Vuitton, Giorgio Armani, Tiffany, Citibank, and JP Morgan Chase vied for architectural dominance. With umbrellas in hand, they would wait for their numbers to grow and then take cues from a few first movers to stand in the middle of moving traffic. Black bloc youngsters would emerge out of nowhere to quickly build barricades with traffic cones and trash bins. Within minutes, the whole street would be filled with the most elegantly dressed and impeccably groomed protesters, peacefully and passionately chanting, "Save students, save PolyU," "Five demands, not one less," and "Fight for freedom, stand with Hong Kong!"

In one of these rallies, before the crowd disrupted traffic, John, a thirty-two-year-old senior executive in Hong Kong's leading bank, caught my eye because of his brightly colored, checkered three-piece suit. He was helping some young women distribute their self-printed flyers. I was first preoccupied with helping protesters collecting umbrellas to bolster the front line where they expected police would appear. At about one in the afternoon, when thousands of people fully took over the roads and filled up all the

3.6 Professionals and white-collar workers in Hong Kong's financial district launched "lunch with you" rallies on the streets in November 2019 to protest against police sieges at the Chinese University and Polytechnic University. Their hand sign signaled the five demands of the antiextradition movement.
CREDIT: Athit Perawongmetha / Reuters Pictures

footbridges above, people took turns leading thunderous chants of slogans and an emotional singing of "Glory to Hong Kong," the unofficial anthem of the city. When I found myself standing next to John again, I struck up some small talk, which led to a longer chat over coffee the following week.

A graduate of an Australian university and soon to be married, John was a staunch believer in using legal, rational, and nonviolent means for democratic struggle. He vowed to have gone to all the rallies that had obtained the "no objection notice" issued by the police. But when indiscriminate violence inflicted by the riot police and gangsters got out of hand, especially the incidents on July 21 (at the Yuen Long train station) and August 31 (at the Mongkok subway station), John was angry and ashamed:

> It's repulsive to see so much injustice and lies [referring to the daily police briefing at four in the afternoon] parading before our eyes every day. During Umbrella I opposed the militants or people waving the American and British flags. My thinking was very simplistic: if

you violate the law, then you are wrong. Why are we so slavish? Why can't Hong Kong people manage our own affairs? Now, I realized those people were five years ahead of me. Today the police can get away with violating the law, and there is no mechanism to make them accountable. Under this situation, demanding protesters' unconditional obedience is an abrogation of justice. Not only do I not blame the young militants anymore, I feel ashamed by their willingness to sacrifice their own future. Without them, the international media would not have paid so much attention to the protests.

For John, the most memorable scene of the movement was the young protesters at the Admiralty intersection between two roads, one leading to the government headquarters and the other toward Central. During the July 1 march, many black bloc youngsters were urging people to go toward the government headquarters to support those breaking into LegCo. Shunning such blatantly "illegal" action instinctively, he was ultimately swayed by the genuine and passionate pleas of the young:

> I saw the insistence on their faces, their tears and hysterical cries from the hearts. I knew they were doing this not for themselves. I was ashamed: we the so-called middle class are willing to slave away our lives for a few million dollars a year and using family and children as excuses to justify our cowardice. These young people, by contrast, use their own money, risk their own safety and freedom to stand up for us and future generations. At that moment, I changed my mind. I took the route toward the government headquarters. I could not bring myself to smash the glass panels of LegCo. But I sat down at the outer rim of "pot bottom" to be with them.
>
> Reclaiming Hong Kong means restoring the "Hong Kong values" prevalent before post-1997 mainlandization. It does not mean returning Hong Kong to British colonialism, because whoever rules Hong Kong—be it China or Great Britain—Hong Kong needs to return to its original core values—judicial independence, clean government, rule of law, mutual respect, freedom of information and expression. I am not pessimistic because I know China needs Hong Kong. Hong Kong is the main platform for 70 percent of foreign capital to go to China and the most important capital market in the world for

Chinese IPOs. Not to mention their massive money laundering here. I believe Hong Kong has bargaining power with China.

New Immigrants, Housewives, and Chinese Republicans

As a demographic group, new immigrants from China and full-time housewives in working-class neighborhoods were often presumed to have a low level of political or rights consciousness, making them easy prey to the petty gift economy pro-Beijing community organizations had used to buy votes and allegiance. But in 2019, they unexpectedly provided inconspicuous but life-saving logistical support to protesters at critical moments, especially after the protesters abandoned "trench warfare" in favor of decentralized flash mobs. Defying stereotypes, these groups' seemingly apolitical, pragmatic, and familial outlooks belied critical political views about China and its agents in their neighborhoods.

Social media clips recorded numerous scenes featuring ordinary citizens in standoffs with the police on a daily basis during the first few months of the antiextradition movement. New immigrants, easily distinguished by their accent, were as articulate and adamant as native Hong Kongers in verbal confrontations with the police. These episodes, playing out in public and often under the intense gaze of press and social media cameras, put a spotlight on the otherwise hidden reservoir of staunch support for human rights and democracy among new immigrants. Their fighting words against the same enemy dissolved the usual divide between immigrants and natives as they stood physically and morally together. One such instance went viral. During evening rush hours on September 29, outside the Admiralty MTR station, amid a huge crowd booing, shouting expletives, and giving middle fingers to busloads of riot police just alighting in the middle of Harcourt Road where police vehicles were blocking traffic, came a high-pitched woman's voice. Leaning against the sidewalk railings near a formation of full-geared gun-wielding riot police, this middle-aged woman shouted in heavily accented Cantonese:

> Your guns should not be pointing at us Hong Kongers. You are totally mistaken. All these people are only demanding democracy. None of the five demands is about Hong Kong independence or splitting the country. (A woman near her trumpeted, "Well said, well said, sister!")

Let's talk reason. Sirs, you are gentlemen. I am a new immigrant. You know how difficult it is for me to become a Hong Konger? (Cheers and applause from the crowd.) If Hong Kong isn't this good, I won't want to come here. You guys grew up here, shouldn't you love Hong Kong more than I do? I love Hong Kong very much. I love Hong Kong very much, sirs. But I wonder if you love Hong Kong. If you love the Greater Bay Area more, then I can't help you. The Sino-British Joint Declaration gives Hong Kongers the right to assemble and protest, but now you don't allow anything. You beat protesters with pepper spray and bullets. This is rule by police, by triad, by Communist Party. Even if the young are wrong, you arrest them, but you cannot beat them up. Answer me, why don't you answer me? (A middle-aged man shouted, "They are dogs, they don't know how to speak!") Why do you become their running dogs? Everyone in Hong Kong is against you now: civil servants, barristers, who don't oppose you? Go home, sleep on my words, think hard if what I say is wrong. I am reasoning with you. Don't just watch CCTV's propaganda. If you love mainland so much, why don't you apply to become a Chinese national?[9]

Many immigrants embraced Hong Kong's rule of law and civil liberty because they had known what it was like to live without them. Their political othering of mainland China came from personal experience there. Away from the limelight was Amy, an immigrant living in North Point, a district famous for its heavy concentration of natives from Fujian Province. Since July, she had been part of an eight-person neighborhood group called North Point Guided Tour on Telegram, providing escape route maps and intelligence to protesters. Having lived in North Point since 2005, and with a brother, a contractor, active in the male-dominated, densely networked community of native place associations funded and coopted by the Hong Kong Liaison Office, Amy was the ideal urban reconnaissance soldier. She usually heard from her brother about planned assaults on protesters by the white shirts (that is, Fujian immigrants mobilized by pro-China forces) and would post warnings on Telegram.

Amy's tortuous route to becoming a Hong Kong citizen taught her the dark truth about the mainland regime. She reckoned, "All my life, I have been exploited by the Communist Party. Now, I want my vote." Her father is a Hong Kong citizen, but she and her brother were born in Fujian. Her dramatic story began when she applied for a one-way visa to settle in Hong Kong, but "mainland officials in the 1980s insisted that every emigrant family must leave one child in China. They wanted to make sure emigrants sent remittances back. Fujianese are traditionally very patriarchal. So my grandparents chose to let my brother go to Hong Kong. They paid a huge sum—50,000 yuan, enough to buy a flat in those days—to bribe the local officials controlling these quotas." When the Hong Kong Court of Final Appeal affirmed their right to live in Hong Kong in 1999, Amy was excited; she arrived in Hong Kong with a tourist visa, planning to change her documents to become a Hong Kong resident. But soon she was caught in a legal limbo, becoming an illegal immigrant when the Hong Kong government sought Beijing's intervention to reinterpret and overturn the court of appeal's decision. She became an activist for a group of about a thousand illegal immigrants like herself, working with social workers, student groups, lawyers, human rights organizations, and the veteran activist Rev. Franco Mella to pressure the Hong Kong government. During those months of mobilization, she saw firsthand how Chinese officials in Hong Kong manipulated immigrants like herself:

> The Liaison Office saw in us a large pool of potential voters. Every one of us has family members, which can be turned into thousands of voters for Beijing. There is a hidden queue for those 150 one-way visas every day. When we were protesting outside the immigrant department building, the Liaison Office people approached us, gave us forms to fill out. Those who promised to vote for pro-establishment candidates, not to protest against Beijing—they said OK to protests against the pan-democrats—and pay HK$100,000 can get the visa to stay. It's exactly the methods they used to manipulate ordinary people in the mainland.

Amy refused and was soon deported. She eventually became a legal Hong Kong citizen by marriage in 2005 and gave birth to a son.

It was an open secret that pro-Beijing forces penetrated grassroots Hong Kong communities by spinning dense networks of patron clientelism, exchanging material benefits for political loyalty. Ordinary citizens used the vernacular term 蛇齋餅粽 (meaning snake soup, vegetarian feast, moon cakes, and dumplings) to vividly sum up the four culinary enticements used to enlist political support among the lower classes and elderlies. Judging from voting surveys, by and large, the strategy had been most effective at the lowest level of consultative governance—the district council—where the pro-China camp dominated. Beyond this politics of petty welfare, another kind of neighborhood politics invited a lot of resentment among the democratically oriented residents. These longtime residents, housewives and retirees who spent their days in the neighborhood, witnessed different forms of political manipulation orchestrated by the Liaison Office. They detested this stealthy colonization and unfair competition. During the 2019 protests, their silent support was a lifeline to many youngsters fleeing the police. They would post security codes of high-rise apartment buildings on Telegram groups or offer their homes as "safe houses" for those on the run.

Mama Cheung, a seventy-year-old self-described "ordinary housewife" living in Tai Po, a densely populated district in the New Territories, has been an activist for three decades in her neighborhood mutual aid committee, akin to a homeowners association. Her passion was to lobby the government on local issues such as bus stops and trash bins. But since 1997, she saw these organizations gradually being overtaken by the blue ribbons (pro-China camp). She lamented this cooptation saying, "I had been chair, but now I am just a committee member. The blue ribbons outnumber us, eight to five. They run meetings that don't allow people to speak. When they stopped me from recording the meeting, I rebutted, saying, 'Why not, even LegCo meetings allow recording!' They are very cunning. They cheat and hide their political affiliation to make themselves look independent. When I volunteered for the Democrats for the district board election, 'volunteers' from the blue-ribbon camp came to ask us how much we were paid. They were astonished to hear that we were unpaid volunteers. They told me a 'manager' bused them from Shenzhen, crossed the border, and gave them some placards to hold. That's HK$500 a day. For those holding signs and chanting slogans in Cantonese, the rate is $1,000. Every time there is an election, I always stick around to observe the vote-counting process because they always scheme to sneak in envelops of fake votes."

Cheung had been a regular at the June 4 and July 1 mass rallies since their beginnings more than two decades ago. I met her in an August citywide multidistrict assembly in Taipo, when she was energetically distributing handbills and urging people to join the general strike. That day, she confronted a group of Raptors who were about to round up half a dozen housewives near a shopping mall in her neighborhood. She was fearless with her fighting words: "Look at you, no official badge, no police number, only tar-tinted teeth, are you sent from the mainland? Who told you to beat up ordinary housewives?" Proudly recalling her participation in the historic anti–Article 23 march on July 1, 2003, with her two young toddlers in tow and a broken ankle, she shared with me her childhood experience of the 1967 riot, the foundation of her political awakening: "Hong Kong needs people like us to come out, because I still remember the leftist rioters planting homemade bombs everywhere in the city. The radio host Lam Bun was murdered just because he criticized the Communist government in his show. Who are the 'rioters'? Carrie Lam, you are a mother, how could you be so ruthless in using police violence against other people's children?" She routinely walked up to protesters, shook their hands, thanked them, and urged them to stay safe. Inspired by her father, she wanted freedom for the future generations: "I only have an elementary school education. My father, a construction site worker, taught us to speak out against injustice. Maybe my father influenced me. He was deeply supportive of the Nationalists in Taiwan. I am old, but I have to oppose this law for the sake of my children and the younger generation."

Echoing many of my interviewees, Mama Cheung wanted to recover a Hong Kong like that of the 1970s, when the colonial government established the Independent Commission Against Corruption and cleansed the police force. Nowadays there was no restraint on the police, who even attacked reporters and treated them as protesters. She launched her own frontline opinion battle with her peers, persuading elderlies to watch not TVB news but the more professional channel of RTHK 32. Sharing livestream videos from all sources with her WhatsApp group, she debated with some blue-ribbon residents: "Look, these youngsters only have cardboards and umbrellas, and the full-geared police hit them with murderous force at their heads every single time. My brother used to be a policeman, and he told me normally police should just hit the limbs, not the heads. But now the police have changed to use augmented batons with steel rings. I always told my friends to join the demonstrations and see the reality with their own eyes."

Another social group harbored political and ideological antipathy against the Communist regime. Mama Cheung mentioned them in passing when she recalled her father's excitement on the annual October 10 commemoration of the establishment of the Republic of China, now represented by the government in Taiwan. In the decades following World War II, these self-professed descendants of Republican China constituted a long-standing political force competing with the Communists, or the "leftist camp," for influence among Hong Kongers. Up until the 1990s, ROC loyalists and sympathizers, commonly called the "rightist camp," assumed a prominent presence in districts such as Tei King Leng and Kowloon City. But since Beijing's resumption of sovereignty and the ascendance of the independent-leaning Democratic Progressive Party in Taiwan at the turn of the new millennium, the rightists in Hong Kong descended into oblivion.

Surprisingly, the "blue sky, white sun, and a wholly red earth" ROC national flag could be seen at almost every protest in 2019. Young men in their twenties took pains, quite literally, to create a formation of ROC flags no matter how chaotic the street confrontations were. The way they talked about their burning desire to raise the ROC flag in a war zone brought to mind the image of American soldiers raising the American flag on Iwo Jima. A curious reemergence of a dormant but sizable political current, they represented another pathway for some Hong Kongers to fervently join the 2019 protest. When Beijing and Carrie Lam assailed the protesters as "rioters," these ROC supporters were the first to shoot back with the inconvenient historical irony that Sun Yat-sen, the founder of the republic, had been branded a "rioter" by the Qing dynasty. Sun, hailed as a national hero by the CCP, had famously said that Hong Kong was the inspiration for the republican revolution.

Bruce, a middle-aged, card-carrying member of Taiwan's Nationalist Party (commonly known as the Kuomingtang, or KMT), managed an NGO affiliated with the KMT in an old neighborhood in Kowloon. He witnessed and participated in the protests "as a Hong Kong citizen," providing and storing supplies and offering refuge to both people fleeing from the police and youngsters disowned by their parents due to their politics. Although his political orientation was well formed before 2019, he was moved by the young protesters around him. In mid-July, he went to Shatin to join a rally and was about to leave when he saw "those nine-year-old, ten-year-old little girls, who could not be more than five feet tall, with arms slimmer than an iron rod. They were dismantling railings on the sidewalk and binding them into triangular barricades. Seeing their willowing bodies, I have no excuse not to pitch in. Gradually, I found myself in the front line. I did not want to be out there to fight. But the police and the government forced a political awakening upon me. One night my wife and I were walking home after dinner. We saw a group of black blocs vandalizing a Bank of China ATM. My wife was shocked because it was her first experience witnessing the violence. I could not help but say 'add oil.' There were a bunch of older blue-ribbon-looking residents right outside the bank and [they] saw everything. I went closer to hear what they were discussing. To my surprise, they were shouting words of support for the protesters. You see, Hong Kongers have been forced to change by this government. Umbrella made me realize I am a Hong Konger. Antiextradition made me a proud Hong Konger."

Mechanisms of Solidarity

Traveling through different biographical and political pathways, the 2019 protesters were driven by a variety of personal beliefs and interests to defend Hong Kong. What happened when these self-mobilized Hong Kongers converged on protest sites? Time and again, I witnessed how the space and ethos of the protests dissolved social differences. The anonymity of the black bloc attire not only removed conventional social markers and allowed a laser focus of their collective consciousness on high-risk action, but the lived and immersive experience in collective anonymity united by common purpose concretized the abstract notion of Hong Kong as a political community among fellow citizens. People always told me, "You did not need to know who the person next to you was, but you knew you would take care of each other." These emergent "communities of action," or what citizens called "communions in resistance," (抗爭共同體), were formed over and over again during a seven-month period, from June 2019 to January 2020, when confrontations occurred in numerous public locations. On closer inspection, four mechanisms of solidarity were at work: mechanical solidarity based on like-mindedness and compassion (conscience), conscious overcoming of past fragmentation (reflexivity), organic solidarity based on a division of labor (organization), and integrating resistance in everyday life (embeddedness). But the 2019 movement had also a dark side that can be called "coercive solidarity."

Collective Conscience

Emile Durkheim's idea of mechanical solidarity was at work everywhere during the movement. The people were bonded to each other by their collective conscience, their common beliefs, objectives, and feelings. The ubiquitous slogan "Five demands, not one less" was the most direct and unifying expression of the collective will. The five demands were full withdrawal of the extradition bill, independent inquiry into police brutality, retraction of the classification of protesters as rioters, amnesty for arrested protesters, and dual universal suffrage (for both legislature and chief executive).[10] Beyond political slogans, collective conscience could be felt by anyone who had been in the midst of the protests in 2019. A few snapshots of compassion and camaraderie at protest sites may help convey how this kind of solidarity, which was not a pregiven, *emerged in action* because of people's care for strangers in pursuit of common goals.

Conflicts flared up often in protest sites due to disagreements about tactics and the timing and location of attack and retreat. Yet even moments of heated altercation were laced with care and respect. Gwyneth Ho, the reporter who livestreamed protesters fleeing the LegCo Complex, captured a typical scene I had witnessed time and again. Around nine in the morning on July 1, protesters were under siege by two formations of riot police near Lung Wu Road. The majority decided to move their barricades back toward LegCo, but a few retorted, "Why should we retreat before the dogs [police] move an inch?" They stood their ground while others rebuilt the barricades closer to LegCo. Then about ten of those rebuilding the barricades returned to this minority group, imploring, "Please come with us. If you stay here, the dogs can easily snatch you when they attack." One guy edged toward the stayers to announce that if they did not move with the rest, they would all stay to defend that intersection, while another asked impatiently, "Do you really want all of us to get beaten up by the police because we want to stay with you?" A young woman among the stayers shot back, "Don't blackmail us with your care." For a long while, in silence, the two groups were locked in piercing stares from behind their half-face gas masks. In the end, the stayers reluctantly conceded, but to save face, they claimed that they needed a cigarette break before moving. Lovingly, before the majority returned to the barricades, they asked the stayers several times for reassurance: "You will be joining us, right?" It was the lived experience of such care among strangers that made the 2019 movement a transformational event for Hong Kong and Hong Kongers.

More often, citizens showed up at protest sites prepared to be supporters for each other in different ways, from offering spanners and snacks to words of encouragement. During the "lunch with you" rally where I met John, the banker, when black bloc protesters took down traffic lights and railings and needed a spanner, a spanner would miraculously be passed up from the crowd. When a smaller spanner was necessary for the task at hand, people shouted "small spanner," and within a minute, a small spanner would travel from the back to the front! People wearing suits or high heels and skirts knew the exact hand signs for hexagons, plastic zip ties, umbrellas, and goggles. They formed resource lines along Peddler Street while the young ones built roadblocks. Among hundreds of well-dressed professionals, I spotted a middle-aged man in a wrinkled white shirt walking around with an equally wrinkled plastic shopping bag. Lo and behold, he was actually carrying different types of metal wrenches and spanners. An elderly lady also milled around the protest crowd, apparently looking for someone. I soon realized her targets were young protesters in black bloc. She had brought sandwiches and soft drinks and wanted to feed them. At around two in the afternoon, after an hour of chanting slogans and blocking traffic, the professionals returned to their offices. Saddened by the dissipating crowd, a young woman in black bloc broke out in tears. An older man told her and her teammates not to despair, saying that they have to live on and well to fight a long battle, while another professional advised another black bloc group scouting on top of a fence to "be ready to leave soon. The riot police like to arrive after most people have left."

Protest sites became live theaters for expressing collective empathy and care for the downtrodden and marginalized, especially the homeless. On October 1, 2019, protesters vowed to "celebrate" the national day of the PRC with fanfare, rebel style. To dilute police deployment capability, the call was to "blossom everywhere," to spread the protest in multiple districts throughout the territory. On Hong Kong Island, thousands of protesters, with gas masks and hard hats, marched from Central to the government headquarters. Along the way, they built roadblocks and cheered on a dozen black bloc men climbing up a half-built structure to take down a red "Celebrate National Day" banner on a Chinese SOE-run construction site on Harcourt Road. As the crowd approached the government complex, people threw stones and Molotov cocktails at one side of the building, and the police shot back with tear gas and rubber bullets. A water canon truck, known to emit a blue, skin-burning chemical, was parked outside the police headquarters nearby. Some protesters took shelter under the Harcourt Road flyover, a spot that allowed them a view of the approaching police on the other side of the road. At that moment, they saw several homeless elderlies under the bridge, with their cardboard beds, some washcloths hanging on the wall, and a few cooking utensils. They were oblivious to the noise, tear gas, and approaching water cannon, which would definitely hurt them. The young protesters tried to yell at the top of their lungs, "Water cannon is coming! It's dangerous! Leave now!" The elderlies, unafraid, went on their business as usual. As one of them was reaching for a thermal bottle next to his pillow, two young men ran toward them, holding their hands and ushering them to the back of a bank building nearby.

A similar act of compassion happened in another intense confrontation with the police in Tsim Sha Tsui. Bruce, the middle-aged ROC sympathizer, was in a large crowd of protesters along Nathan Road, all psyched up as the police had already hoisted a black flag signaling their imminent use of tear gas. All of a sudden, someone yelled, "Give way!" Then everyone was drawn to the sight of a hunchbacked old woman pushing her cart of recycled cardboard through the protest site. One young man then shouted back in foul language, "Give way? Fuck! Come pushing!" Amid thunderous laughter from the crowd, tear gas, and rubber bullets, Bruce and others joined in to push the old lady's cart to safety. He later told me, "People thought protest sites are dangerous and chaotic. They have no idea. I think these sites are more safe and loving than anywhere else in the city."

Reflexivity and Technology

> *Be formless, shapeless like water. Now you put water into a cup, it becomes the cup. You put water into a bottle, it becomes the bottle. You put water in a teapot, it becomes the teapot. Now water can flow or it can crash. Be water, my friend.*
>
> —Bruce Lee

Within the first weeks of the movement, in a conscious attempt to overcome past fragmentation between the moderate and the militant camps, Bruce Lee's poetic musing of his martial art philosophy "be water" was exhumed as a sacrosanct doctrine. The choice was ingenious: Hong Kong's most famous native son, a global household name, a timeless icon of localist pride and prowess. In the ensuing months, the world watched in awe as protesters put into practice Lee's teaching of adaptability, assertiveness, and action: from peaceful rallies to militant confrontations, from trench warfare to decentralized front lines, from making art and memes to Molotov cocktails. All these were accomplished without official leaders or formal organizations but with extraordinary solidarity and agility. Information technology was leveraged to communicate collective preferences and differences, but it was people's will to learn from past failures that accounted for the movement's cohesion.

Much has been written about the power of information and communication technology (ICT), and especially social media, in facilitating a paradigm shift from "collective" to "connective" action, from organization to network. Occupy Wall Street, the Arab Spring in Tahrir Square, antiausterity protests in Spain, protests in Gezi Park in Turkey, and the Umbrella Movement in Hong Kong were just the most famous examples of Internet-mediated struggles that pundits termed the "Facebook Revolutions." Indeed, digital technology allows the masses to signal their shared discontent, synchronize ad hoc actions, and coordinate people connected by weak or nonexistent ties who are scattered in far-flung locations. Over and over again, citizens of a twenty-first-century networked public "could click yes on an electronic invitation to a revolution."[11] Digital tools have an inherent democratizing tendency too, laying the foundation for the culture of "horizontalism" (ethos of equalitarian power) and the capacity for "adhocracy" (in which tasks are accomplished by whoever is available, without prior planning) characteristic of these movements. However, according to experts of these digitally mediated protests, technological affordances come with a critical weakness: "tactical freeze." These movements can go from almost zero to massive within days, but they lack the culture and mechanism for making collective decisions to change course after the initial speedy expansion, navigate the ever-evolving political terrain, or negotiate with their opponents.[12]

The 2019 protesters in Hong Kong proved this technological determinism wrong. The people's willful decision to overcome past fragmentation made ICT technology a tool to achieve tactical flexibility rather than tactical freeze. Their main tool was not Facebook but two social media platforms—LIHKG and Telegram—that had become the proverbial headquarters of the movement. Compared to Facebook, these technological tools offered protesters anonymity, inclusiveness, expansive reach, and flexible scale. Telegram, believed to have better encryption than WhatsApp, allows the formation of numerous chat groups of up to 200,000 members compared to WhatsApp's 256 members. Anyone could join with a fictitious name and a mobile telephone number. Channel owners could decide if the group was open to all or by invitation only. Countless Telegram "open" channels were initiated by citizens during the movement, most of them organized around geographical districts, neighborhoods, occupational groups, protest functions, or ideologies. Small teams had their own private channels for instant communication during protests. One very important function afforded by LIHKG and Telegram was polling, which to a certain extent was a form of deliberation and decision making. Citizens debated and voted online. The results indicated the balance of views, and people made their own decision about what action or position to take. Unlike forums such as Reddit, LIHKG's upvote and downvote indicators did not merely show an aggregated score (that is, the number of upvotes minus the number of downvotes) but also the exact upvote and downvote counts. Telegram polls used simple questionnaires, and channel administrators could report the aggregate results.[13]

Technological affordance only made action *possible*. Purpose and trust in human agency had to be there to activate such affordance. For one thing, Telegram was already available in 2014 when the Umbrella Movement erupted, but it did not help overcome the divisions and strife among the different factions. LIHKG and its predecessor, HKGolden, were popular for discussions on entertainment, food, jokes, current affairs, and everyday social communication. It was only when the antiextradition bill prompted people to act that they were repurposed for political activism.

For ICT to do its magic, protesters' reflexivity on past fragmentation was key to solidarity. A consensus was forged in the early days that this time, people must overcome the acrimonious division between the militants and the moderates that had doomed the Umbrella Movement. One of the most popular posts recognizing the need for both camps appeared on June 17, 2019, the day after the two-million-strong march:

> To the happy resisters [meaning the moderates]: Hong Kong will never obtain any government concession if we only resist with fun and playfulness. But your power is very important because you have public opinion support and can move people's emotion, to plant the seed of democracy by teaching their children about democracy. Your job is to cement public support, and focus on good propaganda. To the militants: you are the big winners of this movement because people now recognize your action has brought results. You should focus

on fighting each street battle well and not on condemning the futility of the happy resisters. Militancy without popular consent will definitely be criticized as riots. Moderates' propaganda warfare can be a very useful supplementary side attack for you.

Other popular posts that were upvoted by many on LIHKG talked about the importance of "not repeating the mistakes of the Umbrella" and urged Hong Kongers to learn from Mao Tse-tung's theory of uniting all secondary enemies to fight the primary enemy. A June 22 post read, "Hong Kong failed in past movements because it was a puddle of sand, with lot of internal strife." As cycles of heated debates emerged over the course of the movement, the keyword count of slogans emphasizing the cardinal principle of solidarity would also jump exponentially. These slogans included "Five demands, not one less," "Climbing the same mountains, each contributes his efforts, going up and down together," "No splitting, no condemnation, no snitching," and "No big stage, no leaders."[14]

The Hong Kong case shows that technology, no matter how advanced or novel, is neutral and does not make or break movements by its mere affordance. Rather, people's reflexivity and collective will to stick together as a community of action determine whether the outcome is tactical freeze, as communication scholars feared, or tactical flexibility, as Hong Kongers demonstrated.

Division of Protest Labor

In addition to mechanical solidarity, the 2019 protests were powerful because of the other kind of solidarity, which Emile Durkheim termed "organic" solidarity. This kind of solidarity arose from an elaborate division of labor among citizens whose specialized task performance formed the basis of mutual dependence on each other. An illustrated manual of twenty "occupations" was widely circulated online with instructions and advice for citizens with different physical strength, interests, and resources to choose from. The monikers for these occupations included "dog killer" (frontline attacker), "magician" (Molotov thrower), "firefighter" (tear gas extinguisher), "weatherman" (blocking cameras with umbrella), "painter" (slogans sprayer), and "school bus driver" (driving getaway cars). Open Telegram channels and LIHKG offered instructions on how to perform these tasks, and numerous small teams were formed either online among strangers or in preexisting social networks—hobby groups, churches, school friends—to coordinate specific action on a particular day.

Avid protesters experimented with different occupations, honing their skills online and on site, making connections with fellow "professionals," and becoming attuned to their overall division of labor in a protest regardless of their own dedicated position. The movement's tactical flexibility was predicated on protesters' willful learning, and determination to overcome physical and psychological hurdles, a process they called "evolution." Typically, a frontline militant began her career as an inexperienced, timid, and law-abiding student hesitant about physical confrontations. Soon, as she became acclimatized and emboldened, she would take up auxiliary frontline roles such as scout or fire extinguisher and then the most dangerous positions of magician and dog killer.

The older generations of social media commentators and key opinion leaders were amazed by the younger generations' unique capacity to collaborate flexibly with total strangers in this elaborate division of labor. Current affairs programs on television explored this topic and concluded that it might have originated from the young's long-term immersion in (read: addiction to) video games. One of the protesters who served as the bearer of the American flag in protests told me his generation grew up playing video games like *League of Legends* and these games taught them a unique skill: teaming up with anonymous online partners from anywhere around the world, all being randomly assigned roles, and playing against another temporary group of strangers. I saw the most vivid evidence of the impact of video game culture on protests in a frontline team of twenty young anime enthusiasts. Drawn together by their love of animation, they had befriended each other several years before in anime-themed festivals, cosplay events, and concerts. The world of Japanese anime series such as *Gundam, Attack on Titan, Code Geass,* and *Neon Genesis Evangelion* taught them the need to fight for justice, to protect homeland and humanity, and to sacrifice for a better future, and 2019 was such a moment of epochal battle against injustice. The leader of these anime militants, a twenty-five-year-old military history buff nicknamed Churchill, explained their division of labor: "Half of the team are intelligence officers, auxiliary resource support, and planning. The rest are a squad in the front line. After we obtained police-grade gas masks and filters, we would test them by running toward tear gas. History tells me we need both the rational and the militant, just like Marin Luther King had Malcom X behind him, like light and shadow." Whether at the level of a small team, a massive rally, a day of action, or the movement as a whole, the actual enactment of a division of labor among protesters created a bond of mutual dependence, adding a layer of organic solidarity to that of mechanical solidarity based on common beliefs.

Embedding Resistance in Everyday Life

A fourth source of solidarity making possible the massive scale of collective action was the widespread practice of citizens incorporating resistance into their everyday life. Ordinary people found ways, in the interstices of their routines, already organized and structured at work or in the neighborhood, to contribute to the movement without explicitly going anywhere. One night in Central, I witnessed how a corporate executive, a group of pedestrians, and a social worker became impromptu supporters of bona fide protesters during the normal course of their daily lives.

It was a late November evening, right after the US Congress passed the Hong Kong Human Rights and Democracy Act, and a Thanksgiving rally was held in Edinburgh Place in Central. I was part of a citizen volunteer group called Protect the Children. Volunteers in groups of seven or eight would show up at protest sites and use their bodies as human shields between the protesters and police when conflict broke out, buying a few seconds' time for the young protesters to flee. Anticipating clashes, my group arrived in Central when the rally had just begun. A busload of riot police arrived and started patrolling the footbridge above the eight-lane Harcourt Road. Our group chose to guard a spot about two hundred feet from the bridge and where we could warn protesters about police presence ahead of time. Echoes of slogan chanting and the singing of "Glory to Hong Kong" filled the brisk autumn air. At about half past nine, when the crowd began dispersing, some protesters were moving traffic cones in preparation of making roadblocks. As the situation became tense, a team of about seven riot police walked toward us and stood next to us, without saying or doing anything, as if they wanted to claim that turf. We did not cede our ground, just standing awkwardly right next to them. Suddenly, a thirty-something young man in a smart suit and tie appeared in our mix. He looked like an accountant working late into the evening and needing a cigarette break and some fresh air.

But why did he insert himself in front of the riot police? The next thing I saw, he began uttering derogatory comments to the police officers, who happened to be smiling and nodding to an odd woman who was walking by, singing their praises, and gesturing a thumbs up. The accountant snapped, "Only low-IQ people will enjoy such praise from a stupid woman . . . you guys are doing nothing good to Hong Kong, losers!" For the next ten minutes, some nasty but low-intensity insults were traded between the accountant and one of the younger officers, who was soon being held back by his senior. Soon, when the police decided to move toward the footbridge, our accountant began walking away in the other direction. He uttered softly to us, "I saw on LIHKG that some bros are thinking of action further down the road. I wanted to distract this group of popo [a derogatory term for the police] to buy them more time."

After most people left the rally, without any incident, our team went to check on the MTR exit, where we saw a huge crowd shouting at the police, "Release him! Release him!" A group of ten to fifteen riot police had stopped and frisked a teenage boy in school uniform who was cornered into a narrow alley. The crowd was made up of middle-aged pedestrians and some senior citizens, who instinctively turned on the flashlight and video functions of their phones, all pointing at the scene, and began chanting antipolice slogans, calling them rapists, murderers, rogue police, and more. Recognizing our vests, they shouted, "Make way for Protect the Children." Within seconds, I was just inches away from the fierce-looking frontline police who cordoned off the area, and behind me was the crowd of about a hundred strangers, yelling one after another, "The kid did nothing, I swear, I saw everything." After some scuffling and interrogation, the police found nothing in the kid's backpack and let him go. The crowd booed the police, who retreated and then went away. Scenes like this had become everyday occurrences in subways and residential neighborhoods. What made that episode particularly memorable to me was its blinding brightness—was it the flashlights, or the glittering golden storefronts of the surrounding luxury brands, or simply the people's conscience and fearlessness?

A few minutes later, our group leader received a message about another police team along Harcourt Road in Sheung Wan. When we arrived, there was a smaller crowd of masked protesters milling around, voicing a litany of expletives and rants at a group of riot police just getting out of their van. The police ordered them to disperse, welding batons and pepper spray canisters.

Amid the usual chaos, a calm but assertive voice blasted from a handheld amplifier. A slight, middle-aged man with a backpack, acting solo, was broadcasting a message: "The world is watching, Hong Kong police.... There is no need to escalate the tension every time you come to the scene.... It is legal in Hong Kong for people to shout foul language in public areas. We still have laws to protect freedom of speech.... You popo, too, can relax, take a deep breath.... You have been too tense lately.... I am a social worker, please follow me to take a deep breath." He kept repeating the same message, like a therapist or hypnotist, moving slowly alongside the police and protesters, who continued to trade insults and threats in a mobile standoff. In the end there were no major clashes that night.

These three instances that I witnessed within a three-hour window and within a one-mile radius from where I began were but tips of an iceberg. Multiply these three scenes throughout Hong Kong during a six-month period and one would understand how citizens from all walks of life had claimed ownership of a movement they could join every day, everywhere, sometimes even in their own workplaces. For instance, many among Hong Kong's about two thousand bartenders, half of whom hailed from the Philippines, Nepal, and Europe, were liberal-leaning pro-democracy sympathizers. The assistance bartenders offered to the protesters was deeply embedded in their daily work and the geography of their business. Most bars were located in the busiest central business and commercial districts, such as Causeway Bay, Mongkok, and Central, which were the default sites of demonstrations and clashes. The bars then became convenient refuges for protesters on the run from the police or storage places for their gear and supplies. Bottles were bartenders' specialty. One activist bartender explained why they were natural partners for protesters: "At the end of any business day, we have tons of empty beer and wine bottles, and instead of disposing them, we left them in our alleys for bros and sisses to pick up. Sometimes our kitchen workers also leave bags of flour. You need it for making petrol bombs.... We bartenders have another protest skill—we are good at throwing bottles. Bartenders do it for showmanship to impress their clients. Some young bartenders would teach protesters in the front line how to throw bottles from a distance. Because we know all the alleys like the back of our hands, we make excellent reconnaissance soldiers, providing intelligence about escape routes and police appearance. During the siege at PolyU, more than twenty members of our group joined the rescue effort. I myself drew maps of escape routes, went to the front line, and asked protesters to take photos of them. Many bars have developed their own security and human intelligence network to protect underage customers from police raids. In 2019, we just repurposed that for the movement."

Gender and Class

For all its legendary achievements in coming together as a collective actor, the solidarity achieved in 2019 had its pernicious and coercive moments. First, a pattern of online misogyny had emerged to mark the front line as a male domain. Online posts in the early months of the movement urged female protesters to refrain from going to the front line and to stay behind to play supporting roles. Some posts ridiculed women's physical weakness, which allegedly "would block the escape routes for male protesters and become a burden to the men who often felt obliged to rescue them when they were being pursued by the police."[15] Discrimination against women was nevertheless restrained by other abiding principles of individual effort and no formal leadership.

One subjugated voice from inside the movement came from some feminists who objected to protesters' discriminatory behavior—harassment of mainland Chinese people (for example, restaurants refusing to serve Mandarin-speaking customers except those from Taiwan), doxing police officers' wives and families, and using derogatory homophobic terms against the police. Under the prevailing sentiment of maintaining solidarity, these criticisms were condemned as betrayal of the cause. The feminists themselves were denounced by right-wing localist opinion leaders, and their Facebook pages received uncivil comments, even violent threats.

Two vocal feminists being targeted called attention to the hierarchy of victimhood and the movement's own "policing" from below. They cautioned that such exclusionary practices would "constrict the space for self-reflection needed for both self-transformation and the transformation of the movement." Whereas the mainstream view prioritized the objectives of universal suffrage and political autonomy over intersectional justice issues, these feminists accused the movement, including some of their feminist colleagues, of creating a new hierarchy of suffering and worthiness:

> This protest movement was repeatedly described as leaderless, but it was not; it had an imaginary leader in a collective sense.... Through populist mythological narratives, the movement established a

particular orthodoxy that prioritized the interests of certain protesters over others. To be accepted within the movement, one had to become a "useful" tool for it, and anyone who did not contribute to the "ultimate victory of the people" in the way the "people" wanted at that moment could be singled out as guilty or kicked out as an enemy. It is in this context that feminists—consciously or unconsciously—came to ignore issues of systemic gender-based violence against women (unless perpetrated by the police), or disadvantaged communities in Hong Kong society.[16]

Elsewhere, some local academics criticized the racial stigmatization, hate speech, and Sinophobia expressed on the social media platform LIHKG and in the mini-posts of Lennon Walls (impromptu use of public space for posting protest messages).[17] Racial tensions had given rise to violent attacks perpetrated by mainland tourists on Hong Kong protesters and vice versa. One scholar underscored the political economic causes underlying Hong Kongers' anti-Chinese sentiments. Mainland Chinese have been used by the regime as the "human vessels of colonial power, as networks and resources are invested in turning them into a bottom-up pro-Beijing force in Hong Kong's civil society.... Anti-Chinese sentiments ... are perhaps not born out of an ethnocratic convention, but a changing power relationship that now favors the Mainland identity over the Hong Kong one."[18] Similarly, protesters' relationship with South Asian minorities (about 3.6 percent of the population) was shaped more by political stance than ethnicity or race. When South Asians showed support for the movement, whether as young frontliners fighting alongside locals or as community residents passing out bottled water at demonstrations, they were embraced as Hong Kongers. But when rumors swirled that South Asians were among those hired by gangsters to attack citizens at the Yuen Long station on July 21, they were harassed, verbally abused. and stereotyped as violent "knifemen."[19]

The People as Historical Agents

If the postcolonial generation spearheading all the protests prior to 2019 were a passionate minority, then the 2019 antiextradition movement had achieved the historical feat of inspiring the pragmatic majority to join the resistance. A Reuters poll conducted at the end of December 2019, after six months of upheaval, found that 59 percent of Hong Kong citizens supported the movement, with about a third of respondents having attended at least one antigovernment protest.[20] Hong Kong researchers called it a "total mobilization."[21] This chapter has probed the range of subjectivities and motivations bringing people from different social strata, generations, and political orientations to the streets. They all had stakes, albeit varied, in resisting the extradition bill and faced mainland China as the source of their discontent. Other scholars have selectively emphasized the role of emotions, fear, and threat.[22] The data here suggest a much more variegated agentic landscape, involving career interests, political visions for Hong Kong, continuing previous movements, neighborhood autonomy, and anti-Communism. A related theoretical insight is the significance of action. Many protesters, especially the youngest cohorts, began as accidental participants with only vague political intentions. But through action in mass protests, they were (re)born as political subjects, and Hong Kong became "a political community in action," a tangible and visible force with real political efficacy. As Fanon famously remarked, "The 'thing' colonized becomes a man through the very process of liberation."[23]

The material conditions for this leap to action were once again a rupture, a crisis in governance created by the regime's political miscalculation and intransigence in the face of mass outrage and accumulated discontent. Building on two decades of activism, disagreements, and failure, people developed a collective reflexivity to overcome these weaknesses in tactics and orientations. The protests of 2019 would be remembered for the stunning level of solidarity in a movement that also aspired to "be water"—leaderless, formless, and boundless. Citizens were largely united by mechanisms of both "mechanical" and "organic" solidarity, made all the more efficacious by mobile communication technology. As confrontations with the regime intensified and spread to all corners of the city around the clock, people integrated acts of resistance into their everyday lives. The self-mobilized populace took up self-assigned positions in the nooks and crannies of what had quickly evolved into an urban guerrilla warfare, giving the 2019 protests a hidden strength. However, all this is not to deny the existence of coercive solidarity and the marginalization of minority voices.

In short, this chapter shows that in 2019, many Hong Kongers reclaimed the history-making collective subjecthood that colonization had repressed. How would they use this newfound agency? The "five demands" in the ubiquitously chanted slogan "Five demands, not one less" were concrete policies, with no mention of decolonization or decoloniality. But just as before 2019, challenges to the colonial order, past and present, did not predicate on the discursive embrace of these terms for those challenges to happen or have effects. We will see in the next chapter how Hong Kongers furthered the breakdown of the four colonial mythologies through confronting various forms of violence. In the process, they would bring Hong Kong's decolonization struggle to a new phase.

CHAPTER FOUR

BENDING THE ARC OF VIOLENCE

ABOUT SIX WEEKS AFTER THE FIRST MILLION-STRONG march in early June, escalating violence began to engulf protesters and police, resulting in more property damage and bodily injuries. Authorities in Beijing and Hong Kong condemned the protesters as rioters, even terrorists, to legitimize repressive policing in the name of restoring law and order. The outsourcing of violence to thugs who indiscriminately assaulted citizens at the Yuen Long train station on July 21 and the use of disproportionate force in pursuit of protesters and innocent passengers alike in the crowded Mongkok subway station on August 31 inflamed an already incendiary atmosphere. Protesters responded with arson at police stations and vigilante justice aimed at law enforcement and regime supporters. The call to paralyze the city with a general strike and mass disobedience in early November brought the conflict to new heights, as two university campuses located atop commanding intersections of major roads and rails became battlefields, besieged and burned. Thousands of mostly young people were arrested and charged with rioting. A shared sense of victimhood unified the citizenry, including parents who were previously pro-regime. Protest chants on the streets darkened from "Hong Kongers, Resist!" to "Hong Kongers, Revenge!" and soon "Hong Kong independence, the only way out!" Foreign governments issued unprecedented travel alerts about public safety in Hong Kong. As the global media broadcast images of thickening tear gas smoke, flames from Molotov cocktails, vandalized stores, and paramilitary police subduing protesters inside shopping malls and smashing their bleeding faces, the movement edged toward a dangerous descent into chaos, unhinged from the moral bearing that had won it global sympathy.

To call this dynamic a metaphorical "spiral" of violence, as most academics and journalists did, is to flatten the political meaning and historical significance of violence in this uprising, reducing it to a mere mechanical response to mutual escalation of physical force. From the beginning, police violence on June 12 became a wake-up call for the masses. Soon, protest banners framed the law as "monstrous" and the movement as one "against institutional violence." In the ensuing months, citizen-protesters wove a tapestry of tactics that defied easy categorization of "violence" and "nonviolence." Pained by the heavy toll exacted by violent street battles, protesters called for three other campaigns to steer the movement off the streets. These attempts included a political consumer movement called the "yellow economy," a new union movement aimed at democracy in the workplace, and an election campaign called "35+" seeking to use constitutional rules to paralyze the government. Along the way, people were forced to revisit and break the colonial boundaries—about the rule of law, market rationality, and stability and prosperity—that had previously limited their politics.

Instead of a spiral, violence in this phase of Hong Kong's decolonization struggle was more like an arc, with a curving trajectory. Militant frontliners and citizen-resisters willfully bent the arc of violence toward an emerging vision of a liberated Hong Kong at the center of the movement's signature slogan. That arc is the subject of this chapter. Beginning with a historically and socially specific contextualization of violence in Hong Kong, I explain why it was such a focal concern in the 2019 movement and how, in the early weeks of protests, an organic pattern of mutual recognition and coordination emerged among militant and peaceful protesters. They were unified by their moral outrage against police violence and a strategic determination to overcome past fractures between the militants and the moderates on issues of violence and nonviolence that had undermined the movement. To illuminate the theory and praxis of violence in Hong Kong's decolonization struggle, I explore the thoughts and actions of three "brave warriors" active on the front line. Following the evolution of the movement, I then track the fortuitous ways Hong Kongers pushed back at the violence of a China-dominated economy and the institutional violence of a biased electoral system.

172 FOREVER HONG KONG

4.1 A rally at Belcher Bay Park in Kennedy Town on August 3, 2019. The banner read, "Against institutional violence: I want genuine universal suffrage."
CREDIT: AP Photo / Kin Cheung

The Local Meaning of Violence

Since Hong Kong's decolonial struggle has been delayed by many decades, the experience of colonial violence in this global city is vastly different from that in Africa, Asia, and Latin America. Anticolonial struggles were inevitably violent affairs if only because colonialism was, as Franz Fanon observed in his classic treatises on the subject. His reference was colonialism and liberation movements in Africa, especially Algeria's war for independence, in which he participated in 1956. Violence suffused every aspect of the colony that was also binarily divided into two groups, the white colonists and the colonized blacks. Their border was represented by "the barracks and the police stations," and the colonized were kept in place "at the point of the bayonet and under cannon fire," "rifle butts and napalm."[1] Violent colonization begets violent decolonization. Fanon drew from his psychiatric knowledge and practice to affirm, even glorify, according to some, the cathartic effects of violence. To him, violence "rids the colonized of their inferiority complex, of their passive and despairing attitude. It emboldens them, and restores their self-confidence."[2]

Even though colonial Hong Kong had witnessed physical violence deployed by police during incidents of civil unrest in the 1950s, 1960s, and early 1970s (as discussed in Chapter 1), physical violence was rare since. Instead, the city prided itself on its rule of law, order, civility, and public safety. Despite the institutional and structural violence inherent in its undemocratic legislature, the ruling elite's economic domination, and colonial control over education and mass media, people did not experience these as violence. Aversion to violence and adherence to the law became central tenets of Hong Kong's civic and protest cultures, marking all subsequent social movements and popular mobilizations, only to become partially undone by the younger generations of activists in the late 2000s. Even then, their so-called direct action was law-abiding. And as late as the Umbrella Movement in 2014, the majority of the population remained decisively in the peaceful, rational, and nonviolent camp. Similarly, after a night of police-civilian clashes in the 2016 Mongkok riot, the majority of the public opposed the use of violence as a means of protest, even though they also blamed the government as the root cause. Unsurprisingly, given this local history, in 2019, violence or nonviolence quickly became the fulcrum on which popular support for the movement would fall or rise.

The centrality of violence and its opposite, the law, in the collective sensibility of Hong Kong explains what on first sight and from afar might have seemed like an oddity. As brutal, abusive, and excessive as the Hong Kong police were in 2019—atrocities detailed in reports by Amnesty International, the *New York Times,* the *Washington Post,* and other NGOs—the level of repression seen in the city was, sadly, typical of protest policing around the world, including in democracies.[3] At times, one might even argue that the level of police violence in Hong Kong paled in comparison to that inflicted on protesters elsewhere. To cite one example: at about the same time that 3 protesters lost an eye to police rubber bullets in Hong Kong, 14 yellow vests protesters lost an eye in France and 285 people suffered severe eye trauma in Chile, mostly from hardened rubber bullets and tear gas canisters fired by Chilean security forces.[4] More deaths were directly related to protests in these other places than in Hong Kong. Notwithstanding the regime's politically motivated use of emergency ordinances to crush dissent, the erosion of the liberal rule of law in Hong Kong in 2019 was nowhere comparable to the pervasive torture, imprisonments, and arbitrary arrests in South Korea under military dictatorship, the Philippines under Marcos, or Egypt under

Mubarak.⁵ So, in the face of comparatively "ordinary" regime violence, what explains the extraordinary scale and duration of the Hong Kong protests and the depths of emotion of the protesters reacting against it?

To the young, police violence and impunity that began as early as June 12 and continued throughout 2019 was a betrayal of the social contract, an assault on the body politic, and an existential violation as traumatic as the 1967 riot was for the older generation. This time, the shock and the necessity to combat violence were compounded by an endgame temporality unique to the Hong Kong struggle. The expiration date for "One Country, Two Systems"—2047—was looming on the horizon. Before this predestined end point of Hong Kong as an autonomous entity, freedom and democracy must be secured if they were to stand any chance of surviving thereafter. This historical temporality translated into a widespread "now or never" determination among the younger cohorts to participate in the movement with great abandon. The movement of 2019 was not just another protest; it was deemed a one-off, all-in, no-holds-barred last stand for the people and the city. Therefore, when filtered through people's views of the past and the future, rather than forensic counts of deaths and injuries, the gravity of police violence and the urgency to fight it in Hong Kong exceeded that in France, Chile, and elsewhere where there was no deadline in sight. But given the hegemony of the law in Hong Kong, protesters faced a dilemma: how to balance the need to literally fight for freedom in the face of overpowering police brutality with the need to shepherd, sway, and sustain public support, bringing into their fold a populace deeply entrained to nonviolence on a journey of boundary-breaking collective transformation, all without central coordination or leadership?

The Choreography of Militant and Peaceful Resistance

A pattern of action resembling an intricate dance between militant and peaceful resisters had already emerged in the first three weeks of protests. Spontaneously, "during the eight days from June 9 to June 16, the movement went through a cycle, from peaceful to militant to peaceful action again, setting up a coordinating tone between the two wings."⁶ People saw the necessity and the power of combining both modes—the two million-strong peaceful demonstrations drew the world's attention but obtained no concession from the government. Then, on June 12, a low level of protest violence (throwing bottles at police and hitting the LegCo Complex with sticks) triggered such disproportionate police violence that mounting popular and global pressure compelled the government to make a token concession: temporarily suspending the legislative process. On social media, especially LIHKG, the overwhelming consensus was that the movement needed both militant and peaceful tactics, both political pressure from confrontational clashes and the moral high ground based on statistics of peaceful participants.

Besides strategic calculation, the dance between the militants and the peaceful camp was guided by a supercharged "emotional unity" engulfing the city. The government's refusal to withdraw the bill, even after the largest march in Hong Kong history, infuriated the millions of peaceful, rational, and nonviolent citizens. When three young people committed protest suicide one after another in the last two weeks of June, the entire city was gripped by grief and anger. Youthful martyrdom, without historical precedent in Hong Kong, made a powerful moral critique of a heartless regime and emotionally bonded the people in collective victimhood. Aggravated, the militants kept up the pressure in two episodes of encircling the police headquarters, throwing eggs at the main building and chanting expletives, while the peaceful resisters pulled off a crowdfunding campaign with lightning speed to advertise Hong Kong's political crisis in major international newspapers ahead of the G20 Summit in Japan (see Chapter 5).

Against this background of common frustration, the storming of the LegCo on July 1 did not trigger any backlash in public opinion beyond the pro-Beijing sectors. Instead, several hours of political vandalism and graffiti spraying produced some of the most iconic and resonant slogans of the entire uprising: "It's you [the regime] who taught us peaceful marches are useless" and "No rioter, only tyranny." These phrases would be sprayed and chanted many times in subsequent protests. The movement breathed a sigh of relief when, the morning after July 1, news reports revealed protesters' principled and methodical exercise of violence—targeting artifacts, such as portraitures of political elite and emblems of government, rather than mindless looting or destruction of the library. Instead of denunciation by the peaceful and rational camp, several lawful marches organized by the elders, mothers, and teachers followed soon after the LegCo break-in. Their message was clear: they sympathized and supported what the young people had done.

Yeung Po, a lifelong peaceful activist with a visceral antipathy to confrontation and a main organizer of the Silver Hair Tribes, admitted her disapproval when she saw those broken glass doors at LegCo: "Like many people, I had many question marks in my head on July 1. You know we elderlies are very afraid of violence. But then I read more about what happened, and I began to see that the young people had clear political targets—the portraits of LegCo chairs and the voting machines on legislators' desks. They were not like those tire-burning mobs in foreign countries. I wanted to do something to let the young people know that they are not alone." As a former student leader in the 1970s, Yeung, exuding calm and confidence, noted with admiration that "When you look at the young today, they gave it all to the struggle so selflessly." Joining with three retirees to obtain a no-objection permit from the police, Yeung knew age was their weapon. On October 17, marching in front and holding a big banner declaring "Support the Youth, Protect Hong Kong," Yeung's rally attracted some ten thousand elders, retirees, and middle-aged professionals, pastors, schoolteachers, and social workers. She recalled seeing about ten senior citizens in wheelchairs and one man with an amputated leg walking with a cane the whole way. Some grannies pleaded with police along the rally route not to hit the youngsters so hard when they made arrests.[7]

As such, in the short space of three extraordinary weeks, an ethics of recognition emerged organically out of shared struggles. The "brave warriors" and the civil resisters began to establish a tacit reciprocal relationship, accepting and appreciating the value of the other as equal but different.[8] A sense of responsibility, a culture of care toward the other camp, and a willingness to facilitate the other side in carrying out their chosen style of resistance were evident at the level of the movement, events, and individuals.

Considering the movement as a whole, a temporal rhythm of weekly collective action emerged. On weekdays, different modes of peaceful and civil action flourished online, in downtown public spaces, and in residential neighborhoods—protest art installations on Lennon Walls, human chains, mass singing of protest songs in shopping malls, community forums on boycotting pro-China businesses, gathering at the airport, and noncooperative action in mass transit. On weekends, the mood would become tense and confrontational. Large rallies or marches showcased large numbers of peaceful, law-abiding citizens, with elders and children in tow, chanting slogans and carrying signs made at home or obtained on site. Yet people knew

4.2 Citizens used sticky notes to create Lennon Walls in public spaces throughout Hong Kong to express their political positions and sentiments. In Taipo, a working-class district in northern Hong Kong, a busy underground walkway became a Lennon Tunnel in July 2019.
CREDIT: Studio Incendo / Flickr

clashes would happen toward the end of the event. Frontline youths in increasingly sophisticated full gear would show up, claiming to protect the marchers, and would start their roadblocks, preparing for a showdown with the increasingly aggressive riot police.

To help netizens keep track of all the events and action, an informational device called Hong Kongers' Schedules circulated widely online. These colorful, at-a-glance schedules listed the dates, locations, and times of the week's action, embellished with protest icons such as Pepe, the LIHKG pig, and a yellow hard hat. Sometimes the schedules included notations of events that might involve confrontations so that people could make their own risk assessment. Otherwise, these schedules visually erased the boundary between militant and civil action by listing them together. For several months, on top of their day jobs, which already demanded some of the longest working hours in the world, Hong Kongers self-mobilized to enroll in different protest occupations during what was left of their waking hours. Like superheroes, they led double or triple lives, combining professional day jobs and activist night shifts: more polite and affective action during the work week and more aggressive and provocative activities on weekends. Businesses near protest sites would close early in anticipation of crowds and clashes; news crews would know where to broadcast the movement live. Drivers would adjust their routes; shoppers and diners made plans accordingly. The city was never so exhausted and edgy, nor so energized and exhilarated.

As the protests evolved, the categorical boundary between "peaceful, rational, and nonviolent" and "the braves and the militants" became ever more elusive thanks to an inclusive ethic of recognition between the two factions. A good example was the Hong Kong Way action. On the thirtieth anniversary of the 370-mile-long Baltic Way human chain formed by citizens across three Baltic states in 1989, Hong Kong netizens announced the Hong Kong Way scheduled for August 23, 2019. On LIHKG posts, initiators explained the historical and global meaning of this preeminently peaceful act, recognized by the EU as the international Black Ribbon Day since 2009, and the logistics for its enactment along subway stations throughout the city. Remarkably, these posts also took pains to address the militant brothers and sisters, lest they feel marginalized. A viral post pleaded with them to join: "Our brave warriors brothers and sisters, we are thankful for all your sacrifices. This action is no exception; we can't do without you. We hope the militants can participate peacefully. But, don't be mistaken, brave warriors cannot retreat. Our resistance has not obtained results. We still need to persist and stay unified. Brothers and sisters go up and down together! No splitting! Never give up until universal suffrage is here!"

All went as planned: peaceful, orderly, spontaneous, even cheerful. It was a rare moment of respite after twelve weeks of intense confrontations with the regime. The thirty-seven-mile Hong Kong Way human chain snaked through all major pedestrian sidewalks along the entire subway system, lit up by the smartphone flashlights of some 210,000 participants. It was so successful that over the next two weeks, students returning to school in early September launched their own human chains in different school districts to mark the start of the new academic year. All told, human chains popped up among some two hundred secondary schools, with their alumni showing up in these early-morning chains before hurrying to their offices to start their work day.

Protest arts also blurred the stark divide between the militants and the moderates. The spectacular explosion of creativity across a variety of media—music, painting, videography, photography, films, literature—during 2019 deserves a monograph of its own. The most impactful and widely distributed medium was graphic design, found on Lennon Walls, online platforms, and political T-shirts. Tens of thousands of artists, designers, advertising professionals, amateur illustrators, and comic book aficionados formed Telegram groups and produced an avalanche of high-quality visual materials depicting and promoting the protests, the protesters, and their causes. One of the most celebrated artists was forty-year-old Abaddon, a veteran designer and entrepreneur in advertising. His pieces were instantly recognizable not just because of their gigantic scale, covering a whole wall in pedestrian tunnels and atriums of public transit. With a mission to forge consensus in a movement fraught with ambiguous moral standards and contending values, Abaddon's works cast the militants in a magisterial, even magical, light, including those executing vigilante justice. Referring to his stunning ensemble portrait titled *Never Surrender—Our Only Weapon,* he said, "I wanted to represent these 16 protesters as super attractive, charismatic heroes, even in their helmets, gas masks and cling wraps, showing a bare-chested young man's six pack abs, with a 'HONG KONG' tattoo on his arm. I wanted to show young people is justice, and justice is stylish; resistance is fashionable, even without clothes." His target audience were the elders and the moderates: "I have talked to grannies and grandpas in the neighborhood. They are avid readers of posters and messages on Lennon Walls; it's part of their morning exercise routines. I can move them and shape their views. I also wanted to show regime supporters that they can never produce this level of work because great art comes from the soul."[9]

Tacit coordination between the militants and the moderates was also evident at the level of protest events. Of all the memorable marches in 2019, the August 18 mobile rally best illustrates how an ethics of recognition bound the militants and the moderates together. Eleven weeks into the protests, the public was reeling from the tragic loss of a woman's eye to police ammunition and the violent clashes during the airport occupation. On August 18, or "8.18," as the march would come to be referred to, a quarter of the population (1.7 million people) showed up for a Victoria Park rally. When the park reached capacity, the organizers improvised a mobile rally, essentially defying the police ban on a march. Peaceful protesters—families with children, elders in

4.3 Protest art featuring the heroism of militant frontliners, titled *Never Surrender, Our Only Weapon*.
CREDIT: Studio Incendo / Flickr

wheelchairs, middle-aged couples holding protest signs, friends coming in groups, and black bloc youngsters—slowly marched along Causeway Bay's six-lane Hennessy Road toward Central and then back. The thundering sound of the torrential rain that afternoon drowned out the chatty noises of private conversations among the solemn crowd. Except for the intermittent eruptions of protest slogans, the procession of 1.7 million in a sea of umbrellas was unusually and eerily quiet, as if people were attending a funeral, not a mass demonstration.

What made 8.18 remarkable was what happened before and after the march. Several days before the event, LIHKG and other social media platforms were rife with discussions about keeping 8.18 free of tear gas or clashes, making it a pure day of "peaceful, rational, and nonviolent" action. The rationale was that after weeks of bloody fighting, the movement needed to show itself and the world the extent of popular support and determination. A widely circulated post demanded that participants follow three principles: no gear, no hurling, and no post-rally action. Some militants expressed their frustration at being marginalized after all their sacrifices, at being told that their three essential markers—mask, helmet, and goggles—were too "menacing" to the public. There was also the view expressed online that whoever broke the peace on 8.18 must be "ghosts"—moles for the regime. No one could predict what would happen. To everyone's surprise, before the march began, a black bloc young man, presumably a self-appointed representative of the frontline militants, held up a self-made sign that went viral: "To the moderates: it's time for us to be your company in your peaceful march today. Thank you for your unwavering support even though you might not agree with our methods!!! 8.18 no more division between the moderates and the brave warriors."

Numerous citizens interviewed by the media that day echoed the sentiment of mutual appreciation, expressing respect for the militants. One said, "I did not feel any violence by the protesters. I only saw police smashing and grinding people's faces on concrete roads, until the bones are visible. If there was no police, all would be safe and peaceful." Some people wore T-shirts bearing the humorous pledge "No split, not even in a nuclear fission." Even more impressive was the understanding that peaceful marchers expressed toward the other wing of the movement. "If we don't show up in large numbers, the young frontliners will be in danger. Large numbers of bodies can protect them and can show the government that citizens would not be afraid of its repression. . . . I won't split with them. I only blame myself for not being as courageous. I have too many burdens and responsibilities. If I were young, I'd become a militant too," said a fifty-year-old woman in tears.[10]

By half past ten at night, the massive crowd had gone home and the rain had stopped, leaving only about a thousand or so black bloc protesters lingering and wandering in small groups along an empty section of road that had seen many clashes. The air was so clean and crisp you could hear both their silence and their chatter. With gas masks and hard hats on, they were ready for combat, just waiting for something to happen. A few climbed atop the water barricades outside the government headquarters to do reconnaissance work. When bored, they played with their laser pens, projecting a dance of light on the wall of the government building, serenaded by an out-of-fashion 1980s Cantopop song, "Under the Laser," playing on one of the black bloc protester's phones. Another group surrounded a cockroach, yelling laughingly at it like the riot police would at protesters, "Don't breach our barricade or we will shoot tear gas!" Soon, a small but passionate few walked up and down the road, urging all to go home: "The whole world, go home! All people, go home!" and "If we fought with the dogs tonight, all the news tomorrow will not be about the 1.7 million march on the street." One woman shot back, "You always say 'liberate,' but I am not seeing how you could liberate Hong Kong by just marching." The other replied in a friendly tone, "Even if we wanted a good fight, today is not the day. Even brave warriors need moderates' back up. There are too few people here for any action." Emotional arguments flared up, but that night, people mostly resolved the tension by patting each other's shoulders, a simple comforting gesture more effective than words. Half past twelve, a middle-aged man, making a last round of "go home" calls, implored, "Reporters, too, please go home, ok?"[11]

The next day, the movement relished in the affirmative global headlines people were hoping for: "Protests in Hong Kong Continue, Remain Peaceful" (NPR), "Hong Kong Protesters Defy Police Ban in Show of Strength" (*New York Times*), "Huge Crowds Rally Peacefully" (BBC), and "Peaceful Hong Kong Protest Puts Onus Back on Beijing" (*Financial Times*).

After the July 21 thug attack and especially after the August 31 police raid in Mongkok, confrontation protests responding to the regime's escalation became more frequent, disrupting the alternation between peaceful weekdays and confrontational weekends. Still, within each event, such as those on August 24 and 31; September 2, 15, and 28; and October 1, a temporal and spatial choreography between the militants and the moderates played out effortlessly, blurring the boundaries between violence and nonviolence. They knew their respective places, each taking their turn, like a team running different laps in a relay or a theater group playing different scenes. During the first two months of the movement, when the police still issued no-objection notices to rally organizers, the moderates would do their orderly marches on the main roads while black bloc militants were busy on the side streets, scouting the surroundings, moving trash cans and wood planks to set up small-scale roadblocks, and stocking resource stations (commonly with bottled water, hard hats, goggles, and umbrellas). Only toward the end of the procession, when demonstrators were done with marching and slogan chanting, would they move to occupy the main road. Teams of black blocs would quickly descend, and major barricades made from bamboo sticks, steel rods, and metal railings would appear as if out of nowhere. The magicians, the firefighters, the dog killers, and the shield soldiers would take their places.

This two-scene or two-shift protest routine became increasingly untenable when, from late August, riot police began using tear gas, rubber bullets, and beanbag rounds to disperse peaceful rallies *in progress*. Other times, in pursuit of protesters, police sent tear gas into densely populated public housing estates or old neighborhoods with many assisted living flats. The spread of confrontation disrupted everyday life in neighborhoods far and wide, engulfing and enrolling, however passively, ordinary citizens in the struggle. The first time tear gas canisters landed in Wong Tai Sin, a concrete forest of working-class public housing blocks, about a thousand residents in flip flops, shorts, and singlets rushed from their homes to the open area downstairs to battle the riot police with expletives. Vendors at news and magazine stalls on the streets began wearing gas masks on a daily basis. Shopping, Hong Kongers' favorite pastime, became a nerve-wracking excursion as malls became sites of police beatings and "kettling" (a policing tactic of cordoning protesters off). Middle-aged housewives learned how to use the bottled water they carried in their handbags to extinguish tear gas canisters landing near them on their way to the wet market. "Eating tear gas" had become a defining experience of Hong Kong life.

Radicalization

With the normalization of everyday violence, a creeping process of radicalization began among local residents and public intellectuals alike. At first, older men and women were merely part of the large crowds yelling at the police, as if they realized verbal, not physical, assaults were their only weapon, and perhaps because their age shielded them from physical abuse. With time, these unlikely protesters would join in making Molotov cocktails for the front line.

One afternoon in late October, I was at one of Kowloon's busiest intersections on Nathan Road, where a huge crowd filled the sidewalks in four directions, surrounding a team of riot police chasing protesters fleeing from another district. One granny shouted, "You have taken money from the CCP, and become their running dogs. Beat me up, beat me up! I am not scared of you." Her friend added, "We have legal right to protest. If you are Hong Kongers, go home and reflect on what you are doing to us; if you are a mainlander, crawl back to China. We Hong Kong people hate you very much!" An enraged old man suddenly stepped onto the road and faced the police at close range, provoking them to hit him: "Beat me to death. I am not worth anything." As the crowd shouted, "Hong Kong police, shame on you," a woman ranted, "We taxpayers have to feed scum like you. Even gods and

4.4 An elderly woman shouted at police officers as they advanced toward protesters in the district of Yuen Long on July 27, 2019.
CREDIT: Getty Images

ghosts hate you. If you have any conscience left, you should resign. If not, heaven will take revenge."

As day turned into night, older folks went home and younger people took over the streets. The standoff had migrated north to other intersections on Nathan Road. The sheer size of the crowd and the anonymity it offered emboldened people to hurl insults at the police. Their verbal assaults usually targeted their masculinity and class status: "Your wife is fucking another guy now, go home quick" and "Your wife shuns your tear gas smell!" When the police unfurled warning flags in red, purple, or black, the crowd would tease them, "Don't just raise your flag [a slang meaning 'erection'], you have to shoot [meaning 'ejaculate']." It was common knowledge that some rank-and-file officers were recruited from high school dropouts with only the inferior diploma qualification. People therefore insulted them as "ngai chun tsai" (毅進仔), which became a pejorative slur for the police as widely heard as "black cops" or "dogs." That night, I was next to a group who got excited when riot police appeared exhausted, stretching their backs and knees. Someone in the crowd yelled, "Haven't you eaten? Go back to your dog house for your dog meat!" When an officer with a baton tripped during a dash for a black bloc, a group of young people burst into laughter, and a two-word chorus, "Po-kai! Po-kai!" (a Cantonese foul word literally meaning falling on the street), erupted. Another man upended the challenge, "If you are a real man, take off your uniform and let's fight. You are nothing without your uniform; you are nothing without your gear, motherfuckers!" Soon, people got wind of an approaching water cannon truck, and as the police pulled out the black flag (signaling the imminent use of tear gas), everyone fled. Scenes like this played out on many nights over six months.

Beyond fighting with words, ordinary citizens and residents in their own neighborhoods learned how to look out for each other in their frequent skirmishes with the police and with Raptors showing up to arrest fleeing protesters. Out of rage but also trying to buy time for those on the run, impromptu groups of middle-aged men and women would argue with the police or plead with them to leave their neighborhood. They had learned from the young that they had to hold onto each other's backpacks or arms in case the police tried to whisk one of them away. By the time of the PolyU siege in mid-November, an array of civilians, including many parents desperate to rescue the students, participated in street clashes with the police. On November 18, thousands of professional men and women just getting off from their office jobs joined grannies and housewives to make Molotov cocktails through the length of Nathan Road. Others helped by digging up bricks, a tactic first used in the Mongkok riot in 2016, to supply the frontline militants who were trying to advance toward PolyU to distract and dilute police deployment there. In the end, their high spirit was not enough to push back the police, who arrested 1,071 "rioters"—the largest number on a single night since the beginning of the 2019 movement.[12]

Evolving in tandem with popular radicalization on the street were critical reflections in public discourse about law and violence. Leading the trend to question the taken-for-granted principle of nonviolence so cherished by the pan-democrats and mainstream society was Joseph Lian Yi-zeng. An influential former editor in chief and columnist at the *Hong Kong Economic Journal* and a former member of the Government Central Policy Unit, Lian became sympathetic to the militant localist cause after the Umbrella Movement and the Fish Ball Revolution. Right after the riot in 2016, he wrote in his column,

> After the Occupy Movement, the SAR Government threw away the restraint on violent suppression.... Young resisters, after gaining the

experience of violence, will turn even more to militant actions. . . .
After failing to achieve democracy through peaceful means, . . . is it
true that [the democrats] still cannot accept "using force against violence," "militant resistance," "fighting against reddening through violence"? Of course, this is not to say that social movements always have
to be violent. The question is, as a matter of principle, can non-peaceful
and violent strategies be included in future protests?[13]

Elsewhere in a public forum, Lian popularized the idea of "violence on the edge," taken from the history of resistance during the martial law era in Taiwan, and approved its use by Hong Kong's militants:

The "theory of violence on the edge" posits that movement activists
would not use violence, but would push their non-violent actions to
the limit of violence, to what the power holders can barely tolerate. It
not only attracts widespread attention in the process but also provokes the regime to employ unjustified violence, which leads people
to condemn the power holders and turn to support the movement.[14]

In 2019, during the months of protracted everyday violence on the streets and campuses, public intellectuals known for their moderate political views began rethinking their moral and legal reasoning about law and violence. In a series of public lectures at local universities, Joseph Chan, a political philosopher of neo-Confucian thought at the University of Hong Kong long known for his political moderation, famously made a case for the use of violence. When the regime had lost its "way," referring to the Confucian notion of a mandate of heaven, he argued, violent resistance may be morally defensible *if* the violence involved was necessary, proportional, and had a legitimate objective and a reasonable prospect of success. Chan rejected, on the one hand, the proestablishment camp's view denouncing all and any violence under any circumstance and, on the other, the most militant groups in the front line who advocated undifferentiated attacks on police and armed uprising for regime change. Confronting the moral ambiguity and conditionality for the use of violence in the movement, Chan implored protesters on the streets to bear in mind that "under an extreme imbalance of power, where the regime can easily defeat resisters, all we have is legitimacy. Losing that, we lose everything."[15]

Likewise, Benny Tai, a law professor who was the main architect of the Occupy Central with Love and Peace campaign in 2014 and a staunch believer in Martin Luther King Jr.'s civil disobedience doctrine, apparently reconsidered his principle of nonviolence in 2019. From "disobeying unjust laws" by nonviolent means, Tai now endorsed "uncivil" resistance. Citing Candice Delmas's *A Duty to Resist: When Disobedience Should be Uncivil*, Tai deplored that Hong Kong had descended into a semiauthoritarian and corrupt regime. He now proposed that resisters could legitimately use illegal and uncivil means to achieve just reform. Given the circumstances, holding all political action to an absolutely sanitized standard of legality would be akin to germophobia. He saw it as an urgent task to shake off this political germophobia, which the government was using to fracture the movement. He reckoned that, "Most vigilantism cannot be legitimate. But against the background of seriously inappropriate official behavior, when the regime assaults its people or fails to protect the people from fatal assaults by others, then vigilantism for protecting oneself or others could become reasonable. The harm brought about by vigilantism should be proportional to the immediate threat to which it responds."[16]

It is difficult to assess the impact of these public discourses on popular acceptance of violence before the 2019 protests. But there is strong academic evidence to show that once the general public were victimized by police violence, the shift was clear. Analyzing the escalation of violence, policing expert Clifford Stott noted of the Hong Kong situation, "Illegitimate and undifferentiated police action created the psychological unity where previously diverse groups with different tactics began to coexist more successfully in order to achieve their common goals. . . . Police tactics then served to legitimize and empower escalating acts of community resistance which amplified ever more intensive forms of police repression until the cycle was broken following the siege of the Polytechnic University in December."[17] One should add to this judicious argument that it was not just the radical groups but ordinary citizens who, over a six-month period, evolved from law-abiding and mostly apolitical bystanders to sympathizers and then participants in protest action. This can be called reactive radicalization, not to undermine the participants' voluntary agency but to highlight the force of circumstance.

A series of polls on popular attitudes toward violence corroborated these points. From June to October, the proportion of respondents who insisted on the necessity of nonviolence in protest dropped from 83 percent to 67 percent. By December, nearly a fifth of Hong Kong voters supported protesters "attacking opponents," hurling bricks and Molotov cocktails, and damaging public facilities such as the subway system.[18] Over the same period, respondents giving a zero trust score to the police increased from 22 percent to 52 percent. When asked who should be held responsible for escalating violence, 70 percent of respondents chose the SAR government and the police in September and October, while only 10 percent chose the protesters. But the largest and most representative poll was the district boards election in November in which pro-movement and pro-democracy candidates, regardless of experience and visibility, scored a landslide victory. Nearly three million voters, or 71 percent of the electorate, turned out to replace pro-establishment representatives with "yellow" candidates who took 80 percent of the 452 seats. District boards did not have legislative powers and were only responsible for overseeing municipal minutiae such as sanitation and recreational facilities. These elections were the only ones using universal suffrage precisely because the regime deemed them harmless. Despite being sleepy events in the past, the timing of the 2019 iteration made this a historic opportunity for people to register their sentiments. Taking place a week after the mayhem at Polytechnic University, the results were widely reported internationally and interpreted as the people's resounding rejection of the regime. It was all the more impressive in the face of the mass media campaigns by government and pro-China forces urging citizens to say no to violence and to split with rioters.

Becoming "Brave Warriors"

Public condonement, and even endorsement, of violence explained its persistence but not its origin. In a society averse to violence, why and how did youngsters become "brave warriors"? Given the extreme imbalance of force—ammunition, personnel, training, resources, and organization—why didn't they see violent combat as an impossible, even foolish, proposition? How did the brave warriors make sense of violence?

At the personal level, there was no romance in violence. Instead of heroism, the valiants spoke of fear, a lot of it, and overcoming fear by training their body and mind. As one described vividly the days of intense fighting at PolyU, "Actually, everyone in the front line lives in constant fear. So you could say there is no 100 percent brave warrior in the world. The difference is more or less fear, or whether you have time to feel the fear. The so-called valiants are just those whose beliefs keep fear at bay for half a second more."

The brave warriors I came to know told their stories not in a grandiose way but with a level-headed pragmatism. Those in the front line did not experience a social movement but a war. For them, resistance, violent or not, was not a choice but a necessity: to defend one's homeland when it was under attack, to protect younger and weaker fellow citizens, to fight for their own future, and to make necessary sacrifices. They also carefully distinguished between senseless violence and principled violence. From the patterns of their violent action, one could discern a moral universe, a "symbolic order of violence."[19] Within that community, there were withering internal criticisms against those who exploited the halo of the brave warriors for personal gains, those inflicting excessive violence, or those retreating cowardly in the front line. Overall, because violence was not instrumentalized, that is, not a calculated tactic to realistically bring about victory, it turned out to be a transformative moral and affective force for its subjects and the larger political community.

Wai: We Are the "Chosen Generation"

One summer day in 2020, after the National Security Law had effectively bulldozed all public acts of defiance, I asked Wai, a seventeen-year-old LegCo-storming political freshman, "What does it mean to be a brave warrior?" He surprised me with a considered answer, as if he had asked himself many times just that: "Being a brave warrior is a state of mind, an attitude, when one willingly confronts fear in order to achieve something. You can be a brave warrior even doing ordinary things, if you look straight at your own fear." Since his narrow escape from the Raptors on June 12, his first encounter with violence, he began a journey traveled by many. Starting with small things (making a triangular barricade), experimenting with a range of protest occupations (from shield soldier and firefighter to dog killer), and learning to use different gear (from the most amateurish hiking sticks to retractable batons and military-grade gas masks), Wai became, in a matter of months, a seasoned frontline militant battling the police in almost every major protest. He was motivated by an obligation to fight: "My generation is chosen by our times to fight. I am now focusing on the revolution. If we can't change this system, what's the point of education, what's the point of studying for our future?" He meant it. The day before taking part in the October 1 Chinese National Day protests, when rumors about Beijing sending in the

People's Liberation Army swirled around the city, many young people left last letters for their loved ones.[20] Wai penned his:

Dear classmates, teachers and friends,

> Four months ago, I was just an ordinary high school student trying to pass his exams. I have ideals and dreams, just no money. June 9 was my first participation ever in social movement and back then I still believed in peaceful and lawful resistance. I never thought our police would turn their guns at citizens. More than 1500 have been arrested. Today is Oct 1. I know the police will use maximum force to protect the regime, and Hong Kongers will confront them with their lives to regain our natural rights and freedom. . . . I am very scared of arrest, and even more scared of dying. . . . But there are more important things than living—freedom and conscience. I will not commit suicide. So if you recover my body and see my motionless face, please be happy because I was always happy when I was with you. You should accompany my last gasp of life with joy . . .
> Glory to Hong Kong!
> Liberate Hong Kong, Revolution of our Times!

Wai

Growing up in a public housing project in Tseun Wan, a working-class district in northwestern Kowloon, Wai was a typical carefree secondary school student with adolescent pimples on his face and little interest in academic subjects but a passion for playing guitar. The 2019 movement reoriented his priority and future plans. He put himself on a strict strength-training regimen, building on the strong foundation of being a distance runner on his school's track team. Eating a diet that focused on a variety of proteins from white meat—he offered me poached chicken breast for lunch—and dietary supplements, he also took up Thai boxing. Martial arts classes had become hugely popular during the movement, as young men and women realized the need to physically protect themselves from the armed police. The term "militia" popped up in many of my conversations with frontline youth.

As someone who had always been athletic, Wai felt a heightened obligation to do "more." A rookie militant, he was overwhelmed with fear. He recalled, "On July 1, my friends and I converted a cardboard trolley into an attack chariot by outfitting it with iron rods. We charged at the glass doors of the LegCo. I was terrified." But the incident gave him the first taste of empowerment: he too "could contribute something to take back what is ours." Two weeks later, in the Shatin skirmish, he threw bricks at the police for the first time in his life. A few weeks later, at the July 21 march in Sheung Wan, he was at the forefront of the massive procession of some four hundred thousand people pressing forward despite numerous rounds of tear gas. It was Wai's first contact with tear gas, made all the more memorable because he was not wearing any underpants. "It was a very hot day, and I just wore a pair of shorts without any underwear. My lungs can take the tear gas, but my private parts were burning. It was fucking painful. From that day on, I always wear long pants," he told me later with a self-mocking laugh. But that day was also a milestone for the entire movement because it was the first time protesters passionately chanted Edward Leung's "Liberate Hong Kong, revolution of our times" as a protest slogan. As night fell, protesters arriving at the Liaison Office pelted it with eggs, sprayed graffiti on its walls, and smeared the PRC emblem with ink. Amid this excited chaos, Wai heard a call for a volunteer to read out a manifesto in front of the media. He surprised himself by coming forward and was even more surprised to hear his own calm voice as he read from a sheet of paper shoved to him just seconds earlier.

That night, on the other side of Hong Kong at the Yuen Long train station, hundreds of thugs connected to pro-establishment politicians indiscriminately assaulted and injured passengers. Police officers were seen walking away from the scene. For Wai, July 21 was a turning point: "I finally got it—we could only count on ourselves. The police will only protect the regime, not citizens. I decided we need to combat violence with violence. I also need to upgrade my gear. At the beginning, when I changed my position from defense to offense, I was very scared, because the police would shoot me with real guns and bullets. With time, I just rely on my instinct. There is no need to overthink. When some of us charge, others will charge together."

July and August were the months when he "evolved" rapidly. Besides learning to become a fire magician based on instructional materials on LIHKG, he absorbed every piece of information from fellow black bloc bros and sisses on site—the effectiveness of "paint bombs" and "water bombs" in hot weather, the assault power of hiking sticks, and, perhaps most significantly, the living examples of fearless courage he witnessed firsthand. On July 27 in Yuen Long, at the end of the large demonstration against the train station attack the week before, Wai was standing among a group of militants bearing the brunt of rubber bullets shot by the riot police. He was proud to find himself holding his ground: "Even when the police were directly pointing their guns at me, I did not move away. The guy next to me took one shot, but he did not retreat. A few minutes later, a reporter approached him, he said nothing except, 'Liberate Hong Kong, revolution of our times.'" In late August, in a clash at Victoria Park, he assaulted riot police—or, in the local slang, "beat the dogs"—for the first time. He clearly remembered the scene: "The police pushed and subdued several protesters on the ground, and someone shouted 'Beat the dogs to rescue people!' Immediately we responded by surging forward, and the police fired, execution style, some thirty to forty rounds of pepper balls. In this chaos, I picked up a retractable police baton from the ground and hit back at the police. Then I heard a real gun shot, and I fled in full speed."

A critical stage in the evolution of many a brave warrior was joining a "small team." Formed by friends, schoolmates, acquaintances, or total strangers who met in frontline action, the size of these teams varied from a handful to twenty or thirty members. Teams provided logistical, tactical, and training support to members and coordinated actions within and across teams. Wai made the fortuitous acquaintance of several black bloc protesters during the airport occupation in August. As the few people "with gear," they hit it off when they started talking during the long sit-in, even making plans for group mixed martial arts training. Most brave warriors belonged to one or more small teams. The bigger teams boasted an internal division of labor with "departments" focusing on tactics (such as paint bombs or water bombs), R&D (for example, triangular wheel nails), and diplomacy (for instance, as a liaison with parent groups). In each protest, three or four members would be responsible for action and eight to twelve for protection, including on-site reconnaissance and remote monitoring of Telegram intelligence about riot police locations. Depending on their physical and mental condition, availability, and preference, frontline militants made their own decisions each time whether they wanted to go solo, form an impromptu team with a few buddies, or join existing small teams that might join forces with other teams. Teams brokered brave warriors' access to networks of safe houses, rescue drivers, underground emergency clinics, and parents who offered anything from cash allowances to temporary lodging and emotional support. Wai had used them all, the groundswell of resources pooled on the basis of trust. Especially after police espionage infiltrating brave warrior teams was revealed in mid-August, trust became a critical resource. When his dad suspended his monthly stipend and Wai had only HK$200 in his savings account, his team reached out to some parent groups who gave him fast food coupons and supermarket gift cards. After each street action, he would hop on rescue vehicles and sought medical help from "studios" (clinics) that his teammates approved.

One resource was particularly critical: combat gear that had to be imported to Hong Kong through illegal channels, mostly from mainland China. As violence intensified, frontline militants had to upgrade their protective and assault gear. Mass-market items such as war-game vests and combat kneepads came in bulk, whereas banned military-grade bulletproof armor, Israeli army gas masks, and tactical batons came in small batches. Frontline militants could tap into this supply chain through their small teams, usually with the financial support of anonymous patrons. Wai had a taser, a bulletproof vest from Germany that cost HK$5,000, a bulletproof helmet, a regular helmet, a collapsible baton, and more. "We are at war," he said. "If I die, I die here. This is my home. Why should I leave because of the enemies?"

The most impressive spirit he witnessed during the whole movement was the battle on November 12 in Mongkok that lasted from around six in the evening to two in the morning. Not wanting to be a burden to his teammates because he was recovering from a rubber bullet wound in his thigh, Wai decided to go solo instead of joining them to fight the siege at CUHK. He arrived around eight in the evening outside the police station, where thousands of protesters were already engaging the police in a street battle aimed at diverting their manpower and resources away from CUHK. Everywhere on Nathan Road he saw bricks piled up and ready to be thrown and bloodstained gas masks and filters abandoned by protesters in retreat. Then someone relayed a message claiming to be from bros and sisses at CUHK that they'd rather commit self-immolation than face arrest. That message sent everyone's blood boiling, and several dozen protesters discussed it and decided on the spot that they should attack the police station. A supply line rapidly took shape, and as in other confrontations, people at the back miraculously sent to the front what the frontline militants wanted: fires, bottles, bricks, umbrellas, and gasoline. There followed rounds of attacks and counterattacks—Molotov cocktails and arrows by protesters and tear gas and rubber bullets by the police. Wai had never seen so many people injured, including South Asian youngsters. He himself was shot in the thigh and was helped to the side by first-aid medics who bandaged his wounds so he could hobble back to the front line. Then, without warning, the riot police came rushing out of the Mongkok station in a mad dash at the protesters. As he was running and approaching a roadblock that was set unusually high, Wai saw a fallen bro who could not climb over due to an injury. As the police charged from several hundred yards away, Wai's first instinct was to carry the boy on his back. The bro urged him to flee for his own life, but Wai refused. "I cannot leave you here, no matter what," he replied, and both had tears rolling down their faces. In the end, they got away from the chase, and first-aiders attended the bro's injury. Wai rested a bit and went back for several more rounds of attacks. He was overwhelmed that, "Our spirit was at the highest because we had a definitive goal that day—to divert police force away from CUHK. This was the kind of solidarity and mutual care I so aspired to in a liberated Hong Kong."[21]

Wai took pains to emphasize that the essence of a brave warrior was not the gear but an all-in determination and fearless fighting spirit, something he found to be in short supply among frontline fighters during the six months of protests. He deplored that "If all the people were determined to charge at the riot police, who should be scared, us or the police? But too many times in critical moments in the fight, the so-called brave warriors turned away just seconds after agreeing to surge forward. Among the three thousand or so people at the PolyU battle, I guess not more than three hundred had the will to die for the revolution. Most people were there with a playful attitude, just for the halo, for taking selfies to post online. I have seen that Hong Kongers actually did not have the will to sacrifice for the revolution. We do not yet have the determination to launch a revolution. Looking back, even I had not done enough."[22] After several days inside PolyU, and realizing the futility of fighting alongside people without determination, he decided to quit. His teammates plotted several escape routes for him to try, and he eventually got out by jumping from bridges, hanging onto train power lines, sustaining deep wounds in his feet, and outrunning the armed police.

Martin: For the Love of Our Land

A couple of weeks after the battle at CUHK, Martin was still intermittently breaking into coughing fits from the countless rounds of tear gas he had inhaled since June 12, most recently at No. 2 Bridge, the front line of the clash

4.5 A police vehicle burned as protesters and police clashed on a bridge at Hong Kong Polytechnic University on November 17, 2019.
CREDIT: Anthony Kwan / Getty Images

in mid-November. A twenty-two-year-old senior in the social sciences at the university, Martin was shot in the head by the police using a new variety of rubber bullets on November 14. It was a long day of fighting. Tear gas began at around one in the afternoon, and after the futile attempt by the university president to negotiate a ceasefire around seven, there was a shower of tear gas canisters from the sky. Martin recalled, "when they [the police] used up the old rubber bullets, they used the new ones which had harder shells. My helmet was dented. I had a concussion, nauseating, nearly lost consciousness for five minutes or so. Some first-aiders pulled me to an emergency aid station. They were crying, worried about my safety. It's very moving to see how they genuinely cared."

Martin, a cohort older than Wai, traced his political baptism to the Umbrella Movement and especially the Fish Ball Revolution in 2016. During Umbrella, he studied for his college entrance exam in the makeshift study room in Admiralty, sometimes even claiming sick leave from school in order to stay overnight. But he was more attracted to the Mongkok site, where he heard militant people who would later form the Hong Kong Indigenous.

Criticizing the futility of carnival-like protests by the nonviolent camp, influential radicals affiliated with the online media site Passion Times were already advocating the need to physically combat violence, to use "bodybuilding to save Hong Kong." Martin recalled proposals at that time about the need for armed struggle to protect Hong Kong, but he did not anticipate it would happen so soon, in 2019. But it was Edward Leung of the Hong Kong Indigenous who had the most influence on him. Recalling his stint as a volunteer for Leung's election campaign in 2016, Martin was certain that "Edward should still recognize me if he sees me. Unlike the pan-democrats who only care about getting elected, his platform shows that he's thinking about Hong Kong's independence and our future generations. Back then, he already talked about building salinization plants to replace buying water from China. I see in him a composite of Hong Kongers, oppressed by China and the regime." Martin witnessed the Mongkok riot—and the Hong Kong Indigenous "blew the whistle" that called on people to join—and he saw a straight line between then and now. To him 2019 was the flower of the seeds sown by Fish Ball: "By refusing to launch any investigation into the root causes of the riot, the government chose to gloss over the deep-seated reservoir of intense animosity among the younger generation toward China. Not just that, 2019 was an endgame for us. There'd be no return. The regime had raised the stake of the game. If they passed the antiextradition law, it meant the legal system would collapse. They could use the law and the court as protective gear to denounce and indict any political opposition."

Like Wai, Martin was not born a brave warrior, and he admitted feeling mortifyingly scared of the police at the beginning: "Tear gas fell like rain that day (June 12). I could totally feel their full intention to kill us. My legs kept trembling . . . there was nothing except some trash and random objects between me and the riot police. But with more practice, my fear dissipated. Soon, I have no qualms about fighting." His small team was made up of half a dozen schoolmates at CUHK, bonded by their shared conviction and presence at the Mongkok riot. Normally, they never talked about their political past, let alone sensitive events such as Fish Ball. But in the dorm, after some beers, Martin and his friends "just unintentionally spill your secrets, and then we realized we were already fellow travelers in 2016. . . . In every action, one of us will always stay behind at the radio station, to collect and screen real-time information. We don't use our personal phones, only very cheap throw-away knock-offs. Same with SIM cards, only disposable unregistered numbers. We exercise a lot of caution to avoid being tracked down. We'd take very convoluted routes to return to CUHK after each action and try changing clothes at each. Say from Admiralty, we'd make three to four extra stops, first to Chai Wan, then take the ferry to Kowloon City, then to Shatin, then to CUHK. But the police are cunning. Once we were caught off guard when thirty Raptors suddenly jumped out of a white van coming from nowhere. We had to jump over water-filled barricades which were quite high. Fortunately, people in our team play varsity sports and are in good shape. I have learned tae kwon do and know which part of the enemy's body to hit. Once a Raptor hit me hard with his baton and snatched me by my backpack. I hit his nose, and he had to let go of my backpack. I know from my martial art training that the nose is the most vulnerable part of the human face."

Martin and his team not only upgraded their gear as police violence intensified but also continued to train rigorously. When they saw an increasing number of protesters being shot in the legs and arms, they began adding combat armor for legs and arms to their gear and practiced running with the armor on campus. The training paid off during the PolyU siege, when they had to climb a high wall and some trees to escape pursuit. Like Wai, Martin also bemoaned the lack of real brave warriors: "That day in Shatin, at the Sha Yan Bridge, there were twenty Raptors but two hundred protesters. Had we all dared to charge at them, guess who would fall off the bridge into the water? We have not applied our maximum impact. The proportion of militants to civilians was still too imbalanced, about one to nine. Many a times, we the militants were constrained and trapped by the civilian masses blocking our escape."

As police escalated from dispersion to kettling and arrests, Martin's team abandoned trench warfare in favor of guerrilla tactics, even though some protesters were still obsessed with positional war, which lent them an illusion of accomplishment. They even tried vigilantism once, attacking a lone policeman, blinding him with a hemp bag, and beating him up, an action that took two months of planning and was extremely scary for the team. What drove Martin to use violence? His response, echoing many others I have come to know, boiled down to his love for Hong Kong and his desire to fight for its future. This was, in his eyes, exactly what the police lacked and hence was their weakness: "Yes, the police was a thirty-thousand-strong force. But what made them fight was money, sheer financial interest. We don't have to kill them all. The death of one or two will scare them because they don't have the will to put themselves in harm's way. We are different: we have beliefs. Like the motto of the antigovernment movie *V for Vendetta*, 'Behind the mask there is an idea, and ideas are bulletproof.'"²³

After 2016, Martin was so despondent about Hong Kong that he only thought about leaving to get a higher degree in a foreign country. But something in him had changed by 2019. He surprised himself by discovering how attached he was to the place: "You know Lo Wai Chung [former police chief] was my high school alum, and Tang Bing-keung [current police chief] lived in my dorm when he was a CUHK student. I felt so ashamed and baffled by their behavior that I called up my secondary school teacher one day. I cried uncontrollably over the phone, asking why these guys could forget what our school had taught them. I realized I was so deeply attached to this city. I even find myself appreciating sunsets in Hong Kong. So much of my memories are here—my first dates, drinking overnight with friends to celebrate admission to CU—and I have seen and felt so much love because of 2019. Despite what people say about social polarization, I have seen unprecedented solidarity and care. Now when I go to 'yellow' restaurants, people would ask if young people like us have enough to eat and urge us to be careful. Who would imagine Hong Kongers to be so caring? On Telegram, there are people providing emotional support to strangers. They talked to me all night long when I was down. I have bipolar disorder, and I appreciate this support. I know it sounds trite and contrived, but this is how I feel: I am willing to sacrifice to protect this city, to defend it, to protect the idea of Hong Kong. Even if I fall or am arrested, I am convinced others would fill my place.... Hatred against the police could at most be an ignitor, a burning aid. It cannot replace the fire itself. Nor can negative feelings of guilt or sadness for imprisoned martyrs. You need a positive force to sustain the fire. For me, it's love, the love to protect and defend this land."

An episode during the CUHK battle illustrated his sense of affective belonging and a natural obligation to protect Hong Kong. After the police fired tear gas on campus, a large number of protesters and alumni rushed to CUHK to reinforce the students' defense. The militants among them did what they had always done, setting up barricades with any materials they could find. When a few of them started demolishing school buses and axing and burning old trees near Bridge No. 2 to make barricades, Martin intervened to stop them. He had feelings "for each grass and each tree," and he recalled saying "You don't have to kill this tree. You could go cut out the wire fences along train station. . . . Sometime later, other outsiders brought along ten or so light pound gas tanks, planning to bomb Bridge No. 2. We from CUHK and they the outsiders had a long and heated discussion about whether this was necessary. In the end, we convinced them bombing and destroying CUHK amounts to bombing and destroying the safe house for bros and sisses because many brave warriors returned to the dorms on campus after each action. They finally agreed to abandon that plan."

Returning again to the idea of love, Martin underscored that "We are gambling with our lives and future. Who'd not prefer risk-free struggle? But under the current circumstances, there is no room for cost-benefit calculation. If Hong Kong becomes another Shenzhen, what kind of future is that for us? How can you stand seeing your own place degenerate? Once you ask if the cause is worth your sacrifice, then it is not worth your sacrifice. Because if you truly love something, you'd not even ask that question of opportunity cost."

The Dragon Slayers and the V Team

The Dragon Slayers, whom the police referred to as "hard-core rioters," were young men in their early twenties infamous for their Molotov attacks on the Raptors and police stations. They formed a group in response to a call to protect black bloc protesters by patrolling streets in Tseun Wan in early August. These patrols followed an indiscriminate attack on citizens by white-shirt thugs, widely believed to have been summoned by pro-establishment elments, on July 21 and another assault in Tsuen Wan in early August. From a vigilante group, they grew into a legendary team of twenty to thirty members known for assaulting on- and off-duty police, rescuing arrested protesters, and setting fire to patrol cars, police stations, and police living quarters.[24] They emphasized inflicting only "effective" violence, that is, force that was targeted at increasing the cost of governance to the regime and the police. Violence should not be for "meaningless" emotional release or pure vengeance. They denounced vigilante justice against blue-ribbon citizens, colloquially teased by young protesters as "elderly junkies." They dismissed the widespread vandalism of the Starbucks and Maxims chains during the movement, arguing that they did not exert any pressure on the government. Famously, one of the team's leaders, twenty-one-year-old George, ridiculed the "fake" valiants as "boy scouts," aimlessly wasting precious Molotov supplies to hit dead objects or burn trash and barricades. George scorned them as, "'half-baked' brave warriors in full gear in the front line, arguing and fighting about charging or retreating. Once they saw the police and tear gas, they would flee like scarred chickens and dogs. We were there not to practice running; we should do real work! Either you give it all, or you should not do it at all."[25]

Another frontline militant team, the V Team, who claimed responsibility for assaulting an off-duty policeman, vowed to limit their targets to the police force, not their families or offspring. The team's Telegram administrator, Victor, explained in an eight-thousand-word manifesto addressed to all Hong Kongers, "We are a revolutionary party, an independent army, and not terrorists. Only Communists and terrorists would attack people based on their family background. During the Cultural Revolution, the mother of our team's second-in-command was beaten and denounced because her parent was a school teacher.... Our team will only kill Hong Kong police. No terrorism. If we kill their families, then we would be reenacting the Cultural Revolution."[26]

Like the Dragon Slayers, Victor's group saw the necessity for violence if the movement was to continue: "Many opinion leaders issuing instructions from their airconditioned rooms preach restraints on the use of force. The result is Hong Kongers have lost hope and cannot see a pathway to victory. They just repeat a cycle: peaceful marches, attacks, more marches, and more attacks. Suppressing our use of force does not bring less casualties. Look at the number of self-immolations in Tibet or deaths in Northern Ireland. The way to victory is not to set up therapy channels or social work groups.... If you are thinking about committing suicide, please join our revolutionary army which is more meaningful than just seeking death. This is a protracted war. An armed force is a sine qua non of a revolution."[27]

In throwing their youthful lives into the uprising and risking their future to confront an overpowering adversary, the most militant of the militants were actually a cool-headed bunch. George of the Dragon Slayers team surmised that they were fighting an unwinnable war: "From the beginning we knew we would certainly lose; we did not stand a chance of beating the Chinese Communist Party. We could not even topple the police, let alone the Communist regime. In their eyes, we were just kids playing with sand.... The best and the worst outcome was scorched-earth. This is the only thing we could achieve." No matter how passionately Hong Kongers chanted "Liberate Hong Kong, revolution of our times," the Dragon Slayers were clear eyed about Hong Kongers' entrenched conservatism: "Mainstream society has never been psychologically and materially prepared to dismantle the regime. Making a revolution is only a pipe dream in Hong Kong.. Our goal is to wake more folks up. We are just a dozen people. We can't hold on for too long. We all have our own dreams but we are willing to sacrifice these because we know without freedom, we cannot realize anything."[28]

Sacrifice was real; their lives were on the line. Their penchant for high-risk action made them frequent targets of the Raptors. Riot police had shot sponge grenades at the team from a short range of fifteen feet, aiming at their chests and faces. One of them was seriously injured by rubber bullets, leaving a big hole at the back of his head. First-aid workers told him that he would have died on the spot if he'd lost any more blood. After several months of sticking their necks out, the Dragon Slayers were forced to disband—some were arrested, while others self-exiled to Taiwan, Australia, or Canada. They made a public announcement about their dissolution in order to stop several fraudulent fundraising campaigns using their name.

Victor of V Team was more sanguine about the revolution: "In response to the police use of unlimited violence, our side has to use even more force in order to tip the balance in our favor. . . . Death and freemen's blood were the price for democracy and revolution." How to beat the CCP? Theirs was a long-term plan to build military capacity for Hong Kong, in part by organizing military training in Taiwan and the United States. Pointing to historical examples gave Victor the conviction that "We are already bigger than what Sun Yat-sen had at the beginning of his career; Che had only twenty men when he launched a guerrilla war in Cuba, and the CCP was founded by twelve people. So we hope to build alliance with other small teams who are willing to sacrifice their lives. Don't belittle yourself. Every regime was started by a few people at the beginning."[29]

On the LIHKG platform, discussions on how to use violence also revealed a persistent concern with self-imposed limits and principles for the use of force. The focus of netizens' discussions shifted as the movement went deeper into the tunnel of violence. A post in mid-August, with 2,016 likes, introduced the political scientist Erica Chenoweth's finding that nonviolent protests are twice as likely to succeed as armed movements (53 percent versus 26 percent). Her tantalizing claim that it takes the participation of around 3.5 percent of a population to bring about serious political change was used by many to urge restraint.

Around that time, vandalism against pro-China businesses went wild, sometimes causing fires that affected nearby residents. LIHKG posts cautioned that the movement could not afford to open another line of battle with public opinion. Protesters then came up with a tricolor rule: "Renovate the Red; Boycott the Blue; Punish the Yellow." The prescription was to sabotage "Red" capital, or Chinese state-owned companies; to boycott blue shops for supporting the CCP; and to "punish" (meaning to make them work harder) pro-democracy yellow shops by patronizing them. Around the same time, a LIHKG post receiving 5,778 likes and 278 dislikes advocated "war disciplines":

> After tonight, does anyone feel that the frontline brothers need a set of military rules? For examples: 1. No beating of journalists; 2. No beating of medical workers; 3. No use of laser pointers or flashlights in the absence of black police; 4. No abuse or torture; 5. No attack on ordinary citizens. Even if this is a war, discipline is of utmost importance to any army. Otherwise, one or two stupid things can destroy [the movement]. When it is a round of peaceful and rational protest, be peaceful and rational. When it is the time for militant protests, then be militant thoroughly.[30]

In short, to the frontline militants, violence was as unnatural as it was demanding. It had to be learned through a deliberate process of overcoming fear, disciplining the body, and sustaining a will to sacrifice. While many talked about their hatred and the desire to take revenge on the police, they made no reference to the cathartic effect of violence, which according to Franz Fanon, frees the colonized from their feeling of inferiority and humiliation.[31] Instead, for the Hong Kong youth, taking up violent resistance was a rite of passage not of their own choosing but an inevitable necessity when their homeland was under attack. They were fighting for their own future in an endgame that had a now-or-never urgency. To justify their use of violence against the regime (police officers, government buildings, pro-China business properties, and public properties such as surveillance cameras and traffic lights), some of them referenced the historical struggles by Nelson Mandela, Malcom X, Che Guevara, Sun Yat-sen, and the people of Ukraine and South Korea. In their action, out of both moral and political considerations, the brave warriors took pain to stipulate limits to violence so that, as the political theorist Michael Walzer would insist, their war against violence would be "just" and "legitimate." At every stage of the movement, the most popular posts on LIHKG always cautioned against violence for violence's sake. Those principles and reasonings delineated a specific symbolic and moral order marking "us," Hong Kong, and "them," the regime. Setting these moral boundaries on social media platforms did not preclude attacks that violated these rules, behavior which would then trigger rigorous denunciations from within the movement.[32]

Second, as illustrated by the open letters of the most militant teams, the brave warriors also intended violence to be more than an instrument to incur higher costs of governance on the regime. It was also, echoing Georges Sorel, used to amplify the moral demands of revolutionary action: "[Violence] provokes hostility, it inspires, it educates and prompts further action. Violence thus moves from being a mere tactical instrument sometimes called upon to facilitate change to being a key element in the moral transformation of humanity. It becomes a means of tutoring and transforming . . . governed by the emerging revolutionary, heroic ethos."[33] And as seen earlier in this chapter, many citizens who showed up in various protests were indeed affected by this ethos of self-sacrifice realized through violence.

Against Market Violence

The antiextradition movement reached an apogee during the bloody month of November. On November 8, a twenty-two-year-old university student, Chow Tsz-lok, died after a mysterious fall from a parking lot near where the police fired multiple rounds of tear gas, rubber bullets, and beanbag rounds to disperse protesters. In a "citizen's press conference" held by protesters following the news of Chow's death, demonstrators said, "In this tragic moment, we plead to all to bear in their heart and mind who the real culprits behind Tsz-lok's death were. His fall was not an unfortunate accident. It was an intentional manslaughter executed by tyranny and the police force."[34] Grief and anger overtook the city, and the public called for a general strike on November 11. In an operation code-named "Dawn," a term taken from the first line of the newly composed Hong Kong protest anthem, "Glory to Hong Kong," protesters self-mobilized to form small teams in different neighborhoods from across the territory to disrupt traffic and set up roadblocks to prevent people from going to work. For instance, a small group of Tseung Kwan O residents who met on a Telegram channel named "TKO dessert club" ambushed a bus terminal in the area and spray-painted the exterior rearview mirrors of all the buses to stop their operation that day. Subway passengers took part in the action by activating emergency alarms in each station, stopping the movement of trains. That day, Molotov cocktails hit police stations in Mongkok where water cannons and armored vehicles marched down the length of Nathan Road, and subway stations were vandalized. Students at CUHK blocked the Tolo Harbor highway, a major artillery connecting the New Territories and Kowloon, leading to serious clashes with the police, who fired more than two thousand tear gas cannisters, a record in a single day. Then came the PolyU siege, where parents and citizens from eleven to eighty-three years old were seen throwing bricks, and many were injured during their rescue action against the police. The arrest of one thousand citizens on November 18 was the largest in a single day since the protests began.

Out of this whirlwind of bloody violence and mounting injuries came a clarion call to open a new frontier for the resistance movement to continue in a less deadly manner. This new sense of urgency "to stop sending people to the guillotine," as the saying at that time went, spurred the rise of a consumer movement called the "yellow economy" and a new union movement to bring about a general strike. Both movements had to work against the grain of Hong Kongers' sacrosanct beliefs in free-market rationality and a strong work ethic (which ruled out absenteeism). But 2019 was such a moment of total rupture that people were compelled, even eager, to jettison or revise old norms and experiment with new ones.

Political Consumerism

There were two types of political consumption during the 2019 protests: boycotting "blue" (pro-China and antimovement) and "Red" (Chinese-owned or China-backed) businesses and buycotting "yellow" (pro-democracy, pro-movement) ones. Before the notion of a "yellow economy" emerged as a political campaign, some restaurants along the route of the two mass demonstrations in June voluntarily handed out bottled water to protesters, while a dozen businesses joined the first call for a market strike on June 12. The following months saw more businesses spontaneously offering donations to relief funds supporting arrested citizens and restaurants installing Lennon Walls for customers to express their solidarity with the movement. A more systematic effort to identify and classify businesses according to their political orientation began in early October, followed by citizens with IT expertise developing mobile apps, directories, and Facebook pages for consumers. Like other aspects of this movement, information about the political color of these businesses was based on crowdsourcing. Netizens classified them based on interior decor, conversations with staff, or social media posts by the owners. Popular interest in the yellow economy grew as clashes intensified on the streets. One study found that social media mentions of the Chinese terms for "boycott" and "buycott" surged in July and August as physical conflict at the protest sites increased, with obvious spikes registered right after the most egregious uses of police force: July 21, August 31, and October 1.[35] Among protesters, as many as 90 percent of respondents in on-site surveys boycotted blue or "Red" businesses and 70–80 percent spent their money in yellow businesses from September to December 2019.[36] In the general population, some 38.5 percent of respondents said they would consider a shop's political affiliation.[37]

According to one of the largest yellow economy databases, Yellowbluemap, there were over six thousand businesses classified as "yellow" as of March 2021; 40 percent of these were restaurants, and the others consisted of industries such as retail, transport, real estate, service, and grocery.[38] Contrary to the blue businesses, which were typically large conglomerates or chain corporations, yellow businesses were locally owned small establishments that, as the protests evolved, also developed connections to each other. Hence the notion of a "yellow economic circle," which went beyond individual-level consumption to include broader visions of the economy. The most widely discussed ideas included an economic system in which all pro-government shops were eliminated from the market; a pro-movement, anywhere-but-China supply chain for retailers; training and employment opportunities for young protesters by pro-movement employers; a "yellow cybercurrency"; and even a sovereign fund. While there was no way to quantify the scale of the yellow economy, given its amorphous boundary, one incident was suggestive of its potential. On May 1, 2020, netizens organized a Hongkonger's 5.1 Golden Week campaign to promote spending at yellow shops, echoing the movement's overall slogan, "Five demands, not one less." It was declared a spectacular success when more than four hundred thousand consumers patronized 2,300 yellow shops, bringing in more than HK$100 million in revenue and prompting Chinese officials in the Liaison Office to condemn it as a "political kidnap of the economy."[39]

While political consumerism is nothing new globally, it was considered subversive in Hong Kong due to the entrenched creed of free-market capitalism. That was why, when the yellow economy was gathering momentum, government officials and pro-establishment key opinion leaders assailed the political consumption movement as an "irrational," "un-Hong Kong way of doing things." The secretary for commerce and economic development objected to what he called the "protectionist" agenda of the yellow economic circle: "We stand oppose to any kind of international protectionism, any trade barriers among nations. . . . There is no real economic entity in the world which locks itself in a self-imposed prison. This is not Hong Kong's economic principle."[40]

What began as a pragmatic economic proposal to leverage the consumption power of two million citizens (the number of people who came out for the mass demonstration on June 16) to sustain the political movement inadvertently spawned a vibrant public discourse about Hong Kong's core value of free-market competition, one of the four pillars of colonial hegemony. Netizens and movement supporters countered these criticisms by pointing to the irrationality of the monopolistic "Red" economic circle and the political imperative to disrupt the government-business alliance. News reports and academic research documented their anticolonial subjectivity without self-consciously using the term: "It [the yellow economy] is a mutual aid economy that can undermine the hegemony of big real estate and conglomerates"; "If Hong Kong goes under, our business becomes meaningless. That's why we must support Hong Kong's revolution"; "Liberate Hong Kong does not merely mean democratic institutions; we must also change our consumption habits, how we buy, eat, travel and live. In the past we got too used to the existence of big businesses."[41]

For months, grievances against Red capital and big business domination over Hong Kongers' lives and the political significance of building a yellow economy could be heard in shopping malls and public spaces in residential neighborhoods. Citizens took it upon themselves to organize open mic events and community forums to promote yellow shops and shopping guides featuring brands of a wide range of consumer products that were made "anywhere but China." On a Saturday afternoon in January 2020, in the atrium of the buzzling Shatin New Town Plaza, I observed retired schoolteacher Lam Sir deliver a speech on the yellow economy, while a small group of young volunteers handed out flyers about the place of origin of different brands of eggs, diapers, toilet paper, detergent, chocolate, beer, and more. Many elders and shoppers stopped and paid attention, while others milled around the displays of QR codes and directories of yellow businesses posted on the walls nearby.

Lam invited people to "Come look the Facebook page of Yellow Economic Front! Come check out these QR codes to find out which brands of shower gel, beers, and chocolate have no contents from mainland China. And don't forget the apps Hong Kong Conscience Guide and the Yellow Blue Business Map. Just press the apps on your phone and they show you all the yellow shops near you. If you don't know how to download, our young volunteers here will help you. . . . I am sure you will be happier if you spend money on yellow businesses. Is it against the principle of free economy? Of course not. It is always our free will which decides how to spend our money. In fact, there has always been a Red economy all around us already, even though it never identifies itself as such. Think about the bookstores you go to; there are all owned by China-controlled companies which do not carry books supportive of the movement. By supporting the yellow economy, we help the movement." About a hundred people applauded him when he was done. Then, the Italian-language teacher and tenor Stefano Lodola, who often showed up at rallies to sing protest arias, performed an Italian version of "Glory to Hong Kong" to the delight of the crowd.

The academic Brian Fong, who was one of the initiators of a new business association among yellow small and medium enterprises, best articulated the political significance of the yellow economy. He wrote, "The rise of the yellow economy marks the awakening of petty capital that has not been part of the ruling coalition between government and big business. Many of them have abandoned their past political conservatism and come out since the movement. They have shaken loose Hong Kong's political economic structure cemented since the 1980s. If we could organize the yellow economic circle, thousands of businesses could together mobilize upward of a million consumers. This would become a gigantic force that can alter the dynamic of the struggle between society and the regime. It may lead to a breakthrough in the democracy movement and a crack at our entrenched class structure."[42]

The campaign was not without controversy. From the beginning, some people asked pointed questions: If yellow shops had harsh labor conditions, were they still yellow? Were yellow shops exploiting the sufferings of protesters for their own profits, or, in colloquial terms, "eating buns made with human blood"? With time, volunteer-run online shopping platforms encountered management, logistics, and financial problems. Some had to close after incidents of fraud fatally damaged their reputation and credibility. But the biggest blow to the yellow economy was police and government harassment in the form of endless inspections and citations. After the enactment of the National Security Law in July 2020, the protest-themed decorations inside many yellow businesses were at risk of being criminalized as "inciting and/or abetting others for the commission of secession and subversion."[43] Still, the yellow economy as a political consumption movement represented a rare awakening of the general public to the market violence inflicted by the structural domination of the government–big businesses alliance. Even though they were not consciously deploying the language of decolonial struggle and were not inspired by ideology or theory, their pragmatic action to build a yellow economy was anticolonial in its political effect.

The New Union Movement

Like the yellow economy campaign, the new union movement had its beginning in the early days of the antiextradition movement. But it was not until the mass arrests and injuries in the wake of the battles at the two universities that it picked up substantial momentum. The rationale was that unions were still a legal institution, endorsed by the Basic Law and Hong Kong's labor law, not to mention a powerful organizational weapon to achieve an elusive goal of the movement: a general strike. By early 2020, some 45 openly pro-movement new unions were formed. Official statistics showed that 1,600 unions were waiting for official approval in the first quarter of 2020, a "tsunami-like surge" that, according to the labor minister, would take his staff fifty years to process.[44] For these new unions, a major goal was the general strike. Netizens had made three attempts, on August 5, September 2–3, and November 11, for a citywide "triple strike," that is, labor, school, and market strikes, with varying degrees of public support. An estimated 350,000 employees called in sick or used their personal leave to join the first strike. Some 40,000 people showed up in rallies on the second, and widespread disruptions of public transportation on November 11 prevented many from getting to their workplaces. Yet the general populace had always been divided on the rationale of a general strike. On the one side was the argument that the vast majority of the working class could not afford the financial cost of absenteeism and the likely retribution by employers. On the other, supporters argued that if young protesters were willing to dodge bullets and sacrifice their future for Hong Kong, why would the public not reciprocate with a one-day strike?

True to form, the new union movement was the result of anonymous, decentralized, self-mobilized efforts. In the first days of the 2019 movement, young activists of the Hong Kong Confederation of Trade Unions (HKCTU), an independent alliance of some sixty affiliated unions with a total membership of 160,000, were braced for an imminent political storm. On June 12, milling around the tens of thousands of protesters encircling the LegCo Complex, they handed out flyers with legal rights and postarrest assistance information on one side and propaganda about union formation and strikes as a method of resistance on the other. Disagreeing with HKCTU senior management's assessment of popular support for a strike, these young unionists, in their late twenties and mid-thirties and more in tune with the pulse of the streets, patiently planted calls for unionism on Telegram channels. They leveraged the surge in popular anger after each political incident and netizens' spontaneous initiatives to find "fellow travelers" (a code word for movement supporters) in the same occupation to brainstorm possible collective action. By the time of the first strike in early August, a Save Hong Kong platform already connected twenty-four Telegram groups organized along occupational or sectoral lines.

In early October, a group called Two Million Three Strikes, an interunion front, appeared on Telegram. The initiators included two sophomores in a local university and a graduate student just returning from his studies abroad. Without any actual experience in union organizing, and not knowing each other, these "commanders in air-conditioned rooms," a nickname given by street protesters, were able to ride the waves of popular desperation to promote action items on social media. Gabriel, a skinny, nerdy, and bookish twenty-year-old with a short ponytail, was inspired by the many online signature campaigns among college and high school students. He believed there was a reservoir of self-organizing energy among the young and that a platform would add wind to the fire of occupational networking. Soon, the young activists of the HKCTU met in person with him and others who until then were just online personas with fictitious names. A spirited and affable group, fluent in both Rosa Luxemburg's mass strike theory and Cantonese foul vocabulary, with sophisticated taste buds for Japanese sake and fine whiskey, they talked a lot about "imaginaries"—setting up a new union every week, joining forces with students and yellow businesses, unionism without unions, and occupational visions for a postliberation Hong Kong. They had to toe a fine line between being mistaken for the commanding leadership disavowed by the movement and providing logistical infrastructure and bureaucratic assistance for union formation. Their efforts paid off. After November 2019, street booths for new unions, adorned with banners bearing their names and providing a human contact point for curious potential members and the concerned general public, became a common sight in downtown and residential neighborhoods. Internally, the Two Million Three Strikes alliance instilled a culture of cross-union dialogue, refurbishing the image of trade unions long jettisoned as irrelevant and outdated.

The novelty of the new unions stemmed from their middle-class roots and their brand of political unionism. The vast majority of the forty-five new unions joining the Two Million Three Strikes alliance hailed from the professions. The most active were unions representing nurses and medical personnel; therapists; IT experts; accountants; financial workers; designers; public relations and communications specialists; aviation, hotel, and tourism employees; engineers; civil servants; white-collar employees and clerks; marketing employees; bartenders; and performance artists. All the unions began with a Telegram channel for people to sign up. According to one of the initiators of the IT channel, "Almost immediately after I opened the channel, some three thousand people signed up, and over a hundred expressed an interest in forming a union. People's original motivation was only political—to further the movement. In our profession, we do not have conventional labor issues such as wage default or industrial safety. The major grievance is the lack of overtime compensation. Soon, people begin to realize how underpaid they are when they talk within the channel about their salaries. One solution is salary transparency."[45]

With college degrees and professional qualifications, these unionists were articulate, savvy, and independent thinkers and organizers. Some were inspired by the Umbrella Movement and had dabbled in new party politics in its aftermath. Others were political freshmen prompted to act by a strong sense of natural justice and a desire to defend their city. Eddie, the thirty-something chair of the financial employees' union, was clear about the group's two priorities: the political movement and labor rights. An actuary by training who was now working for an international bank, Eddie was pleasantly surprised that his members, in their first general meeting, approved a political strike. He explained, "In Hong Kong, finance absorbs the crème de la crème. We have global knowledge and know how unreasonable it is that the government has been using institutional violence of the law to repress young people's political aspirations. We all have grudges but because of our family responsibilities, we cannot join the fight in the front line. But in our heart, we want to contribute, using our professional voice, to criticize the government and to protect Hong Kong's interest. That interest is our interest because we cannot make money without it."

During interunion meetings, amid sparks of merriment, contention, and jaunty curses, Eddie's tone was always serious, bordering on arrogant. His assertiveness probably came from his experience as a founding member of Youngspiration, one of the political parties formed after the Umbrella Movement. Self mockingly he recalled "At that time, we still believed in fighting an electoral battle, not a union struggle." He quit the party due to disagreements with the leadership. The Telegram group called "Financial Sector Fellow Travelers" was the catalyst for the formation of the Financial Industry Employees General Union in 2019. What Eddie described as the unhealthy professional ecology in finance reflected the general discontent of other professional sectors such as IT, accounting, and design: "My working hours are 8 a.m. to 9 p.m., and weekend, all without overtime salary. Because our hours are so insanely long, our hourly rate is lower than that of taxi drivers! I see my Australian counterparts getting off from work on time and never reply to emails after 5 p.m. Why? Because they have unions." But the biggest threat was the repression by corporations, especially Chinese corporations: "What Chinese capital wanted to suppress is our professional consciousness. Finance employees in Hong Kong have a strong professional identity and attitude. You cannot bribe me to betray my professional judgment in order to write a good report for your company. This is the fundamental reason Shanghai and Shenzhen cannot replace Hong Kong as a global financial center. Our professional culture is very entrenched, but China is a society used to making knockoffs and copycats. Chinese capital has now controlled half of the financial sector, and Chinese employers still do not understand why Hong Kong financial professionals are so 'stubborn.' The Bank of Communications' attack and dismissal of its chief economist, Law Kachung, is a good example. He was dismissed for voicing his professional research-based assessment that the Hong Kong economy was hit more by SARS in 2003 than the protests of 2019. If the numbers in your reports are not what they'd prefer to see, they'll punish you."[46]

To many activists, unionism was an extension of the antiextradition movement. An energetic and expressive group of speech therapists' union organizers summed this up succinctly, saying to me, "No antiextradition, no new unions. As simple as that. Before the movement, we had zero interest in strikes, and we did not know what unions were. We felt it was not for us."[47] Its core leadership consisted of seven twentysomething, newly minted professional speech therapists, all recent graduates of the University of Hong Kong. Earning twice the salary of average college graduates and buoyed by a tight labor market with high demand for their expertise, they admitted they had no discontent at work. Moreover, before 2019, they ridiculed unions as "plastic" (a Cantonese slang for dogmatic, rigid, and unappealing) and a hopeless vehicle for politics. In their minds, "Unions are part of the institution. And the Labor Party even embraces the idea of Greater China." The union chair had her first political experience in waging a successful "anti-Red" campaign at the University of Hong Kong, reversing the domination of the student union by mainland Chinese students. After this first taste of success, she was active in the democracy deliberation days proposed by the law professor Benny Tai in preparation for his Occupy Central campaign in 2013–2014. After the failure of Umbrella and especially Edward Leung's electoral disqualification and imprisonment for the Mongkok riot, she shunned "institutional resistance." In 2019, the airport sit-in and subway blockades were a revelation to her and her peers, as they recalled with lingering excitement, "We realized if people do not go to work, a lot of manpower can be released for the movement!" But their profession was small—only about 1,200 graduates in speech therapy in the city—and their colleagues, whom they said were second-best wannabe dentists and doctors, were obsessed with maintaining stability. Still, they saw a niche for their union: "We have discursive capacity. We can explain and express." Indeed, no one could have imagined that such an innocuous aspiration would one year later lead to the arrest of five of them. Their crimes? Conspiring to publish and distribute three "seditious" children's books depicting protesters as sheep and police as wolves.[48]

In some professions, more than one new union emerged to represent different political visions. Accountants, for instance, could choose between the one emphasizing member interests and playing the institutional game and the other advocating strikes, social movements, and building a yellow economy to resist the established "Red" economy. Tellingly, initiators of both accountants' unions were inspired by the mass movement to mobilize fellow professionals to do something about long-standing workplace grievances in the face of big capital and Red capital, which increasingly were becoming one. Extremely long working hours plagued the profession, but there was no "labor" voice within the profession's regulatory body, the Hong Kong Institute of Certified Public Accountants, which was dominated by "blue" (establishment) and "red" interests. One account unionist explained the connection between the profession's labor problem and the political intrusion of Red capital:

> During the peak season, or when I had an IPO [initial public offering] job, my normal working hours are from 10 a.m. to 3 a.m., sometimes even two straight days with only a shower break. Now 80 percent of Hong Kong's listed companies are mainland Chinese. They have a tendency of cutting job prices, ruining the market. You simply can't say no. What we need is a statutory limit of maximum working hours. . . . I speak from my own experience of handling Chinese IPOs in Hong Kong. The auditing standards have been compromised. Our role has changed from a gatekeeper of standards to creative paper pushers. For example, you saw that 23 percent of your client's earning is false. And your boss turns a blind eye. What we have to do is to wander in the grey zone, trying to find ways to change yes to no and no to yes. This amounts to a lot of creative labor, which explains why our work hours are getting longer and longer. China defines national security so broadly it includes the economy. I suspect one of the goals of the National Security Law is to allow it financial governing power.[49]

Even though the other new union in accounting was more oriented to social movements and saw strikes as an important weapon available to them, its leadership saw the possibility of combining labor rights with the larger political agenda of independence from the Red economy. A twenty-nine-year-old accountant who initiated this union was so moved by the acts of solidarity during the storming of LegCo on July 1 that he decided to do something: "That interview by Stand News Sister [nickname of reporter Gywneth Ho] about the girl in tears explaining why they had to rescue the martyrs inside was like a moral calling to me. I said to myself, if those young kids could give up everything, why can't I do a little something?" After recruiting ten fellow workers in accounting, they set their union priority as assisting frontline protesters who had sacrificed their school work and job opportunities. In addition to tutoring young protestors interested in doing auditing work, they came up with a longer-term plan: "To counter the Red economy, we need to grow our own yellow economy. We have developed a job placement platform connecting frontline bros and sisses, unions, and yellow businesses. Here's how it works: yellow businesses which need auditing or accounting services will find yellow local accounting firms which hire and train frontline bros and sisses who are college or secondary school students. Our union councilors thought that this would be a viable path for the movement."[50]

Among the most cherished core values of Hong Kong as an affluent financial and knowledge-driven economy was professionalism—the dispassionate adherence to principles and standards of specialized work defined by international professional communities. In the past few decades, this culture of professionalism had spread to many occupations that now require licenses, certification, and degrees. Employees in a broad array of occupations, such as real estate management, tourism, and construction, go through training that emphasizes professional identities, norms, and standards. During the 2019 protests, the conflict between professionalism and its blatant violation by the "politics in command" of Red capital and the Hong Kong authorities spurred even the apolitical fraction of the professional class into unionism.

A prime example was the real estate employees' union. High-rise condominium managers and security guards were ubiquitous in every private housing development throughout Hong Kong. The Telegram group for this sector was launched on August 1, 2019, and by December 2019, it had 1,300 members. Like many in this industry, Zero, a thirtysomething with a decade's worth of experience managing private residential complexes and one of the union councilors, was career driven but politically agnostic. In 2019, though, he was awakened to the close tie between the movement and his profession. Too many times, police barged into private condominium complexes or shopping malls in search of protesters, all without court permission or registration. There were many examples of police trespassing into private premises to make arrests: "Regency Gardens, Long Ping Court, Ma On Shan shopping mall . . . in Tun Mun's Siu Hing Court, they even made residents squat down and register their names when they looked for suspects. All these violate our professional principle of protecting lives and property of the homeowners. How can we face the homeowners, our clients? On our

BENDING THE ARC OF VIOLENCE 215

Telegram channel, people debated how and when we security managers should control the police who have lost self-control. They [the police] are now the ones who disrupt order. According to the law, even policemen need to register with the security staff, and we have rights to refuse their entry. What is ironic is that in the past, when we called the police in to deal with crimes or offences, they were too lazy to do their job, saying it's security staff's duty in private premises. But today, the same police argue they could enforce law in private property."⁵¹ It did not help that many property management companies in Hong Kong are now owned by mainland or pro-regime corporations.

Similarly, drivers of subway trains formed the new MTR union, Railway Power, as a protest against police attacks on their professional obligations. Station managers and train captains were appalled by what happened on July 21 in the Yuen Long railway station and August 31 in the Mongkok subway station. "How can police allow and use violence within the premises of MTR which always talks up the importance of passenger safety? How dare they storm MTR stations with tear gas in Tai Koo and Kwai Fong? Citizens are outraged by MTR's silence in the face of such violence. They hate us now, which is dangerous for frontline employees. Younger colleagues were angered and concerned. They signed a petition letter to management, but there was no response, no accountability, no explanation. They became the backbone for the preparatory committee. Our average age is twenty-seven. Some of them made a political stance on August 5 by donning a hard hat and gas mask while driving the train," recalled Mike, the union chair, with pride.⁵² Another impetus for setting up a new union was to beat back at the Communist penetration represented by five of the existing seven unions. In the face of these subsidiaries of the pro-China HKFTU, the new unionists wanted to create a countervailing political voice. Rumor had it that pro-China unions had proposed shutting down an MTR station for the first time on August 24 in Kwun Tong to impede protesters escaping from the police.

Partly motivated by the political objective of bolstering the new union movement, activists forming the literary, dramatic, and creative professionals' union also had their sights on using their new union to counter the negative impact of the China factor and the government's cultural policies. In the past two decades, local craft production of stage costumes, props, and lighting had disappeared because labor costs in China were much cheaper. Dependency on China had drastically limited jobs and opportunities for

Hong Kongers, depleting the performing arts of young talent. The government's policy of renting performance venues also strongly favored groups supported by pro-China community organizations, so much so that a local theater group could not compete with elderly singing ladies who used the Tsuen Wan city hall regularly to stage salacious shows, basically to flirt and make money from elderly men's tips. The government gave all its support to the largest eight performing arts companies and none to independent artists. In fact, union discussions regularly brought to light common concerns about Hong Kong's unhealthy dependence on Chinese capital and the government's failure to mitigate sky-high land prices.

Communist-backed HKFTU subsidiaries had long existed in almost all sectors of the labor market. Flushed with seemingly unlimited funding from the HKFTU and pro-Beijing forces, these unions grew a broad-based but passive membership by offering adult and community classes throughout the city, discounts for Chinese medicine and health services, dried goods, supermarkets, banquets, and even home-buying tours to the Pearl River Delta. According to the new unionists, these welfarist unions were like old fossils, invisible and inactive, not interested in recruiting or representing employees, let alone advancing worker interests or confronting employers. Those affiliated with the independent HKCTU were more energetic, especially in assisting workers with wage arrears, hosting press conferences or organizing petitions on labor-related policies, and joining forces with civil society to put pressure on the government. Some of the new unions chose to operate as subsidiaries of HKCTU to take advantage of its legal and secretarial support. Others opted to avoid HKCTU due to its affiliation with the Labor Party and its pan-democratic establishment leadership. The third organized force the new unions had to contend with were the professional societies, which functioned as both regulatory authorities and social clubs. Dominated by senior, high-status, pro-employer employees approaching retirement, and thus with a "harvesters' mentality," the professional societies were unlikely to be a vehicle of change in a time of political crisis. The influx of Red capital also saw the strengthening of pro-Beijing and pro-government representatives in these bodies.

In short, united by a single target—the SAR-Communist regime—these unions opened up a dual political front, both internal and external. First, organizing inside the professions and the workplace brought them face to face with Red capital from China as well as the entrenched professional associations and unions China has long sponsored and penetrated within each sector. From these struggles came an incisive critique of Red capital and government complicity. Oftentimes, their most abiding complaint was not exploitative labor practices but, as the examples above show, the erosion and destruction of professional standards and values. Second, as part of the resistance movement, they sought to instrumentalize unions for the purpose of political strikes to compel concessions from the regime. Shunning formal political parties and bureaucratic unions, their passion was in impactful mobilization. Their political allegiance was to the resistance movement, and the unannounced goal for the most active unionists was "liberate Hong Kong." While these expressions were too risky to be included in their constitutions, they were conveyed by visual symbols on flyers, social media, and websites, featuring the LIHKG piggy, Pepe the frog, the color yellow, hashtags associated with #hongkongprotests, and background sketches of protest slogans and scenes. In the boisterous interunion meetings, heated discussions often revolved around how their strategies might contribute to the political movement.

This localist political aspiration marked them apart from the historical political unionism dominant in pre-1970s Hong Kong. Then, most unions were the local arm of either the CCP on the mainland or the KMT in Taiwan. Their strategies of maintaining allegiance focused on educational, cultural, and welfare services, areas the colonial regime ignored. An independent wing of the union movement, represented first by the CIC (Christian Industrial Committee, established in 1967) and then by the HKCTU (formed in 1990), was oriented toward sectoral interests and workplace rights rather than general political development.[53] This history was not lost on some of the new unionists. A thoughtful and widely circulated commentary written by a member of the new construction and engineers' union reflected on the failure of the CCP's own political unionism in Hong Kong and proposed a path for the new unions. Drawing parallels between the sociopolitical discontent in the 1960s and 2020, this union member concluded that Hong Kong was still in the midst of an "anticolonial struggle":

> In the past, CCP-controlled leftist unions were so obsessed with Maoist thoughts that they squandered the solidarity among workers and became a mere strike machine. This type of unionism fanned the flame of nationalism and ignored workers' interests and rights. When

the CCP withdrew its big stage support, the local unions, unmoored from the masses, lost their directions.... During the 1960s, numerous civilian conflicts with the regime happened due to youth unemployment, workers' harsh livelihood, lack of labor rights protection, and police corruption. All these led to riots, led by the leftists but joined also by groups disaffected by the colonial regime. In 2020, we see wealth gaps, economic inequity, outdated labor law, corrupt police, illegitimate government, and regressive politics. It seems Hong Kong's anticolonial resistance never ends. How can we who pursue universal values and social justice learn from our own historical experience and once gain regain power from the colonialists? How can we, standing on the side of labor, use unions to connect with the masses, raise public concerns about their own labor rights as a means to achieve civic awakening?[54]

In fact, within six months of this article's publication, Hong Kong's new union movement had answered this question with two bittersweet episodes of collective action.

A Historic Strike and a Failed Referendum

The new union movement had its first taste of success when one of its member unions pulled off a political, public interest, and professional strike that also raised public awareness about workers' collective potential. It was a perfect storm fomented by public panic about the arrival of the coronavirus outbreak from the mainland in late January 2020, triggering traumatic memories of SARS in 2003. In both cases, the public was outraged by the government's failure to stem the spread of a public health crisis from China and provide adequate support for frontline medical professionals. This time, in the wake of seven months of mass protests, the fledgling Hospital Authority Employees' Alliance (HAEA) leveraged the wave of popular distrust of the Carrie Lam administration and aligned their professional interests with public interests. Demanding the government close all borders with the mainland, and using the slogan "Strike to Protect Hong Kong," HAEA mixed political and labor rights issues in the five demands they presented to the Hong Kong government: (1) forbid all Chinese travelers from entering Hong Kong; (2) implement constructive measures to ensure a sufficient supply of masks to the public and ensure a safe working environment for its staff; (3) provide sufficient isolation wards and stop all nonemergency services; (4) provide sufficient support and facilitation for health-care staff caring for quarantined patients; and (5) commit publicly not to take any reprisals in retaliation for striking.

The enthusiastic response exceeded even HAEA's expectations. From a membership of two thousand on January 23, when the union called its first emergency general meeting, it grew nine times to become an eighteen-thousand-strong union at the beginning of the five-day strike on February 3. In addition, an opinion poll showed that more than 60 percent of the general public supported the action. A nurse in the strike articulated a general public sentiment at that time: "Legally speaking, we are using the rights to which we are entitled by the Basic Law [Article 27], to freely join the unions and to strike. It relates to our workplace safety! Once more infected patients come to Hong Kong, the risk of medical workers getting infected is higher. We are using our lives to protect citizens' health. We are not afraid of death—since we chose this occupation, we are fully aware of the risks and our responsibility to the patients—but we do not want to be at risk because of the government's inaction.... If this strike has anything to do with politics, I think it is in the sense of getting everyone involved and together pushing the government to prioritize the public's interest [in public health] rather than political considerations [to please the Chinese government]."[55]

Even though the government stopped short of fully closing all Hong Kong's borders with the mainland, it did suspend all land traffic. But when officials and the Hospital Authority did not respond to any of the five demands and the union asked for the mandate to extend the strike, only an inadequate quorum of three thousand voted yes. All told, at its peak, some eight thousand members joined the strike, and HAEA union membership grew to more than twenty thousand in the wake of the action.

In an internal evaluation meeting more than a month after the strike, the dozen or so core leaders still relished the mass support during those miraculous days. Since the union did not yet have a bank account, people had to show up in person with cash in hand to become members. When they called for a strike, they had neither basic supplies—folding tables, handheld amplifiers, or volunteers—nor techniques—speaking to the media, negotiating with the Hospital Authority, or communicating to the public and fellow unions. It was all exhaustion, chaos, and a total lack of division of labor.

Winnie, the chairwoman, laughed in disbelief that she was making endless rounds moving from the membership desk to speaking with reporters to the negotiation table with the head of the Hospital Authority. "We learn to walk and run at the same time," she teased. But who could forget the long queues of nurses and medics, some waiting up to eight hours outside the union's office, to submit membership forms and dues in cash so they could vote for the strike? It was a memorable scene that was also a shot in the arm for other new unions. Winnie's vice-chair, Ivan, reckoned, "It was a huge deal because NHS [National Health Service in the United Kingdom] medics usually only strike for a day or two. Ours was five days!"

However, the majority of union members, the general workforce, and the citizenry were not yet receptive to unions as a weapon for transformative change. Several months after the HAEA strike, an interunion call for a referendum—to oppose the soon-to-be-enacted National Security Law and launch a general strike—revealed the shallow base of the new union movement. In late May, after Beijing floated a draft of the National Security Law that would criminalize civil society activities as sedition or terrorism, the Two Million Three Strikes alliance called an action meeting attended by two dozen new unions. The mood was somber and stoic, without the usual riotous banter. Unionists agreed that they had to make a stand. Eddie, the finance union chair, made a firm announcement that his council had decided to go ahead with a strike, to which a young woman from HAEA echoed with news that her union was ready for another strike and wanted to use this joint action as a mobilizing exercise to grow membership. By and large, they concurred on holding an indoor referendum at a school a church, concentrating all union members who would vote on two motions: opposing the National Security Law and agreeing to call a strike. Their assumption was that if people were upset by the draconian law, they would join the unions in order to endorse a strike, as happened with the HAEA strike.

It was not a promising moment to propose a mass strike. COVID-19 had wreaked havoc on the economy, especially for those in retail, tourism, personal services, and aviation. At the emergency general meeting of the aviation union, flight attendants and ground crews of major airlines were forthcoming about their reservations: "Are we aiming at paralyzing the Hong Kong airspace for a couple of days, to repeat what happened in August? If so, we would need to secure the participation of the very few but very important guys at the control tower. Back then they called in sick and forced one of the runways to shut down. How many of our union members work in the control tower? It does not matter how many of us strike; it matters whether these few strike." Another confessed the painful reality flight attendants were facing during the COVID-19 shutdown, admitting that "I have stopped flying for two months; I was forced to take no pay leave for two months, just staying at home every day. Striking is not a matter of making an emotional assault. In my heart, of course, I totally oppose the National Security Law, but is it realistic to strike now? This is an impossible time." Another member countered, "If only flight attendants strike, there will be zero effect because there are no flights, no passengers at the airport. Our airport is now running at 5 percent capacity. But we should try a 'precision' attack—the cargo and engineering departments can bring the government to its knees. The question is can we convince them?" A voice came from behind, yelling, "No fucking chance. Many of them are deep blue! And they'd ridicule us as crazy to call a strike now." A countervailing argument pushed back: "We will never know what will happen. We all came from the movement, right? Without the brave warriors coming out in June, we would already be living under the extradition law. If we don't try, how do we know we can?"[56]

With the full force of the Communist regime behind its imposition, the National Security Law stoked such widespread fear and paralyzing despair that the strike referendum solicited, unsurprisingly, only an anemic response from the public. Just shy of 9,000 among the 140,000 members of the two dozen unions cast their votes. While 95 percent voted to oppose the new law and to strike, this result fell far short of the unions' own threshold of a two-thirds majority among a targeted total of 60,000 voters. In front of a huge press entourage, union representatives bowed to thank their members and admitted their disappointment and failure: no general strike.

"If We Burn, You Burn with Us"

Under the double weight of the National Security Law and a pandemic-induced recession, the new unions' effort to mobilize a general strike fell flat. But this setback had not dampened the political will of the most committed unionists and other political activists to continue, even escalate, the struggle against Beijing's autocratic control. This time, their combat zone was the legislature—the cornerstone of the regime's institutional power and one that Beijing had deliberately engineered to preempt a democratic majority.

Succinctly summed up in the slogan "35+," the pan-democratic camp's goal was to exploit the aroused political consciousness among the electorate and some wavering liberal politicians to win a simple majority in the seventy-seat legislature in the 2020 territory-wide election, scheduled to take place in September. A pipe dream to many people, this action plan, if realized, would allow the pan-democrats to trigger a political crisis from within the existing constitutional order laid down by the Basic Law.

According to the architect of this audacious campaign, Benny Tai, the following imaginary sequence would unfold once the pan-democrats became the majority in the LegCo. First, they would exercise their constitutional power to veto the government's budget. This would compel the chief executive to dissolve the legislature and call a new election. If the democrats won the majority again, the chief executive would have to resign and trigger a constitutional crisis, at which point the Chinese government, short of agreeing to the democrats' demand for universal suffrage, would likely take direct control over Hong Kong and formally terminate "One Country, Two Systems." In doing so, China would have violated the international treaty it signed with Britain, with the likely consequences of provoking severe international sanctions and a massive popular uprising at home. According to Tai, Hong Kong's odds of autonomous survival were so small that only by pushing China and Hong Kong to this profound crisis would the city and its people stand a chance of finding a way out. "There is no more alternative now that Hong Kong is at the brink. Instead of begging the regime for forgiveness at a cliff's edge, we should proactively fight back, bring it down with us, and see who can find a lifeline during the fall," he lamented in a manifesto-like piece in the *Apple Daily* on April 28, 2020. Tai cautioned that at every step along the way, many uncertainties could derail this mutual destruction strategy. Needless to say, no one could predict how the international community and local people would react to the premature demise of "One Country, Two Systems" in Hong Kong.

Benny Tai's metamorphosis from a moderate law professor committed to defending the rule of law to a civil disobedience advocate and then an institutional warrior embracing mutual destruction, landing him today in prison for ten years, was in many ways the most poignant individual embodiment of wider societal change. Like many Hong Kongers, he had been radicalized by the regime's aggravation of physical and institutional violence. After being marginalized as weak and compromising by the younger generations of activists, he emerged as a radical voice bringing together different factions of the pan-democrats, localists, and independents to wage a last-ditch, and knowingly impossible, effort to legally dislodge China's dominance. The message of the 35+ campaign was clear to the public: the law and political institutions themselves were violent. The erstwhile binary distinction between "lawful institution" as orderly and rational and "violence" as chaos and savage no longer held.

Mutual destruction, or in vernacular Cantonese, *laam caao*, (攬炒) first emerged in late June 2019. A netizen adopting the moniker "I want *laam caao*" on LIHKG came to prominence after he successfully organized a crowdfunding campaign to advertise protesters' demands in dozens of international newspapers, which the next chapter discusses in detail. The idea referred to a high-stakes, scorched-earth strategy in Hong Kong's improbable fight against Beijing. "If we burn, you burn with us" was the slogan the protesters adopted from the movie *The Hunger Games*. "Burnism" was another popular expression for the same protest mentality. The significance of young people's embrace of "burnism" cannot be overstated in a society whose motto had for generations been "stability and prosperity." "Burnism" turned this prized tenet upside down: not only was "stability and prosperity" inadequate as the primary feature of a good society, but in order to have a viable future for Hong Kong, people had to create instability.

Rejecting the primacy of stability and legality was nothing new to the postcolonial generation, who were disheartened by the disqualification of their political leaders in 2016. But it was a cognitive breakthrough to the majority of the citizenry. Some 610,000 voters participated in an unofficial primary among more than fifty pro-democratic candidates supportive of Benny Tai's 35+ campaign.[57] This was a resounding turnout in the face of legal threats by the government and at the height of the COVID-19 pandemic. Many of the candidates explicitly ran on a "burnism" platform. Among them were leaders of the new union movement, including Winnie Yu, the chairwoman of the HAEA who shot to fame during the hospital strike. She could not bring herself to physically fight on the street, but she believed unions and elections were the quintessential institutional means to combat institutional violence. At a meeting about the future of the new union movement, her vice-chair and comrades in arm at HAEA declared their commitment to burnism:

> The HAEA strike told us that people joined us because they wanted to strike and because they wanted to continue the movement. We

4.6 Scorched-earth gamble.
PHOTO CREDIT: Tyrone Siu / Reuters Pictures

attracted members because our banner read "Liberate Hong Kong." So in light of the upcoming election [2021 LegCo], we do not want to see any more compromises with the regime; we want *laam caao*. What unions can do is to encourage members to vote in *laam caao* candidates in order to realize this institutional *laam caao*. But don't forget there is an occupational or sectoral *laam caao*. We need to push people to have visions about what a liberated Hong Kong will be like. Simply put, what an independent Hong Kong will look like. Of course this phrase won't appear in our public statements [*laughs*]. We hope to use the election as a means to stimulate discussion of what each sector should do to achieve the liberation of Hong Kong.[58]

One of the most articulate and committed candidates in the 35+ electoral campaign was thirty-year-old Gwyneth Ho. Widely and endearingly known as Stand News Sister thanks to her viral livestream reporting on the July 1 protesters, Gwyneth famously jettisoned her press card for a shot at the legislature. No one had talked with as much clarity and eloquence about the logic, hope, and demand of "burnism" as resistance to the institutional violence inherent in Hong Kong's electoral system:

We need to nullify the function of LegCo and its zombies who keep assaulting people. Because LegCo is a hurdle for a normal Hong Kong, we need to stop it from sustaining itself. . . . Election has been a black hole: it's a machine that sucks up and wastes our political capacity. I always feel our Umbrella generation has come of age under the logic of traditional democratization. We try to shake it off, expending a lot of internal energy, but cannot totally get away from its inherent conservatism. It has taken us a long time to combat our own or the masses' obsession with nonviolence. On top of that, we are facing a devastating storm from the outside. But, those teenagers today . . . their first political act is already being fire magicians [throwing Molotov cocktails]. That unleashes their political imaginations. They are not constrained by the traditional political environment, even though the cruelest thing is this generation will have to face imprisonment.

We, the so-called Umbrella Generation, are only a transit station. That is, we are the bridge that allows others to jump to a higher level. It's like an old sheep and a young sheep at a cliff, trying to cross to the other side of the valley. If they jump together, both will die. The old one will die anyway, its only value is to jump to the middle, becoming a stepping stone for the young to land on the other side. I don't think the Umbrella Generation will make it, but maybe the next generation. . . . I think the best outcome for this campaign will be we achieve 35+, and even seize the chair position. At that moment, CCP will not be able to tolerate, and may send the police to arrest all of us and charge us with the National Security Law. Our historical significance is to die, and not fucking hang on for a last gasp of life.[59]

Gwyneth was prescient. The Hong Kong government invoked the National Security Law on January 6, 2021, to launch a mass raid at the break of dawn and arrested all fifty-five candidates and organizers participating in the primaries. A month later, on February 28, forty-seven of them were charged with conspiracy to subvert the state, a move that startled local society and the world alike. It was by far the clearest incident of institutional violence Hong Kongers had ever seen—a peaceful primary voting exercise participated in by 610,000 voters was now declared a crime against the state. In May 2023, after pleading not guilty to the charge of subversion, Gwyneth used her testimonial in court to enunciate the goal of the movement and "burnism": "Since July [2019], the essence of the movement was to change the institutional injustice of Hong Kong's political system.... Laam caao is not the goal, but a spirit of knowingly accepting an enormous personal cost, that is to burn oneself, in order to do the right thing.... As people resist, they will at the same time build up something that will end up weakening the regime. In the process, many spaces will be opened up. This is the true contribution of the movement."[60] Found guilty of subversion, Ho was sentenced to seven years in prison in November 2024, while the other forty-four fellow activists received jail terms from four years and two months to ten years.[61]

The 2019 Protests as a Lesson in Violence and Sacrifice

Until 2019, Hong Kong citizens were ardent supporters of the rule of law, and the majority would only endorse social movements that used peaceful, rational, and nonviolent means. The law as the opposite of violence was a colonial mythology manufactured by a retreating British colonial government and leveraged by the Chinese Communist regime to secure popular submission to its rule. After 1997, Beijing's high-handed interventions into the judicial decisions of the Hong Kong court, by imposing Chinese state interpretations of the Basic Law on matters ranging from procedures of political reform to clarifying the length of the term of the succeeding chief executive to disqualifications of electoral candidates and lawmakers due to the disapproval of various forms of oath taking, made increasingly visible state violence against the city's trademark cherished value.[62] Still, as late as the Fish Ball Revolution in 2016, the general public overwhelmingly objected to the use of violence. But the antiextradition movement in 2019 offered a transformative lesson in violence, albeit a costly one. As of mid-2024, more than ten thousand people had been arrested, and about three thousand prosecuted, while others were in remand awaiting trial. An advocacy group in the United States put the number of political prisoners at 1,916 (as of December 2024), more than three-fourths of them under the age of thirty.[63]

This chapter chronicled how popular participation in various forms of collective action—rallies, marches, clashes with the police, the yellow economy, new unions, and election primaries—broke down the schism between lawful and violent resistance. First came the police use of disproportionate force, which challenged people's entrenched beliefs in a stark opposition between "law and order" and "violence and chaos." Nothing united an enraged population like violent law enforcement throughout the territory. According to the Hong Kong police's own account, they fired a total of 19 live rounds, 16,191 tear gas rounds, 10,100 rubber bullets, 1,880 react rounds, 2,033 beanbag rounds, and 1,491 bottles of pepper spray when handling large-scale disorder related to the protests.[64] Thanks to the euphoria and exigencies of a mass movement, more Hong Kongers than ever before became directly involved in confrontations with state violence—offering transportation and safe houses to protesters, becoming reconnaissance volunteers, helping prepare Molotov cocktails, fighting and distracting riot police with words, and more. The spirit of sacrifice among the young "brave warriors" who were willing to combat violence with force became a moral challenge to the otherwise law-abiding populace. In both practice and cognition, what used to be a self-evident and unbridgeable boundary was transcended. The 2019 protest and its aftermath had busted the "rule by law" myth in Hong Kong like never before.

Empirical evidence of this transformation can be found in two surveys commissioned by Benny Tai himself. In a 2015 "rule of law" culture survey of 3,500 randomly chosen respondents, almost 60 percent agreed that maintaining social order is more important than protection of individual freedoms, that it was proper for civil society organizations to be supervised by government agents, and the media had a duty to promote government policies. A whopping 81 percent said they would follow the law even if they did not agree with it. Tai concluded that the legal culture of the general public showed an entrenched conservative "pragmatism"—belief in rule of law as regulation by law, rather than limitation on government or justice through law.[65] People were willing to support liberal ideals—such as equality and liberty—when they were framed in general and abstract terms, yet they might tilt toward conservatism when social order seemed to be in conflict with those values. Five years later, Tai commissioned another random survey in November 2020, just three months before he was arrested and charged with conspiracy to commit subversion, and the results were flipped. When asked about the purpose of the law, 61 percent of the respondents now chose "higher order" definitions such as law for justice, limitation of government power, and conflict resolution. Only 28 percent agreed that the law's most important objective was to maintain social order and 10 percent thought it was to provide behavioral guidance. Among eighteen-to-twenty-nine-year-olds, 60.5

percent selected "realizing justice" as the primary purpose of the law. Equally important, the public had a very poor assessment of Hong Kong's rule-of-law performance. Only between 15 and 27 percent of the respondents said the rule of law had been realized in Hong Kong according to each of the five criteria.[66] Overall, from July 1997 to July 2021, public rating of the rule of law in Hong Kong dropped from 6.9 out of 10 to 4.5.[67]

Public consciousness about the violence of the "free-market economy" was also heightened during the 2019 protests. Mass political consumption to build and support the yellow economy and the professional middle class's turn to new unionism were united by their shared critique of the domination of Red capital. On the streets, in the media and social media, and in union meetings, discussions turned to the deep-seated structural inequality in Hong Kong's economy and workplaces, the persistence of the government–big business alliance since the colonial era, the new erosion of professionalism by Red capital from mainland China, and visions for an anywhere-but-China supply chain. No other social movement before 2019 had popularized these critical reflections on the oligopolistic political economy of Hong Kong to such a great extent.

Finally, activists made an improbable bid to win an electoral majority using constitutionally prescribed rules within an electoral system designed to keep them a permanent minority. When their primary polls showed solid popular support, Beijing resorted to a new National Security Law to criminalize their peaceful primaries, thereby exposing the naked violence of so-called lawful institutions for all to see. The campaign platform of "mutual destruction," that is, destabilizing the status quo for a better future, had become a popular political vision. At least among the 610,000 voters in the primaries, "stability and prosperity" as an untouchable core value had been turned on its head. As the prominent cultural critic Law Wing-sang noted, it was the regime's obtuse resort to outright violence to crush the movement in 2019 that most effectively shattered the two-decade-old illusion that Hong Kong's future had been peacefully resolved by the handover. To him, the call for *laam caao* marked the explosion of a decolonization struggle whose target was none other than the institutional violence hidden in Hong Kong's colonial power structure.[68]

For all the breakthroughs in challenging the colonial hegemony of rule of law, 2019 also revealed the uneven and at times shallow roots of resistance. On the one hand, there were moments when Hong Kongers seemed to approach what one protester called a "communion in suffering," where people empathized with each other in suffering and cherished each other's sacrifice and took every struggle of resistance as recognition, and ratification, of those who marched on this path before us in hardship.[69] On the other hand, accounts in this chapter allude to brave warriors fleeing from protests, and court testimonies reveal fraudulent use of public donations by some militants. The new unions' referendum to call a strike against the National Security Law failed spectacularly, and unionism remained a fringe idea. Hong Kongers' critique of Red capital also did not extend to homegrown tycoons. When the city's richest man, Li Ka Shing, put out some cryptic newspaper ads that were interpreted as a call for leniency toward the young protesters, he was deemed a hero rather than a leader of the dominant class in the colonial order.

As one exiled activist admitted, Hong Kongers were just beginning to learn that resistance demanded sacrifice. Admiring South Korean workers' will to fight and die under military rule and Ukrainians' physical stamina in the Maidan winter uprising, the veteran leftist Jaco bemoaned the lack of a tradition of sacrifice among Hong Kongers:

> I used to know some leftists from Greece. There they have family traditions of resistance. Several generations—grandfathers, fathers, uncles, brothers—all joined the radical Communist struggle against the government, going in and out of prison. When they were out of prison, they lived on welfare. They were fine with not making money. We Hong Kongers, on the other hand, would naturally consider the opportunity cost of activism and prison terms too high to bear. Me too. In the past, I wagered I could bear a maximum of a year or so jail time. Now with National Security Law, ten or more years of prison, I am so scared that I decamped.... That's the difference: there is a limit to what Hong Kongers are willing to sacrifice.[70]

Jaco now lives in Taiwan. Tens of thousands of Hong Kong citizens, professionals, middle-class families, and young university graduates had also emigrated to Great Britain, Canada, Australia, and beyond. The National Security Law and colonial-era sedition-related offences in the Crimes Ordinance lend the government wide latitude to criminalize political dissent, dealing an insurmountable existential blow to Hong Kong's civil society. Opposition newspapers, yellow businesses, trade and student unions, independent bookstores, veteran nongovernmental organizations, and political parties were shut down or forced to disband.[71] One group, however, managed to continue the struggle overseas. The next chapter looks at how the exiled dissidents, political emigrants, and diaspora practiced "be water" abroad and reimagined Hong Kong's destiny beyond China.

CHAPTER FIVE

"BE WATER" GOES GLOBAL

THE TERM "GLOBAL CITY" ACQUIRED TWO new meanings for Hong Kong during the 2019 protests. In addition to its venerable status as a global hub for commerce and finance, the city was now also deemed the front line of a global pushback against Chinese Communist authoritarianism. For locals, "global city" was no longer just a descriptive category; it became a category of political practice. It was the first time that Hong Kong citizens en masse leveraged transnational forces to circumvent the power of its national sovereign. The masses, not the few political heavyweights with international name recognition and connections, consciously made and maintained an "international front" (國際線). This front entailed crowdfunding campaigns, lobbying foreign governments, engaging in public diplomacy via foreign media and social media, appropriating symbols and discourses from other countries' democratic struggles, and mobilizing Hong Kong emigrants around the world. Netizens and street protesters alike were keenly aware of the need to articulate this international front with local action. Never far from their minds was the world's perception of and reaction to their peaceful demonstrations, violent clashes with the police, turnout rates at local elections, and so on.

This global turn was stunning because, as late as the 2014 Umbrella Movement, activists strategically framed their struggle for autonomy largely within a national framework. As seen in Chapter 2, seeking foreign support was considered treasonous by Beijing and the local populace. But by 2019,

Hong Kongers found themselves inside the breaking waves of a perfect storm: a fallout between China and the West; a sympathetic global media transfixed by the cause, scale, and duration of the protests; the affordances of social media; and the radicalization and proliferation of dispersed leadership in and beyond the city. When all these elements congealed into a force majeure, transborder protest ideas and tactics erupted. None of this should be taken for granted. During the Cold War, even though the city was also geopolitically perched on the edge of an epochal contest between the liberal West and the Communist East, there was no collective action to harness the conflict for local politics. Hong Kongers' agency to challenge China's monopoly on its destiny has to be accounted for. What and who had inspired this scaling up of the decolonization struggle from the local to the international arena?

This chapter chronicles how Hong Kongers applied the principle of "be water" on the global stage through five events during and after 2019: crowdfunding campaigns, advocacy for international sanctions, lobbying the US Congress to pass the Hong Kong Human Rights and Democracy Act, cross-movement solidarity building, and diasporic activism. Once again, the postcolonial generation provided the impetus behind these mobilizations, often with essential but unexpected support from the previous generations of émigré activists whose quiet groundwork had become a legacy to build on. Their activism punctured the colonial mythology of "China as destiny" and unleashed a search for alternative political visions that are still amorphous and tentative. Like in previous chapters, the analysis here centers on the formation of decolonizing subjectivities and the political economic conditions and relational processes that produced breakthroughs and limitations for Hong Kong's decolonization from below.

Business and Political Elite Forerunners

To appreciate the novelty of this global turn in Hong Kong's decolonization movement, we should put it in historical perspective. In the past, the arena of international political economy was the exclusive playground of Hong Kong's business and political leaders. The citizenry seldom took an active part in reaching out to the world for political purpose. For many decades before the handover, Hong Kong was *made* a global city by the entrepreneurialism of the capitalist class, many of whom were emigrants fleeing China's Communist regime under Mao. The historian Peter Hamilton called them "straddling merchants"—the interconnected, mobile, pragmatic, and adaptive clusters of émigré bankers, industrialists, lawyers, executives, academics, and former Nationalist technocrats. They played the role of strategic middlemen between European colonial regimes and Chinese and Southeast Asian economies since the late Qing dynasty. After World War II and the decline of the British empire, these multigenerational elite families pursued modern education as an investment and exploited their native ties to reorient Hong Kong's commercial and education system toward the United States. As China's reform and opening up began, and despite personal anti-Communist sentiment, the straddling elites rebalanced their network strategies between China and the United States. They thrived by "bridging both the production and the sales ends of their commodity chains" and "the world's largest source of labor power and the world's largest consumer market."[1] At the sub-elite level, Gary Hamilton similarly described a cosmopolitan capitalist class consisting mostly of small- and medium-sized firms producing first rattan furniture, plastic flowers, and textiles and later garments, watches, toys, and transistor radios. Grouped in small, loosely organized subcontracting networks, they used their commercial knowledge and a lot of hard work to hunt for and link up with big buyers in the United States, Great Britain, and Germany.[2]

Among the political elite, there was a brief period in the post–World War II era when attempts were made to engage international institutions to initiate constitutional reform in Hong Kong. It was a period of global decolonization, and Hong Kong was still on the United Nations' list of dependent territories whose right to self-determination was affirmed by the UN's Declaration on the Granting of Independence to Colonial Countries and People. A coalition of local Chinese, expatriates, and exiled mainland Chinese activists, including Ma Man Fai, G. S. Kenned-Skipton, and Sun Baogang, formed political organizations and parties to push for self-government, universal suffrage, and democratic elections. As leaders of the United Nations Association of Hong Kong and the Democratic Self-Government Party of Hong Kong, these political elites lobbied members of Parliament, sent open letters to British newspapers, and debated officials in the United Kingdom in support of Hong Kong's autonomy.[3] This short-lived and conflict-ridden reform movement in the 1950s and 1960s did not survive the PRC's entry into the United Nations and Beijing's success, with British acquiescence, to remove Hong Kong from the UN list of dependent territories.

In the mid-1980s, after Britain and the PRC declared that Hong Kong would return to Chinese sovereignty in 1997, the first attempts to alert the world about Hong Kong's uncertain future and the need for full democracy were made by the British-trained barrister Martin Chu-ming Lee. He lobbied members of Parliament in the UK to advance the timetable for direct elections in Hong Kong, Canadian politicians for visa-free arrangements for Hong Kong SAR passport holders, and American legislators to unconditionally renew China's most favored nation trading status (as a way to improve the rule of law in China).[4] In the aftermath of the Tiananmen incident in 1989, Lee found in the West a ready audience doubtful about the Chinese regime's determination to liberalize. As the founder and leader of the political party with the largest number of elected legislators in Hong Kong, he was taken seriously by the West. Famously, in a week-long lobbying trip to Washington, DC, in 1996, he managed to "penetrate almost the same level of seniority in the Congress and the Administration as the Governor David Wilson."[5] Some of these politicians, including Nancy Pelosi, who was then a junior congresswoman from California, would rise to the top of American politics three decades later and play a pivotal role in supporting Hong Kong protesters in 2019.

Among the politicians Lee came to know in the early 1990s was Mitch McConnell, who at that time was a junior Republican senator from Kentucky in search of an issue to define himself. It was unclear if Lee had to lobby for what would become McConnell's bill, officially known as the United States-Hong Kong Policy Act of 1992. American interests alone were strong enough for the bill's passage. It was the beginning of the end of the Cold War, but Hong Kong was at risk because, as a *New York Times* op-ed put it, "its 7 million citizens will be heading into 1997 in the opposite direction to those hundreds of millions of people around the world who are embracing freedom and the free market."[6] The bill was passed with bipartisan support and reassured jittery American businesspeople that the United States would firmly support Hong Kong after it reverted to Chinese control in July 1997. It advanced American interests by requiring presidential reports to Congress on the fulfillment of Hong Kong's full autonomy in such crucial areas as commerce, communications, culture, economics, and finance. Human rights were mentioned in the preamble, but McConnell made it clear he was not picking a fight with China over touchy subjects: "U.S. economic interests require the bill. . . . With over 22,000 Americans living here, over 900 U.S.

firms located here, and 99 billion U.S. dollars deposited here, it's a gross understatement to say our economic interests are significant."[7]

After China joined the WTO, ushering in a Chimerica boom, the American political establishment shifted its attention away from China as an adversary.[8] Their abiding focus was then global terrorism, Afghanistan, and the Middle East. Except for one congressional hearing in March 2004, Hong Kong dropped off the political radar of Capitol Hill.[9] In the 2010s, as China's policy in Hong Kong took an interventionist turn and Beijing repeatedly stalled the process toward genuine universal suffrage, Martin Lee, along with Anson Chan, the former top civil servant turned democratic politician, visited the United States, the UK, Australia, and Europe to express concerns about China's tightened control, interference in press freedoms, and erosion of judicial independence. They laid the groundwork of personal contacts on Capitol Hill that they would later pass on to the younger generation of advocates such as Joshua Wong. In those years, to their dismay, Western politicians were keener on staying in China's good graces, thanks to their commercial interests, than in promoting Hong Kong's democracy. In Lee and Chan's visit to London in July 2014, for instance, the British prime minister David Cameron famously refused to even meet with them. Regardless, Beijing was enraged, and the Chinese press lambasted them for "inviting foreign intervention" and acting as foreign agents with a "fetish for Western authority."[10] The demonization campaign by Beijing was so effective that even Benny Tai, one of the three leaders of the Occupy Central campaign in 2014, declared that he would not seek foreign support because the movement was a "purely local" one. The fear of being branded as a traitor was also palpable among the student leaders of the Umbrella Movement. Nathan Law recalled that "the whole political community in Hong Kong was allergic to international lobbying. Martin Lee was accused not just by the CCP but also some sectors in society as 'a traitor against Han Chinese.' For me as a budding politician, such stigma was disconcerting. . . . But there was no international support for Hong Kong either. China then enjoyed friendly relations with the US. Obama did not express any support for Umbrella; the UK was talking about a 'golden era' [with China], and the EU, oh well. Politicians and international NGOs paid little attention to us."[11]

Between the end of Umbrella and the beginning of 2019, the reluctance to reach for international support subsided. The unstoppable and shrewd Joshua Wong saw the first glimpse of an international front after *Time* put

5.1 *Time* cover.
CREDIT: *Time* 184, no. 15

James Nachtwey's photo of him on its cover—a skinny teenager sporting a bowl cut, wielding a smartphone in the midst of a sea of protesters, taking a break to strategize the next step for the movement he had unleashed. As the face of this unprecedented movement, Joshua soon developed a multi-pronged international strategy that would find its moment several years later as US-China relations deteriorated. He and his peers in the newly formed political party Demosisto exploited his international star power—they liked to call it "halo"—to build the relational infrastructure for lobbying Washington. They also pioneered the use of Twitter and social media as tools of public diplomacy.

With his trademark quick wit, he explained, "Once Umbrella was over, we began asking, 'What else can be done?' The picture of me on *Time* magazine made me think more consciously about ways to use international attention to spread our message. Hong Kong's political freedom depends on Beijing, but Hong Kong's economic freedom depends on the US and the West. So we need a long-term presence in Washington. The Netflix documentary [*Joshua: Teenager vs. Superpower,* 2017] helped a lot. That's why I am about to publish a book called *Unfree Speech* that will be translated into six languages. As long as China is a keyword and a forever issue in international politics, we are bound to find some anti-China politicians in one country or another. Umbrella is a good name, so people are willing to meet with us. And when the West wants to find an opposition voice about China's policy and future, they talk to us because mainland Chinese dissidents are either in jail or cannot speak English."[12]

Then there was Twitter. Beaming with excitement and pride, Joshua boasted confidently, "I dare say I was the first and only one to use Twitter as an international front in 2016! Today [2020] I have five hundred thousand followers, more than my Facebook page. Tweeting in Chinese I got four hundred thousand, number one in Hong Kong. Agnes Chow [another student leader affiliated with Scholarism and Demosisto] tweeting in Japanese also gets more than two hundred thousand." He relished his political stardom, which opened many doors for him to talk to the world about Hong Kong: "Why would the editorial board at the *New York Times,* the *Wall Street Journal,* and a dozen reporters spare an hour listening to our thoughts about Hong Kong? It's not necessarily because we have new ideas but because they respect our reputation."[13]

Between 2015 and 2019, the political inclination of the locals also began to change. "With localism gaining ground among the Hong Kong people after 2014, we saw a popular mandate to connect Hong Kong identity with the world. People want a global Hong Kong, not a Chinese Hong Kong. This gave us courage to ignore CCP press' labeling," explained Nathan Law. However, he and Joshua saw only limited international opportunities. They accepted invitations to give talks at American universities and saw their task as raising global consciousness about Hong Kong's struggle. Whenever they got an invitation to visit college campuses in New York, they would add a stop in DC. Chris Smith's Hong Kong Human Rights and Democracy Act, first introduced in 2015, did not find enough momentum on Capitol Hill but gave them a tangible objective. Yet they were also fully cognizant that "Hong Kong is always a derivative issue, tethered to China-US relations. When the latter is a hot topic, we have some space. But it was not something for which we can be in the driver's seat."[14]

The Global Media

By 2019, the deterioration in Sino-US relations was one of the most important backdrops that opened up previously unimaginable opportunities for the masses to advance an international front. The Trump administration's hawkish rhetoric and trade war with China found a receptive audience among American industrial titans, who were losing out to Chinese companies after years of commercial espionage and unfair market policies under Chinese state capitalism. Anti-Communist Republicans and human-rights advocates among the Democrats forged a bipartisan stance against China.[15] Beyond the United States, since the second half of the 2010s, Western public opinion had become increasingly unfavorable toward China, suspicious of its global expansion in Africa, Latin America, and Asia. Pew opinion polls show a precipitous deterioration in China's image around the world during Xi Jinping's tenure. His Belt and Road Initiative, military buildup in the South China Sea, and increased infiltration in domestic politics in Australia, New Zealand, and Canada all raised the ire of the West. A Pew research study concluded, "Alongside its growing influence is a sense that China is a growing *threat*. Roughly half or more in South Korea, Japan, the Philippines, Australia and the U.S. said China's power and influence was a major threat to their country in 2018. But even outside these particular countries, around half or more of the population in every country but Tunisia said China's power and influence posed either a major *or* minor threat."[16] This was the context in which Hong Kongers' resistance against Beijing's authoritarian encroachment found resonance in many parts of the world. A key intermediary in disseminating the Hong Kong story to the world was the global media.

From the beginning, the 2019 protests in Hong Kong were energized by sympathetic coverage by all the major news organizations in the world around the clock. For six months, a symbiotic relationship developed between global media and citizen action. Knowing that the world was watching, and seeking to sway international public opinion in favor of the movement, citizens consciously played up their cosmopolitan sensibilities with innovative and photogenic street action. As a foreign correspondent noted, "From Oslo to Osaka, Congress to the United Nations, Taiwan to Twitter, Hong Kongers have taken their DIY approach to protest to a global audience. Celebrity supporters testify in high-profile settings; highly targeted, crowd-funded media campaigns aim to keep the issue in the spotlight; and viral videos, catchy slogans, and even a movement anthem and flag help magnify the message on social media."[17]

Self-mobilized citizens initiated collective action on LIHKG and Facebook to connect Hong Kong's movement to global ones. A consistent message was that Hong Kong's fight was a global fight and that Hong Kongers stood in solidarity with other peoples. There were numerous outdoor community screenings of the Netflix documentary *Winter on Fire*, about Ukraine's Maidan protests, and the South Korean film *1987: When the Day Comes*, about the death of a student protester during police interrogation that led to the June Democratic Uprising.[18] Protesters held several airport sit-ins with the explicit purpose of drawing international visitors' attention to the plight of the city. Then, on August 23, netizens called for a commemoration of the thirtieth anniversary of the Baltic Way. Hong Kongers organized the Hong Kong Way to create a glittering fifty-kilometer human chain along major highways and metro stations on both sides of Victoria Harbour and up the landmark Lion Rock Hill (see Chapter 4). There were the ubiquitous English slogans, mass singing sessions in the malls, op-eds and letters to the editors of various international newspapers, sign language for mobilizing protective gear, and a strong presence of international flags at most rallies, appealing to a dozen or more countries and territories. The US flag was featured most prominently as the Hong Kong Human Rights and Democracy Act was making its way through the US Congress.[19]

A veteran journalist who had covered Hong Kong and Asia for twenty years for a major international news agency pointed to the irresistible appeal and global significance of the Hong Kong story. To him, the 2019 movement was the most emotionally consuming and important event he had ever covered: "It was no doubt the biggest story in the world that year. Everyone I knew in journalism was here. It had a simplistic and innocent thrust—freedom-loving youngsters taking on a dictatorship which was also challenging the US. Everyone could grasp its compelling, almost biblical, narrative of good against evil. It is often difficult for a global audience to handle too much complexity or local details. But the Hong Kong story had the advantage of being uncomplicated: the cause was the extradition bill. And over several months, we saw the evolution of the protests—how peaceful they were at the beginning and then how the government refused to concede. The timing was ripe too. Under Trump, Washington came to a bipartisan position about China. That chimed with the dynamic in Hong Kong and amplified it. The legislative moves in the US were massive as they have found a unifying issue to seize upon against China. . . . Every media outlet was sending people here, not just for short stays but for months. The amount of resources being pumped into this story was incredible. Everyone was competing to find a fresh angle; the drones were taking shots that wow the audience. Many of my colleagues who have covered war zones were extremely moved by the PolyU siege. In this part of the world, there has not been anything like it in recent decades: anarchy in one of the world's modern metropolises! No one had expected it in a way one might expect everyday violence in Gaza or Israel. In the eyes of the editors, this was the news value."[20]

Indeed, even though there were numerous protests around the world in 2019—from the yellow vests in France to massive demonstrations in Lebanon, Gaza, Chile, Ecuador, and Haiti, just to name a few—Hong Kong protesters received the most frequent and favorable coverage.[21] Chinese and Hong Kong officials seized upon this bias to criticize the Western media's anti-China conspiracy. In return, the West pointed to China's warfare of misinformation against the protesters.[22] Regardless, there was no mistaking that the stunning visuals, the simplicity and moral clarity of the cause, and the arc of the story captivated the world, endearing the protesters to the global public. Among the protesters, the prevailing perception was that the international front would be effective. In a protest-site survey conducted on August 31, 68.7 percent of the respondents believed it was very or quite likely that "the international society's attitude" could force the Hong Kong and Chinese governments to concede to the movement's demands. A majority of them (75.9 percent) believed it was very or quite likely that the China-US trade war could force the government to concede.[23] Such views were buoyed by academics and public intellectuals popularizing the view that China's globalizing economy still needed Hong Kong as an offshore exchange hub for the official Chinese currency, RMB, and as a platform for the IPOs of Chinese corporations.[24]

Grassroots International Front

Let us now go inside the international front to understand the cast of characters and the motives, logic, and limits of their activism. Piecing together first-person accounts by key figures involved in different tracks of the international front reveals one heartening and unexpected lesson: the international front in 2019 had a decades-long lineage. Previous bouts of democracy activism abroad had emerged and subsided at different political junctures but, like a winding, silent spring, had quietly continued to flow. Contacts, networks, organizations, and aspirations accumulated one event at a time. They might lie dormant for years only to be reactivated when the next event came about, be it in 1989, 2003, 2012, 2014, or 2019. The key to their continuity was people's unrequited attachment to Hong Kong, through thick and thin. For these emigrants, politics and protests were never their full-time occupation. Yet when the time was ripe, their contributions as business owners, community organizers, accountants, foreign citizens, professionals, students, and professors would prove critical. This history is instructive because now that 2019 had become part of that past, we can begin to envision its possible legacy for the future.

Massive participation by the local citizenry and the Hong Kong diaspora notwithstanding, entrepreneurial drivers of three global-facing campaigns in 2019—crowdfunding, international sanction, and the Hong Kong Human Rights and Democracy (HKHRD) Act—had hailed from the postcolonial generation based abroad. Their audacious sensibility that Hong Kong belonged to the world, not China, was matched by their timely capacity to collaborate transnationally. The modus operandi seemed to follow this sequence: (1) ideas and proposals were put forth anonymously on social media; (2) those attracting strong support (quantifiable as the number of upvotes) were hotly debated; (3) entrepreneurial netizens moved the discussion to Telegram and took up the role of "administrators"; (4) task-oriented Telegram groups would form among volunteer recruits; (5) mass campaigns took shape, attracting global media reports; (6) old and new activists, both local and overseas, converted global attention into political capital and capacity; and (7) global responses boosted local morale, incentivizing more innovative ideas and proposals on social media.

Crowdfunding for Global Advertisements

The opening salvos of the international front were launched by young Hong Kongers studying and working overseas. Glued to their smartphones and transfixed by livestreamed videos of the historic march on June 9, police violence, and the government's callous insistence on tabling the extradition bill on June 12, they shared their fellow citizens' euphoria and rage instantaneously. Only one difference set them apart: a profound sense of guilt for their absence on the streets that was so overwhelming they sublimated it by taking action abroad. The LIHKG platform was filled with lively tactical discussions, but people in Hong Kong were too consumed by daily events to realize proposals that called for a more complex division of labor. Hong Kongers overseas pitched in because they could not participate on the streets. Their dispersal around the world in different time zones, their sensitivity to international public opinion, and the affordance of messaging platforms allowed them to quickly source from a global pool of talent. They worked together around the clock to make the Hong Kong protests politically legible to and emotionally resonant with the global community.

Anna Kwok, a.k.a. "Knorr macaroni" on LIHKG and "random" on Telegram, was a junior at New York University studying visual art and philosophy in 2019. Her first political activity was attending the mass rally against national education in 2012 when she was a high school student in Hong Kong. That experience made her realize that politics was not the privilege of "older men in suits" and that high school students could also wield discursive power in public affairs. Rebelling against the examination system in Hong Kong, Anna charted her own path to attend an international baccalaureate program in Norway in 2014. When Umbrella broke out, she could only follow the movement via the discussion platform HKGolden. While she was saddened by the fractures and animosity among the occupiers, she was also moved by people's willingness to confront tear gas and pepper spray. Seeing her previously apolitical friends confronting the police was also a revelation. Not able to join them in person, Anna nevertheless made presentations on her campus in a small Norwegian town, explaining to locals the difference between Hong Kong and China. She was part of the postcolonial generation who naturally embraced the vision of an independent Hong Kong. Without ambivalence, she was clear that "I have no emotional connection with China. I grew up with news reports about China's fake eggs, tofu-dregs projects, land grabs, and corruption. In a child's mind, there is only black and white, and China to me was all uncivilized and evil. Once I was in Lo Wu [a border town in mainland China] with my parents, and someone tried to grab me from their hands. It's so terrifying that I still remember it to this day. Later on, I read about the rampant networks of human traffickers. Everything about China goes against my values."[25]

As fate would have it, Anna was also not in Hong Kong when protests erupted in June 2019. Her first act was to set up a Facebook page to offer support for those who stayed overnight on June 11 near the government headquarters. Some overseas Hong Kongers joined the page to translate news from Chinese into English for the international media, and some started a letter campaign spamming the United Nations and other international agencies. Anna recalled,

> Around mid-June, I saw a LIHKG post saying G20 is happening soon [June 28–29], and that an advertisement on the front page of all international newspapers will persuade political leaders of major countries to help stop the extradition bill. I saw several thousand positive replies, but after searching through forty pages of comments, I could not find anyone actually doing anything. I decided to propose forming a small public group on Telegram, and then with another netizen we became the leaders and started basic screening of members. I coordinated people to do advertising and writing statements, and he worked on fundraising. We formed subgroups for different countries, for translation and editing details and country-specific designs. As soon as we announced the link for sending in donations, the response was so overwhelming that the crowdfunding platform had to shut us down because they suspected us of money laundering. We have to call its customer service to reopen our link. . . . Everything is so organic and so fast—only two days from crowdfunding to publishing the advertisements! I guess facing a hard deadline unified us all and suppressed dissent. Trust was amazing and pure between the public and us and among us. Our motive was very pure: Hong Kongers could not believe the crazy thing that was happening in the city, and we wanted the world to know about it. We were not expecting the G20 leaders to take concrete action on our behalf, but at least we wanted the world to directly hear our authentic voices, our newly formulated five demands.[26]

They published an audit report on the Facebook page called Freedom Hong Kong on August 23, informing the public that twenty-one advertisements were published between June 27 and 29 in major international newspapers such as *The Guardian, Le Monde,* the *New York Times,* the *Washington Post, Japan Times, Asahi Shimbun,* and *Chosun Ilbo.* They received twenty-two thousand donations, pledging a total of HK$6.73 million. After paying for the advertisement, the remaining HK$157,000 was handed over to the 612

Humanitarian Relief Fund. The same report also revealed that the average donation was only HK$304, the largest single donation was only HK$30,000, and the smallest was HK$4.[27]

How much impact the campaign had was unclear, though the Japanese prime minister Shinzo Abe did bring up Hong Kong's protests with the Chinese leader Xi Jinping when the two met on the sidelines of the summit. Regardless, the success in pulling off such a feat in record speed was a tremendous boost to the protesters' morale and sense of efficacy. They were confident that the movement could tap into the wealth, generosity, and solidarity of Hong Kongers. A second crowdfunding campaign happened in mid-August, around the time the police deployed tear gas in the city's subway for the first time and a young woman lost an eye to a rubber bullet. By then, they were joined by Stand with Hong Kong (SWHK), a team formed by UK-based Finn Lau, a.k.a. "Brother Laam Caao" (meaning "mutual destruction"). There was overlapping personnel across the two teams, each made up of both overseas and locally based members. This drive was for another round of global advertisements, and people responded enthusiastically: HK$3 million in half a working day and a grand total of HK$10 million. In the UK, SWHK used half the funds to hire a lobbying firm to compensate for their lack of lobbying experience and elite contacts. There was also a desire to insert the Hong Kong issue in the upcoming UK election at the end of 2019. Taking a leaf from Boris Johnson's campaign playbook, they rented a double-decker bus that was splashed with the question "Will Boris Johnson Kowtow to China?" and toured around London. Some two hundred Hong Kongers attended, but the event received negligible media attention.

Anna recalled that "in the second campaign, we had more internal conflicts and mistrust across teams, maybe because there was no definitive deadline, unlike the case of the G20 meeting. A third global advertising campaign was on October 1, urging foreign companies not to do business with China. So our message shifted from Hong Kong itself to Hong Kong as the testing ground for China's encroachment in the rest of the world. Thereafter, the political atmosphere became too tense for us to continue." Right before the National Security Law in May–July 2020, and expecting the imminent crackdown would put an end to crowdfunding in the future, SWHK organized a final campaign raising HK$12 million from civil society groups around the world.

Crowdfunding is now used by social movement activists around the world. But the challenge is how to maintain participants' anonymity when crowdfunding platforms have stringent internal and external regulations to prevent money laundering. To overcome this hurdle, the crowdfunding campaigns in 2019 received critical help from Hong Kong emigrants with foreign citizenship. These individuals were willing to use their real identities to set up a trust outside of Hong Kong as the legal recipient of the multimillion-dollar donations. Credibility was of the essence. Layers of interpersonal ties connected young activists like Anna and Finn with these veteran emigrant organizers whose reputations were rooted in years of community activism abroad for Hong Kong. One of these emigrant activists explained,

> Because the G20 campaign and SWHK were not legal entities, the platform was suspicious of money laundering. Whenever you have money, you need a registered organization, and registration requires legal identity. Friends of friends were frantically looking for figureheads willing to stake their real names to set up a trust so the donations can be transferred from the platform to the movement. My wife agreed to let me do it [*laughs*], as long as I would give up ever returning to Hong Kong. So the trust was set up with me and another Hong Konger with US citizenship. But my job is limited to writing checks, not organizing and executing action. All together we had raised several million US dollars. . . . They used it for foreign newspapers advertising, hiring professional lobbyists, and funding some small projects by overseas Hong Kongers for Hong Kong.[28]

Beyond crowdfunding, the Hong Kong diaspora around the world contributed different kinds of unique assistance. When the city saw a severe shortage of goggles, gas masks, and filters, Hong Kongers living near airports and those working in the aviation industry formed an impromptu supply chain. A participant in such an operation recalled, "For two months, the apartment I rented became a warehouse of face masks, goggles, and other gear that were brought and sent by overseas Hongkongers. I personally delivered this stuff to flight crews bound for Hong Kong. It was like smuggling narcotics. They dropped a message to me via Telegram when they were about to board, and I had to carry two big bags of gear to meet them."[29] In Taiwan, a land of motorcycles, the Hong Kong diaspora organized a donation drive for helmets. They also offered material and psychological support to many of the estimated five hundred to one thousand (by 2021) young escapees facing or fearing prosecution who had arrived in Taiwan, which was just an hour's flight from Hong Kong. Similar "haven assistance" networks were formed in Europe, the UK, and the United States in the aftermath of the protests. Finally, established diaspora organizations formed in support of the 1989 pro-democracy movement or the 2014 Umbrella Movement joined with new ones formed in 2019 to hold global solidarity rallies in twenty-two cities on June 12, thirty-six cities on August 17–18, and sixty-five cities on September 29.[30]

Campaigning for International Sanctions

Like publishing global advertisements, the idea to solicit foreign sanctions against Hong Kong officials emerged initially from LIHKG and very soon found strong support among netizens, college students, community organizers, and politicians. People pointed to the Sino-British Joint Declaration (1985), the Hong Kong Policy Act (1992), and the Hong Kong Human Rights and Democracy Act (2015, 2016, 2017, 2019) as legal and legislative justifications for foreign intervention. In the end, protesters claimed victory when the HKHRD Act was passed by the US Congress and signed into law by President Donald Trump in late November 2019. The law, a singular breakthrough by Hong Kong's international front, was made possible by Hong Kongers overseas working together with local activists across several generations to harness American political interests to intervene in Hong Kong.

Among the first activists to propose the idea of seeking foreign sanctions on Hong Kong officials was Finn Lau, a professional surveyor working in London. On June 9, he posted his first message on LIHKG under the moniker "I want laam caao" (我要攬炒) to recruit foot soldiers. Finn did not foresee that his idea of burnism would spread like wildfire in the following months. It expressed such a radical paradigm shift that the Communist regime would later devote a whole press conference to denounce it. Finn's trajectory from an ordinary netizen with a catchy fictitious name, Brother Laam Caao, to a movement influencer epitomized the organic fluidity and dispersed capacity of modern mass movements. Amazingly, even though Finn had never participated in any social movements or campus politics while he was in college in Hong Kong, he shared the political ethos of his peers. One step and one idea at a time, Finn was propelled forward by the amount of mass support on LIHKG, reflected in the number of likes and comments his posts received. He began with a simple idea: to punish legislators supporting the extradition bill by targeting the foreign passports of those with dual citizenship. His childhood memory of the 2003 protest kicked in: "I was thinking about the lesson in 2003. It was the negative votes by the Liberal Party politicians that finally forced the government to withdraw the Article 23 legislation. So we could compel the legislators to vote against the extradition bill by having foreign governments revoke their passports if they vote yes. So the first thing we need to do is to dig up information about the passport status and foreign assets of the several dozen pro-China legislators."[31]

His June 9 LIHKG post, which garnered seven thousand positive replies, stated,

> Tonight many martyrs are arrested. But don't despair, because we can still win. . . . We know all top officials have to give up their foreign passports as a condition of their appointment. We should target foreign governments to revoke the right to regain their passports when they step down. This is the only way to burn them, and force them to change course on June 12. . . . I will open a Telegram group, and call on all those who want to work seriously, on turbo mode, those who can afford the time, have good English skills and legal knowledge, please leave us your Telegram info. Four teams: A. research team finding out the legal grounds for depriving them the right to reinstate their foreign passports, one person per country; B. opposition research on senior officials, to find out the nationality of the top 16 political appointees, their immediate family members and then their deputies; C. opposition research on pro-establishment politicians, their nationalities and email addresses; D. a writing team will draft letters to be sent to foreign governments, and to inform our targets of this "big present."

Several years later, he still remembered the outpour of enthusiasm: "I got two thousand replies within one day but only thirty hours until legislators cast their votes. I selected about thirty people based on their time zones, skill sets, and professional experience; 60 to 70 percent are based overseas. I'd at least talk to each of them once and feel them out. Within one or two days, we released our reports under the Chinese name 'Laam Caao Team' or 'Hong Kong Liberty' for the international audience, including one about police violence on June 12 that we submitted to Amnesty International and the United Nations. The response was overwhelming: twenty positive responses in one minute, and soon our posts were pushed to the top, and that generated more views, likes, and replies."[32]

The simultaneity of experience made possible by social media allowed Finn to closely monitor popular impulses. After the two-million-strong march on June 16, when he saw signs of fragmentation and old animosity between the militant and moderate camps, he wrote another post advocating unity: "The moderate camp is like the shield, and the militants are the swords." It touched a nerve, attracting a whopping twelve thousand positive replies. He recalled, "I never thought I'd be so popular. This is another encouraging turning point. We were all excited when our teammates had their letter to the editor published in the *Financial Times* [June 26, 2019]." When the crowd stormed the LegCo building on July 1, Finn and another group of overseas Hong Kongers drafted and posted two Hong Kongers' declarations on LIHKG. In the end, the protesters inside the chamber scrolled on LIHKG and read the one that concisely stated the five demands. Finn's was apparently too wordy for the occasion. The next day, Finn was shocked to find London's newsstands all plastered with the photo of the Hong Kong colonial flag hoisted inside the ransacked LegCo chamber. He had an epiphany: "All the major newspapers featured that flag on their front page. A light bulb went off in my mind. I suddenly realized Britain still feels for Hong Kong, which is really surprising for me. I then posted a message on LIHKG about opening a front focusing on China's violation of the Sino-British Joint Declaration. When I got more than ten thousand likes, I formed a new team called Stand with Hong Kong. The idea was to put pressure on the UK government to take action, which will then facilitate the US to revoke the Hong Kong Policy Act. We had six subteams targeting different countries and regions: Japan, EU, UK, US, Northern Europe, and cross-countries."[33]

Before 2019, appealing to foreign countries for intervention was stigmatized by Beijing and the public as collusion with foreign forces. But in 2019, the people were ready for Finn's idea of *laam caao,* which according to him basically said, "'We are not afraid of upsetting the CCP.' When the CCP collapses, Hong Kongers will have a new space for survival. In September 2019, I wrote in *Stand News* that Hong Kongers will have to die first in order to be reborn. We just need to bear the short-term pain of burning with China in order to have a future in the long term. The peaceful camp made their best effort in Umbrella 2014. The militants did the same in Fish Ball 2016. We have tried it all, except a third tactic: the international. What we need is all these fronts together at the same time. People were very supportive of burnism."[34] Indeed, a representative opinion survey at the time showed that 64 percent supported the HKHRD Act and its sanctions against the police.[35]

Back in Hong Kong, it was all quiet on the international front in July 2019, when the movement's energy was focused on shifting from trench warfare to flash mobs in dispersed neighborhoods. But an August 16 mass rally, organized by university students of the Hong Kong Higher Institutions International Affairs Delegation (HKIAD), rekindled citizens' concern for international lobbying. The rally saw the first public cooperation of local and overseas activists, joined by a common agenda targeting the US and UK governments—the United States because of its Hong Kong Policy Act and Hong Kong Human Rights and Democracy Act and the UK as the signatory of the Sino-British Joint Declaration. The event featured a broad spectrum of political figures across several generations, all expressing a strong sense of solidarity on the necessity of an international front. Riding on his fame as the mysterious and faceless Brother Laam Caao, Finn made a recorded speech to energize the crowd at the end of the rally. Thunderous cheers and applause echoed his commanding voice broadcast from behind a black cloth screen fluttering in the wind as he explained the idea of burnism if sanctions were available: "Pro-establishment politicians will not be able to reclaim their foreign passports and will be forced to stay forever in China to face the same 'bright' future as us. If Hong Kongers burn, they burn with us."[36]

The university students behind the international front came to the idea of capitalizing on geopolitical tensions for advancing the movement through a different venue. Their spokesperson, Sunny Cheung, a University of Hong Kong student union representative in 2019, formed the HKIAD by bringing together twelve student unions throughout the territory. A veteran of the Umbrella Movement, Sunny was most inspired by the role of overseas Taiwanese, especially the Formosan Association for Public Affairs, in galvanizing American support for the island's democratization. The idea of building an international front was planted during a summer workshop in 2018 at Taiwan's Academia Sinica, where he learned about Taiwan's democratization history and the role of the Taiwanese diaspora. He was particularly impressed by the book *Forty Years of Taiwan Independence Movement Overseas*. When the 2019 movement erupted, he sought to put his knowledge into practice. But partly he was also swayed by discussion on LIHKG that "to pressure the government to withdraw the bill, we need foreign investors to care because they would be subject to it too. The logic was that even though the regime cared little about citizens, it would worry about *guilos* [foreigners]. The essence of the fugitive act provides a platform and rationale for an international front because it claims to cover everyone everywhere."[37] He understood that university students had moral capital. In Hong Kong, this halo effect was augmented by financial resources: student union membership fees were collected automatically by the universities.

A remarkable departure from the older generation of prodemocracy activists, Sunny was adamant that "Never for a second did we worry about being lambasted as 'traitors' of the Chinese people because most of us do not consider ourselves Chinese. If they denounce us as traitors, we would consider that an honor. To us 'Two Systems' are more important than 'One Country.' Whatever international advocacy we do, it's not Beijing's business because it's our own autonomy and decision to reach out to the world. I just felt it's our naturally born intrinsic right to do it. Not just us, but the whole society did not see anything wrong with seeking international support. The only opposition voice then was some old pan-dem professional groups like the Denis Kwok and Charles Mok delegation in 2019 who found calls for sanctions [HKHRD Act] too provocative to Beijing. I was proud of our rhyming theme of the rally 'UK-US-HK alliance, sovereignty by the people' [英美港盟 主權在民]."[38]

Buoyed by the high morale after the success of the crowdfunding campaign for the G20 advertisements, Sunny was very excited to see that protesters collectively created a slogan to address an international audience—"Stand with Hong Kong." It was, of course, the name of Finn's team. To leverage Brother Laam Caao's online fame and his innovative proposals for international campaigns, Sunny approached Finn, who remained anonymous and faceless in their messaging and conference calls.

Their advocacy targeted the revocation of the Hong Kong Policy Act, denouncing China's abrogation of the Joint Declaration, and sanctions of key officials, especially Carrie Lam. On behalf of HKIAD, Sunny met with legislators in Australia, the UK, Germany, and the United States, where he spoke in a Congressional-Executive Commission on China (CECC) hearing on September 17, 2019. In reaching out to foreign politicians, he tapped into the contacts of other veteran activists, such as Joshua Wong and Martin Lee, and lobbying groups such as the UK-based Hong Kong Watch. Other times, he sent emails requesting meetings to the top brass of the political parties whose public profiles indicated possible interest in countering China. His experience revealed an uneven global landscape for Hong Kong lobbying: "Germany was very disappointing. I met with politicians from all five major political parties to find a bipartisan consensus—Germany will never have a Malinsky Act because they claimed that Germany was a peace-loving country with no tradition or intention to intervene in other states' affairs. They wanted to leave it to the EU to deal with human rights. . . . Australia had no interest in supporting the Hong Kong movement before 2019. But they have changed because they now have problems with China's interference in domestic politics. It's all about countries' geopolitical interest."[39]

Sunny's team consisted of university students who formed work groups to conduct legal research and proposed terms and texts for the HKHRD Act. He was bemused to find that "Congressional staffers love and appreciate our reports because they have to handle too many issues and do not have time to find basic facts. The US has for the longest time prioritized the Middle East and global terrorism. A former National Security Council member told me that after 9/11, China was dropped out of the White House conversation for twenty years. There's very little background knowledge about China, let alone Hong Kong. North Korea is a nuclear power, so there is significant expertise."[40]

Sammy, one of Sunny's twenty-six team members, was a political science student from a local university and part of an interuniversity study group devouring classics on "nationalism, Sinophone studies, linguistic oppression," and more.[41] Like many of his generation, he was inspired by Joshua Wong to care about student rights, and Edward Leung's sacrifice during the Fish Ball Revolution compelled him to seek redemption by contributing to the movement. Knowing that he would "not survive prison" if he were charged with rioting, he focused on research, putting to good use his self-professed strength in "assembling texts." He continued, "We study the US Hong Kong Policy Act and the HKHRD bill and write amendments to expand the scope of sanctionable violations and the type of personnels covered by sanctions: not only senior government officials but judges too; not just the suppression of protests but all kinds of human rights violations. We also propose easing the application process for Hong Kongers to obtain US visas. We do profiling of foreign politicians by searching interview transcripts and speeches for mentions about Communism, authoritarianism, Tibet to identify those who may be inclined to support Hong Kong. We always used 'the free world' in the headline of our narratives. Our talking point was always that China uses Hong Kong to steal US technology."[42]

These students' clear-eyed assessment of the geopolitical situation was that the United States did not care about democracy in Hong Kong but only about how China's intervention in Hong Kong might adversely affect American business interests. They fully foresaw the possibility that Americans would sacrifice Hong Kong in order to strike a trade deal with China. Yet they tried their best regardless. After his exile to the United States, Sunny was less sanguine:

> In 2019 we were hopeful that international pressure would work. Our logic was that the CCP was not fearful of Hong Kongers but it did care about the international community. We needed the US to play its hands, otherwise China would not concede. Hong Kong was the last straw to tell the world about the essence of CCP. But looking back, I now realize that Hong Kong was just one factor in a long process of changing US-China relations; it was not a decisive factor for overhauling their relation. Besides the US, other Western countries had all kinds of complicated ties with China. Still, the HKHRD Act is a starting point of a new era of US-China relations.[43]

Lobbying the US Congress

How to convert the momentum of street protests in Hong Kong into a concrete legislation passed by the US Congress, all without the financial wherewithal to hire professional lobbyists? Reconstructing the campaign from first-person narratives of the key activists, I discover the pivotal role played by young US-based Hong Kongers whose political imagination escaped the confines of the OCTS endorsed by their veteran predecessors, such as Martin Lee and Anson Chan. Like Sunny and Anna, their generation did not feel beholden to China. Their efforts, with critical help from the Hong Kong diaspora, would bring about a fundamental change in the nature of the "Hong Kong question" as a fulcrum in US-China relations, from one driven by trade, transport, and investments to one of human rights and democracy. But even these young advocates would emphasize one important lesson: without mass action, nothing would have happened.

Jeffrey Ngo was a New York University sophomore majoring in history in 2014 when he joined a global action day in New York City, organized by the diaspora organization New York for Hong Kong (NY4HK), in support of the Umbrella Movement in Hong Kong. A chance encounter there with a dissident foundation from China led him to a meeting in Washington, DC, with Frank Wolf, a congressman known for his hawkish position on China's human rights record and a cosponsor of the first version of the Hong Kong Human Rights and Democracy Act along with Chris Smith and Nancy Pelosi. All three American politicians have a long-term interest in Chinese human rights, and the Umbrella Movement was the impetus for the first draft of the bill in the House of Representatives in 2015. The timing of the bill and Jeffrey's East Coast location sparked his interest in advocacy for Hong Kong. As part of NY4HK and a self-made advocate, he began collecting business cards of legislators and congressional staffers. A critical moment came in September 2015 when Joshua Wong arrived in New York with Martin Lee after they received a Freedom House human rights award. At a dinner in Chinatown with the Hong Kong community, Jeffrey was taken by Joshua's clear political vision, which was representative of their generation:

> Martin was reiterating the old idea of fighting for universal suffrage under the framework of OCTS. But when Joshua took the floor, he simply said, "It does not matter what we say now, the important thing is whether Hong Kong can have self-determination in 2047." This was the first time anyone applied the term "self-determination" to the Hong Kong context. Martin Lee's generation will not talk about 2047 because they'll be gone. But our generation will live beyond 2047. I can see right there that Joshua is a gifted politician who has a knack for opening up a new terrain of political action with his unique vision. The reason why he could come up with that idea was that after Umbrella, young people were convinced that OCTS would never lead to democracy. We had pushed civil disobedience to its limit, and we began to see the problem was political imagination. So by 2015, young people were already talking about independence, brushing aside the Basic Law. That's the natural conclusion after many years of struggle. The failure of Umbrella opened a floodgate for alternative political ideas—of the city-state, return to British colonialism, independence, etc. And Joshua added self-determination—a human right recognized universally. It's better than "independence," which is one of the possible outcomes of self-determination. This vision appeals to me

because basically he is saying Hong Kongers did not have the right to determine our future in 1997. But we must exercise our right in deciding our future beyond 2047. Joshua and I continued to talk after the dinner. To him, I am also unique because I am of his generation but an international student in the US, based in the East Coast, and had already independently started lobbying legislators. You could say there was mutual attraction. For me, it's his ideas; for him, my background and location.[44]

The star power of Joshua Wong allowed American politicians to put a face on Hong Kong's struggle, humanizing it for themselves and their constituencies. The meetings with big shots such as Pelosi, Mike Pompeo, and Marco Rubio were typically brief, fifteen to thirty minutes, more photo opportunities than policy discussion. But establishing human connections was very significant because politicians need to feel for the issue and see it as a priority so that "Hong Kong will move from the back to the front of their minds," Jeffrey observed. He himself worked on a lower level of the political hierarchy: the professional staffers who were instrumental in defining and carrying out the politicians' priorities and routinely solicited input from credible people and legitimate organizations with local expertise about Hong Kong. Beginning in 2016, Jeffrey harnessed Joshua's international recognition and made regular visits to congressional staffers' offices on behalf of their political party, Demosisto. After he moved to Washington, DC, for his doctoral degree in history at Georgetown, he kept Hong Kong alive as an issue on Capitol Hill by constantly knocking on their doors.

Wearing a sunny and mocking smile, Jeffrey was confident of his effectiveness as an advocate: "We are not well-heeled professional lobbyists. We are grassroots and youth-led, but I understand American culture enough to get acquainted with them. . . . Pulling school connections—many staffers have Georgetown roots—and striking up small talks about pop stars while feeding them information about development in Hong Kong, be it the Lantau Vision plan, disqualification of pro-independence political candidates, or the national anthem bill . . . Hong Kongers like me are more plugged into US culture than, say, advocates from Thailand, Burma, or Taiwan because we are more internationally savvy and connected."[45]

Building on the Washington contacts accumulated by Martin Lee and Anson Chan, who were willing to pass the advocacy baton to the younger generation, Jeffrey and Joshua also developed new connections. By 2016, the champion of the HKHRD Act had become Florida Republican senator Marco Rubio, who was searching for a signature issue to burnish his self-branding as a China hawk. In the wake of Rubio's defeat for the Republican presidential nomination and the abduction of the Causeway Bay booksellers, Hong Kong became an appealing cause for him. Playing up his Cuban descent in a political exile household, he introduced a stronger Senate version of the House bill by Chris Smith. Incidentally, that same year, Congress enacted the Global Magnitsky Human Rights Accountability Act, providing for American sanctions on human rights abusers around the world. Applied to Hong Kong, Rubio's version of the HKHRD Act turned what was more like messaging legislation into legislation with teeth, calling for a report by the secretary of state on Hong Kong's autonomy as well as sanctions against officials. Both Joshua and Jeffrey found Rubio genuine in his concern about Hong Kong. He would personally go on Twitter to monitor and comment on events such as the Yuen Long assault on July 21. Netizens based in Hong Kong enthusiastically reciprocated, thanking him and retweeting his posts as a way to publicize the city's situation among the American public.

A passionate minority in Congress committed to the bill, while necessary to keep the issue alive, was not sufficient to elevate it to the level of the House or Senate leadership. Less than 10 percent of all the bills sponsored by the House and Senate get passed in any particular year, as numerous priorities compete for attention in Washington's rapidly shifting political cycles. By mid-June 2019, when the two-million-strong marches became household news in the United States, the stars were aligned in Washington for the Hong Kong bill. Rubio had become the cochair of the CECC, Nancy Pelosi the Speaker of the House, and Jim McGovern, another Democrat supporter of human rights, chair of the House Rules Committee (which controls which bills come to the floor of the House). What was missing was political organizing to focus all these energies to "resurrect the HK bill from the abyss,"[46] in the words of Samuel Chu, who succeeded in doing just that.

Samuel's trajectory to this pivotal role in the international front of the Hong Kong movement was a reminder that the lineage of activism was not a straight line. There was no clear model of diasporic activism for Hong Kong to follow. A Hong Kong–born American citizen in his early forties, Samuel had been a Los Angeles–based community organizer for almost two decades, working at the intersection of religion and social justice issues such as hunger, affordable housing, and LGBT rights. Before 2019, his work had nothing to do with Hong Kong, despite being the son of Rev. Chu Yiu Ming, one of the three founders of the Occupy Central campaign in 2014. An accidental invitation by a journalist friend brought him to Hong Kong in the summer of 2019, where he saw real political opportunity: "Congress is dead in the summer. I was worried that the marches would end and the news cycle would move on to something else. Then we would just see another iteration of Umbrella—every five years Hong Kong becomes a photo op, a news story, occasional lobbying by Martin, but nothing concrete will come out. I said to myself if these guys [Hong Kongers] could hang on for several more months, I could use this window to build a political machine to push the bill."[47]

While in Hong Kong, Samuel met with several democratic political leaders who supported the idea of establishing a permanent DC-based entity funded and run by American Hong Kongers but totally separate from the movement in Hong Kong. His years of organizing and acquaintance with legislators and congressional staff were a boon to the cause, allowing him to set up a nonprofit, the Hong Kong Democracy Council (HKDC), in a matter of weeks. Some of the original sponsors of HKDC were emigrant activists who came together in support of the pro-democracy demonstrations in Beijing in 1989 and Hong Kong in 2014. They formed organizations in major US and Canadian cities, including NY4HK (New York), Canada-Hong Kong Link (Toronto), NorCal HK Club (San Francisco), Hong Kong Forum (Los Angeles), Vancouver Society in Support of Democratic Movement, and an umbrella organization called the Alliance of Hong Kong Chinese in America with chapters in California, New York, Chicago, and Washington, DC. Besides June 4 commemorations, they also organized global solidarity actions echoing those in Hong Kong.[48]

Sustained and favorable coverage by the global media on street protests in Hong Kong gave HKDC the most valuable currency that Samuel and Jeffrey could capitalize on in dealing with American politicians: exposure. This was why it was immensely important that people stayed on the streets. Samuel's years of lobbying suggested to him that "foreign policy is not something that Americans vote on. But foreign policy is great for political attention; it generates exposure that is unique. You cannot underestimate how much they [politicians] crave any sort of attention. Like in the past three days, everyone was talking about Russia, not because they think people would vote on Russia, but because that's where the political attention is. And the Hong Kong movement was really relatable to the US audience. It was 'clean,' untainted by any complications such as the genocide of Rohingyas condoned by a Burmese rights leader. The Hong Kong issue is appetizing, something people can gain and profit from politically. It feeds into the political narrative about China. A lot of people can relate to Hong Kong in ways that they cannot relate to Tibet, Myanmar or Iran. Not only had they never been. But these places feel foreign to them. It's also that people like me, Martin, and Joshua speak English. That's a whole different game you can leverage. The mass protest does matter also because people can relate to things they can see. You don't get that coverage in Iran, for example. You only have grainy videos about people being beaten up. That's a whole different thing than professional news cameras and drone filming."[49]

Like Samuel, Jeffrey's experience from numerous visits to Congress came down to the political significance of news headlines, especially those from CNN, a fixture of congressional offices around the clock. He was elated to observe that, "The television [in these offices] is always muted, which means no one is listening to the reports. But, above the running banner at the bottom of the screen is one line announcing the news of the hour. For months in 2019, Hong Kong protests occupied that space. This is why Hong Kong, and not a million other issues, got Congress to act."[50] Media attention signaled to politicians that this issue was one they could exploit to create political capital. For those who were longtime supporters of the cause, the world's attention on Hong Kong could finally catalyze tangible legislation.

The role of a lobby organization such as HKDC, first managed by Samuel and then by Anna, with veteran student leaders turned exiles Brian Leung and Alex Chow on the board of directors, was to placate different people's political needs and interests at that moment. Samuel explained, "For Pelosi, Hong Kong was on brand for her. It's who she is. It's in her DNA to do it. Her first overseas trip was to China and Hong Kong back in 1991. She kept up these relationships. The moment I knew Pelosi was to continue as Speaker, I knew Hong Kong would get visibility because her brand was China and human rights. . . . Rubio failed miserably in 2016 and was cut out from the center of power in his party running against Trump, who won. He needed to carve out something to claim as a champion. And he was fighting with Josh Hawley and Ted Cruz on who can oust China. . . . After Josh Hawley was elected to the Senate, I got a call from his staff saying the senator was interested in going to Hong Kong. I helped organize the trip, including whom he should talk to."[51]

Two months after the bill was passed, Joshua Wong reckoned that Twitter also played a role in translating clashes on the street into political pressure in Washington: "There were a lot of accidents. We can never prove what was the most important factor. But combining news reports and what staffers mentioned to us afterwards, you'll get the picture that one of the factors was Hong Kongers' rigorous Twitter campaign. The large number of tags mentioning McConnell, Rubio, Pelosi, and Trump must have created immense pressure on them."[52] Indeed, it has been documented that these names were the top accounts on the Twitter "target list" of movement supporters in 2019–2020.[53]

Ultimately, individual, organizational, and mass lobbying for Hong Kong had real limits. These efforts had little influence on how the bill was written, what details were included, and whether it would be taken to the floor. As the protests entered the most violent phase on the campuses of CUHK and PolyU, political momentum to pass the bill reached a high point, hastening US legislators to act expediently.[54] Jeffrey was in constant communication with congressional staffers, feeding them information about the emergency situation in Hong Kong. He also got wind that Mitch McConnell's staffers were trying to delay the bill's passage in the Senate, but the development at PolyU shocked Rubio into confronting a reluctant McConnell, who eventually agreed to take the bill to a floor vote on November 20. However, certain business interests interfered at the final Senate stage, resulting in the addition of a five-year sunset clause to the final bill.[55]

In sum, the international front in 2019 was spearheaded by young activists such as Anna, Finn, Sunny, Jeffrey, Joshua, and Samuel with the assistance of veteran politicians and the Hong Kong diaspora. The postcolonial generation's unequivocal turn to international politics and the global public was a bold step, defying the power of the sovereign by subjecting it to the constraint of international norms and transnational forces. US sanctions against Hong Kong and Chinese officials triggered a tit-for-tat reaction—the Hong Kong government issued warrants for the most high-profile exiled activists. Under the National Security Law, their activism was criminalized as subversion of the state and collusion with foreign forces. From time to time, bounties were announced for the capture of these exiled activists, triggering a new round of condemnations of transnational repression by the governments in the United States, the UK, and Australia, now the host lands of these exiles. Such was the paradoxical effect of the National Security Law that the international spotlight on Hong Kong had both dimmed and lingered.

Cross-Movement Global Solidarity in 2019

So far, we have examined the international front's harnessing of global elite power, such as international institutions (G20, United Nations human rights mechanisms, and global media) and foreign government sanctions and legislations (the UK and the United States). But in the peripheral field of action and vision of the protesters in 2019, there was another dimension of the international front that engaged the power of popular uprisings outside Hong Kong. A prime example was a solidarity rally held simultaneously in Hong Kong and Barcelona on October 24, 2019. A thousand protesters in Central shouted the slogan "Stand with Catalonia, stand with Hong Kong" and waved the Estelada—the unofficial flag of the Catalan independence movement. Earlier that month, Barcelona also saw escalating street protests against the Spanish court's sentencing of Catalan independence activists to long prison terms of up to thirteen years. Catalonians explicitly referenced Hong Kong as the inspiration for their protests, with a group of youth occupying the local airport reportedly shouted, "We are going to do a Hong Kong!"[56] A public forum organized by a grassroots group was titled "Experiences of the Use of New Technologies in the Nonviolent Struggle: The Case of Hong Kong." The Facebook page of a protest group called Picnic x República listed several Hong Kong protest-related Telegram channels, with links in Catalan, as sources of inspiration and information, as well as photos of Hong Kong protesters' street-level organization. One of their representatives told the press, "The images and videos showing Hong Kongers' discipline passing messages and goods all along the lines of action made a strong impression on us, although we are not sure we could achieve such perfection. Maybe, with some time and practice!"[57] In response to the police violence both movements faced, the Hong Kong protesters chanted, "Fight against oppression" and "Fight for freedom together."[58]

Another example of cross-movement solidarity was the Milk Tea Alliance. Inventively named after a sweet drink popular throughout Asia, the hashtag #MilkTeaAlliance was born during a meme war in early 2020. After Chinese nationalist netizens attacked two Thai celebrities for supporting Hong Kong and Taiwan independence, a series of collaborative protests emerged with Hong Kongers' participation: a Twitter war, boycott action against cotton produced by forced labor in Xinjiang, and solidarity rallies for each other's pro-democracy protests. Soon, activists from the Philippines,

5.2 A solidary rally with Catalonia in Central Hong Kong on October 24, 2019.
CREDIT: *Hong Kong Free Press*

Indonesia, Malaysia, and Myanmar joined. A number of other movements from around the globe also dropped in and out of using the hashtag to raise awareness.[59] Throughout 2019, technologically savvy young protesters in Thailand, Myanmar, and Indonesia translated and shared manuals of Hong Kong protest tactics, detailing the building blocks of protests, from gears and infographics to slogans (including "be water") and concrete actions. They practiced them in their own protests.[60] In Myanmar, "protesters told Reuters that social media helps them borrow symbols and ideas from elsewhere, like using Hong Kong-style flash mobs, rapidly shifting hashtags and colorful meme artworks."[61]

Solidarity with the Black Lives Matter movement in the United States proved to be more controversial, exposing the Hong Kong movement's internal fissures. Even though activists eventually failed to realize any BLM-related action similar to the one supporting Catalonia, the debates pointed to people's imagination of a global field of action. The two movements shared striking similarities: both were leaderless, decentralized, sustained protests with police brutality a central target, and both enjoyed enormous international support. Attempts to organize a BLM solidarity rally in Hong Kong never materialized due to organizers' reluctance to criticize the Trump administration, which they deemed an ally to Hong Kongers' fight against China. When the protests erupted in late May 2020 in response to the police killing of George Floyd in Minnesota, Hong Kong Internet users shared tips with Americans on how to defuse tear gas canisters and how to "be water" when overwhelmed by riot police. Many identified strongly with the movement. But others wanted to keep a distance from BLM due to reports of lootings and indiscriminate destruction of private property. This did not sit well with Hong Kong protesters' ideal imagery of their own movement, even though it had its own share of vandalism and violence. When Trump railed against BLM and the American police used excessive force, many in Hong Kong were torn: "supporting whoever will stand with us and do something, but unfortunately it's only Trump, so Trump it is."[62]

Other than these three instances of movement outreach, Hong Kong protesters had been quite oblivious to the many struggles they had unwittingly inspired around the world in 2019. But the reality remained that learning and diffusion of tactics across movements certainly put Hong Kong in a prominent place in what can be called a "global 2019." According to one count, "37 countries experienced massive anti-government movements in the last few months of 2019 alone. And over the course of 2019, anti-government protests occurred in 114 countries—31 percent more than a decade ago."[63] It is no exaggeration to describe these as mass uprisings as the sheer size of the protests was remarkable. In at least three cases, a quarter of their respective populations went on the streets: 2 million in Hong Kong; 1.2 million in Santiago, Chile; and 1 million in Lebanon.

Intense international coverage of the Hong Kong protests in 2019 fueled a diffusion process that was reminiscent of other tidal waves of regional or transnational uprising in 1968, 1989, and 2011.[64] Digital connectivity, made possible by ubiquitous access to ICT and social media, provided the infrastructure for the process of diffusion. Besides the previously mentioned examples of Spain and Southeast Asia, Hong Kongers' innovative protest tactics were emulated far and wide. In Chile and Iraq, the laser pointer popularized by Hong Kongers in early August 2019 as a tool of defiance was eagerly adopted in street confrontations with the police in the following months. Lasers were used "to distract or obstruct riot police and their cameras and drones, as a colorful way to celebrate and show solidarity in groups, or as a method of communication."[65] In Lebanon, "Protesters began to use high-powered lasers and blinding lights to distract and confuse security forces—something they had never done before. We also learned how to

5.3 Graffiti in Beirut, November 20, 2019.
CREDIT: Joey Ayoub

neutralize tear gas based on tactics from Hong Kong."⁶⁶ In December 2019, during India's movement against the Modi government's Citizenship Amendment Act, which would block Muslim refugees from the neighboring countries of Pakistan, Afghanistan, and Bangladesh, many protesters took a page from the Hong Kong protesters' playbook. Besides sharing many of the characteristics of the Hong Kong movement—organic, leaderless, dispersed—Indian protesters switched from WhatsApp to Bridgefy after a local government imposed an Internet blackout. Bridgefy allowed mobile phone users to communicate with each other without any active Internet or phone connections, relying on Bluetooth connectivity among the users instead. In 2019, protesters in Hong Kong were using this software to communicate amid rumors that the city's government could shut down mobile networks.⁶⁷ In Peru, protesters faced with similarly intense police deployment organized into "brigades," like those among Hong Kongers. Each "consists of around 60 people, including paramedics, deactivators and 'front-line' activists who stand in the middle of protesters and police with shields, in an effort to block any pellets or tear gas police may fire into the crowd."⁶⁸ In particular, people learned how to be 'deactivators'—running toward instead of away from tear gas shot by police, "donning gas masks, safety goggles and thick gloves, these volunteers grab the hot canisters and toss them inside large plastic bottles filled with a mixture of water, baking soda and vinegar."[69]

In short, whether people were aware of it or not, Hong Kong's uprising was an ineluctable part of a global phenomenon in 2019. Outreach, learning, and diffusion of ideas and tactics from either direction had connected Hong Kongers with protesters elsewhere. But the dilemma posed by BLM for Hong Kong protesters also illustrated the limits of transnational solidarity against the complex matrix of national and international politics. This matrix of power was also one the Hong Kong diaspora had to engage and exploit.

Multiscalar Diasporic Activism

In the wake of the National Security Law and Beijing's unrelenting purge of all major liberal institutions in Hong Kong, an exodus of educated youths and middle-class families followed. The first two years after the law took effect, more than 150,000 had settled in the UK and 33,000 in Canada, with more expected to leave in the next few years.[70] With this wave of repression-induced emigration, a new global agenda had emerged among the Hong Kong diaspora. Like other diasporic communities, Hong Kongers' diasporic activism typically entails three types of action: cultural mobilization to preserve diasporic identity, political mobilization around homeland politics, and lobbying host governments.[71] During the 2019 movement, one study found 69 active Hong Kong diasporic groups in different countries organizing 139 solidarity protests responding to homeland political events.[72] These groups had gathered for networking and strategic discussions at several summits and retreats. For instance, several dozen diasporic organizations in the United States came together in March 2020, July 2022, and July 2023 in Washington, DC. A Montreal retreat in April 2023 featured prominent activists who discussed pathways to liberation. In March 2023, the UK-Hong Kong Summit in London was attended by representatives from more than sixty organizations of various sizes located all over the country.

If the previous waves of emigration from Hong Kong consisted of individual and family decisions induced by political anxiety, the post-2019 exodus was marked by a collective trauma in the homeland. The special immigration pathways offered by the British and Canadian governments to Hong Kongers in response to the National Security Law unceremoniously put an imprimatur on the new emigrants' political identity.[73] Prominent

Hong Kong political exiles are now regularly invited to appear in international forums to talk about their personal experience in terms of China's encroachment on human rights. Are they taking the international front in new directions? Lobbying host governments for policies facilitating Hong Kongers' emigration remains the main focus for organizations such as HKDC and Canada-Hong Kong Link. But others are discovering new advocacy possibilities at the transnational, national, subnational, cross-movement, and individual levels. Their search for ways to "liberate Hong Kong" is transforming Hong Kong from a "homeland"—a bounded geographical location they dream of living *in* once again—into a "heartland" they live *with* and carry forward as a life force informed by their shared history and suffering.[74]

At the most global level, one approach has been to assert the right to self-determination through UN human rights platforms, national legislative hearings, and other alternative global political spaces for unrepresented nations and marginalized and indigenous peoples. Legal scholars have argued for such an agenda and have shown how both the British and Chinese governments have colluded in depriving Hong Kongers of this universal human right.[75] Carole Petersen, for instance, pointed to customary international law on the rights of colonized peoples as the source of Hong Kong's right to autonomy and internal self-determination. She argued that in 1972, China's residual territorial claim to the New Territories portion of Hong Kong—and the United Kingdom's own geopolitical interests—ultimately prevented the people of Hong Kong from exercising external self-determination. Instead, the Sino-British Joint Declaration, as a tool for "resolving, in a peaceful manner, conflicts between the normal rights of a colonized people and a neighboring state's territorial claim," stipulated internal self-determination for Hong Kong as an autonomous region. But now that neither autonomy nor self-governance has been realized, the UN General Assembly has an obligation to bring China back into compliance. The UN Human Rights Council monitors China's Universal Periodic Review, while the UN Human Rights Committee monitors Hong Kong's compliance with the International Covenant on Civil and Political Rights, and the International Court of Justice has confirmed the UN's obligation to promote the right to self-determination even after a territory is delisted. In various diasporic forums, the reassertion of Hong Kong's right to self-determination had emerged as an action item. When a US-based activist reminded more than a hundred of his fellow Hong Kongers that the current UN power structure was consolidated at a particular historical moment—the end of World War II, when Japan and Germany were not given a seat on the Security Council but China and the United States were, someone in the audience asked what would happen if one day China lost its seat on the Security Council. What was done can be undone, they concluded. There have also been suggestions for campaigns to work with other peoples, including Tibetans, Uyghurs, and Ukrainians, to push the argument that Russia's and China's imperialist authoritarianism requires additions to the UN's list of non-self-governing territories. In meetings among diaspora groups, people also invoked the examples of the formation of Israel as a nation-state and Taiwan's achievement as a de facto independent political entity.

Another international space where overseas Hong Kongers have begun to show up after 2019 is transnational human rights advocacy. Conferences such as the Oslo Freedom Forum, Copenhagen Democracy Summit, Geneva Summit for Human Rights and Democracy, Interparliamentary Alliance on China, and more have featured young activists speaking out against tyranny and rights violations in Hong Kong. Personal testimonies of victimization are more valuable than abstract moral principles, since they make the stakes relatable, compelling, and urgent. In human rights conferences, activists' speeches could move and motivate politicians to take up their causes, for instance, by promoting sanctions against autocrats. Several Hong Kongers in exile—Nathan Law, Finn Lau, Anna Kwok, Glacier Kwong, and Francis Hui, among others—have been thrust into this role. For instance, Nathan, building on his track record as a student leader of the Umbrella Movement and the youngest elected legislator in Hong Kong's history, has become a prominent face of Hong Kong's exiled community and its international human rights cause. A frequent speaker in the world of human rights campaigning, he sees a niche for himself: "I as a Hong Konger represent a 'Chinese' liberal voice in international public discourse, something mainland dissidents cannot provide. They are too aligned with American right-wing conservatives."[76]

At a Prague conference hosted by the Interparliamentary Alliance on China in September 2023, Finn Lau shared his experience of having a bounty issued by the Hong Kong police for his arrest in violation of the National Security Law, reminding the attending legislators and human rights activists about the 1,900 political prisoners serving more than 770 years of imprisonment in Hong Kong. Self-mockingly, he came to realize that "my role is as a mascot, making a dry issue more human. The bounty shocked them. Many came up to me over the three days of meeting and told me they were moved by my story. A Bolivian legislator offered to show me around their parliament if I travel there, and a German Green Party legislator even encouraged me to run for office in the UK. Meetings like this are the beginning of a beginning, alerting them to the Hong Kong situation, building personal relations that may years later be helpful for Hong Kong."[77]

Another avenue for continuing the international front beyond 2019 was the idea of city diplomacy. After pro-movement candidates' landslide victory at the district board election in November 2019, netizens on LIHKG toyed with the idea of forging sister-city agreements between the district boards and cities in foreign countries, for example, Shatin with Geneva or Wong Tai Sin with London. The argument was that because district board representatives were generated by direct election, they had legitimacy equivalent to the British Lower House, as Finn Lau wrote in a vision statement for a liberated Hong Kong published in *Stand News* before the National Security Law took effect. Simon Cheng, a thirty-two-year-old political exile who founded and chaired Hong Kongers in Britain, a diaspora organization serving emigrants, was accidentally inducted into this realm of "city diplomacy" when he attended the Budapest Forum organized by the Pact of Free Cities in 2022. Founded by the mayors of Warsaw, Prague, Bratislava, and Budapest in 2019, the pact is an alliance of city mayors from around the world promoting progressive values to counter the nationalistic populism prevalent in many national legislatures. City diplomacy, in their view, was a space to circumvent the monopoly of power wielded by the national elites.

After delivering a keynote about Hong Kong's democracy struggle at the Budapest Forum, Simon reaffirmed his belief in the importance of inserting Hong Kong into this global narrative of freedom and human rights: "Mere talks and pledges of human rights won't change the political economic power structure of the world. But, once the latter is loosened by whatever forces, as it did when the Soviet Union collapsed, narratives will realize their weight. Public opinion is a war front of its own. That's why the Budapest Forum's partners included the German Marshall Fund and NATO."[78] Representing his NGO, Simon had joined others to submit implementation reviews to the UN Human Rights Committee documenting the deteriorating human rights conditions in Hong Kong, which is a signatory of the ICCPR. "If one day, China would loosen its grip in Hong Kong, public opinion, debates, narratives, political ideologies could amount to a countervailing mechanism. They may generate enough pressure to intervene in international law and force the withdrawal of National Security Law. It's part of a long-term strategy," Simon wagered.[79]

Emigrants settling into their communities overseas had discovered a new realm of local advocacy for Hong Kong. During a lively discussion session at the UK-Hong Kong Summit in 2023, one resident of Brighton questioned why Hong Kongers only asked the world to "Stand with Hong Kong" and not the other way around. When he recounted how he was inspired by the sight of a "Ukraine Stands with LGBTQ" banner at the Brighton pride parade, many in the audience nodded with approval. Building on this new comparative perspective, another participant admonished Hong Kongers' tendency to "peddle plight" (賣慘) as ineffective because their sufferings were nothing like those of Ukrainians or Afghans. In the same summit, embedding Hong Kong issues into the agenda of council and national electoral campaigns was proposed as a mode of everyday advocacy. "Just like what the Indians have done so successfully," one participant referenced the then newly minted British prime minister of Indian descent, Rishi Sunak, "Hong Kongers can one day be king makers too. . . . As part of the electorate, we could grill candidates about their positions on Hong Kong issues: government procurement from China, police violence, the trial of Jimmy Lai who is a British citizen, Hong Kong government's compliance with international conventions on torture."

On the cultural front, community activities aiming at preserving Hong Kong identity abound in the UK thanks to the large number of new immigrants. Art and craft shows, food bazars and festivals, popular history talks, book exhibitions, a mobile library, a literary club, and film festivals, however small and local, were means for sustaining a sense of history and belonging among Hong Kongers. Organizers also talked of sending a message to the British public that Hong Kongers are a community distinct from mainland Chinese. Cross-movement solidarity is yet another strategy to strengthen Hong Kong's cause. Some Hong Kongers joined the training camps, rallies, and signature campaigns organized by Uyghurs and Tibetan activists. Other proposed forming a Hong Kong Assembly resembling the World Uyghur Congress or the Central Tibetan Administration that can articulate a strong, legitimate voice representing the diaspora to lobby MPs, the British government, or the international community. Some ex-frontline valiant Hong Kongers even urged the diaspora to prepare for the takeover of the Hong

Kong administration when liberation comes. One of them implored the UK summit audience, "We need people with the psychological preparedness, knowledge and training in military affairs, strong and healthy fighters, and experience in running democratic government." Unlike most recent emigrants, these young activists are keeping up the fight abroad if only because their frontline bros and sisses are still in jail in Hong Kong. Their dream of returning to and retaking Hong Kong is very much alive.

Across the pond, one asylum seeker in the United States reckoned another kind of international front: to integrate into the elite institutions of the host country. In his late twenties, this young man's idea of Hong Kong advocacy has broadened after 2019. Pondering his future, he said "Sooner or later, when I become a naturalized Hong Kong-American, with my memory of Hong Kong, and my mindset, I can join the staff of the Pentagon, Congress, or the US government. Many Taiwanese Americans have done just that. I keep 'indoctrinating' [haha!] my friends around me that we can play many roles that a lobby organization like HKDC cannot. Everyone in the diaspora, as an individual, can connect his or her career path with advocacy for Hong Kong. Once you open this Pandora's box, a lot can be done by Hong Kongers. I prefer an interdisciplinary approach, not counting on any one organization. Of course, I'd like to return to Hong Kong in my lifetime. But no one knows how long this is going to take. All I know is this [international] path must have a long timeline."[80]

Hong Kong Unbound

A major breakthrough in Hong Kong's decolonization struggle in 2019 was the mass adoption of an international front—swaying international politics and the global public to circumvent the autocratic power of the nation-state. Young activists had no qualms about challenging China's sovereignty, which to them was imposed and external to their sense of personal and collective being. Coming of age in a postcolonial and global Hong Kong, habituated to a culture of protest, and embracing the quest for freedom and democracy as a universal right, they became localists and globalists for whom nationalism is an alien force, trumpeted by a one-party state. This generation's instinctual orientation to connect Hong Kong's localist demands with global norms was something the Chinese Communist regime had failed to grasp. Yet no amount of decolonizing agency alone could have succeeded in creating a popularly supported international front had there not been geopolitical tensions between China and the US-led West.

The passage of US legislation sanctioning officials and judges infringing on Hong Kongers' rights only materialized when bipartisan politicians agreed on confronting the Chinese Communist regime. This is why the HKHRD Act did not come to the floor of Congress before 2019. American legislative action was always tied to the interests of American politicians. In 2019, Hong Kongers' mass street action created so much attention and affection among the American public that politicians acting out of either calculation or conviction had to take a stance for their own good. The prime mover, as this chapter has shown, was not any organization, individual lobbyist, or American legislator but the sustained spectacle of Hong Kongers' mass mobilization. Alas, aligning the interests and power of foreign politicians with the cause of Hong Kong required the right conjuncture in the world of international politics, by nature fleeting and unpredictable.

A seasoned transnational human rights advocate working on China and Hong Kong had a sobering observation about Hong Kong's future in international politics: "We have lost on Hong Kong. We've got what we were going to get, and we are not going to get more because there is not adequate pressure for more. It's a very sad situation, but it is the reality. When we had two million people on the street, a lot of noise in the media and in Parliament, then we [activists in the UK] got some perfunctory stuff going, statement of concerns but absolutely no accountability measures for Hong Kong. Even at the height of the movement and with the UK having the most skin in the game, we only got the BNO scheme, which is not an accountability measure. And it's all because Hong Kongers can prop up the UK economy. Governments never care and will never on their own hurt business relations for the sake of human rights. They have to be pressured. London just announced a new trade commissioner for China and Hong Kong. The US did not do anything visa-wise for Hong Kongers."[81]

His support for Hong Kongers notwithstanding, he was frustrated not just by the instrumentalism of foreign governments but also by the lingering colonial mentality he observed among the new émigrés. His observation was that "Hong Kongers in the UK have been extremely deferential; it's very rare that they make demands publicly or in parliamentary hearings. Even the most famous dissidents. It is as if they say 'let's be good citizens,' rather than demand our rights. I feel like they treat this as their new borrowed home, feeling lucky to be taken care of. But no! You are entitled to these things, and by the way, the UK betrayed you very badly. I think this deferential posture arises perhaps from decades of disempowerment and colonialism. They are grateful for receiving crumbs. They need to take agency of their own rights."[82]

Hong Kong's decolonizing struggle has a long and treacherous road ahead. However, observing emigrants in action in the UK and the United States suggests, to me at least, that something profound has taken place. Hong Kong to them is no longer just a distant location they call their "homeland." The city has become a claim to action, a project, a cause, not limited to the territory within the Chinese borders. Still experimenting with multiscalar activism, without any guarantee of success, at least they had achieved the cognitive liberation from the colonial myth that China is Hong Kong's only destiny. From a comparative historical perspective, these diasporic activists are in a similar political location as their counterparts during the global wave of decolonization in the 1950s and 1960s. At that time, spearheaded by intellectuals and politicians, including those in exile and in the metropoles, projects such as Eurasia, Eurafrica, and Afroasia emerged to reimagine political relationships beyond the confines of either "colonial empires" or "nation-states." These cross-continental, postimperial constructions envisioned that groups with different ethnic origins and religions could share a historically conditioned capacity for alliance in a multinational polity.[83] That these movements eventually failed to mobilize people in widely varying localities and circumstances, especially compared to national elites championing national independence, suggests that efforts to continue the international front of the movement are neither easy nor necessarily effective. Yet, as this chapter has shown, no action is too small. No citizen making a private decision to join the peaceful marches in June 2019 would have foreseen the political tsunami they helped unleash. Nor could Martin Lee have predicted that Nancy Pelosi, with whom he maintained a personal relationship for decades, would one day climb to the top of American politics. The seeds that diaspora activists are sowing today, no matter how mundane or miniscule, may be of unimaginable significance when the right moment arrives.

CHAPTER SIX

TO BE CONTINUED

> *Even in the darkest of times we have the right to expect some illumination, and that such illumination may well come less from theories and concepts than from the uncertain, flickering, and often weak light that some men and women, in their lives and their works, will kindle under almost all circumstances and shed over the time span that was given them on earth.... Eyes so used to darkness as ours will hardly be able to tell whether their light was the light of a candle or that of a blazing sun.*
>
> —Hannah Arendt

IN 2024, FIVE YEARS AFTER THE INITIAL ERUPTION of the massive antiextradition movement, this quote from Hannah Arendt's *Men in Dark Times* (1968) was making its rounds on Hong Kong social media. Living under the totalitarian rule of not just one but two national security laws, netizens were gingerly searching for words of hope and comfort.[1] In this city of light, people gravitated toward a rumination about darkness. The paradox is as stark as it is sobering. Was the 2019 protest, and the broader decolonization struggle of which it was a part, a candlelight or a blazing sun? In this conclusion, I follow Arendt's sage advice: "Such objective evaluation seems to me a matter of secondary importance which can be safely left to posterity."[2] Of more immediate significance is to reflect on what Hong Kong's case suggests about colonization and decolonization. Looking ahead, all signs suggest the struggle has continued, if only because Beijing has publicly and emphatically announced, in the wake of the 2019 uprising, its own project to "decolonize" Hong Kong from above. This chapter summarizes what decolonization from below entailed in Hong Kong as a historical process and what analytical lessons the Hong Kong experience offers about the sociology of decolonization. Broaching this ongoing process without the distorting lens of a known end point, I conclude this book by sketching the clashing visions of decolonization proposed by Chinese Communist officials and their scholarly elite as opposed to those by Hong Kong activists and intellectuals. These imaginaries all intimate the global and epochal significance of Hong Kong's ongoing contestation.

Decolonization: What Has Changed?

A major claim this book makes is that since the late 1990s, a quarter century of resistance by the people of Hong Kong amounted to a decolonization struggle that chipped away at the foundations of a 180-year-old colonial order. While the result was not taking hold of the state or declaring political independence, their activism shattered the colonial boundaries of the political and forged people's subjecthood as makers of their own history. Focusing on people's decolonial praxis—the assemblage of thought-action-reflection—I showed that Hong Kong's decolonization did not begin with a master plan or a visionary ideology, organization, or leadership. It gathered momentum, haphazardly and haltingly, one campaign after another, championing an array of causes—from universal suffrage and electoral reforms to urban planning, cultural and education policies, immigration, and police accountability. This echoed Fanon's observation that decolonization "cannot be accomplished by the wave of a magic wand, a natural cataclysm, or a gentleman's agreement. . . . It can only find its significance and become self-coherent in so far as we can discern the history making movement which gives it form and substance."[3] At the forefront were the young postcolonial generation, who succeeded in enrolling an ever-expanding number of their fellow citizens. Invoking the rhetoric of decolonization unevenly across campaigns and constituencies, the summation of their agitation was the crumbling of the core pillars of a colonial hegemony coproduced by Britain and China that had limited Hong Kongers' political imagination, agency, and capacity. Why and how did colonized subjects remake themselves into subjects of decolonization? What changes had they brought about through two decades of popular uprising?

To understand Hong Kong's decolonizing trajectory, one must revisit its colonial past. Officially a British colony, the city was actually subjected to double colonialization, with China (under the Qing dynasty and Republican and Communist governments) always asserting a phantom influence. Ideological animosity notwithstanding, Britain and China were complicit in denying Hong Kongers the right to self-determination thanks to their shared interest in keeping the city a depoliticized economic colony. British policies, from brutal repression of dissent and blatant neglect of social welfare for more than a century to late colonial social and political reform, were made so often with an eye toward China's reaction that the Communist regime was practically a cocolonizer. Under this situation of double colonization, where political aspirations and activism were severely punished, and where the alternative to colonialism was Communism, Hong Kongers, who were mostly refugees and immigrants from the mainland, developed a survivalist culture of pragmatism. Coupled with sustained postwar economic growth, British colonialists' deliberate social reforms had absorbed and pacified the brief bout of anticolonial rebellions in the 1960s and 1970s. From then on, for about a quarter century, Britain and China forged a colonial rule by consent in anticipation of the empire's honorable retreat and China's resumption of national sovereignty. Despite their intense tussle over the pace and extent of democratization in the last five years of formal British rule, the two colonial masters shared an abiding interest in sustaining a colonial hegemony built around four tenets—prosperity and stability, the rule of law, a free-market economy, and China as destiny. These core values had been trumpeted as the eternal truths of Hong Kong's success story. But as Chapter 1 argues, these were myths that obliterated the history of colonial repression and reduced people's aspirations to the status quo on the eve of the handover. Since the mid-1980s, when the two colonizers decided to transfer the city's sovereignty from one to the other, taking pains to exclude Hong Kongers from their negotiations, the local populace embraced these mythologies to sublimate their powerlessness and anxiety and acquiesced to a future thrust upon them. The long absence of a struggle for decolonization before the 1997 handover was therefore the result of an overwhelming imbalance of power between the colonizers and the colonized and the depoliticizing lure of economic prosperity.

Yet the colonizers' plan of simply transferring sovereignty over the proverbial "goose that lays the golden egg" from one to the other did not go as planned. After 1997, colonial mythologies that previously secured rule by consent became antiregime critique when they were violated by external shocks, opening up possibilities, capacities, and identities that were constituted and contested through collective action. In specific terms, Hong Kong's decolonizing struggle erupted in the post-handover era when the city became the eye of a perfect storm where three powerful forces converged and collided: the economic turbulence of neoliberal capitalism hitting a global city, the contradictory imperatives of globalizing Chinese state capitalism, and a young political generation interpellated to become masters of their postcolony. They were in a hurry to do so thanks to the imminent expiration date of China's promise of "One Country, Two Systems."

During the first decade of Chinese rule, Hong Kong as a global city was exposed to the devastating volatility of capitalist neoliberalization and its nemesis, the global justice movement. The former ignited discontent and doubts about Hong Kong's mythologies of success while the latter provided inspiration for people to challenge the status quo. The Asian financial crisis, the bust of property market speculations (a precursor of the 2008 Wall Street meltdown), the SARS epidemic (a precursor of COVID-19), and government mismanagement alienated the middle class. They also shattered the inherited wisdom that a free-market economy, the rule of law, and a popular abstention from politics would guarantee prosperity and stability. Taking inspiration from the global social justice movement and empowered by social media and advances in communication technology, a minority of activists asserted their democratic right to the city, proposed a new notion of a good society, and challenged the behavioral norm of polite politics. Unwittingly, and with hindsight, these fringe movements had enough of a domino effect across society to set Hong Kong on a decolonizing path.

Then, since the early 2010s, as a globalizing China flexed its economic, political, and cultural muscle around the world, including in Hong Kong, the city's popular protests became ever more focused on China. Under Xi Jinping, Beijing felt assured of its economic prowess but was haunted by the collapse of Soviet and Eastern European Communism. Global economic integration proceeded apace in tandem with heightened national securitization. The same contradictory impulses motivated Beijing's policy toward Hong Kong. On the one hand, an instrumental imperative to preserve Hong Kong's status as an indispensable broker for China to access Western capital and technology compelled Beijing to leave intact the city's major liberal institutions and ways of life. This was also a condition explicitly prescribed by the 1992 United States-Hong Kong Policy Act. The remnants of colonial liberalism inadvertently provided the necessary political space for Hong Kong's decolonizing agitation to take off. On the other hand, an imperialistic impulse dictated a clear shift toward tightening control and stalling democratic reform, sparking widespread discontent. Beijing's goal was to remake the city's liberal institutions—media, education, civil service, election, law enforcement, and criminal justice—in its own Communist image. But mainlandization of everything was perceived by Hong Kongers, especially the younger generations, as an existential crisis, an external, colonial invasion of the homeland. The anti-national education campaign (2012), the Umbrella Movement (2014), the Fish Ball Revolution (2015), and the antiextradition movement (2019) were all rebellions against what people experienced as recolonization.

Even as two decades of popular mobilization (1997–2020) had not resulted in the removal of external political and military control, they had led to an unmistakable change in the political subjectivity of the people. First, under colonial rule, "stability and prosperity" was hailed as the gold standard of a good society, and no politics could threaten or question this achievement. Political economic upheavals and social movements since 1997 had burst the myth that "stability and prosperity" could be maintained without "democracy and freedom," now considered the more fundamental and desirable sine qua non of a good society. By 2019, the popular idea of "burnism," or mutual destruction, went as far as advocating destabilizing the status quo in order for Hong Kong to have a future of democracy and autonomy.

Second, Hong Kongers' commitment to the rule of law and a polite culture of protest was subverted through two decades of decolonizing struggle. Gone was people's submission to the principle of peaceful, rational, and nonviolent resistance. Especially after the Umbrella Movement in 2014, as Beijing and the Hong Kong government weaponized the law and the judiciary to disqualify opposition political representatives from election, curb civil liberty, impose harsh sentences on dissidents, and allow the police to inflict disproportionate violence on protesters with impunity, the line between law and violence was blurred in the public consciousness. In 2019, the motto "be water" signaled a drastic expansion of the repertoire of legitimate resistance, which now included violating the law for justice. With the implementation of the National Security Law, gone was the popular naivete about law as synonymous with justice and impartiality.

Third, popular belief in Hong Kong as a free-market economy was so entrenched that before 1997, the colonial government was able to keep demands for social spending at bay while drawing attention away from oligopolies, many of British origin. But the local version of the global justice movement erupting at the turn of the millennium sustained an enduring critique against profit-driven developmentalism and socioeconomic disparity caused by oligopolistic capital in real estate and Red capital from China. In 2019, the political consumer movement popularized the idea of a prodemocracy "yellow economy" with a supply chain free from dependence on China. The new unionism movement against Red capital's erosion of professionalism also brought new attention to the ineluctable connection between politics and economy, busting the myth of Hong Kong as a "free" market economy.

Finally, through their action and slogans, the younger generation openly declared the bankruptcy of the "China as destiny" myth. The popularity of a variety of localist ideologies intensified in tandem with Beijing's violation of its own "One Country, Two Systems" promise, which had the unintended effect of liberating people's political imagination from the confines of this blueprint. Self-determination and Hong Kong independence were publicly discussed in the election platforms of new political parties formed after the Umbrella Movement. By 2019, "Hong Kong independence, the only way out" became the ubiquitous protest chant. An international front of the movement arose to garner the support of the global public and foreign governments to counter China's sovereign authority. Emigrants and exiles had vowed to continue this unfinished project of "liberating" Hong Kong, now taking uncertain postnational directions.

It must be emphasized that the breakdown of the colonial order and the rise of decolonizing subjecthood had been uneven. This book has focused on the "postcolonial" generations coming of age in the post-1997 era who were the leading force of decolonization, a demographic and political constituency whose collective interests were most implicated by the 2047 expiration date of "One Country, Two Systems." In a population of 7.5 million, they were a numerical minority, but their passion, ideas, and action had an outsize impact on the pragmatic majority, who in ordinary times were preoccupied with life's routines and the pursuit of private interests. But in extraordinary moments, as during the mass uprising in 2019, they had shown up to an unprecedented extent, joining the struggle that caught the regime by surprise. As we have seen, many were transformed by the movement they helped unleash, while others retreated to their rearguard positions at critical junctures, be it the referendum for a general strike or during the many frontline battles with the riot police.

The conservatism of the pragmatic majority was in no small measure attributable to the Chinese regime's vast machinery of patron-clientelism, which had penetrated all corners of society and coopted citizens from all walks of life. At the top of the power structure, Beijing's largesse had for years groomed politicians and political parties to do its bidding in the Hong Kong legislature and rewarded the "patriotic" pro-China business elite with honorific titles useful for their expansion on the mainland. Thanks to the domination of Chinese capital, professional associations in accountancy, medicine, law, engineering, and more also saw the rise of pro-China representatives. At the grassroots level, the united front apparatus was given a strong organizational and financial boost in the aftermath of the 2003 antigovernment rally. The Liaison Office, tasked to create a second governance ladder in Hong Kong and to change the hearts and minds of the people, had overseen an expansion of mass organizations throughout the territory. Hometown and clan associations, women's federations, neighborhood committees, and new immigrants' organizations were given generous budgets to literally buy the allegiance of grassroots clients. In short, whether out of interest, identity, ideology, or inertia, there was no lack of support for the establishment. As in other decolonization struggles, opposition to change came not just from the regime but from a society already fractured and structured by colonial forces.

Contemporary Decolonization

Against the most canonized historical cases of decolonization in the academic literature, certain characteristics of Hong Kong's contemporary experience are anomalous. First, at the perceptual level, Hong Kong's fight for decolonization was not always recognized as such. Absent from this twenty-first-century decolonization struggle in a cosmopolitan global financial center was the abject brutality of slavery and the destructive violence of torture, racial segregation and oppression, poverty, diseases, and wretched dispossession commonly found in accounts of decolonization in Haiti, Algeria, Kenya, Namibia, Congo, and elsewhere. In Hong Kong, for most of its existence, colonial violence has taken the more insidious and "productive" forms of institutional, symbolic, and identity violence. As a consequence, the decolonization struggle of the city also manifested itself as institutional, symbolic, and identity politics and mobilizations around election, education, cultural preservation, and identity claims.

Second, whereas scholars tend to focus on racialized capitalism as *the* structural political economic impetus of colonialism, and therefore of decolonization resistance, the Hong Kong story complicates this analysis. In addition to British imperialism as an expression of the expansionist logic of capitalism, Hong Kong's colonial situation brings to light an additional force: actually existing Communism. Before 1997, it was the complicity and competition between the two powers that formed the structural basis of double colonization in Hong Kong, and for the colonized subjects, British imperialism was experienced as less oppressive than Chinese Communism. After the handover, the Chinese Communist regime instituted a state capitalism and racialized nationalism on the colony that proved to be another form of colonization. While contemporary scholarship accords theoretical priority to racialized capitalism, the trajectory of Hong Kong's decolonization struggle sheds light on the understudied coloniality of Chinese Communism and the complex configuration of multiple colonizations that obfuscate the oppression of racial capitalism in the lived experience of the colonized subjects.

Also, Hong Kong's colonial experience suggests the multiple logics of racialization. While, before 1997, race was deployed by the British colonialists as a politics of difference and exclusion, the colonial relationship between China and Hong Kong illustrates a logic of racial domination grounded on claims of sameness and unity. China's semicolonialization by Western colonial powers in what the Chinese called "a century of humiliation" spawned a state nationalism that sought to reverse this wrong as a remedy to all problems.[4] As the self-professed redeemer of a metaphysical unity that was split by foreign powers, the CCP's ideologies and policies since 1949 have established the domination of the Han majority through the coercive assimilation of ethnic and religious minorities within its territory. In post-1997 Hong Kong, where the majority are Han, Beijing's practice of racial nationalism (in education, media, and political appointment) demanded loyalty to the party-state on the basis of racial similarity, primordial blood ties, and shared cultural origin. The historian Arif Dirlik's remark about the insidious coloniality of Chinese nationalism as a former victim of colonization is instructive: "Nationalism itself [i]s a form of colonialism—not in the ordinary sense of nations colonizing other nations or ethnicities, but in the sense of nation-building itself as colonial activity. Coloniality in nation-building is relieved somewhat by the real or imagined cultural proximity of the subjects of the nation, as well as the promise of political empowerment, most importantly in their remaking as citizens with 'the right to have rights' which distinguish the colonialism in nationalism from colonial relations nations. It is more readily visible where the nation-state denies citizenship rights to its subjects while imposing upon them obligations of loyalty and service to abstract notions of nationhood embodied in the state, or, more concretely, as in the case of the PRC, in the party-state."[5]

Finally, unlike historical studies of decolonization with the end of the story already known (that is, nationalist triumph), this book tracks an ongoing struggle whose eventuality is wide open. Whereas the former condition often leads historians to read backward and produce unidirectional metanarratives of nationalist triumph subsuming all other struggles, the latter allows us to see the messy politics and ambivalent subjectivities inside decolonization in progress. As a subject-oriented deep dive into Hong Kong's decolonial struggle over twenty years, this book reveals that decolonizing resistance is demanding, ambivalent, and reversible for the people involved. The treacherous entanglement of coloniality and decoloniality is most obvious in the Hong Kong case whereby, in countering Chinese colonial claims of *sameness,* the colonized subjects ironically drew on their historical experience with British colonialism to develop discourses of civic, cultural, and historical *difference* to legitimize their demands for autonomy. Colonial mythologies of the rule of law, civic liberty, prosperity and stability, and a fair and free market economy became the ideological standpoints to criticize and subvert the coloniality of Chinese racial nationalism. Through various campaigns, drawing inspiration globally, people reimagined various elements of the colonial modernity they inherited. From the colonized subjects' perspective, their struggle was neither a total rejection nor a total embrace of colonial modernity, making it difficult to assert from the outside an a priori definition or normative end point of decolonization.

As a process rather than an outcome of struggle, decolonization is reversible and its subjects defective. For more than twenty years, especially in 2019, Hong Kong protests demonstrated the essential spirit of decolonization, characterized as the citizens' "will to community," "to stand up on one's own and to create a heritage . . . making possible the manifestation of one's own power of genesis, one's own capacity for articulating difference and for expressing a positive force."[6] Activists' self-narratives throughout the book attest to their determination to make sacrifices, build a legacy, and forge a political community. But they were also constantly assessing the legal liability of their action and the threshold of personal sacrifice, weighing the balance of heroic camaraderie and apprehensive retreat among fellow citizens at critical moments of resistance. The Hong Kong resistance movement was able to sustain itself for as long as it did in large part because of the Chinese regime's recalcitrant refusal to reform, bargain, or concede. If China had abided by "One Country, Two Systems" or not been constrained by its own interest to preserve Hong Kong's civil liberty for so long, allowing the decolonial movement to acquire organizing, ideological, and reflexive capacity, or had the Hong Kong government yielded to some of the five demands early on in 2019, decolonization resistance would not have exploded into a citywide, cross-class, cross-generation uprising. The decolonizing subject was therefore by turns quixotic and timid, committed and calculating, unyielding and compromising.

Clashing Imaginaries of Decolonization

As I ponder the future of Hong Kong, two clashing visions of decolonization loom on the horizon. On the one hand, Communist officials and establishment intellectuals call for a comprehensive decolonization of Hong Kong to cleanse its people's hearts and minds already corrupted by Western colonialism's toxic vestiges. And, beyond just a governance strategy under Chinese sovereignty, decolonizing Hong Kong is part of a broader project—as a "border" experiment and a "method" for developing a China-centered world empire. On the other hand, a diametrically opposite view of decolonization emerging from the resistance movement was articulated by Hong Kong activists and public intellectuals. They outlined visions of citizenship, community, and revolution and, like their Communist counterparts, saw decolonization as a global project involving transnational alliances championing relational equality in the broadest sense.

China: Hong Kong Decolonization as a Method of Empire

In the writings and speeches of Communist officials, the governance problems China faced in post-1997 Hong Kong originated from the city's century-old coloniality, deeply entrenched in its institutions, ideology, and identity. Ignoring its own historical complicity in perpetuating Hong Kong as a colony before the handover, Beijing now bemoaned the lack of national identification among Hong Kong people, which according to officials' diagnosis was a main reason for the wave after wave of social protests under Chinese rule. The other main reason was foreign, particularly American, manipulation á la the color revolutions in the early 2000s. Since the half-million-strong protest on July 1, 2003, scholar-officials sent to tackle what has since been called the "hearts and minds" problem in Hong Kong began to reengineer people's identity. Over the past twenty years, and especially after 2019, under the rubric of "decolonization," Beijing has forcefully implemented its own colonization by transplanting mainland institutions to Hong Kong. The list of its (de)colonization programs kept growing: patriotic education curriculum, propaganda campaigns in mass media, expansion in clientelist networks in communities, the rise of a second echelon of political leaders under Beijing's direct control to replace homegrown allies, the appointment of patriotic judges and electoral vetting of patriotic candidates, mandatory pledge of political loyalty by civil servants, and the eradication of liberal civil society organizations. On a more pedestrian level, decolonization had a symbolic front, with patriotic legislators floating proposals to rename public parks (Victoria Park), streets (Hennessy Road), and schools (Queen Elizabeth School) bearing the "humiliating" imprint of Hong Kong's colonial history.[7]

Chinese thinking of "decolonization" as both a national and global agenda can be found in the writings of a number of establishment scholar-officials who were either dispatched to the Liaison Office in Hong Kong to conduct research and write up policy documents or professional academics already employed in local universities. Defending and justifying Xi's regime with academic analyses and concepts, these authoritarian scholars came mostly from the fields of legal and political studies and write in prose of varying degree of coherence and clarity. They were equally deft in citing ancient Chinese thinkers who counseled stern rulership and contemporary Western critics of liberal political traditions, meandering between the leftist traditions of Antonio Gramsci and subaltern studies and the statist theories of the Nazi jurist Carl Schmitt.[8] "Decolonization" for them is a statecraft for nationalizing Hong Kong, which is conceived as both a proving ground for exercising a sovereignist rule of law within the country and as a new borderland of a China-centered civilizational global order.

A prominent voice justifying Beijing's decolonization as a necessary policy to realize, rather than violate, "One Country, Two System" came from the sociologist and CCP political advisor Lau Siu-kai. Thanks to the fame he won by writing influential scholarship on British colonial governance and the Hong Kong Chinese culture of political apathy (discussed in Chapter 1), Lau had assumed a leadership role in the Chinese Association of Hong Kong and Macau Studies, a think tank under the State Council's Hong Kong and Macau Work Office. Drawing on his academic publications on how Britain implemented a historically unique "decolonization without independence" in Hong Kong, in recent years Lau churned out public-facing diatribes, defending China's decolonization as a response to the damage done by Britain's decolonization.[9] He called it "de-decolonization." For him, British decolonization entailed a series of hurried reforms in the run-up to 1997—electoral and legal reforms, expanding popular franchise and human rights, checks on executive power, empowering democratic political parties, and so forth. These measures, all designed to maximize British influence and citizens' identification with colonial culture and institutions, resulted in an anti-China and anti-Communist Hong Kong. Such British decolonization was therefore an abomination sabotaging "One Country, Two Systems" in the Sino-British Declaration, which stipulated that Hong Kong should be executive led, ruled by patriots, and never a bastion of subversion. With this "proper" historical perspective, Lau shot back at local and international critics accusing China of abrogating an international treaty and betraying the people of Hong Kong. Chinese rather than British decolonization was the true way to realize OCTS. He envisioned that "even though Hong Kong has been returned to its motherland for more than 25 years, Beijing's 'de-decolonization' project has yet to be fully accomplished. Unremitting efforts at 'de-decolonization' will continue to shape the configuration of politics in Hong Kong in the years ahead."[10]

For the law professor Tian Feilong, one of Lau's directors at the same think tank, decolonization was at heart about transforming culture and law. The root cause of the 2019 protests was the city's "twisted" education and culture, Tian reckoned, noting that "in the name of freedom, people perpetuated their position as colonized subjects and refused a national education founded on patriotism."[11] Writing in the wake of the forced dissolution of a fifty-year-old educators' union, he accused the organization of being a radicalizing tool of Hong Kong's "color revolution" and a vestige of colonial civil society aimed at destroying "One Country, Two Systems" through the education system. For him, decolonization should go together with delocalization because colonialism and localism had colluded, bringing about slogans such as "Liberate Hong Kong, revolution of our times." Finally, to add even more moral heft to China's project of decolonizing, Tian invoked the term "transition justice" to justify the need to remove the deep-seated relics of colonialism and establish a cultural order and psychology compatible with OCTS.[12]

Decolonization as cultural overhaul was also emphasized by Yan Xiaojun, a mainland-born, Harvard-educated, pro-establishment political scientist now at the University of Hong Kong. Joining an official craze of "decolonization" opinion pieces in the press, he argued that three aspects of Hong Kong's colonial culture had to be overhauled in order for the city to develop and innovate. Citing subaltern scholars on British colonialism in India as a cultural project, Yan argued that (1) a highly contentious political discourse was developed by the retreating British empire to resist China through democratization; (2) the colonial governance philosophy of "small government, big society" became a constraint on the power of the post-handover government; and (3) the general colonial cultural order had adversely affected the younger generation in Hong Kong.[13]

Among these so-called statist intellectuals promoting and rationalizing the Communist regime's authoritarian worldview in the Xi Jinping era, it was the writings of Jiang Shigong that were the most revelatory on Chinese decolonization in Hong Kong. A law professor from Beijing who was sent to the research department of the Liaison Office in Hong Kong (2004–2007) after the mass demonstration in 2003, Jiang was widely considered the architect of China's hardline turn in Hong Kong. After his stint in the city, Jiang returned to Beijing as a vice dean at the Peking University Law School, and his prolific writings continued to amplify two main strands of regime thinking—sovereignty and empire—that situate Hong Kong decolonization within the national and international contexts. First, Jiang asserted that China enjoyed absolute and substantive sovereignty, or "comprehensive jurisdiction," over Hong Kong, a concept he expounded on in a 2014 white paper on "One Country, Two Systems" issued by Beijing that triggered the Umbrella Movement. Jiang and other faculty at the Peking University Law School, heavily influenced by the Nazi legal theorist Carl Schmitt, developed a "sovereignist" school of legal thinking. He put forth the idea of an "absolute constitution," defined as "the concrete wholeness of a given country's territorial unity and social order," to subordinate the rule of law in Hong Kong. The assault on Hong Kong's legal and judicial systems under "comprehensive jurisdiction" was part of a broader theoretical critique of liberal theories of law. Their writings and policies echoed Schmitt's idea of sovereignty as the state's monopoly over the ability to define friend and enemy, both internally and externally, and to decide upon a "state of emergency" in which politics (the friend/enemy distinction) takes precedence over the rule of law. Moreover, it is the party, not the state, that embodies sovereignty. In Jiang's view, "The highest power of interpretation of the constitution should . . . lie with the Party rather than with the state, because it has the power not only to interpret the letter of the law or to protect citizens from the state, as in Western systems, but to preserve the balance between Party, state, and social ethics."[14]

Beyond being a proving ground for a sovereignist model of governance within China, Jiang saw in Hong Kong people's resistance to Chinese rule a telltale sign of a fundamental problem for China on a global scale: "In a post-Cold War world, when the ideology of 'end of history' has spread globally, Hong Kong has leveraged its ideological and cultural leadership to contest the central government's political domination. . . . Even though China is legally a sovereign state with the power of political domination [over Hong Kong], its discursive power is constricted by the cultural domination of a US-led world imperial system."[15] From what he called a transcivilizational perspective, Hong Kong as a border (just as Taiwan, Tibet, and Xinjiang are also borders) is not a "problem" but a "method" for China's "unfinished project" of constructing a "civilizational empire."[16] He distinguished a "Confucianist empire," which is benign domination based on morality and norms, from the exploitative and extractive British empire, the expansionist Roman empire, and the cultural supremacy of the American empire. According to Jiang, "the Hong Kong question is at the core of Chinese civilization revival," and the China in "One Country, Two Systems" is not a nation-state but a Chinese civilizational order.[17] Governing Hong Kong is an experiment for China to develop the flexible statecraft that can accommodate diversity within this imagined centralized civilizational order, or "a world empire 2.0."[18]

Hong Kong: Decolonization as Relational Equality and Self-Determination

In stark contrast to the idea of decolonization as a method for world empire building, imaginaries of decolonization from within Hong Kong and its diaspora emphasize various modalities of relational equality. The first entry into this repository of intellectual resources dated back to the pre-1997 social movements. As explained in Chapter 1, the city was never a land known for radical ideology or anticolonial thoughts because, for the people at that time, fighting against British colonialism from a nationalist position meant accepting Chinese Communism. But out of this complex political landscape came a small group of radical thinkers, part of the global 1960s cohort, seeking an alternative path of political ideology for Hong Kong. One of them was Ng Chung-yin. Beginning as the leader of a campus rebellion criticizing authoritarian control by the administration of a local college, Ng became a central figure in the so-called fiery era of the 1970s and was among a group of young intellectuals behind the bilingual publication *The 70s Weekly*. Regarded as a magazine of the "New Left," which differentiated it from publications of the mainstream Left defined by the CCP, and later as a journal of "youth radicalism" with anarchist coloring, it was an alternative creative and political space. Their critical writings targeted all forms of authority, including colonialism, imperialism, Chinese Communism, and the mass media, and advocated direct action such as street protests and autonomous, bottom-up self-organizations.[19] In a recent review of Ng's radical writings published mostly in the *70s Weekly*, Law Wing Sang highlighted their contemporary resonance. First, inspired by the youth rebellions in the 1960s, Ng considered young students the most important revolutionary agents. Second, even in an era of political cynicism and pessimism, Ng proposed a vision of a "third revolution" in the Hong Kong–China context. It would emerge out of the failures of the previous two, namely, the Republican revolution led by Dr. Sun Yat-sen and the Communist revolution led by Mao Zedong. It would be a revolution against all ruling powers—colonialism, capitalism, nationalism, and the CCP—and would require the awakening of an internationalist solidarity with oppressed people all over the world. Third, like Fanon, Ng emphasized the transformative potential of "action," which will overcome fatalistic determinism and lay the groundwork for genuine revolution. Hence his active role in the Chinese as official language movement and the defend the Diaoyutai movement in the mid-1970s. Although he admitted that "we do not have any grounds to be optimistic about replacing British colonialism, let alone CCP rule in China; yet combating against colonial rule in Hong Kong is still our immediate task—simply because the immediacy of colonial rule provides a starting point to awaken people from all these different versions of fatalistic determinism."[20]

Launching a double critique of British capitalist colonialism and the CCP's bureaucratic authoritarianism, and believing that all oppression would generate its resistance, Ng envisioned a mutuality between Hong Kong's and China's revolutions. He tried different ways to foster cooperation between activists on both sides of the border, as well as forming cross-class alliances with young workers by organizing the Revolutionary Marxist League. Before Ng died in 1994 at the age of forty-eight, he and his associates created a niche of radical politics and discourse at the grassroots level. Their activism declined precipitously in the run-up to 1997, when democratic political reform by the colonial regime and China's turn to capitalism became the political economic games of the day. Still, the questions Ng tackled—the relationship between Hong Kong's and China's popular movements and the class divide among citizens—have not lost their relevance.

After 1997, the most influential decolonial thinker is Law Wing Sang, a cultural studies scholar who is also a well-known columnist using the pen name 安徒 in the intellectual newspaper *Ming Pao*. As a faculty member in the Cultural Studies Department at Lingnan University, he and his colleagues saw cultural critique as political intervention, and in their role as activist scholars, they instilled in their students a passion for social activism. In 1982, Law's anticolonial stand prompted him to lead a small student protest against the continuation of British colonial rule beyond 1997, a proposal Margaret Thatcher was then taking to Beijing. His dissertation, which became the seminal book *Collaborative Colonial Power* (2009), offers an incisive and critical history of the indigenization of British colonial power through selected Chinese elite, as well as their impact on the making of Hong Kong Chinese identity. Shunning academic production catering to a small, professional knowledge elite, Law writes mostly in Chinese for public consumption.[21] One of his consistent critiques of post-1997 Hong Kong mainstream politics was the idea of "virtual liberalism." This refers to the illusionary freedom and democracy that political parties and civil society conjured with their participation in the structurally biased electoral system and large-scale ritualistic rallies. For him, these were performative and carnival-like politics that did not truly empower citizens. People's repeated performances simply made freedom and democracy *feel* real and romantic but avoided serious reflections on the political structure, the internal fractures in civil society, and the CCP's cooptation of the elite and the grassroots. Exactly because virtual liberalism could not address the structural causes of Hong Kongers' discontent, the younger generation was compelled to look to radical alternatives outside institutionalized politics and polite civil society. In Law's assessment, the movements documented in this book broke the spell of virtual liberalism.

Another important aspect of Law's critique of Hong Kong's coloniality was the absence of historical subjectivity. In the post-handover period, even in light of an unmistakable rise in local identity and consciousness, Law cautions that Hong Kongers' localism lacks reflexive agency, creativity, and autonomy. In his view, Hong Kongers' local consciousness has long remained at the level of lifestyle, core values, and institutions. It lacks critical and honest reflections of their collective past struggles, due in no small part to the obliteration of local history in the colonial education system. Decolonial subjects must seek to regain their historical reflexivity.[22] Given how colonialism and nationalism have intertwined in Hong Kong's development, he argues, the constitution of agentic local subjectivity would call for a careful dissection of Hong Kongers' entanglement with these forces.[23]

Law's advocacy for decolonial subjectivity was a thoughtful intervention in post-Umbrella identity politics leading up to the 2019 uprising. The basic questions people were grappling with are still relevant today: What kind of political community are Hong Kongers aiming to create? How do we define who is or is not a Hong Konger? As seen in Chapters 2, 3, and 4, acrimonious divides based on ethnicity/race, gender, class, and tactical preference persisted, coming to the surface at various moments. The most salient fracture was the opposition between two ideas of community—the nativists' ethnic-based, essentialist "communitarianism" and the progressives' abstract, value-neutral, individualistic "liberalism." Law proposed a third alternative, "civic republicanism," that defined the constitution of a political community as a continuous process of civic praxis and struggle for equal rights of participation, a process that *coproduced* the political community as well as the citizenry through action that now transcended their original cultural, linguistic, and religious identities. For him, this was what a truly "decolonized imaginary of political community" should strive for.[24]

Among the younger generation of public intellectuals, there was an earnest search for postcolonial forms for Hong Kong as a political community. Various strands of nationalism and proposals for nation building traveled beyond the walls of academia into the public domain. Editors of student magazines and academics with policy orientations floated ideas such as civic nationalism, stateless nationalism, peripheral nationalism, and permanent autonomy. As a provocation countervailing China's ethnic/racial nationalism and some Hong Kongers' nativist localism, Brian Leung, the editor in chief of the University of Hong Kong's *Undergrad* magazine, appropriated Benedict Anderson's concept of "imagined community" to say that Hong Kongers were forming a political community based on civic nationalism.[25] Membership in this community should be based not on ascriptive status but on subscription to the values of Hong Kong and willingness to protect its interests. He used the hotly debated issue of new immigrants' entitlement to welfare to make the point that immigrants who have established their credential for mutual obligation and responsibility should have the same right to welfare as locally born citizens.[26]

Brian Fong, a social scientist at the Education University of Hong Kong, together with more than a dozen young academics, issued a manifesto-like *Discourse on Reforming Hong Kong* advocating permanent self-government under Chinese sovereignty.[27] Fong found parallels between Hong Kongers' aspiration for autonomy and nationhood and that among the Scots, Quebecois, and Catalonians. He argued that Hong Kong had since 1949 developed into a "stateless nation," or "a political community that lacks a state of its own but consciously self-identifies itself as distinct people with enough cohesion to seek some sort of greater self-government."[28] Under British rule, territorial border controls separating the city from China and the informal devolution of autonomous power from London to Hong Kong in budgetary and financial matters, coupled with the city's bilateral agreements with other nation-states and membership in international organizations, jump-started Hong Kong's stateless nation-building process. After 1997, Fong conceded that the fate of Hong Kong as a stateless nation, or its permanent autonomy, had been linked to China's political trajectory. It had more or less autonomy depending on whether China was under decentralized or centralized authoritarianism. With cautious optimism, Fong wrote, "Stateless nations are usually powerless in changing the nature of the state structures that constrain them.... However, history tells that stateless nations can survive and even remobilize despite continuous suppression under centralized authoritarianism. The survival of Catalans under Franco's dictatorship in 1936–1975 and their remobilization in democratizing Spain in 1979 are illustrative."[29]

Going beyond the nation-state, an energetic collective of young activist-scholars, based locally and abroad, have added insights to the Hong Kong repertoire of "decolonial thoughts" (their term) from the position of the internationalist Left. Their anthology *Reorienting Hong Kong's Resistance* (2022) argues that the "political futures of Hong Kong cannot rely solely on an analysis of the 'China factor,' on uncritical support for the benevolence of Britain as a former colonizer, or on the desired model of liberal democracy represented by the US. Rather, Hong Kong's decolonial and leftist possibilities must draw from and build upon critiques of frameworks of empire and imperialism, continuous coloniality and (non)sovereignty, and the debates around border, migration, and transnational solidarity."[30] For instance, they alluded to the parallels between Taiwan and Hong Kong, caught in the geopolitics of the United States and China. They spotlighted American exploitation of Southeast Asia creating a mass labor migration that ends up in Hong Kong and asked if there might be space for an alliance between Hong Kongers and minoritized, colonized, and oppressed people around the world. Similarly, their critique of police brutality in Hong Kong pointed to the possibility and urgency of joining forces with antipolice abolitionists in the Black Lives Matter movement in the United States and beyond to effect true change against the carceral logic of the capitalist state. These normative propositions may not find resonance among local protesters and citizens caught in contradictory positions between supporting BLM and supporting the Trump administration. Regardless of their impact, we should note that these diasporic and transnational positionalities have historically made Hong Kong a global city.

The internationalist orientations implicated in these decolonization imaginaries have parallels with those envisioned in an earlier age by black Anglophone anticolonial critics and nationalists, such as Nnamdi Azikiwe, W.E.B. Du Bois, Michael Manley, Kwame Nkrumah, Julius Nyerere, George Padmore, and Eric Williams. Self-determination for them was not just about national independence and the elimination of alien rule. It entailed the creation of a world of nondomination and equal integration to be secured by juridical, political, and economic institutions in the international realm. As Adom Getachew emphasized, decolonization was a project of reordering the world that sought to create a domination-free and egalitarian international order. Anticolonial nationalists were also world makers rather than solely nation builders.[31] Writing from a similarly global perspective, the political theorist Shuk Ying Chan rediscovered one essential normative vision shared by intellectuals and national liberation leaders in the anticolonial tradition, including Fanon, Aimé Césaire, Kwame Nkrumah, and Jawaharlal Nehru. What was core to their project was not nation building or independence but relational equality in the broadest sense: "Anticolonial thinkers had broader and more radical egalitarian aspirations that went beyond national self-determination. . . . They were egalitarians whose nationalism grew out of a particular historical juncture."[32] That historical juncture was the persistent opposition from European metropoles to these leaders' initial experiments with different kinds of proposals short of national independence, from republican federation with the metropole to departmentalization on the basis of equality to comprehensive economic planning or expansion of labor rights. Only when these failed did anticolonial leaders realize that national independence was an important way to compel white Europeans to regard them as moral equals. Given the many internal hierarchies of inequality inside Hong Kong's decolonizing struggle, Chan's argument holds out a tantalizing vision: "The moral claim against colonialism is not dependent on showing that colonizers and subjects have come to bear different identities, or even that they were different throughout history. Rather, it is a claim against relational inequality."[33]

To conclude this book with a juxtaposition of two opposing views of decolonization is to emphasize its capacious and contested nature. On the one hand, decolonization is an agenda of domination, in the name of anti-Western imperialism, Chinese nationalism, and civilizational order, over subjects and territories controlled by the Chinese Communist Party. On the other hand, emerging from the Hong Kong experience, decolonization is a liberatory project for relational equality in the broadest sense: among citizens, classes, races, cultures, and nations. Postimperial possibilities include stateless nationhood, city diplomacy, transnational governance, and regional solidarity networks. I do not know which of these decolonization imaginaries might prevail or how they would translate into political action. What seems certain is that through a *longue durée* and transnational lens, Hong Kong's decolonization struggle has only just begun. And this book has only covered its first chapter.

NOTES

INTRODUCTION

1   Richard Hughes, *Borrowed Place, Borrowed Time: Hong Kong and Its Many Faces* (London: Deutsch, 1976).
2   Interview, July 5, 2023.
3   Quoted in Law Wing-sang, "The Impossible Decolonization and the Radical Thought of Ng Chung-Yin," in *The 70s Weekly: Social Activism and Alternative Cultural Production in the 1970s Hong Kong*, ed. Lu Pan (Hong Kong: Hong Kong University Press, 2023), 36.
4   Clay Chandler, "Discontents Afflicts Hong Kong," *Washington Post*, June 28, 2000.
5   For a good critical review, see William I. Robinson, "Saskia Sassen and the Sociology of Globalization: A Critical Assessment," *Sociological Analysis* 3, no. 1 (2009): 5–29. For a Hong Kong case study as a global city, see Stephen Chiu and Tailok Lui, *Becoming a Chinese Global City* (New York: Routledge, 2009).
6   Its GDP per capita (PPP) ranked thirteenth in 2023, according to World Bank data. https://data.worldbank.org/indicator/NY.GDP.PCAP.PP.CD?most_recent_value_desc=true&year_high_desc=true. See https://www.cia.gov/the-world-factbook/field/gini-index-coefficient-distribution-of-family-income/country-comparison/.
7   Examples: Francis L. F. Lee and Joseph Chan, *Media and Protest Logics in the Digital Era: The Umbrella Movement in Hong Kong* (Oxford University Press, 2018), and *Media, Social Mobilization, and Mass Protests in Post-Colonial Hong Kong: The Power of a Critical Event* (New York: Routledge, 2011); Edmund Cheng et al., "Total Mobilization from Below: Hong Kong's Freedom Summer," *China Quarterly* 251 (2022): 629–659; Edmund Cheng and Francis L. F. Lee, eds., "Hybrid Protest Logics and Relational Dynamics against Institutional Decay: Networked Movements in Asia," special issue, *Social Movement Studies* 22, no. 5–6 (2023).
8   Andrew G. Walder, "Political Sociology and Social Movement," *Annual Review of Sociology* 35 (2009): 397–398.

9   Social theories, despite their purported generality and universality, are products of specific circumstances. Social movement theories as we know them today were formulated in the 1970s in the era of organized capitalism when social movements lost their counter-hegemonic radicalism and became an incorporated, managed, and professionalized institution in Western democracies. Hence the theories' focus on the technicality of mobilization and organization. To squeeze the Hong Kong case into the straightjacket of these presumably universal social movement theories is to misunderstand the essence and obliterate the totality of these struggles. Similarly, global cities theories, as an intellectual response in the 1980s to the shift from national to transnational capitalism, from manufacturing to service industries, are more concerned with the economic sovereignty of nation-states and economic citizenship of corporations. They are less interested in the cultural political consequences of geopolitical rivalry, the transnational flows of ideas, or the intensified social ravages resulting from market instability on the citizens of global cities.

10   Jiang Shigong, *China's Hong Kong: The New Frontier Between Civilizations*, rev. and enlarged ed. (Hong Kong: Joint Publishing, 2022), 5 [in Chinese].

11   Yang Li-shan, "Hong Kong Must Completely and Thoroughly Remove the Influence of Colonial Governance," Think Hong Kong, December 7, 2022, https://www.thinkhk.com/article/2022-12/07/58462.html.

12   For examples, Franz Fanon, *The Wretched of the Earth* (New York: Grove Press, 1963); Pierre Bourdieu and Abdelmalek Sayad, "Colonial Rule and Cultural Sabir," *Ethnography* 5, no. 4 (2004): 445–486; Caroline Elkins, *Legacy of Violence: A History of the British Empire* (New York: Alfred A. Knopf, 2022); Alexandre I. R. White, "Who Can Lead the Revolution?," *Theory and Society* 51 (2022): 457–485; Adam Hochschild, *King Leopold's Ghost: A Story of Greed, Terror and Heroism in Colonial Africa* (Houghton Mifflin, 1999); George Steinmetz, *The Devil's Handwriting: Precoloniality and the German Colonial State in Qingdao, Samoa, and Southwest Africa* (Chicago: University of Chicago Press, 2007).

13   Shuk Ying Chan, *Postcolonial Global Justice* (Princeton, NJ: Princeton University Press, 2025) chapter 1.

14   Walter D. Mignolo and Catherine E. Walsh, *On Decoloniality: Concepts, Analytics and Praxis* (Durham, NC: Duke University Press, 2018), 136.

15   I am deeply grateful to Wing Sang Law and Shuk Ying Chan for their advice on decolonial theorization.

16   David Meyer Temin, "A Decolonial Wrong Turn: Walter Mignolo's Epistemic Politics," *Constellations*, published ahead of print, March 6, 2024, https://onlinelibrary.wiley.com/doi/epdf/10.1111/1467-8675.12744.

17   Madina Tlostanova, "Decoloniality between a Travelling Concept and a Relational Onto-epistemic Political Stance," in *Coloniality and Decolonization in the Nordic Region*, ed. Adrian Groglopo and Julia Suarez-Krabbe (London: Routledge, 2023), 152; Miri Davidson, "Sea and Earth," *New Left Review Sidecar*, April 4, 2024, https://newleftreview.org/sidecar/posts/sea-and-earth.

18 Timothy Synder, "The War in Ukraine Is a Colonial War," *New Yorker*, April 28, 2022; Botakoz Kassymbekovo, "How Western Scholars Overlooked Russian Imperialism," *Al Jazeera*, January 24, 2023, https://www.aljazeera.com/opinions/2023/1/24/how-western-scholars-overlooked-russian-imperialism; Nitasha Kaul, "Kashmir Is Under the Heel of India's Colonialism," *Foreign Policy*, August 13, 2019, https://foreignpolicy.com/2019/08/13/kashmir-is-under-the-heel-of-indias-colonialism/; Rashid Khalidi, *The Hundred Year's War on Palestine* (New York: Metropolitan Books, 2021).

19 Raewyn Connell, "Decolonizing Sociology," *Contemporary Sociology* 47, no. 4 (2018): 399–407; Michael Burawoy, "Decolonizing Sociology: The Significance of W.E.B. Du Bois," *Critical Sociology* 47, no. 4–5 (2021): 545–554; Julian Go, "Decolonizing Sociology: Epistemic Inequality and Sociological Thought," *Social Problems* 64 (2017): 194–199, and "Thinking against Empire: Anti-Colonial Thought as Social Theory," *British Journal of Sociology* 74 (2023): 279–293; George Steinmetz, ed., *Sociology and Empire* (Durham, NC: Duke University Press, 2013); Jose Itzigsohn and Karida Brown, *The Sociology of W.E.B. Du Bois: Racialized Modernity and the Global Color Line* (New York: New York University Press, 2020).

20 Ricarda Hammer and Jose Itzigsohn, "Rethinking Historical Sociology," *Du Bois Review: Social Science Research on Race, First View*, (2024): 1–19; Julian Go, "Postcolonial Possibilities for the Sociology of Race," *Sociology of Race and Ethnicity* 4, no. 4 (2018): 439–451.

21 Mignolo and Walsh, *On Decoloniality*, 28

22 Jose Itzigsohn, "On Decolonial Sociology," *Transilvania*, no. 4 (2023): 1–12. On postcolonial sociology, see Julian Go, *Postcolonial Thought and Social Theory* (New York: Oxford University Press, 2016).

23 Ricarda Hammer and Alexandre I. R. White, "Toward a Sociology of Colonial Subjectivity: Political Agency in Haiti and Liberia," *Sociology of Race and Ethnicity* 5, no. 2 (2019): 215–228; Adom Getachew, *Worldmaking after Empire* (Princeton, NJ: Princeton University Press, 2019); Jean Casimir, *The Haitians: A Decolonial History* (Chapel Hill: University of North Carolina Press, 2020); Chan, *Postcolonial Global Justice*.

24 E. P. Thompson, *The Making of the English Working Class* (London: Vintage, 1963), preface.

25 Rosalind O'Hanlon, "Recovering the Subject: Subaltern Studies and Histories of Resistance in Colonial South Asia," *Modern Asian Studies* 22, no. 1 (1988), 204–205.

26 Achille Mbembe, *Out of the Dark Night* (New York: Columbia University Press, 2021), 2–3.

27 "Hong Kong Was Not British Colony as China Did Not Recognise Unequal Treaties Ceding City to Britain, New Textbooks Reveal," *South China Morning Post*, June 13, 2022, https://www.scmp.com/news/hong-kong/education/article/3181560/hong-kong-was-not-british-colony-china-did-not-recognise.

28 Fanon, *The Wretched of the Earth*, 149.
29 Milan Kundera, *The Book of Laughter and Forgetting* trans. Michael Henry Heim (New York, Alfred A. Knopf, 1980), 3

1. COLONIAL MYTHOLOGIES

1 Chris Patten, *The Hong Kong Diaries* (London: Allen Lane, 2022), 57.
2 Jan C. Jansen and Jurgen Osterhammel, *Decolonization: A Short History*, trans. Jeremieh Riemer (Princeton, NJ: Princeton University Press, 2017).
3 Prasenjit Duara, *Decolonization: Perspectives from Now and Then* (London: Routledge, 2003), 12.
4 Chi-Kwan Mark, "Lack of Means or Loss of Will? The United Kingdom and the Decolonization of Hong Kong, 1957–1967," *International History Review* 31, no. 1: 45–71 (2009); Jeffrey C. H. Ngo, "Betraying Self-Determination: Inside One Tanzanian Ambassador's Quest against Taiwan, Hong Kong, and Macau, 1970–72" (paper presented at the "After Bandung: Africa and China in a New Era" conference, Yale University, New Haven, CT, April 21–22, 2023).
5 During the nineteenth century, Britain concluded three treaties with China: the Treaty of Nanjing in 1842 (ratified in 1843), which ceded Hong Kong Island; the Convention of Peking in 1860, which ceded the southern part of the Kowloon peninsula and Stonecutters Island; and the Convention of 1898, under which the New Territories (NT) were leased for ninety-nine years. Comprising 92 percent of the integrated whole, it was not possible to divide the NT from Hong Kong on the expiry of the lease. See the introduction to "A Draft Agreement between the Government of the United Kingdom of Great Britain and Northern Ireland and the Government of the People's Republic of China on the Future of Hong Kong" [the Sino British Joint Declaration] (Hong Kong, Government Printer, September 26, 1984), p. 8, para. 29. See *International Legal Materials* 23, no. 6 (November 1984): 1366–1387.
6 For a cultural historical analysis of Sino-British collaboration in shaping the identity and meaning of Hong Kong Chinese, see Wing Sang Law, *Collaborative Colonial Power: The Making of Hong Kong Chinese* (Hong Kong: Hong Kong University Press, 2009). Where his book focuses on collaboration, I argue in this book that double coloniality was also based on tacit compliance and collusion, even competition, between the two colonial masters.
7 John M. Carroll, *Edge of Empires: Chinese Elites and British Colonials in Hong Kong* (Cambridge, MA: Harvard University Press, 2005).
8 Ma Ngok, *Political Development in Hong Kong: State, Political Society and Civil Society* (Hong Kong: Hong Kong University Press, 2007), chap. 4.
9 Richard Klein, "Law and Racism in an Asian Setting: An Analysis of the British Rule of Hong Kong," *Hastings International and Comparative Law*

Review 18, no. 2 (1995); Ming K. Chan, "The Legacy of the British Administration of Hong Kong: A Hong Kong View of Hong Kong," *China Quarterly*, no. 151 (September 1997): 567–582.

10 Cited in Suzanne Pepper, *Keeping Democracy at Bay: Hong Kong and the Challenge of Chinese Political Reform* (Lanham, MD: Rowman and Littlefield, 2008), 141.

11 Ho-fung Hung, *City on the Edge: Hong Kong Under Chinese Rule* (Cambridge: Cambridge University Press, 2022), 131.

12 Aime Cesaire, *Discourses on Colonization* (New York: Monthly Review, 1952), 42. Hammer and White, "Toward a Sociology of Colonial Subjectivity."

13 "Word of a Prince and a President: Continuity, Change and Assurances" The *New York Times*, July 1, 1997. https://www.nytimes.com/1997/07/01/world/words-of-a-prince-and-a-president-continuity-change-and-assurances.html.

14 Government Information Services, *Daily Information Bulletin, June 30, 1997*. https://www.info.gov.hk/gia/general/dib/19970630.htm.

15 John Wong, "Constructing the Legitimacy of Governance in Hong Kong: 'Prosperity and Stability' Meets 'Democracy and Freedom,'" *Journal of Asian Studies* 81 (2022), 47.

16 Wong, 48.

17 Siu-kai Lau, *Society and Politics in Hong Kong* (Hong Kong: Chinese University Press, 1982), 67–119. As an undergraduate student in the same department as Lau, and reading his book in my sophomore year, I was totally blown away by the elegance of his theorization. Celebrated as a landmark study of Hong Kong, its analysis resonated with my experience growing up in the 1970s.

18 Lau, 65–66.

19 Lau, 165–166 (emphasis mine).

20 These social scientists, based at the two universities in Hong Kong, include Ambrose Y. C. King, N. J. Miners, Peter Harris, and Siu-lun Wong. For a critique of their bias of ignoring external forces shaping Hong Kong and only focusing on the state's administrative absorption of politics and people's political apathy, see John D. Young, "The Building Years: Maintaining a China-Hong Kong-Britain Equilibrium, 1950–71," in *Precarious Balance: Hong Kong between China and Britain 1842–1992*, ed. Ming K. Chan, 131–147 (Armonk, NY: M. E. Sharpe, 1994). Even Queen Elizabeth II made the same argument about Hong Kong in her first visit in 1975: "The fabric of your community is strengthened by family ties which are still stronger here and more durable than now exist in most other parts of the world. Chinese tradition and British liberalism had combined to produce a heartwarming range of practical achievements: you have a totally free press and an independent judiciary, you have evolved a cosmopolitan community which owes much to both Chinese and British traditions." https://www.youtube.com/watch?v=3S2nb8YH9EM&t=7s.

21 To his credit, Lau did admit in the book that he took "liberty to let his creativity and imagination take charge, without being encumbered at every point by well-established and jealously-defended dogmas and perspectives." Lau, *Society and Politics in Hong Kong*, ix.

22 Jung-fang Tsai, "From Anti-foreignism to Popular Nationalism: Hong Kong between China and Britain, 1839–1911," in *Precarious Balance: Hong Kong between China and Britain 1842–1992*, ed. Ming K. Chan, 9–25 (Armonk, NY: M. E. Sharpe, 1994).

23 Ming K. Chan, "Hong Kong in Sino-British Conflict: Mass Mobilization and the Crisis of Legitimacy, 1912–26," in *Precarious Balance: Hong Kong between China and Britain 1842–1992*, ed. Ming K. Chan (Armonk, NY: M. E. Sharpe, 1994), 45. See also his PhD dissertation, Ming K. Chan, "Labor and Empire: The Chinese Labor Movement in the Canton Delta 1895–1927" (PhD diss., Stanford University, 1975).

24 Lu Yan, *Crossed Paths: Labor Activism and Colonial Governance in Hong Kong, 1938–1958* (Ithaca, NY: Cornell East Asia Studies, 2019), 173–175.

25 Yan, 261–280.

26 Yan, 297–321; Hong Kong Government, *Reports on the Riots in Kowloon and Tseun Wan, October 10th to 12th, 1956* (Hong Kong: Hong Kong Government Printer, 1957).

27 Commission of Inquiry, *Kowloon Disturbances 1966: Report of Commission of Inquiry* (Hong Kong: Hong Kong Government Printer, 1967).

28 Ray Yep and Robert Bickers, "Studying the 1967 Riot: An Overdue Project," in *May Days in Hong Kong: Riots and Emergency in 1967*, 1–18 (Hong Kong: Hong Kong University Press, 2009).

29 Commission of Inquiry, *Kowloon Disturbances 1966*, 125–128.

30 "C M MacLehose to Sir Leslie Monson, Mr Wilford, Mr Morgan and Mr Laird," October 16, 1971, The National Archives in Kew Garden (TNA), FCO 40/329, cited in Ray Yep and Tai-lok Lui, "Revisiting the Golden Era of Mac Lehose and the Dynamics of Social Reforms," *China Information* 24, no. 3 (2010): 249–272.

31 Pepper, *Keeping Democracy at Bay*, 139–140; Steve Tsang, *Hong Kong: An Appointment with China* (London: I. B. Tauris, 1997), chap. 4.

32 "Planning Paper on Hong Kong," 12, TNA, FCO 40/704, cited in Yep and Lui, "Revisiting the Golden Era."

33 "MacLehose to Callaghan: The Future of Hong Kong," February 12, 1976, TNA, FCO 40/713, cited in Yep and Lui, "Revisiting the Golden Era."

34 Tai-lok Lui, "Flying MPs and . . . Yep and Lui, "Revisiting the Golden Era."

35 Michael Ng, *Political Censorship in British Hong Kong: Freedom of Expression and the Law (1842–1997)* (Cambridge: Cambridge University Press, 2022), 135.

36 John D. Wong, "Between Two Episodes of Social Unrest below Lion Rock: From the 1967 Riots to the 2014 Umbrella Movement," in *Civil Unrest and*

Governance in Hong Kong, ed. Michael H. K. Ng and John D. Wong (London: Routledge, 2017), 103.

37 Leo F. Goodstadt, *Profits, Politics and Panics: Hong Kong's Banks and the Making of a Miracle Economy, 1935–1985* (Hong Kong: Hong Kong University Press, 2007).

38 Wong, "Between Two Episodes of Social Unrest," 104.

39 Lu Pan, ed., *The 70's Biweekly: Social Activism and Alternative Cultural Production in 1970s Hong Kong* (Hong Kong: Hong Kong University Press, 2023).

40 Essays in Law Wing Sang, *Thinking Hong Kong* (Hong Kong: Oxford University Press, 2020) [in Chinese].

41 Alvin Y. So and Ludmilla Kwitko, "The Transformation of Urban Movements in Hong Kong, 1970–1990," *Bulletin of Concerned Asian Scholars* 24, no. 4 (1992): 32–43.

42 Siu-kai Lau and Hsin-chi Kuan, *The Ethos of the Hong Kong Chinese* (Hong Kong: Chinese University Press, 1988), 58, 73, 102.

43 Lau and Kuan, 94.

44 See also the "bloom and doom" described in Ackbar Abbas, *Hong Kong: Culture and the Politics of Disappearance* (Minneapolis: University of Minnesota Press, 1997).

45 Two hundred professionals published a declaration to defend Hong Kong's core values in 2004 in the wake of China's interference in Hong Kong affairs. Ambrose Leung, "Push to Defend City's Core Values," *South China Morning Post*, June 7, 2004. https://www.scmp.com/article/458500/push-defend-citys-core-values.

46 Ming Sing, *Hong Kong's Tortuous Democratization: A Comparative Analysis* (London: Routledge Curzon, 2004), 141.

47 Law Wing Sang [An To, pseud.], "The End of Virtual Liberalism," in *Rewriting the History of Hong Kong*, ed. Po-keung Hui, 3–12 (Hong Kong: Oxford University Press) [in Chinese].

48 Private communication with Michael Ng, a legal historian at the University of Hong Kong.

49 Citing James Fitzjames Stephen, in Caroline Elkins, *Legacy of Violence: A History of the British Empire* (New York: Alfred A. Knopf, 2022), 13.

50 Peter Wesley-Smith, "Anti-Chinese Legislation in Hong Kong," in *Precarious Balance: Hong Kong between China and Britain 1842–1992*, ed. Ming K. Chan, 91–105 (Armonk, NY: M. E. Sharpe, 1994).

51 Christopher N. J. Roberts, "From the State of Emergency to the Rule of Law: The Evolution of Repressive Legality in the Nineteenth Century British Empire," *Chicago Journal of International Law* 20, no. 1 (2019), art. 1; Carol A. G. Jones, "A Ruling Idea of the Time? The Rule of Law in Pre- and Post-1997 Hong Kong," in *From a British to a Chinese Colony? Hong Kong before and after the 1997 Handover,* ed. Gary Chi-hung Luk, 112–140 (Berkeley, CA: IEAS China Research, 2017).

52 Elkins, *Legacy of Violence*, 582.
53 Jones, "A Ruling Idea of the Time?" 121.
54 Ng, *Political Censorship in British Hong Kong*, 87.
55 For a full list of emergency regulations, see Max W. L. Wong, *Re-ordering Hong Kong: Decolonization and the Hong Kong Bill of Rights Ordinance* (London: Wildy, Simmonds & Hill Publishing, 2017), 45–59.
56 Ng, *Political Censorship in British Hong Kong*, chaps. 2–4.
57 Tsang, *Hong Kong: An Appointment with China*, 117.
58 Cited in Tsang, 69.
59 Pepper, *Keeping Democracy at Bay*, 101; Tsang, *Hong Kong: An Appointment with China*, 78.
60 Cited in Sing, *Hong Kong's Tortuous Democratization*, 36–37.
61 Tsang, *Hong Kong: An Appointment with China*, 120.
62 Mark Hampton, "British Legal Culture and Colonial Governance: The Attack on Corruption in Hong Kong, 1968–1974," *Britain and the World* 5, no. 2 (2012): 223–239.
63 Gary Ka-Wai Cheung, *Secrets from the British Archives: Hong Kong and Its Post-Colonial Future* (Hong Kong: City University of Hong Kong, 2022), 61 [in Chinese].
64 Wong, *Re-ordering Hong Kong*, 41–43.
65 Both before and after the official handover, the PRC repealed an entrenchment clause in the Bill of Rights, which means the Basic Law can override the BOR. See Wong, *Re-ordering Hong Kong*, 212–213.
66 Ng, *Political Censorship in British Hong Kong*, 193.
67 Jones, "A Ruling Idea of the Time?," 125–126.
68 John Flowerdew, "The Discourse of Colonial Withdrawal: A Case Study in the Creation of Mythic Discourse," *Discourse & Society* 8, no. 4 (1997): 453–477, and *The Final Years of British Hong Kong: The Discourse of Colonial Withdrawal* (New York: St. Martin's Press, 1998).
69 Lau and Kuan, *The Ethos of the Hong Kong Chinese*, 139.
70 Benny Tai, *Rule of Law and Legal Culture in Hong Kong*, 2017, 42 and 65.
71 Leo Goodstadt, *Poverty in the Midst of Affluence: How Hong Kong Mismanaged Its Prosperity* (Hong Kong: Hong Kong University Press, 2014), 73–74.
72 Ng, *Political Censorship in British Hong Kong*, 192.
73 Jamie Peck, "Milton's Paradise: Situating Hong Kong in Neoliberal Lore," *Journal of Law and Political Economy* 1, no. 2 (2021), 190.
74 M. Friedman and R. Friedman, *Free to Choose: A Personal Statement* (Harvest Press, 1990), 34, cited in Stephen W. K. Chiu and Kaxton Y. K. Siu, *Hong Kong Society: High-Definition Stories beyond the Spectacle of East-Meets-West* (Singapore: Springer Nature, 2022), 140.
75 Leo Goodstadt, *Uneasy Partners: The Conflict between Public Interest and Private Profit in Hong Kong* (Hong Kong: Hong Kong University Press, 2009), 120–121.

76 Policy speech from 1992, cited in Flowerdew, "The Discourse of Colonial Withdrawal," 195.

77 Hong Kong Economic and Trade Office, Berlin, "Hong Kong Tops Economic Freedom Index Again" (n.d.), https://www.hketoberlin.gov.hk/en/newsletter/2019/203.html.

78 J. R. Schiffer, "State Policy and Economic Growth: A Note on the Hong Kong Model," *International Journal of Urban and Regional Research* 15, no. 2 (1991): 180–196.

79 Stephen W. K. Chiu and Kaxton Y. K. Siu, "Hong Kong as an Economic Miracle? The Myth of Laissez-faire," in *Hong Kong Society: High-Definition Stories beyond the Spectacle of East-Meets-West* (Singapore: Springer Nature, 2022), 147.

80 Tak-wing Ngo, "Colonialism in Hong Kong Revisited," in *Hong Kong's History: State and Society under Colonial Rule* (London: Routledge, 1999), 4–5.

81 Goodstadt, *Uneasy Partners*, 159.

82 Marcus W. Brauchli and G. Bruce Knecht, "False Image: A Free-Market Hong Kong Is Belied by Oligopolies," *Asian Wall Street Journal*, September 17, 1998.

83 "Planet Plutocrat," *The Economist*, March 15, 2014, https://www.economist.com/international/2014/03/15/planet-plutocrat.

84 Peter E. Hamilton, *Made in Hong Kong: Transpacific Networks and a New History of Globalization* (New York: Columbia University Press, 2021); Gary G. Hamilton, ed., *Cosmopolitan Capitalists: Hong Kong and the Chinese Diaspora at the End of the Twentieth Century* (Seattle: University of Washington Press, 1999).

85 Stephen Chiu and Tai-lok Liu, *Hong Kong: Becoming a Chinese Global City* (New York: Routledge, 2009).

86 Siu-kai Lau and Hsin-chi Kuan, "Public Attitude toward Laissez Faire in Hong Kong," *Asian Survey* 30, no. 8 (1990), 770.

87 Lau and Kuan, 778.

88 Goodstadt, *Uneasy Partners*, 122.

89 Tsang, *Hong Kong: An Appointment with China*, chaps. 3 and 4.

90 Tsang, 70–71.

91 Tsang, 75–76.

92 Pepper, *Keeping Democracy at Bay*, 127–137.

93 Pepper, 139.

94 Pepper, 141.

95 Cited in Patricia A. Dagati, "Hong Kong's Lost Right to Self-Determination: A Denial of Due Process in the United Nations," *New York Law School Journal of International and Comparative Law* 13, no. 1 (1992), 154.

96 The letter states, "As is known to all, the questions of Hong Kong and Macau belong to the category of questions resulting from the series of unequal treaties left over by history, treaties which the imperialists imposed on China. Hong Kong and Macau are part of Chinese territory occupied by the British and Portuguese authorities. The settlement of the questions of Hong Kong and Macau

is entirely within China's sovereign right and does not at all fall under the ordinary category of 'colonial territories.' Consequently, they should not be included in the list of colonial Territories covered by the Declaration on the Granting of Independence to Colonial Countries and Peoples. With regard to the questions of Hong Kong and Macau, the Chinese Government has consistently held that they should be settled in an appropriate way when conditions are ripe. The United Nations has no right to discuss those questions. For the above reasons, the Chinese delegation is opposed to including Hong Kong and Macau in the list of colonial Territories covered by the Declaration and requests that the erroneous wording that Hong Kong and Macau fall under the category of so-called 'colonial Territories' be immediately removed from the documents of the Special Committee and all other United Nations documents" (cited in Dagati, "Hong Kong's Lost Right to Self-Determination," 166).

97 Ngo, "Betraying Self-Determination."

98 Nelson K. Lee, "The Changing Nature of Border, Scale and Production of Hong Kong's Water Supply System since 1959," *International Journal of Urban and Regional Research* 38, no. 3 (2014), 914.

99 Siu-keung Cheung, "Reunification through Water and Food: The Other Battle for Lives and Bodies in China's Hong Kong Policy," *China Quarterly* 220 (2014), 1023.

100 Cheung, 1021.

101 Chi-kwan Mark, "Decolonizing Britishness? The 1981 British Nationality Act and the Identity Crisis of Hong Kong Elites," *Journal of Imperial and Commonwealth History* 48, no. 3 (2020): 565–590.

102 Gary Cheung, *Secrets from the British Archives: Hong Kong and Its Post-Colonial Future* (Hong Kong: City University of Hong Kong, 2022), 59–60 [in Chinese].

103 Record of a discussion at No. 10 Downing Street on March 7, 1983, TNA, PREM 19/1054, cited in Cheung, 78.

104 Cheung, 101.

105 Tsang, *Hong Kong: An Appointment with China*, 107–109.

106 Lau and Kuan 1988, 62–63.

107 Siu-Kai Lau, "Hongkongese or Chinese: The Problem of Identity on the Eve of Resumption of Chinese Sovereignty over Hong Kong" (occasional paper no. 65, Hong Kong Institute of Asia-Pacific Studies, 1997), 5.

108 Lam Ka-sing, "Exodus of Hongkongers Triggered by National Security Law Unlikely to Dent City's Home Prices, Say Analysts," *South China Morning Post*, June 6, 2021; Ronald Skeldon, "Hong Kong in an International Migration System," in *Reluctant Exiles? Migration from Hong Kong and the New Overseas Chinese* (Armonk, NY: M. E. Sharpe, 1994), 30.

109 For a historical overview of the development of local consciousness, see Law Wing Sang, "The Past and Present of Hong Kong's Local Consciousness,"

in *Thinking Hong Kong,* 187–222 (Hong Kong: Oxford University Press, 2020) [in Chinese].

110 Sang, 14–30.

111 Interview, September 16, 2022. See also his memoir, Lee Wing-tat, *Reflections on the Eve of Sentencing* (Hong Kong: Lee Wing-tat, 2019) [in Chinese]. The themes articulated by Lee echo those found in a small but growing literature of oral histories and autobiographies by Hong Kong political figures. These include Ma Ngok, ed., *An Oral History of Democratic Movement of Hong Kong in the 1980s* (Hong Kong: City University of Hong Kong Press, 2012) [in Chinese]; Yeung Sum, *Restarting the Journey: Chronicle of Yeung Sum's Political Career* (Hong Kong: Greenfield Bookstore, 2008) [in Chinese]; Szeto Wah, *A Mighty River Runs East* (Hong Kong: Oxford University Press, 2011) [in Chinese].

2. PRACTICING POSTCOLONIALITY

1 Antonio Gramsci, *Selections from the Prison Notebooks,* trans. Nowell-Smith Hoare (London: Lawrence & Wishart, 2003), 276

2 Rune Moller Stahl, "Ruling the Interregnum: Politics and Ideology in Non-Hegemonic Times," *Politics and Society* 47, no. 3 (2019): 333–360.

3 Ho-fung Hung, *City on the Edge: Hong Kong under Chinese Rule* (Cambridge: Cambridge University Press, 2022), chap. 3.

4 Ching Kwan Lee, *Hong Kong: Global China's Restive Frontier* (Cambridge: Cambridge University Press, 2022).

5 Francis L. F. Lee and Joseph M. Chan, *Memories of Tiananmen: Politics and Processes of Collective Remembering in Hong Kong: 1989–2021* (Amsterdam: Amsterdam University Press, 2021); Edmund Cheng and Samson Yuen, "Memory in Movement: Collective Identity and Memory Contestation in Hong Kong's Tiananmen Vigils," *Mobilization* 24, no. 4 (2019): 419–437.

6 Ming Sing, *Hong Kong's Tortuous Democratization: A Comparative Analysis* (New York: Routledge Curzon, 2004), 116–117.

7 Anson Chan, chief secretary, August 14, 1998. Speech at the Hong Kong Economic and Trade Office in Singapore, http://www.info.gov.hk/gia/general/199808/14/0814048.htm.

8 Tai-lok Lui, "Under Fire: Hong Kong's Middle Class after 1997," in *The July 1 Protest Rally: Interpreting a Historic Event,* ed. Joseph Y. S. Cheng (Hong Kong: City University of Hong Kong Press, 2005), 292.

9 Francis L. F. Lee and Joseph M. Chan, *Media, Social Mobilization, and Mass Protests in Post-Colonial Hong Kong: The Power of a Critical Event* (New York: Routledge, 2011), 147.

10 Lee and Chan, 182.

11 S. K. Lau, M. K. Lee, P. S. Wan, and S. L. Wong, *Indicators of Social Development: Hong Kong 1999* (Hong Kong: Hong Kong Institute of Asia-Pacific Studies, 2001).

12 Tai-lok Lui, "Rearguard Politics: Hong Kong's Middle Class," *Developing Economies* XLI-2 (June 2003), 162.

13 Wing Sang Law, *Beyond Colonialization and the Nation-State* (Hong Kong: Oxford University Press, 2014), 38 [in Chinese].

14 Interview, December 17, 2020.

15 Interview, August 25, 2020.

16 Nathan Law, *Freedom: How We Lose it and How We Fight Back* (New York: The Experiment, 2021), 39, 46–47.

17 *Ten Years of Civil Human Rights Front: The Story of Seven Million* (Hong Kong, Civil Human Rights Front, 2013), 148–149, https://issuu.com/wchk/docs/book-final.

18 Jason Kwun-hong Chan and Rami Hin-yeung Chan, "Learn to Disobey: Evolution of 'Civil Disobedience' and the Transforming Sociopolitical Context of Hong Kong," *Asian Politics & Policy* 12 (2020):516–538.

19 Adjusting for inflation, the growth in median income between 1976 and 1981 and between 1981 and 1986 was 36 percent and 11 percent respectively. From 1986 to 1996, real income growth hit 144 percent. In stark contrast, from 1996 to 2006, the rate stayed flat at 4 percent. From 2001 to 2011, the average worker saw actual income (after inflation) decline, as income grew by 12 percent and inflation by 12 percent. John D. Wong, "Between Two Episodes of Social Unrest below Lion Rock: From the 1967 Riots to the 2014 Umbrella Movement," in *Civil Unrest and Governance in Hong Kong,* ed. Michael Ng and John D. Wong (New York: Routledge, 2017), 103.

20 Stephan W. K. Chui and Tai-lok Lui, "Testing the Global City-Social Polarization Thesis: Hong Kong since the 1990s," *Urban Studies* 41, no. 10 (2004): 1863–1888.

21 Timothy K. Y. Wong, Po-San Wan, and Kenneth W. K. Law, "Public Perceptions of Income Inequality in Hong Kong: Trends, Causes and Implications," *Journal of Contemporary China* 18, no. 61 (2009): 657–673.

22 Alice Poon Wai-han, *Land and the Ruling Class in Hong Kong* (Richmond, Canada, 2005; Chinese trans., Hong Kong: Enrich Publishing, 2010).

23 Agnes S. Ku and Clarence Hong Chee Tsui, "The Global City as a Cultural Project: The Case of the West Kowloon Cultural District," in *Hong Kong Mobile: Making a Global Population,* ed. Helen Siu and Agnes S. Ku (Hong Kong: Hong Kong University Press, 2008).

24 J. Ho, "Lobbying Underway to Secure WTO Talks," *South China Morning Post,* February 28, 2004.

25 Y. C. Chen and M. Szeto, "The Forgotten Road of Progressive Localism: New Preservation Movement in Hong Kong," *Inter-Asia Cultural Studies* 16, no. 3 (2015): 436–453.

26 Eddie Chu, "From the Queen's Pier, I See to the Shackles on My Body," *Ming Pao*, April 29, 2007.

27 Lam Sum, Documentary film "Queen's Pier" 人在皇后 (2007).

28 Chow Sze Chung, interview, December 28, 2020.

29 Chung, interview.

30 Dennis Leung Ka Kuen, "Constituting and Engaging in Transnational (Media) Activism Locally: The Case of Hong Kong In-media," *Media Asia* 41, no. 3 (2014): 227–239.

31 Interview, December 28, 2020.

32 Interview.

33 Interview, December 17, 2020.

34 Interview.

35 Interview.

36 Interview, December 28, 2020.

37 Interview, November 29, 2016.

38 Interview.

39 Interview, November 28, 2022.

40 Joshua Wong, "Scholarism on the March," *New Left Review* 92 (March–April 2015), 44.

41 Joshua Wong (with Jason Y. Ng), *Unfree Speech: The Threat to Global Democracy and Why We Must Act, Now* (London: Penguin Books, 2020), 18–19.

42 Wong, 23–24.

43 Lee, *Hong Kong: Global China's Restive Frontier*, 11–17.

44 Hung, *City on the Edge*, 136.

45 Whereas in the colonial era, the standard curriculum sought to cultivate an apolitical and anti-Communist, ethno-cultural Chinese identity among local students, ever since the handover, the SAR government had been under mounting pressure from Beijing and pro-Beijing forces to implement "national" and "nationalistic" education. In the first decade after 1997, official strategies for raising national consciousness entailed mainly nonmandatory extracurricular activities—museum visits, military youth camps, and Chinese calligraphy and folk dancing classes. Even when a general reform of the school curriculum identified "moral and civic education" as a curricular area in 2000, the SAR government took a soft approach to national identity and emphasized global citizenship. But after President Hu Jintao in 2007 (on the tenth anniversary of the SAR) explicitly emphasized the need for national education and surveys consistently showed young people's strong identification as either Hong Kong people or Hong Kong Chinese rather than Chinese, the SAR government was compelled to act. Tracy C. Lau, Thomas Tse, and Y. W. Leung, "Dynamics of Chinese Nationalistic Education in Hong Kong from 1945 to 2012." *Oxford Review of Education* 42, no. 3 (2006): 677–691.

46 Catherine Lai, "Ex-Xinhua Hong Kong Chief Blames Separatism on 150 Years of 'Colonial Brainwashing,' Urges National Education," *Hong Kong Free*

Press, June 20, 2017, https://hongkongfp.com/2017/06/20/ex-xinhua-hong-kong-chief-blames-separatism-150-years-colonial-brainwashing-urges-national-education/.

47 Wong, *Unfree Speech,* 28.

48 Interview, July 17, 2021.

49 Tony Cheung, "A History of How National Education Was Introduced in Hong Kong," *South China Morning Post,* September 9, 2012; Klavier Jie Ying Wong, "Mobilizing Resources to the Square: Hong Kong's Anti-moral and National Education Movement as Precursor to the Umbrella Movement," *International Journal of Cultural Studies* 20, no. 2 (2017): 127–145. According to a high-level government source who insisted on anonymity, the government's decision to back down was partly due to the magnitude of societal opposition and the possible political consequences of the students' hunger strike and partly due to the fact that the newly installed chief executive, C. Y. Leung, did not want to see his own popularity tarnished by this first policy issue of his term and one that was left over by his predecessor, Donald Tsang.

50 Wong, *Unfree Speech,* 35–37.

51 Interview, September 5, 2022.

52 Interview.

53 Interview, March 15, 2024.

54 Interview, July 17, 2021.

55 Interview, July 21, 2021.

56 Interview, May 3, 2021.

57 Interview, September 5, 2022.

58 Published in 2012, from the personal archive of Yeung Chun Yin, president of the CUHK student union in 2012; See the banner of "anti-colonial, anti-national education" in the Voice of America report, https://www.voacantonese.com/a/hk-universities-students-boycotting-class-live-qa/1505819.html.

59 Ngok Ma, "The Rise of 'Anti-China' Sentiments in Hong Kong and the 2012 Legislative Council Elections," *China Review* 15, no. 1 (2015), 62.

60 Eric Ma, "Grassroots Nationalism: Changing Identity in a Changing Context," *China Review* 7, no. 2 (2007): 149–167; Chi Kit Chan, "China as Other: Resistance to and Ambivalence toward National Identity in Hong Kong," *China Perspectives* 1 (2014): 25–34.

61 https://www.reuters.com/article/idUSTRE65O0W9/.

62 Benny Tai, "Nonviolent Civil Disobedience: The Story of Hong Kong's Fight for Democracy," in *This Is an Uprising: How Nonviolent Revolt Is Shaping the Twenty-First Century,* by Mark Engler and Paul Engler, trans. Edmond Chung (Taipei: 3space, 2021), 457–458 [in Chinese].

63 Benny Tai, *Occupy Central: Psychological War Chamber of Peaceful Resistance* (Hong Kong: Enrich Publishing, 2013), 198–207 [in Chinese].

64 Francis L. F. Lee and Joseph M. Chan, "Appendix: Profiling the Umbrella Movement Participants," in *Media and Protest Logics in the Digital Era:*

The Umbrella Movement in Hong Kong (New York: Oxford University Press, 2018), 207–233.

65 Samson Yuen and Edmund W. Cheng, "Neither Repression nor Concession? A Regime's Attrition against Mass Protests," *Political Studies* 65, no. 3 (2017): 611–630.

66 Alex Chow, "After Umbrella, Is Revolution the Only Way Out?" *Initium*, September 28, 2015, https://theinitium.com/article/20150928-opinion-alexchow-evaluation/ [in Chinese].

67 Chow, "After Umbrella."

68 Jason Y. Ng, *Umbrellas in Bloom: Hong Kong's Occupy Movement Uncovered* (Hong Kong: Blacksmiths Book, 2016), 126–127.

69 Sebastian Veg, "Legalistic vs Utopian: Hong Kong's Umbrella Movement," *New Left Review* 92 (March–April 2015): 55–73.

70 Based on interviews with multiple leaders of the Occupy movement.

71 Interview, September 3, 2022.

72 Federation of Students class boycott statement on September 22, 2014, in *Collection of Writings by Federation of Students Cohorts 56, 57, 58*, ed. Chan Man Hei (Hong Kong: HKFS, 2017), 227–229 [in Chinese].

73 Some of the texts of these public lectures, including this one by Lee Chun Wing, "Democratic Politics and Hong Kong's Financial and Taxation Systems," are found in Ip Am Chong and Chan King Fai, eds., *Boycotting Classes without Boycotting Learning* (Hong Kong: Stepforward Multi-media Publishing, 2015), 323 [in Chinese].

74 Alex Chow, "Prefigurative Politics of the Umbrella Movement: An Ethnography of Its Promise and Predicament," in *Take Back Our Future: An Eventful Sociology of the Hong Kong Umbrella Movement*, ed. Ching Kwan Lee and Ming Sing (Ithaca, NY: Cornell University Press, 2019), 34–51.

75 Samson Yuen, "Transgressive Politics in Occupy Mongkok," in *Take Back Our Future: An Eventful Sociology of the Hong Kong Umbrella Movement*, ed. Ching Kwan Lee and Ming Sing (Ithaca, NY: Cornell University Press, 2019), 52–73. A total of 50 percent of Mongkok protesters, compared to 44 percent in Admiralty, self-identified as "grassroots," and 54 percent actually had attended tertiary institutions.

76 Lam Yi Ting, "Mongkok Youth, Misunderstood Battle," *Initium*, September 21, 2015, https://theinitium.com/article/20150921-hongkong-occupycentraloneyear02/.

77 Ting.

78 Interview, November 28, 2022.

79 Interview, September 20, 2022.

80 Interview, September 18, 2022.

81 Interview, September 20, 2022.

82 Brian Leung, "Violence, Space Differential and Ethic," *Stand News*, June 25, 2018, [in Chinese].

83 Interview, June 23, 2023.

84 K. M. Chan, "The Seduction of Revolution," *Initium*, September 27, 2015, https://theinitium.com/article/20150928-opinion-chankinman-evaluation/ [in Chinese].

85 Interviews with various Mongkok protesters in 2022.

86 Zhang Jieping, "Showhand: Resistance Generation" in *Three Years in Hong Kong*, ed. Zhang Jieping and Chung Kim Wah. (Hong Kong: Oxford University Press, 2016), 62 [in Chinese].

87 Ting, "Mongkok Youth."

88 Ng, *Umbrellas in Bloom*, 276.

89 Wing Sang Law, *Thinking Hong Kong* (Hong Kong: Oxford University Press, 2020), 187–222 [in Chinese].

90 Vera Taylor, "Social Movement Continuity: The Women's Movement in Abeyance," *American Sociological Review* 54, no. 5 (1989): 761-775.

91 Samson Yuen and Chit Wai John Mok, "Groundwork for Democracy? Community Abeyance and Lived Citizenship in Hong Kong," *The China Journal*, no. 90 (2023): 78-105.

92 Interview, May 24, 2017.

93 Wai-man Lam, "Changing Political Activism: Before and after the Umbrella Movement," *Hong Kong 20 Years after the Handover*, ed. Brian C. H. Fong and Tai-lok Lui (London: Palgrave, 2017); Ngok Ma, "The Plebeian Moment and Its Traces: Post-UM Professional Groups in Hong Kong," in *Sunflowers and Umbrellas*, ed. Thomas B. Gold and Sebastian Veg (Berkeley, CA: Institute for East Asian Studies, 2020).

94 Interview, September 9, 2022.

95 May 24, 2015, YouTube video, by Passion Times.hk, "Ah Bi: Establishing the Spirit of Localism on June 4th," https://www.youtube.com/watch?v=YG78FmezYas.

96 The Individual Visit Scheme was introduced in 2003 and was expanded to become multiple IVS in 2009, resulting in an annual influx of twenty-eight million mainland visitors in 2011 and hovering between forty million and fifty million each year between 2014 and 2018. See Jackson Yeh Kuo Hao, "China's Influence on Hong Kong's Economy: Lessons from Mainland Tourism," in *China's Influence and the Center-Periphery Tug of War in Hong Kong, Taiwan and Indo-Pacific*, ed. Brian C. H. Fong, Wu Jieh-Min, and Andrew J. Nathan (London: Routledge, 2012), 105–120.

97 Interview, December 20, 2022.

98 Interview, September 20, 2022.

99 Interview.

100 Interview.

101 Kong Tsung-gan, "Justice It Ain't" Hong Kong Free Press, June 17, 2018, https://hongkongfp.com/2018/06/17/justice-aint-repercussions-implications-hong-kongs-mong-kok-riot-trials.

102 For an eyewitness-based account of the Mongkok civil unrest, see Francis L. F. Lee, Pro-Democracy *Contention in Hong Kong: Relational Dynamics between the Umbrella Movement and the Anti-Extradition Protests* (New York: SUNY Press, 2025), chap. 3.

103 Lee.

104 The documentary *Black Bauhinia* (2020) directed by Malte Philipp Kaeding, https://www.imdb.com/title/tt16235812/.

105 Interview, September 20, 2022.

106 The documentary *Lost in the Fumes* (2017) directed by Nora Lam chronicles Edward Leung's political activism and his 2016 electoral campaign, https://www.imdb.com/title/tt7875626/.

107 Lee, *Prodemocracy Contentions in Hong Kong*.

108 Kevin Carrico, *Two Systems Two Countries: A Nationalist Guide to Hong Kong* (Berkeley: University of California Press, 2022), 89–102.

109 Demosisto, *Determine Our Future: New Generation LegCo* (Hong Kong: Demosisto, 2016), 6.

110 Carrico, *Two Systems Two Countries*, 59–111.

111 Interview, March 15, 2024.

112 Carrico, *Two Systems Two Countries*, 94.

113 Radio Free Asia interview with Edward Leung, June 16, 2017.

114 Radio Free Asia interview with Edward Leung, April 29, 2016, https://www.rfa.org/cantonese/features/teahouse/sat-callin-show-05072016080532.html?encoding=traditional.

115 Gene Lin, "CUHK Poll Finds Nearly 40% of Young Hong Kongers Want Independence after 2047," *Hong Kong Free Press*, July 25, 2016, https://hongkongfp.com/2016/07/25/17-hongkongers-support-independence-2047-especially-youth-cuhk-survery/.

116 See https://time.com/4856181/hong-kong-lawmakers-oath-china-disqualified/.

117 Goran Therborn, *The Ideology of Power and the Power of Ideology* (London: Verso, 1980).

118 Frederick Cooper, *Decolonization and African Society: The Labor Question in French and British Africa* (Cambridge: Cambridge University Press, 1996); Frederick Cooper, "Labor, Politics and the End of Empire in French Africa," in *Colonialism in Question: Theory, Knowledge, History* (Berkeley: University of California Press, 2005), 204–230.

119 Karl Mannheim, "The Problem of Generations," in *Essays on the Sociology of Knowledge* (1923; repr., London: Routledge Kegan Paul, 1952), 303.

120 Mannheim, 309.

121 "Taking Back Hong Kong's Future," *New York Times*, October 29, 2014.

122 Iam-chong Ip, *Hong Kong's New Identity Politics: Longing for the Local in the Shadow of China* (New York: Routledge, 2020), chap. 4.

123 Law, *Thinking Hong Kong*, 229–230.

3. "HONG KONGERS" (RE)BORN IN ACTION

1 Achille Mbembe, *Out of the Dark Night: Essays on Decolonization* (New York: Columbia University Press, 2021), 2.

2 "Timeline: Key Dates for Hong Kong Extradition Bill and Protests," *Reuters*, July 1, 2019, https://www.reuters.com/article/idUSKCN1TW14F/.

3 David Lague, James Pomfret, and Greg Torode, "How Murders, Kipnappings and Miscalculation Set Off Hong Kong's Revolt," *Reuters*, December 20, 2019, https://www.reuters.com/investigates/special-report/hongkong-protests-extradition-narrative/.

4 Edmund Cheng and Samson Yuen, *The Making of Leaderful Mobilization* (Cambridge: Cambridge University Press, 2025).

5 These accounts were collected between July 2019 and March 2020 in Hong Kong. To protect their identities, all names used are fictitious, with the dates of the interviews and observations removed.

6 Edmund Cheng and Samson Yuen, "Anti-Extradition Movement (Hong Kong)," in *The Wiley Blackwell Encyclopedia of Social and Political Movements*, 2nd ed., ed. David Snow, Donatella della Porta, and Doug McAdam (Hoboken, New Jersey: Wiley Blackwell, 2022), 992–996.

7 Original interview with *Stand News* published on October 18, 2019; a summary in English can be found at Petula Sik Ying Ho, "Queering the Valiant: an Alternative Perspective on the Hong Kong Protest Movement," *Feminista Journal*, August 3, 2020, https://feministajournal.com/queering-the-valiant-an-alternative-perspective-on-the-hong-kong-protest-movement.

8 Hong Kong Free Press, "Activist Brian Leung at Storming of the Legislature" July 1, 2019, https://www.youtube.com/watch?v=n3EsrjpgKbQ.

9 YouTube video, HK Hope China, "An Immigrant Auntie Shouts at Police" [in Chinese] September 29, 2019, https://www.youtube.com/watch?v=7H-YefqPf50.

10 Wong Tsuui-kai, "Hong Kong Protests: What Are the 'Five Demands'? What Do Protesters Want?" August 19, 2019, *South China Morning Post*, https://www.scmp.com/yp/discover/news/hong-kong/article/3065950/hong-kong-protests-what-are-five-demands-what-do.

11 Zeynep Tufekci, *Twitter and Tear Gas: The Power and Fragility of Networked Protest* (New Haven, CT: Yale University Press, 2017), 27.

12 Tufekci, 71.

13 Yong Ming Kow, Bonnie Nardi, and Wai Kuen Cheng, "Be Water: Technologies in the Leaderless Anti-ELAB Movement in Hong Kong," in *CHI'20: Proceedings of the 2020 CHI Conference on Human Factors in Computing Systems*, 2020. Association for Computing Machinary Digital Library, https://dl.acm.org/doi/10.1145/3313831.3376634.

14 Francis L. F. Lee, "Solidarity in the Anti-Extradition Bill Movement," *Critical Asian Studies* 52, no. 1 (2020): 18–32.

15   Susanne Y. P. Choi, "Doing and Undoing Gender: Women on the Frontline of Hong Kong's Anti-Extradition Bill Movement," *Social Movement Studies* 22, no. 5–6 (2023): 786–801.

16   Petula Sik Ying Ho and Minnie Ming Li, "A Feminist Snap: Has Feminism in Hong Kong Been Defeated?," in "Being Water," special issue, *Made in China* 3 (September–December 2021): 89. See also Priscilla Sham, "Who Deserves Compassion: A Hierarchy of Suffering," *Medium*, February 22, 2020, https://medium.com/@priscillasham/who-deserves-compassion-a-hierarchy-of-suffering-in-hong-kongs-anti-extradition-movement-a12592950c4b.

17   David Palmer, "Black Bloc against Red China," *HAU: Journal of Ethnographic Theory* 10, no. 2 (2020): 325–332.

18   Katy Chan, "Behind the 'Racism' of the 2019 Hong Kong Protests," *HAU: Journal of Ethnographic Theory* 11, no. 2 (2012), 867–868.

19   Jessie Lau, "Hong Kong's Minorities Face Racism from Police and Protesters," *Foreign Policy*, November 7, 2019, https://foreignpolicy.com/2019/11/07/hong-kong-protests-minorities-face-violence-racism-police/.

20   James Pomfret and Clare Jim, "Exclusive: Hong Kongers Support Protester Demands; Minority Wants Independence from China," *Reuters*, December 31, 2019, https://www.reuters.com/article/idUSKBN1YZ0VI/.

21   Edmund Cheng, Francis Lee, Samson Yuen, and Gary Tang, "Total Mobilization from Below: Hong Kong's Freedom Summer," *China Quarterly* 251 (2022): 629–659.

22   John Mok, "Violent Repression, Relational Positions, and Emotional Mechanisms in Hong Kong's Anti-extradition Movement," *Mobilization* 27, no. 3 (2022): 297–317; Cheng et al., "Total Mobilization from Below"; Sara Liao, "Feeling the 2019 Hong Kong Anti-ELAB Movement: Emotion and Affect on the Lennon Walls," *Chinese Journal of Communication* 15, no. 3 (2021): 355–377.

23   Franz Fanon, *The Wretched of the Earth* (New York: Grove Press, 1963), 2.

4. BENDING THE ARC OF VIOLENCE

1   Franz Fanon, *The Wretched of the Earth* (New York: Grove Press, 1963), 2–4.

2   Fanon, *The Wretched of the Earth*, 51.

3   Amnesty International, "Hong Kong: Arbitrary Arrests, Brutal Beatings and Torture Revealed" September 19, 2019, https://www.amnesty.org/en/latest/press-release/2019/09/hong-kong-arbitrary-arrests-brutal-beatings-and-torture-in-police-detention-revealed/; Shibani Mahtani et al., "In Hong Kong Crackdown, Police Repeatedly Broke Their Own Rules," *The Washington Post*, December 24, 2019, https://www.washingtonpost.com/graphics/2019/world/hong-kong-protests-excessive-force/; Javier C Hernandez et al., "Did Hong Kong Police Abuse Protesters? What Videos Show," June 30, 2019, *New York*

Times, https://www.nytimes.com/2019/06/30/world/asia/did-hong-kong-police-abuse-protesters-what-videos-show.html.

4 Brent McDonald, "A Bullet to the Eye Is the Price of Protesting in Chile," *New York Times*, November 19, 2019, https://www.nytimes.com/2019/11/19/world/americas/chile-protests-eye-injuries.html.

5 Personal communication with historian Perry Anderson.

6 Ngok Ma, *The Resistant Community: The 2019 Anti-Extradition Movement in Hong Kong* (Xinbei, Taiwan: RiverGauche, 2020), 106 [in Chinese].

7 *Apple Daily*, August 1, 2019.

8 Nancy Fraser's original theory makes the distinction between the struggle for recognition and that for redistribution. Commonly known as identity politics in the West, recognition highlights the psychological effects of racism, sexism, colonization, and cultural imperialism. Recognition is about establishing a reciprocal relationship among subjects who see each other as equally valued but separate, even different. Misrecognition is the denial of value by the dominant group and the deprivation of a healthy self-identity among the disesteemed groups. See Nancy Fraser, *Justice Interruptus: Critical Reflections on the Postsocialist Condition* (New York: Routledge, 1997).

9 *Stand News*, April 15, 2020, https://collection.news/thestandnews/articles/115993 [in Chinese]; interview with artists F and Childe Abbadon, October 23, 2019, online news outlet Mosttv.com, report titled "Art on the Wall." (in Chinese; removed].

10 *Stand News*, "8.18 No Smoke Part 1," August 19, 2019 [in Chinese; website no longer available].

11 *Stand News*, August 19, 2019 [in Chinese].

12 Vivian Wai-Wan Tam, *Voices Out of the Darkness: Stories from the Hong Kong 2019 Protests* (Hong Kong: Breakthrough, 2020), 383–393 [in Chinese].

13 Cited in Francis L. F. Lee, *Prodemocracy Contention in Hong Kong* (New York: SUNY Press, 2025), 144.

14 "Joseph Lian: Theory of Violence on the Edge—A Possible Point of Convergence of the Route of Resistance of the Three Camps," *Initium*, September 28, 2015, https://theinitium.com/article/20150928-opinion-lianyizheng-evaluation/, cited in Lee, 144.

15 "Political Ethics of the Use of Violence," *Stand News*, November 20, 2019 [in Chinese].

16 "Anti-authoritarianism and Political Germaphobia," *Apple Daily*, October 15, 2019, https://apple-daily.eth.limo/20191015/LNN2YZNKQ6NWLCJ5SKBEGFJ54E/index.html [in Chinese].

17 Clifford Stott, Lawrence Ho, Matt Radburn, Ying Tung Chan, Arabella Kyprianides, and Patricio Saavedra Morales, "Patterns of 'Disorder' during the 2019 Protests in Hong Kong: Policing, Social Identity, Intergroup Dynamics, and Radicalization," *Policing: A Journal of Policy and Practice* 14, no. 4 (2020), 833.

18 Sum Lok-kei, "Nearly a Fifth of Hong Kong Voters Say They Support Violent Actions by Protesters," *South China Morning Post*, December 21, 2019, https://www.scmp.com/news/hong-kong/politics/article/3043073/nearly-fifth-voters-say-they-support-violent-actions.

19 Karl von Holdt, "The Violence of Order, Orders of Violence: Between Fanon and Bourdieu," *Current Sociology* 61, no. 2 (2012): 112–131.

20 Cora Engelbrecht, "In Hong Kong, Gasoline Bombs, Masks and . . . Last Letters," *New York Times,* October 20, 2019, https://www.nytimes.com/2019/10/20/world/asia/hong-kong-protesters-letters.html.

21 Wai, Interview, August 17, 2020.

22 Interview.

23 Joanne Ma, "Why Movie 'V for Vendetta' Has Become Part of Hong Kong Protests," *South China Morning Post*, October 21, 2019, https://www.scmp.com/yp/discover/lifestyle/features/article/3067925/why-movie-v-vendetta-has-become-part-hong-kong.

24 Five team members were arrested in December 2019 and charged under the antiterrorism law. Their testimonies in court in 2024 can be found in a series of reports by the Hong Kong Free Press, "Dragon Slayers," https://hongkongfp.com/tag/dragon-slayers/.

25 Interview by *Stand News*, November 8, 2019 [in Chinese; removed].

26 Originally published on Telegram [in Chinese; removed].

27 Originally published on Telegram [in Chinese; removed].

28 Interview by *Stand News*, November 8, 2019 [in Chinese; removed].

29 "2019 Revolutionary Manifesto from the Frontline," circulated on social media September 3, 2019 [in Chinese].

30 Cited in Lee, Prodemocracy Contention in Hong Kong, 240.

31 Fanon, *Wretched of the Earth*.

32 Examples included the beating of a mainland Chinese man during the airport occupation on August 12, 2019, and a man doused with flammable liquid and set on fire by protesters on the day the police shot at an unarmed protester, November 11, 2019. See Mike Ives, Ezra Cheung and Elsie Chen, "Chaos Grips Hong Kong's Airport as Police Clash with Protesters," *New York Times,* August 12, 2019, https://www.nytimes.com/2019/08/12/world/asia/hong-kong-airport-protest.html, and Bill Chappell, "Hong Kong in Tumult," National Public Radio, November 11, 2019, https://www.npr.org/2019/11/11/778204680/hong-kong-in-tumult-man-is-set-on-fire-after-police-shoot-protester.

33 Cited in Christopher J. Finlay, "Violence and Revolutionary Subjectivity," *European Journal of Political Theory* 5, no. 4 (2006): 373–347. See also Georges Sorel, *Reflections on Violence*, edited by Jeremy Jennings (Cambridge: Cambridge University Press, 1999).

34 Lily Kuo, "Hong Kong Protests," *The Guardian*, November 8, 2019, https://www.theguardian.com/world/2019/nov/08/hong-kong-protests-student-who-fell-from-parking-lot-during-demonstrations-dies. In 2021, a jury told the

coroner's court that they were unable to determine the causes and circumstances of his death.

35 Francis L. F. Lee and Ivy W. Y. Fong, "The Construction and Mobilization of Political Consumerism through Digital Media in a Networked Social Movement," *New Media and Society* 25, no. 12 (2012), 3582.

36 Cited in Debby Sze wan Chan, "The Consumption Power of the Politically Powerless: The Yellow Economy in Hong Kong," *Journal of Civil Society* 18, no. 1 (2022), 78.

37 Matthew Y. H. Wong, Ying-ho Kwong, and Edward K. F. Chan, "Political Consumerism in Hong Kong: China's Economic Intervention, Identity Politics, or Political Participation?," *China Perspectives* no. 3 (2021), 63.

38 Interviews and Facebook page of the Yellowbluemap at https://www.facebook.com/yellowbluemap.

39 Wong et al., "Political Consumerism in Hong Kong," 63.

40 *Stand News,* December 19, 2019.

41 Chan, "The Consumption Power of the Politically Powerless", "Consumption Must Take Side," *Apple Daily,* December 5, 2019 [in Chinese; removed].

42 Liu Xiu-wen,"The Ideals and Struggles of the Yellow Economy," *Initium,* May 6, 2020, https://theinitium.com/article/20200506-hongkong-yellow-economic-circle-firstofmay [in Chinese].

43 Yanni Chow and Carol Mang, "New Security Law Starts to Break Down Hong Kong's Prodemocracy Economy," *Reuters,* July 6, 2020, https://www.reuters.com/article/idUSKBN24800K/.

44 Natalie Wong, "Tsuanmi-like Surge in Applications to Form Unions," *South China Morning Post,* May 16, 2021, https://www.scmp.com/news/hong-kong/society/article/3133696/hong-kong-labour-minister-vows-kick-out-unions-do-not-abide.

45 Interview, March 5, 2020.

46 Interview, March 30, 2020.

47 Interview, March 6, 2020.

48 John Yoon, "Hong Kong Sentences 5 to 19 Months for Children's Books Deemed 'Seditious,'" *New York Times,* September 10, 2022, https://www.nytimes.com/2022/09/10/world/asia/hong-kong-childrens-books-free-speech.html.

49 Interview, May 27, 2020.

50 Interview, April 9, 2020.

51 Interview, May 13, 2020.

52 Interview, January 17, 2020.

53 David A. Levin and Stephen W. K. Chiu, "Trade Union Growth Waves in Hong Kong," *Labour History,* no. 75 (1998), 40–56.

54 C. P. Lau, "Anti-colonial Unionism," on the Facebook page of the Hong Kong Construction and Engineering Employees' General Union, May 2, 2020 (removed).

55 Yao-tai Li and Jenna Ng, "Moral Dilemma of Striking: A Medical Worker's Response to Job Duty, Public Health Protection and the Politicization of Strike," *Work, Employment and Society* 36, no. 5 (2022), 972.

56 Fieldwork, June 8, 2020.

57 Rachel Wong, "'Hong Kong People Made History Again': Over 600,000 Vote in Democrats' Primaries," *Hong Kong Free Press*, July 12, 2020, https://hongkongfp.com/2020/07/12/hong-kong-people-made-history-again-over-600000-vote-in-democrats-primaries-as-co-organiser-hails-miracle-turnout/.

58 Interunion meeting, March 21, 2020.

59 Interview, July 23, 2020.

60 "Ho Kwai Lam's Testimonials," *Inmedia*, July 18, 2023, https://www.inmediahk.net/node/1097326/ [in Chinese].

61 Jeffie Lam, Brian Wong, Kaliz Lee and Marcelo Duhalde, "Hong Kong 47 and Their Jail Time after Longest National Security Law Trial," *South China Morning Post*, November 20, 2024, https://multimedia.scmp.com/infographics/news/hong-kong/article/3286769/hk47sentence/index.html.

62 Yan-ho Lai, "The Judiciary," in *Contemporary Hong Kong Government and Politics*, ed. Lam Wai Man, Percy Luen-tim Lui, and Wilson Wong (Hong Kong: Hong Kong University Press, 2024), 76–110. For an analysis China's assault on Hong Kong's rule of law and the response of the legal profession, see Yan-ho Lai, *Defending the Rule of Law: Hong Kong's Resistance to Authoritarianism* (Amsterdam: Amsterdam University Press, 2025).

63 Hong Kong Democracy Council, "Hong Kong Political Prisoners," https://www.hkdc.us/hong-kong-political-prisoners.

64 Tom Grundy, "Hong Kong Police Watchdog Clears Force of Misconduct," *Hong Kong Free Press*, May 15, 2020, https://hongkongfp.com/2020/05/15/in-full-hong-kong-police-watchdog-releases-report-on-protest-conduct-but-no-evidence-of-yuen-long-mob-attack-collusion/.

65 Benny Tai, "Challenges to the Rule of Law in Semi-authoritarian Hong Kong," *Social and Legal Studies* 29, no. 1 (2020): 110–128.

66 Benny Tai, "Rule of Law Is Not Just about Maintaining Social Order," *Ming Pao*, December 31, 2020 [in Chinese].

67 Lai, "The Judiciary."

68 Law Wing-sang, "'Laam Caao' Is a Type of Decolonization," *Ming Pao*, September 20, 2019 [in Chinese; removed].

69 Original interview with *Stand News* published on October 18, 2019; English translation in Petula Sik Ying Ho, "Queering the Valiant," *Feminista Journal*, March 8, 2020, https://feministajournal.com/queering-the-valiant-an-alternative-perspective-on-the-hong-kong-protest-movement.

70 Interview, November 28, 2022.

71 Olivia Chow, Thomas E. Kellogg, and Eric Yan-ho Lai, *Anatomy of a Crackdown: The Hong Kong National Security Law and Restrictions on Civil Society*

(Washington, DC: Center for Asian Law, Georgetown Law, 2024), https:// www.law.georgetown.edu/law-asia/wp-content/uploads/sites/31/2024/03/24 _ASIAN_LAW_NGO_REPORT_FINAL.pdf.

5. "BE WATER" GOES GLOBAL

1 Peter E. Hamilton, *Made in Hong Kong: Transpacific Networks and a New History of Globalization* (New York: Columbia University Press, 2021), 283.

2 Gary Hamilton, "Hong Kong and the Rise of Capitalism in Asia," in *Cosmopolitan Capitalists: Hong Kong and the Chinese Diaspora at the End of the 20th Century*, ed. Gary Hamilton, 14–34 (Seattle: University of Washington Press, 1999).

3 Suzanne Pepper, *Keeping Democracy at Bay: Hong Kong and the Challenge of Chinese Political Reform* (Lanham, MD: Rowman and Littlefield, 2008); Kenneth Yung, "Decolonization and the Triangular Collaboration for Democracy in Cold War Hong Kong" (unpublished manuscript, 2023).

4 Ann Quonn, "Beaten but Unbowed," *South China Morning Post*, January 23, 1988; Louis Won, "International Status 'Gives Life to Territory,'" *South China Morning Post*, May 6, 1996.

5 Michael Chugani, "Lee Determined to Spread the Word," *South China Morning Post*, May 7, 1990.

6 Andrew B. Brick, "Time Passes for Hong Kong and Still Bush Waits," *International Herald Tribune*, April 16, 1992.

7 Gene Linn, "US Senator Defends Hong Kong Act," *United Press International*, April 22, 1992, https://www.upi.com/Archives/1992/04/22/US-senator -defends-Hong-Kong-act/7158703915200//print/. By 2018, these numbers grew to 85,000 and 1,300 respectively.

8 Historian Niall Ferguson and economist Moritz Schularick first coined the term *Chimerica* in late 2006 to describe the symbiotic relationship between American overspending and Chinese export earnings deposited as American government securities.

9 Senate Hearing 108-480—Democracy in Hong Kong. March 4, 2004. US Government Publishing Office. https://www.congress.gov/event/108th -congress/senate-event/LC13856/text?s=1&r=45.

10 Tanna Chong, "China Propaganda Organs Slam Anson Chan, Martin Lee over American Trip," *South China Morning Post*, April 20, 2014, https://www .scmp.com/news/hong-kong/article/1490014/china-propaganda-organs-slam -anson-chan-martin-lee-over-america-trip.

11 Nathan Law, interview, September 3, 2022.

12 Interview, January 9, 2020.

13 Interview.

14 Interview, September 3, 2022.

15 Ho-fung Hung, "The US-China Rivalry Is about Capitalist Competition," *Jacobin,* July 11, 2020, https://jacobin.com/2020/07/us-china-competition-capitalism-rivalry.

16 Laura Silver, Christine Huang, and Laura Clancy, "How Global Public Opinion of China Has Shifted in the Xi Era," Pew Research Center, September 28, 2022, https://www.pewresearch.org/global/2022/09/28/how-global-public-opinion-of-china-has-shifted-in-the-xi-era/.

17 Chris Horton, "Hong Kong's Protesters Are Outfoxing Beijing Worldwide," *The Atlantic,* September 29, 2019, https://www.theatlantic.com/international/archive/2019/09/hong-kong-public-opinion-beijing/599059/.

18 Hillary Leung, "Hong Kong's Summer of Unrest Has Been Drawing Inspiration from Ukraine's *Winter on Fire,*" *Time,* September 24, 2019, https://time.com/5682003/winter-on-fire-hong-kong-protests-ukraine/.

19 Photo at Teddy Ng, "Chinese State Media Denounces Hong Kong Protesters Seeking U.S. Support," *South China Morning Post,* September 9, 2019, https://www.politico.com/story/2019/09/09/hong-kong-protesters-1486227.

20 Interview, July 5, 2023.

21 Alan Macleod, "With People in the Streets Worldwide, Media Focus Uniquely on Hong Kong," December 6, 2019, https://fair.org/home/with-people-in-the-streets-worldwide-media-focus-uniquely-on-hong-kong/.

22 Bernard Chan, "Western Media Reports on the Hong Kong Protests Tell Just One of Many Stories," *South China Morning Post,* December 20, 2019, https://www.scmp.com/comment/opinion/article/3042655/western-media-reports-hong-kong-protests-tell-just-one-many-stories; "Biased Western Media are Fueling HK Riots," *Global Times,* November 12, 2019, https://www.globaltimes.cn/page/201911/1169821.shtml; Steven Lee Myers and Paul Mozur, "China is Waging a Disinformation War Against Hong Kong Protesters," *New York Times,* August 13, 2019, https://www.nytimes.com/2019/08/13/world/asia/hong-kong-protests-china.html.

23 Francis L. F. Lee, "Proactive Internationalization and Diaspora Mobilization in a Networked Movement: The Case of Hong Kong's Anti-Extradition Bill Protests," *Social Movement Studies* 22, no. 2 (2023): 232–249. See also Edward Wong, "Hong Kong Protesters Call for U.S. Help: China Sees a Conspiracy," *New York Times,* November 3, 2019, https://www.nytimes.com/2019/11/03/world/asia/hong-kong-protesters-call-for-us-help-china-sees-a-conspiracy.html?searchResultPosition=1.

24 B. Fong, "The Future of Hong Kong's Autonomy: How Will China and the West Respond to the Water Revolution?," *The Diplomat,* October 29, 2019; H. F. Hung, "The Political Economy of Mutual Destruction," *Ming Pao,* November 11, 2019 [in Chinese].

25 Interview, June 24, 2023.

26 Interview.

27 Cheung Bo Sang, "G20 Crowdfunding Announces June Data," *HK01*, August 23, 2019, https://www.hk01.com/article/367200?utm_source=01articlecopy&utm_medium=referral [in Chinese].

28 Interview, June 30, 2023.

29 Ming-Sho Ho, "Hongkongers' International Front: Diaspora Activism during and after the 2019 Anti-extradition Protest," *Journal of Contemporary Asia* 54, no. 2 (2024): 238–259.

30 Ho, 2024; see also Lee, "Proactive Internationalization and Diaspora Mobilization," 241.

31 Interview, September 29, 2022.

32 Interview.

33 Interview, September 12, 2022.

34 Interview, September 29, 2022.

35 Hong Kong Public Opinion Research Institute, "Civic Sociey Sponsorship Scheme: Survey Report (3)," November 22, 2019, https://www.pori.hk/wp-content/uploads/2021/01/sp_rpt_csss_sanctionpolice_2019nov22_FINAL_v3.pdf.

36 YouTube video, "Stand With Hong Kong Power to the People 2/2," SocRec, August 16, 2019, https://www.youtube.com/watch?v=HQKHMdeJTV8.

37 Interview, October 29, 2019.

38 Interview, June 23, 2023.

39 Interview, October 29, 2019.

40 Interview, June 23, 2023.

41 Interview, October 25, 2019.

42 Interview.

43 Interview, June 23, 2023.

44 Interview, June 24, 2023.

45 Interview.

46 Samuel Chu, interview, June 26, 2023.

47 Chu, Interview.

48 Ho, "Hongkongers' International Front."

49 Chu, Interview.

50 Interview, August 3, 2023.

51 Chu, Interview.

52 Interview, January 9, 2020.

53 Cheryl S. Y. Shea and Francis L. F. Lee, "Public Diplomacy via Twitter: Opportunities and Tensions," *Chinese Journal of Communication* 15, no. 3 (2022): 449–462.

54 Patricia Zengerle, "U.S. Senators Push for Vote on Hong Kong Rights Bill as Violence Rises," *Reuters*, November 13, 2019, https://www.reuters.com/article/uk-hongkong-protests-usa/u-s-senators-push-for-vote-on-hong-kong-rights-bill-as-violence-rises-idINKBN1XM2VO.

55 In December 2024, the HKHRD Act was extended for another five years by President Joe Biden. See Mark Magnier, "Biden Signs Pentagon Budget Bill that Extends Sanctions on Hong Kong Officials," *South China Morning Post*, December 25, 2024, https://www.scmp.com/news/china/diplomacy/article/3292206/biden-signs-pentagon-budget-bill-extends-sanctions-hong-kong-officials.

56 Mary Hui, "Hong Kong is Exporting its Protest Techniques around the World," *Quartz*, October 16, 2019, https://qz.com/1728078/be-water-catalonia-protesters-learn-from-hong-kong.

57 Hui.

58 Holmes Chan, "'Fight against Oppression': Hong Kong and Catalan Protesters Hold Parallel Solidarity Rally," *Hong Kong Free Press*, October 16, 2019, https://hongkongfp.com/2019/10/25/fight-oppression-hong-kong-catalan-protesters-hold-parallel-solidarity-rallies/.

59 Laignee Barron, "We Share the Ideals of Democracy," *Time*, October 28, 2020, https://time.com/5904114/milk-tea-alliance/; Xun-ling Au, "The #Milk-TeaAlliance: Why Does It Matter?," *Medium*, May 14, 2021, https://xunling.medium.com/the-milkteaalliance-why-does-it-matter-8bed98c4098e.

60 William Yang, "How Hong Kong Protests Are Inspiring Movements Worldwide," DW, October 22, 2019, https://www.dw.com/en/how-hong-kong-protests-are-inspiring-movements-worldwide/a-50935907.

61 "Power in Solidarity: Myanmar Protesters Inspired by Hong Kong and Thailand," *Reuters*, February 9, 2021, https://www.reuters.com/article/us-myanmar-politics-protests/power-in-solidarity-myanmar-protesters-inspired-by-hong-kong-and-thailand-idUSKBN2A913H.

62 Helen Davidson, "How the Killing of George Floyd Exposed Hong Kong Activists' Uneasy Relationship with Donald Trump," *The Guardian*, June 14, 2020, https://www.theguardian.com/world/2020/jun/14/how-the-killing-of-george-floyd-exposed-hong-kong-activists-uneasy-relationship-with-donald-trump.

63 Samuel Brannen, Christian S. Haig, and Katherine Schmidt, *The Age of Mass Protests: Understanding an Escalating Global Trend* (Washington, DC: Center for Strategic and International Studies, 2020), 1.

64 Political currents defy neat calendrical boundaries, so the listed years only mark the high points of their respective periods of social upheaval.

65 Alan Taylor, "The Lasers of Discontents," *The Atlantic*, November 19, 2019, https://www.theatlantic.com/photo/2019/11/photos-lasers-discontent/602263/.

66 Elia J. Ayoub and Lausan Collective, "Revolution Everywhere: A Conversation between Hong Kong and Lebanese Protesters," *Lausan*, June 13, 2020, https://lausancollective.com/2020/revolution-everywhere-conversation-between-hong-kong-and-lebanon/.

67 Kunal Purohit, "WhatsApp to Bridgefy, What Hong Kong Taught India's Leaderless Protesters," *South China Morning Post,* December 18, 2019, https://www.scmp.com/week-asia/politics/article/3042633/whatsapp-bridgefy-what-hong-kong-taught-indias-leaderless?module=hard_link&pgtype=article.

68 Associated Press, "Peru's Protest 'Deactivators' Run toward Tear Gas to Stop It," January 23, 2023, https://www.voanews.com/a/peru-s-protest-deactivators-run-toward-tear-gas-to-stop-it/6939496.html.

69 Associated Press January 23, 2023.

70 William Yiu, "Canada Targets Hong Kong's Young and Well-educated," *South China Morning Post,* January 9, 2023, https://www.scmp.com/news/hong-kong/society/article/3206004/canada-targets-hong-kongs-young-and-well-educated-grants-1700-permanent-residence-and-33000-work?module=hard_link&pgtype=article.

71 Connor Kopchick, Kathleen Cunningham, Erin Jenne, and Stephen Saideman, "Emerging Diasporas: Exploring Mobilization outside the Homeland," *Journal of Peace Research* 59, no. 2 (2022): 107–121.

72 Brian Fong, "Diaspora Formation and Mobilization: The Emerging Hong Kong Diaspora in the Anti-extradition Bill Movement," *Nations and Nationalism* 28, no. 3 (2022): 1061–1079.

73 The British government's interest in this was twofold—economic and moral. On the one hand, the naturalization of Hong Kong's middle class was expected to boost the British economy by 2.4–2.9 billion pounds, mostly from tax revenue. On the other, the British government recognized its historic and moral commitment to BNO holders now that the Chinese state had violated the Sino-British Joint Declaration. See The Home Office, "Impact Assessment: Hong Kong British (Overseas) Visa," October 22, 2020, https://www.legislation.gov.uk/ukia/2020/70/pdfs/ukia_20200070_en.pdf. For the Canadian government, which had issued twenty-one thousand work permits by spring 2023 to young and educated Hong Kongers with a pathway to permanent residency, replenishing a depleted labor force of retiring baby boomers was the main concern. Laura Westbrook and William Yiu, "21,000 Hongkongers Granted Canadian Work Permits," *South China Morning Post,* March 18, 2023, https://www.scmp.com/news/hong-kong/society/article/3213831/greener-pastures-more-red-tape-canadas-migration-pathways-draw-young-hongkongers-some-trip-over.

74 This idea was adapted from Tahseen Shams's conceptualization of the Muslim diaspora. Tahseen Sham, "Homeland and Heartland: Conceptualizing the 'Muslim' 'Diaspora,'" *Diaspora: A Journal of Transnational Studies* 21, no. 1 (2021): 47–63.

75 Carole J. Petersen, "Not an Internal Affair: Hong Kong's Right to Autonomy and Self-Determination under International Law," *Hong Kong Law Journal* 49 (2019): 883–904; Max Wong, *Reordering Hong Kong: Decolonization*

and the Hong Kong Bill of Rights Ordinance (Wildy, Simmonds & Hill Publishing, 2017), 43.

76 Interview, September 3, 2022.
77 Interview, September 11, 2023.
78 Interview, September 27, 2022.
79 Interview.
80 Interview, June 23, 2023.
81 Interview, September 18, 2023.
82 Interview.
83 Frederick Cooper and Jane Burbank, *Post-Imperial Possibilities: Eurasia, Eurafrica, Afroasia* (Princeton, NJ: Princeton University Press, 2023).

6. TO BE CONTINUED

1 Beijing directly imposed the National Security Law on Hong Kong in July 2020, and the Hong Kong legislature passed a second, homegrown version in March 2024, expanding the scope of national security crimes. See Chris Lau, "Hong Kong Passes Second National Security Law," *CNN World*, March 20, 2024, https://edition.cnn.com/2024/03/19/china/hong-kong-second-national-security-law-passed-intl-hnk/index.html.

2 Hannah Adrendt, *Men in Dark Times* (New York: Houghton Mifflin Harcourt, 1970), 9.

3 Franz Fanon, *The Wretched of the Earth,* trans. Richard Philcox (1963; repr., New York: Grove Press, 2004), 2.

4 Kevin Carrico, "National Identity Deconstruction: Revisiting the Debate on Chinese Nationalism via Hong Kong Nationalism," *Nations and Nationalism* 29, no. 2 (2023): 768–783.

5 Arif Dirlik, "Taiwan: The Land Colonialisms Made," *Boundary 2* 45, no. 3 (2018), 5–6.

6 Achille Mbembe, *Out of the Dark Night* (New York: Columbia University Press, 2021), 2–3.

7 Karen Cheung, "'Decolonize Hong Kong Street Names,'" *Hong Kong Free Press*, March 5, 2018, https://hongkongfp.com/2018/03/05/decolonise-hong-kong-street-names-suggests-member-beijings-top-advisory-body/.

8 For a profile of some of these scholars, see Chris Buckley, "'Clean Up This Mess': The Chinese Thinkers behind Xi's Hard Line," *New York Times*, August 2, 2020, https://www.nytimes.com/2020/08/02/world/asia/china-hong-kong-national-security-law.html.

9 Lau Siu-kai, "Decolonisation á la Hong Kong: Britain's Search for Governability and Exit with Glory," *Journal of Commonwealth and Comparative Politics* 35, no. 2 (1997): 28–54.

10 Lau Siu-kai, "De-decolonization Achieves Remarkable Results but Is Far from Complete," *China Daily,* August 31, 2022.

11 Tian Feilong, "Rectifying the Teachers' Union Is a Necessary Remedy for Hong Kong's Decolonization," *am730,* August 9, 2021 [in Chinese].

12 Tian.

13 Yan Xiaojun, "Hong Kong Reform Must Break Colonialism's Cultural Influence," *Ming Pao,* August 26, 2024 [in Chinese].

14 These ideas are analyzed in Sebastian Veg, "The Rise of China's Statist Intellectuals: Law, Sovereignty, and 'Repoliticization,'" *China Journal,* no. 82 (2019): 39.

15 Jiang Shigong, *China's Hong Kong: The New Frontiers between Civilizations,* rev. and enlarged ed. (Hong Kong: Joint Publishing, 2023), 6–7 [in Chinese].

16 Jiang, 22.

17 Jiang, 381. See also Koon-chung Chan, *Chinese Imperial Ideology and Hong Kong* (Hong Kong: Oxford University Press, 2012), 87–127 [in Chinese].

18 Jiang Shigong, "The Internal Logic of Super-Sized Political Entities: 'Empire' and World Order," *Aisixiang,* April 6, 2019, http://www.aisixiang.com/data/115799.html. English translation available at https://www.readingthechinadream.com/jiang-shigong-empire-and-world-order.html.

19 Lu Pan, introduction to *The 70s Bi-weekly: Social Activism and Alternative Cultural Production in 1970s Hong Kong* (Hong Kong: Hong Kong University Press, 2023), 5–6.

20 Wing-sang Law, "The Impossible Decolonization and the Radical Thought of Ng Chung-Yin," in *The 70s Weekly: Social Activism and Alternative Cultural Production in the 1970s Hong Kong,* ed. Lu Pan (Hong Kong: Hong Kong University Press, 2023), 39.

21 Collections of his Chinese newspaper commentaries and conference papers are published as Law Wing-sang, *Retheorizing Colonial Power* (Hong Kong: Oxford University Press, 2007), *Beyond Colony and Nation* (Hong Kong: Oxford University Press, 2014), *Thinking Hong Kong* (Hong Kong: Oxford University Press, 2020), and *Counter Narratives about My City* (Hong Kong: Arcadia Press, 2020). All are in Chinese.

22 Law, *Beyond Colony and Nation,* 25.

23 Law, *Thinking Hong Kong,* 221.

24 Law, 44–48.

25 Benedict Anderson, *Imagined Communities: Reflections on the Origin and Spread of Nationalism* (London: Verso, 1983).

26 Brian Leung, "The Controversy over Social Assistance and Localist Political Community," in *On the Hong Kong Nation,* ed. 2013 Undergrad Editorial Board (Hong Kong: HKUSU, 2014), 23–31 [in Chinese].

27 Brian Fong, ed., *Discourse on Reforming Hong Kong* (Taipei: Azoth-Books, 2015) [in Chinese].

28 Brian Fong, "Stateless Nation within a Nationless State: The Political Past, Present, and Future of Hongkongers, 1949–2019," *Nation and Nationalism* 26 (2020), 1070.

29 Fong, 1081.

30 Wen Liu, J. N. Chien, Christina Chung, and Ellie Tse, eds., *Reorienting Hong Kong's Resistance: Leftism, Decoloniality and Internationalism* (Singapore: Palgrave Macmillan, 2022), xx.

31 Adom Getachew, *Worldmaking after Empire: The Rise and Fall of Self-Determination* (Princeton, NJ: Princeton University Press, 2019).

32 Shuk Ying Chan, *Postcolonial Global Justice* (Princeton, NJ: Princeton University Press, 2025), 33.

33 Chan, 34.

ACKNOWLEDGMENTS

It was an unparalleled privilege to be in the company of millions of fellow Hong Kongers, to experience and observe firsthand what had turned out to be the city's most fateful political upheaval. Writing this book allowed me to relive and reinscribe events in 2019–2021, and render them historically and sociologically legible. Now at the end of this journey, with thoughts and emotions unloaded onto these pages, what came to my mind most vividly was Charles Dickens. His poetic reflection on London and Paris in another epoch of revolution has become an apt summary of Hong Kong: "It was the best of times, it was the worst of times, it was the age of wisdom, it was the age of foolishness, it was the epoch of belief, it was the epoch of incredulity, it was the season of Light, it was the season of Darkness, it was the spring of hope, it was the winter of despair, we had everything before us, we had nothing before us" (*A Tale of Two Cities*, 1859). Hong Kongers could perhaps find comfort in this memorable prose, knowing they are now part of a universal human struggle.

I would like to thank all the citizens and activists who were featured in this book. Your willingness to share with me your views and experiences, even in the face of grave political risks, made my research possible. As a newcomer to Hong Kong Studies, I have counted on the outstanding scholarship and deep knowledge of many colleagues based in Hong Kong and beyond. For their insightful criticisms and constructive feedback on the draft manuscript, I am particularly grateful to Law Wing-sang, Jeffrey Ngo, Rey Yap, Chris Chan, Alex Chow, Chan Shuk-ying, Eric Lai, and Joseph Chan.

At Harvard University Press, I was fortunate to work with editor Joseph Pomp, whose enthusiasm for the project, exquisite intellectual taste, and sage counsel at every step made writing this book a most gratifying undertaking. HUP's team of designers, editorial assistants, project manager, and copyeditor are among the best I have ever worked with.

During my two years (2019–2021) in Hong Kong, I was on the faculty of the Hong Kong University of Science and Technology. For all the opportunities and support they had generously offered me, and their ardent efforts to preserve academic freedom during a challenging time, I thank President Wei Shyy and Dean Kellee Tsai. Returning to UCLA, I was grateful to Darnell Hunt, then the Social Science Dean, for providing a seed grant for an online Global Hong Kong Studies initiative I launched with colleagues from several UC campuses. Seeing young scholars from around the world and members of the global public joining our book talks, symposia, and panel discussions has given me hope that Hong Kong will remain an inextinguishable subject of scholarly interest.

INDEX

Page numbers in *italics* refer to photographs.

Abe, Shinzo, 244
Afghanistan, 72, 235, 262, 267
Africa, 5, 6, 19, 61, 116, 172, 238
Ai Weiwei, 86
Algeria, 5, 172, 277
Alliance in Support of Patriotic Democratic Movements in China, 63
Alliance of Hong Kong Chinese in America, 256
American Revolution, 18
Anderson, Benedict, 82, 112, 288
"anticolonial," use of the term, 7
antieviction riot (1948), 29
antiforeignism, 27
antiglobalization movement, 60–61, 69, 71, 72, 81
anti–national education campaign, 77–81, 82, 85, 87, 89, 116, 126, 275
antiprivatization, 12, 116
anti-West Rail campaign, 12, 74, 76, 116
anti-WTO protests, 69, 71–72, 73, 115, 116, 126, 131
Arab Spring, 78, 81, 135, 159
Arendt, Hannah, 271
assimilation, coercive, 23, 60, 278
"Autonomous Destiny," 91
Azikiwe, Nnamdi, 289

Banking Ordinance, 43
Basic Law, 53, 56, 64, 86, 88, 91, 108, 111, 144, 208, 219, 222, 226, 253

Belt and Road Initiative, 238
"be water," 158, 168, 230, 232, 260–261, 275
Bill of Rights, 39, 64
Bill of Rights Ordinary (BOR), 39
Black Lives Matter movement, 260–261, 263, 289
Black Ribbon Day, 178
Bourdieu, Pierre, 5
Boxer Uprising, 27
boycotts, 27–28, 202, 205; anti-Japanese boycott, 28; cotton boycott, 259; general strike boycott, 28; student class boycotts, 85, 89, 93; tram boycott, 27
brainwashing, colonial, 79–80, 82
"brave warriors," 188–203
British Dependent Territories citizens (BDTC), 50, 51
British National (Overseas) (BNO), 50–51, 269
bubbles, speculative, 11, 63, 144
burnism, 223–224, 225, 246, 249, 255, 275

Cameron, David, 235
Cao Erbao, 78
Catalan independence movement, 259, *260*
Cesaire, Aime, 22
Chan, Alan, 114
Chan, Anson, 235, 252, 254
Chan, Joseph, 186
Chan, Shuk Ying, 289–290
Chan Ho Tin, Andy, 110

325

Chan Kin Man, 88, 99
Charles III, 25
Chen, Y. C., 74–76
Cheng, Edmund, 2
Cheng, Simon, 266
Chenoweth, Erica, 201
Cheung, Mama, 152–154
Cheung, Sunny, 249–252, 258
Chiang Kai-shek, 46
Chimerica, 58, 235
"China as destiny," 11–13, 45–54, 91, 100–109, 115, 232, 273, 276
Chinese Association of Hong Kong and Macau Studies, 282
Chinese language, 23, 32–33, 112, 285
Chinese Manufacturers' Association, 43
Chinese Reform Club, 47
Chinese University of Hong Kong (CUHK), 105, 193–194, 196–199, 204, 258
Chin Wan, 104, 111
Chow, Agnes, 237
Chow, Alex, 89, 91, 99, 257
Chow, Jaco, 76, 96, 229
Chow, Jason, 110
Chow Hang Tung, 113
Chow Sze-chung, 71–72, 73–74
Chow Tsz-lok, 203
Christian Industrial Committee (CIC), 217
Christianity, 76, 133
Chu, Samuel, 255–258
Chu Hoi-dick, Eddie, 65–66, 70, 72–74, 76, 210–211, 220
Chung Yiu Wah, 100
Chu Yiu Ming, 88, 256
city diplomacy, 266–267
Civic Square, 82, 84, 89, 136
Civil Human Rights Front, 67, 120
civil liberty, 24, 38, 41, 60, 67, 74, 86, 150, 275, 280
coercion, 23, 166; coercive assimilation, 23, 60, 278; coercive sameness, 8; coercive solidarity, 12, 155, 168
Cold War, 17, 32, 44, 47, 232, 234, 284

colonial mythologies, 23–24. *See also* China as destiny; free-market utopia; prosperity and stability; rule of law
colonial nostalgia, 75, 78, 117
colonial othering, 7–9, 21–22, 60, 143, 150
color revolutions, 64, 78, 81, 92, 281, 282
Comitium (Hong Kong National Party journal), 112
comprador class, 20, 47
Confucianism, 21, 48, 78, 186, 284
Convention of 1898, 294n5
Convention of Peking, 294n5
COVID-19 pandemic, 14, 220, 221, 223
Cowperthwaite, John, 41
Crimes Ordinance, 36, 229
crony-capitalism index, 44
crowdfunding, 241–246
Cruz, Ted, 257
Cuba, 18, 201, 255
cultural economy, 68–69
Cultural Revolution, 29, 46, 132, 200
Cyberport, 68
Czechoslovakia, 99

Dapiran, Antony, 2
Du Bois, W.E.B., 289
Declaration on the Granting of Independence to Colonial Countries and People, 19, 48, 49, 233, 300n96
decolonial subjectivities, 115–118
decolonization, 2–9, 272–277; Chinese imaginaries of, 280–284; contemporary, 277–280; Hong Kong imaginaries of, 284–290
"decolonization," use of the term, 7
"decolonizing," use of the term, 7
Delmas, Candice, 187
Democratic Party, 55, 86–87
Democratic Progressive Party, 154
Democratic Self-Governing Party, 47, 233
Demosisto, 111, 236, 237, 254
Deng Xiaoping, 39, 51, 78

deregulation, 43, 63
developmentalism, 11, 61, 68, 70, 276
Diaoyutai, 23, 33, 37, 73, 285
diaspora, Hong Kong, 245–246, 252–253, 255, 258, 263–268
diasporic activism, multiscalar, 263–268
Dirlik, Arif, 278
dispossession, 5, 18, 116, 277
double colonialization, 18–23, 112, 273, 278
double coloniality, 3, 9, 12, 19, 22, 36, 57, 59, 119, 273
Dragon Slayers, 199–201
Durkheim, Emile, 155, 161

education campaign, anti-national, 77–81, 82, 85, 87, 89, 116, 126, 275
Education Ordinance, 36
Education Regulations, 36
Egypt, 135, 159
8.18 march, 179–181
Elizabeth II, 25, 295n20
emergency regulations, 35–36, 47
English language, 21
epistemology, 7–8
European Convention on Human Rights, 35
Executive Council, 21

"Facebook Revolutions," 159
Falklands War, 51
Fanon, Franz, 5, 13, 15–16, 168, 172, 202, 272, 285, 290
Federation of Hong Kong Industries, 43
Federation of Students, 67, 80, 85, 88–89, 92, 93, 95, 97, 99, 111, 112, 118
feminism, 166–167
fiery era, 23, 32, 285
Film Censorship Regulations, 36
financial crises: Asian financial crisis, 11, 63–64; 2008 financial crisis, 78, 115, 274
Fish Ball Revolution, 106, 110, 114, 116, 120, 195, 248, 251, 275
Fixing Hong Kong, 101, 102
Floyd, George, 261

Fong, Brian, 207, 288
food security, 50
Franco, Francisco, 288
Fraser, Nancy, 310n8
free market utopia, 10, 11, 23, 41–45, 54, 67–71, 77, 115
Friedman, Milton, 41

gaps, income and wealth, 68, 218
GDP, 32, 291n6
Geneva Summit for Human Rights and Democracy, 265
gentrification, 4
Getachew, Adom, 289
Ghana, 8
global cities, 4, 67–72, 115–116, 231–232, 274, 289
Global Magnitsky Human Rights Accountability Act (US), 255
global media, 238–241
Godber, Peter Fitzroy, 32
Golden (social media platform), 83–84
Goodstadt, Leo, 44
graffiti, 1, 140, 175, 191, 262
Gramsci, Antonio, 59, 281
Grantham, Alexander, 31, 37
Greenpeace, 71–72, 73
guerrilla warfare, 1, 107, 168, 197, 201
Guevara, Che, 202

Haddon-Cave, Philip, 41
Haiti, 8, 18, 240, 277
Hamilton, Gary, 233
Hamilton, Peter, 233
Han nationalism, 22, 92, 235, 278
hate speech, 167
Hawley, Josh, 257
HKGolden internet forum, 160, 242
Ho, Gwyneth, 141, 156, 224, 226
Homo economicus, 22, 58
Hong Kong Civic Association, 47
Hong Kong Confederation of Trade Unions (HKCTU), 209, 216–217
Hong Kong Human Rights and Democracy Act (US), 13, 163, 232, 237, 239, 241, 246, 249–253, 255, 269

Hong Kong Indigenous, 96, 105–110, 138, 195–196
Hong Kong In-media, 71
Hong Kong National Party, 110–112, 114
Hong Kong Policy Act (US), 60, 78, 111, 234, 246, 248–251, 274
Hong Kong Polytechnic University (PolyU), 146, 165, 185, 187–188, 194–195, 197, 204, 240, 258
Hong Kong United Nations Association, 47
Hong Kong Watch, 250
Hong Kong Way, 178, 239
Hospital Authority Employees' Alliance (HAEA) strike, 218–221, 223–224
Hui, Francis, 265
human rights advocacy, 265–266
Hundred Days' Reform, 27
Hung, Ho-fung, 2
Hunger Games, The (film), 223
hunger strikes, 29, 30, 70, 73, 80, 81, 83, 84, 105

icons, protest, 177, 217
Independent Commission Against Corruption, 31, 38, 153
Independent Media Center (Indymedia), 71
India, 7, 51, 262, 267, 283
Individual Visit Scheme, 306n96
inequality, 4, 6, 32, 68, 76–77, 94–96, 228, 290
information and communication technology (ICT), 159–160, 261
International Covenant on Civil and Political Rights, 38, 264
Interparliamentary Alliance on China, 265–266
interregnum (between colonialities), 59–62
Ip, Regina, 83
Iran, 72, 257
Itzigsohn, Jose, 8

Japan, 33, 110–111, 244; anime, 83, 126, 162; anti-Japanese boycott, 28; G20 Summit in, 175; occupation of Hong Kong, 28; Sino-Japanese War, 27; United Nations and, 265; World War II and, 46, 265
Jiang Shigong, 78, 283–284
Jiang Zemin, 25
Joint Declaration. *See* Sino-British Joint Declaration
Jones, Carol, 40
July 1, 2003, protest, 12, 62, 64, 71, 78, 97, 116, 138, 142, 145, 148, 153, 156, 281
July 1 annual marches, 64–67, *90*, 120, *141*
June 4 vigils, 63–66, 81–82, 113, 152, 256
June Democratic Uprising (South Korea), 239
justice movements, 7–8, 11, 69, 71, 73, 274, 276

Kenned-Skipton, G. S., 233
King, Martin Luther, Jr., 87, 107, 163, 187
Korean War, 46, 56
Kowloon riots (1956), 29
Kuan, Hsin-chi, 44
Kundera, Milan, 16
Kuomingtang (KMT), 28, 30, 36, 46, 154, 217
Kwok, Anna, 242–245, 252, 257, 258, 265
Kwong, Glacier, 265

Labour Party (Hong Kong), 45, 47
Labour Party (UK), 31
Lai, Jimmy, 267
laissez-faire economics, 26, 41–42, 44–45
Lam, Carrie, 70, 74, 120, 121, 123–124, 129, 138, 153, 154, 218, 250
Lam, Ivan, 79, 82, 83, 84, 89
Lam Bun, 153
Lam Sir, 206–207
Lau, Finn, 244, 246, 265–266
Lau Siu-kai, 26, 44, 282, 295n17, 296n21
Law, Nathan, 66–67, 89, 92, 111, 235, 237, 265
lawful protests, 67
Law Wing Sang, 54–55, 285, 286–287
Lee, Bruce, 158–159

Lee, Martin Chu-ming, 55, 56, 84–85, 92, 234–235, 250, 252, 253, 254, 270
Lee Wing-tat, 55–57
Legislative Council, 39, 48, 54–55, 86, 105, 123, 141
Legislative Council (LegCo) Complex, 105, 121, 123, 127, 131–132, 138, *141*, 156, 175, 209
Lennon Walls, 167, 176–177, 179, 204
Leung, Baggio, 110, 145
Leung, Brian, 82, 98, 112, 117, 140–141, *141*, 257, 288
Leung, C. Y., 86
Leung, Edward, 106, 108–109, *109*, 110, 113–114, 117, 138, 143, 145, 191, 196, 212, 251
Leung Kam Shing, 104
Leung Ling Kit, 136, 137
LGBTQ communities, 256, 267
Liaison Office, 78, 83, 145, 150–152, 191, 205, 277, 281
Lian Yizeng, Joseph, 104, 107, 185–186
Liberal Party, 64, 247
"Liberate Hong Kong, Revolution of Our Times," 1, 114, 136, 144, 145, 190, 191, 192, 200, 283
Liberia, 8
LIHKG social media platform, 159–162, 167, 175, 177–178, 201–202, 242–243, 246–249
Li Ka Shing, 229
Lim, Louisa, 2
Li Wangyang, 86
lobbying, congressional, 252–258
Local Action, 73, 74
localism: against "China as Destiny," 100–109; communal localism, 101–102; global origins of, 71–75; militant localism, 102–107; political parties, 107–109
Lugard, Frederick, 27
"lunch with you" rallies, 146, *147*, 157
Luxemburg, Rosa, 209

Macau, 19, 46, 48–49
MacLehose, Murray, 30–32, 38

Mahtani, Shibani, 2
Malcolm X, 107, 163, 202
Ma Man Fai, 47, 233
Mandela, Nelson, 107, 202
Manley, Michael, 289
Mao Tse-tung, 32, 37, 46, 161, 217, 232–233, 285
Marcuse, Herbert, 22
margin epistemology, 8
martial arts, 158–159, 190, 192, 197
martial law, 62, 63, 186
Marxism, 59
Mbembe, Achille, 9
McConnell, Mitch, 234–235, 258
McGovern, Jim, 255
McLaughlin, Timothy, 2
Mella, Franco, 151
Mignolo, Walter D., 6, 7
Milk Tea Alliance, 259
Ming Pao (newspaper), 105, 126, 286
misogyny, 166
Myanmar, 144, 260
mythologies. *See* colonial mythologies

Nachtwey, James, 90
Napoleonic Wars, 18
Nationalist Party (Taiwan), 28, 30, 36, 46, 154, 217
Nationality Act (UK), 45, 50, 51
National People's Congress Standing Committee (NPCSC), 86, 89, 111, 114
National Security Law, 36, 64, 67, 123, 189, 208, 220–221, 228–229, 258, 263–267
nation building, 19, 111, 113, 287–290
NATO, 266
neoliberalism, 2, 3, 9, 11, 42, 58–64, 70–75, 115, 274
New Territories (NT), 46, 51, 152, 204, 264, 294n5
new union movement, 208–218
New York for Hong Kong (NY4HK), 253, 256
Ng, Jason, 100
Ng, Michael, 39, 41
Ng Chung-yin, 285–286

Ngo, Jeffrey, 252–258
1911 Revolution, 27
1966 riots, 29, *30*, 48
1967 riots, 29–30, 38, 48, 153, 174
Nkrumah, Kwame, 289, 290
Non-Aligned Movement, 46
nongovernmental organizations (NGOs), 71, 154, 173, 230, 235, 266
North Korea, 251
nostalgia, 15, 71, 75, 78, 117
Nyerere, Julius, 289

Obama, Barack, 92, 235
Occupy Admiralty, 89, 93–100, 105
Occupy Central with Love and Peace (OCLP), 12, 76, 87–89, 96, 116, 118, 186–187, 212, 235, 256
Occupy Mongkok, 94–100, 102–104, 106, 107–110
Occupy Tamar, 81
Occupy Trio, 88–89, 95, 99–100
Occupy Wall Street, 76, 81, 159
oil crisis (1970s), 32, 36
Olympics (Beijing), 81, 82
"One Country, Two Systems" (OCTS), 9, 12, 18, 58, 78, 86, 102, 104, 108, 222, 252–253, 282–283
othering, 7–9, 21–22, 60, 143, 150

Pact of Free Cities, 266
Padmore, George, 289
Palestine, 7, 72
Passion Times, 102, 196
Patten, Chris, 17, 39–40, 42
Peace Preservation Ordinance, 27
Pelosi, Nancy, 234, 253, 254, 255, 257, 258, 270
pepper spray, 89, 95, 98, 106, 124, 129, 150, 165, 192, 227, 242
Petersen, Carole, 264
Poland, 99
polarization, social, 4, 67, 198
political consumerism, 204–208. *See also* yellow economy campaign
politics of difference, 8, 278
Pompeo, Mike, 254

preservation campaigns, 75–76
privatization, 12, 75–76, 116
professionalism, 214, 228
prosperity and stability, 24–34
protest arts, 179, *180*
Public Order Ordinance, 36, 67, 75, 100, 133

Qing dynasty, 27, 154, 233, 273
Queen's Pier, 12, 69–70, 72–73, 101, 116
Quiyano, Anibal, 6

racialization, 8, 18, 22, 28, 111, 116, 278
racial segregation, 21, 35, 277
racism, 5, 8
radicalization, 183–188
Railway Power, 215
Red capital, 61, 76, 206, 213–214, 216–217, 228–229, 276
Reform Club, 47
Reorienting Hong Kong's Resistance, 289
Rubio, Marco, 254, 255
rule of law, 10–13, 23–25, 34–41, 54, 173, 227–228, 273–275

sanctions, campaigning for international, 246–252
SARS epidemic, 60, 64, 66, 211, 218, 274
Schmitt, Carl, 281, 283–284
Scholarism, 79–85, 88–89, 111, 118, 237
Seattle anti-WTO protests, 71–72, 73, 116
sedition, 220, 229
Sedition Ordinance, 36
segregation, racial, 21, 35, 277
70s Weekly, The, 285
sexism, 118, 166
Shek Kip Mei shantytown fire, 29
Shum, Lester, 89
Sincere Department Store, 47
Sino-British Joint Declaration, 3–4, 9, 39, 43–44, 72, 150, 246, 248–249, 264, 282
Sino-French War, 27
Sino-Japanese War, 27
Sinophobia, 112, 167, 251
Smith, Chris, 237, 253, 255
Socialist Democratic Party, 47

social movement theories, 292n9
solidarity: coercive solidarity, 12, 155, 168; collective conscience and, 155–158; cross-movement solidarity, 259–263; division of labor protest and, 162–163; everyday resistance and, 163–166; roles of gender and class in, 166–167; roles of reflexivity and technology in, 158–161
Solidarity movement (Poland), 99
Sorel, Georges, 203
South China Morning Post, 25
South Korea, 63, 69, 71, 72, 73, 116, 131, 173, 202, 229, 238, 239
special administrative region (SAR), 44, 64, 81, 86, 91, 100, 140, 185, 188, 234
stability. *See* prosperity and stability
Standing Committee on Pressure Groups, 33
Stand with Hong Kong (SWHK), 244–245
Star Ferry, 12, 29, 30, 33, 69–70, 72–73, 101, 116
Statute of Westminster (UK), 19
Stott, Clifford, 187
subjectivities, decolonial, 115–118
suicide attacks and protests, 99, 136
Sunak, Rishi, 267
Sun Baogang, 233
Sunflower Movement, 116, 140
Sun Yat-sen, 27, 154, 201, 202, 285

Tahrir Square protests (Egypt), 135, 159
Tai, Benny, 87–88, 107, 186–187, 212, 222–223, 227, 235
Taiwan, 75, 121, 153–154, 201, 245, 249
Tang, Leo, 66
Tang Bing-keung, 198
Tanzania, 8
Telecommunication Ordinance, 36
Telegram social media app, 146, 150, 159–161, 209–211, 214–215, 241, 247
Thailand, 50, 63, 144, 254, 260
Thatcher, Margaret, 39, 42, 49, 51–52, 55, 286
35+ election campaign, 13, 171, 222–225

Thompson, E. P., 8
Tiananmen Square protests, 34, 39, 53, 56, 62–63, 79, 82, 86, 115–116, 234
Tian Feilong, 282–283
To Kwan Hang, 67
tourism, 64, 69, 85, 94–95, 103–106
Treaty of Nanjing, 294n5
Trench, David, 31, 38
trench warfare, 1, 149, 159, 197, 249
Trump, Donald, 238, 239, 246, 257–258, 260–261, 289
Tsoi Yuen Village, 70
Tung Chee-hwa, 66
Tung Tau fire, 29
Twitter, 236, 237, 238, 255, 258, 259
2014 Hong Kong protests. *See* Umbrella Movement
2019 Hong Kong protests: "brave warriors" and, 188–203; Chinese republican protesters, 153–154; division of protest labor, 161–163; everyday-life resistance and, 163–166; as lesson in violence and sacrifice, 226–230; middle-class and professional-class protesters, 142–149; new immigrant protesters, 149–151; ordinary citizen protesters, 151–153, 154–155; protester solidarity, 155–167; public support for, 167–168; roles of gender and class in, 166–167; roles of reflexivity and technology in, 158–161; Umbrella Movement and, 132–142; young protesters, 124
2019 Hong Kong extradition bill, 137, 156, 160, 168, 239, 241, 243, 246–247, 1210129
Two Million Three Strikes, 209–210, 220

UK-Hong Kong Summit (2023), 263, 267
Ukraine, 202, 265, 267; Revolution of Dignity, 99–100, 116, 229, 239; Russian invasion of, 7; *Winter on Fire* (documentary), 239

Umbrella Movement, 12, 66, 76, 87–100; class differences and internal friction, 92–100; localism in post-Umbrella Movement, 100–109; 2019 Hong Kong protests and, 132–142
Undergrad (student magazine), 98, 111, 113, 117, 288
United Democrats, 63
United Nations, 243, 247, 259, 264–265; Charter, 48; Declaration on the Granting of Independence to Colonial Countries and People, 19, 48, 49, 233, 300n96; decolonization agenda, 46; International Covenant on Civil and Political Rights, 38, 264; Joint Declaration and, 52; list of non-self-governing territories, 19, 49, 233, 265; PRC joining the, 48
United Nations Association (UNA) of Hong Kong, 47, 233
United Nations Human Rights Committee, 264, 266
United Nations Human Rights Council, 264
University of Hong Kong, 98, 102, 107, 111, 212, 249, 283, 288
utilitarian familism, 26

Vancouver Society in Support of Democratic Movement, 256
Velvet Revolution, 99
Victoria Harbour, 17, 41, 69, 239
Victoria Park, 37, 63, 64, 66, 81, 103, 179, 192, 281
Victoria Road Detention Centre, 36
vigilantism, 86, 104, 170, 187, 197, 199
Vine, Stephen, 2
violence: alternative forms of resistance, 203–221; "arc" of, 171; "brave warriors" and, 188–203; cycle of militant and peaceful resistance, 174–183; local meaning of, 172–174; police violence, 146, 153, 171, 173–175, 187, 241, 257, 259, 267; public opinion on, 187–188; radicalization and, 183–188; "spiral" of, 171
virtual liberalism, 34–35, 286–287
V Team, 200, 201

Walsh, Catherine, 6
Walzer, Michael, 202–203
WeChat app, 132
Wedding Card Street, 69, 70
Williams, Eric, 289
will to community, 9, 119, 279
Wilson, David, 234
Wong, John, 25
Wong, Joshua, 76, 79, 81, 83, 88, 89–90, 92, 105, 111, 117, 235, 250, 251, 253–254, 258
Wong, Ray, 96, 97–98, 99, 104–106, *109*, 145
World Expo (Shanghai), 81, 82
World Trade Organization (WTO), 69, 71–72, 115, 116, 126, 131–132, 235
World Trade Organization Ministerial Conference of 2005, 69, 72, 126, 131, 132
World War II, 46, 233

xenophobic, 117
Xiao Jianhua, 121
Xi Jinping, 121, 126, 133, 238, 244, 274, 281, 283

Yan Xiaojun, 283
yellow economy campaign, 13, 171, 204–208, 210, 212, 214, 226, 228, 229, 276
Yellow Emperor, 22, 112
"yellow locusts," 85, 104, 117
yellow vests protests, 173, 240
Yeung Po, 176
Young, Mark, 37
Youngspiration, 108, 110, 114, 211
Yuen, Samson, 2
Yuen Long railway station attack and protests, 144, 147, 167, 170, 191–192, 215, 255

Zhao Lianhai, 86